ASSASSINATION CLASSROOM

YUSEI MATSUI

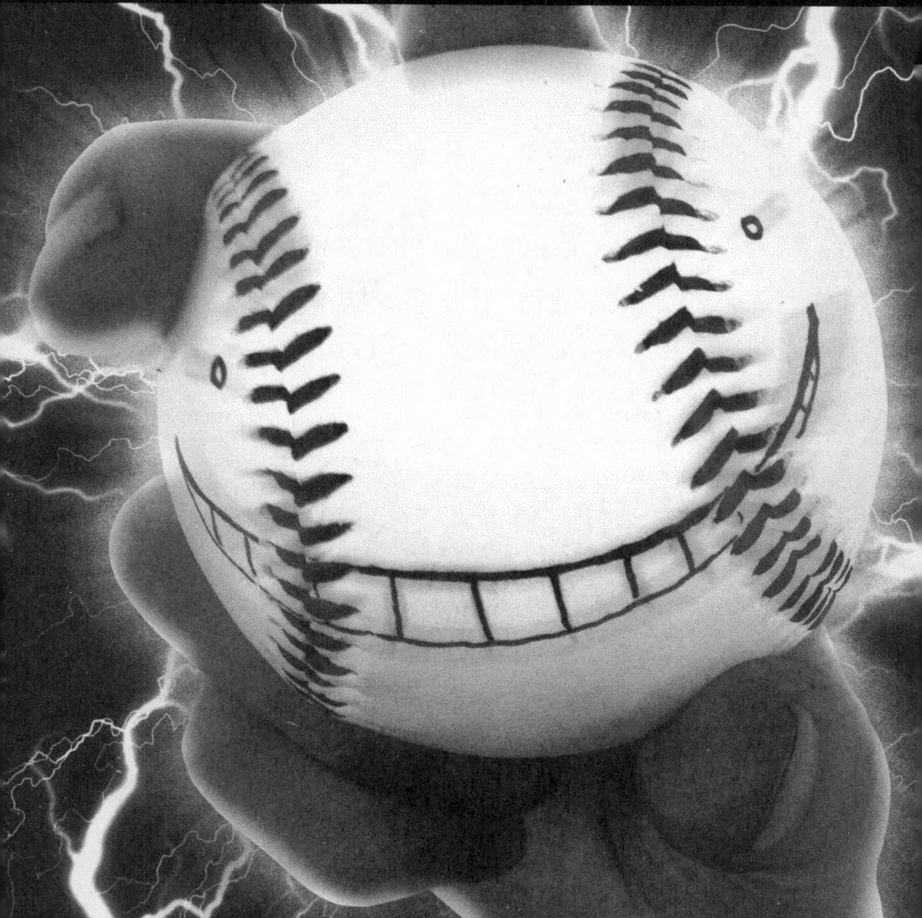

4

TIME TO FACE THE UNBELIEVABLE

SHONEN JUMP ADVANCED

Koro Tribune

May Issue

Published by: Class 3-E Newspaper Staff

Our new teacher is a creature who plans to destroy the world...?!

Story Thus Far

One day, something destroyed most of the moon.

I'M THE ONE WHO DISINTEGRATED PART OF THE MOON.
AND NEXT YEAR AT THIS TIME I'M GOING TO DO THE SAME THING TO YOUR PLANET EARTH.
ALSO, I'M YOUR NEW TEACHER. I HOPE WE

A mysterious creature showed up in our junior high classroom claiming that he had attacked the moon and promising to destroy the earth next March. And then... he took over as our teacher. What the—?! Faced with a creature beyond human understanding that no army could kill, the leaders of the world had no choice but to rely on the students of Kunugigaoka Junior High, Class 3-E, to do the job. For a reward of ten billion yen (100 million dollars)... SIGN ME UP!! Will the students of the so-called End Class, filled with losers and rejects, be able to kill their target, Koro Sensei, by graduation...?!

Koro Sensei

TWTCH
TWTCH

A mysterious octopus-like creature whose nickname is a play on the words "koro senai," which means "can't be killed." He is capable of flying at Mach 20 and his versatile tentacles protect him from attacks and aid him in everyday activities. Nobody knows why he wants to teach Class 3-E, but he has proven to be an extremely capable teacher.

And he enjoys a good bath!

Kaede Kayano

Class E student. She's the one who named Koro Sensei. Sits at the desk next to Nagisa, and they seem to get along well.

Nagisa Shiota

Class E student. Skilled at information gathering, he has been taking notes on Koro Sensei's weaknesses.

Karma Akabane

Class E student. A quick thinker skilled at surprise attacks. Succeeded in injuring Koro Sensei a few times.

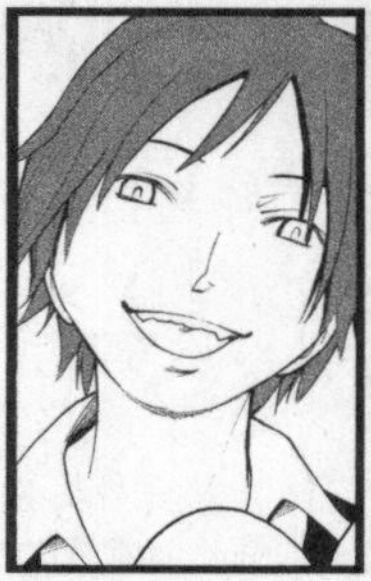

Ryunosuke Chiba

No one in 3-E has ever seen his eyes. Rumor has it that even his parents haven't seen them for the past year.

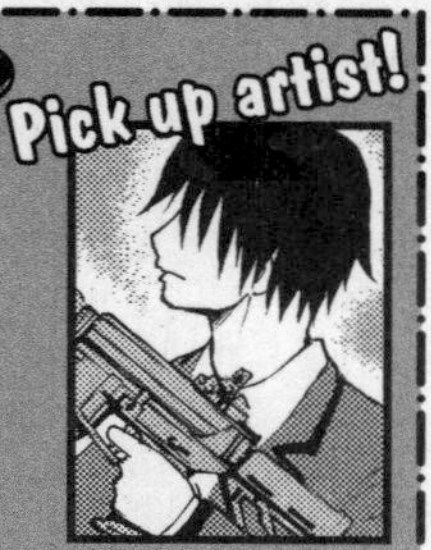
Pick up artist!

Ritsu (Autonomous Intelligence Fixed Artillery)

Transfer Student Assassin, a self-evolving fixed artillery weapon created with top military technology. She succeeded in blowing off Koro Sensei's finger.

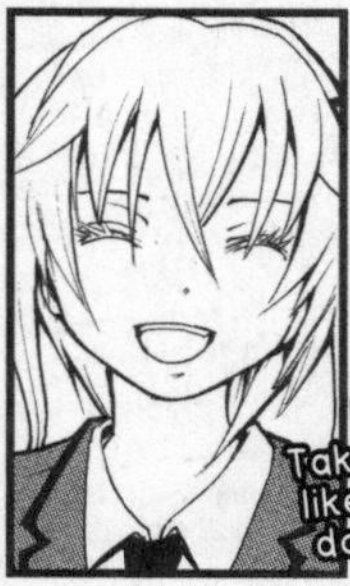

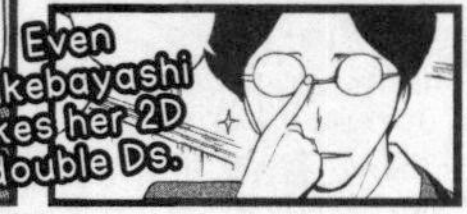
Even Takebayashi likes her 2D double Ds.

Kanzaki gets into a huge fight with her father over her choice of career!

Apparently, she elegantly told him to "stick it" when he said she had to become a lawyer. She wants to be a social worker instead. Are lawyers capable of being social?

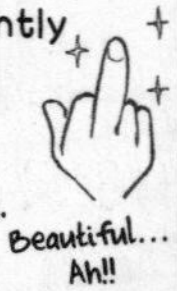
Beautiful... Ah!!

Tadaomi Karasuma

Member of the Ministry of Defense and the Class E students' P.E. teacher. Also in charge of managing visiting assassins.

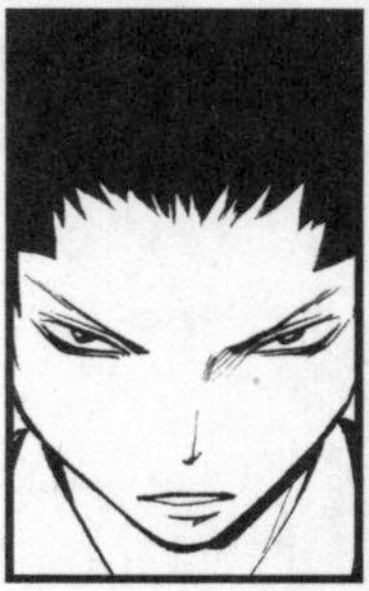

Irina Jelavich

A sexy assassin hired as an English teacher. She's known for using her "womanly charms" to get close to a target, but has failed to kill Koro Sensei—yet.

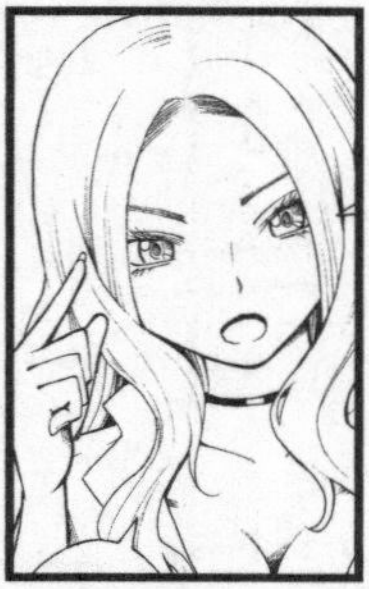

Gakuho Asano

The principal of Kunugigaoka Academy, who built this academically competitive school based on his faith in rationality and hierarchy.

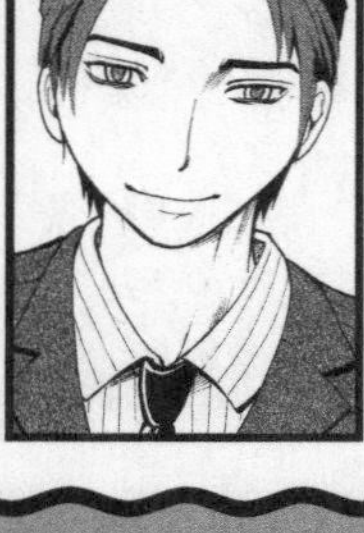

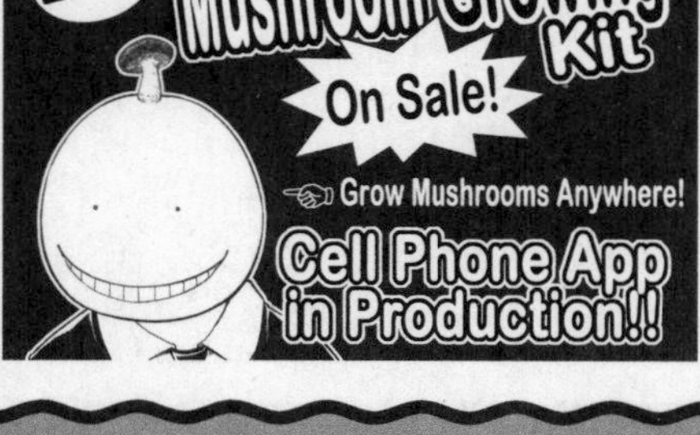
Easy!
Mushroom Growing Kit
On Sale!
Grow Mushrooms Anywhere!
Cell Phone App in Production!!

ASSASSINATION CLASSROOM ④ CONTENTS

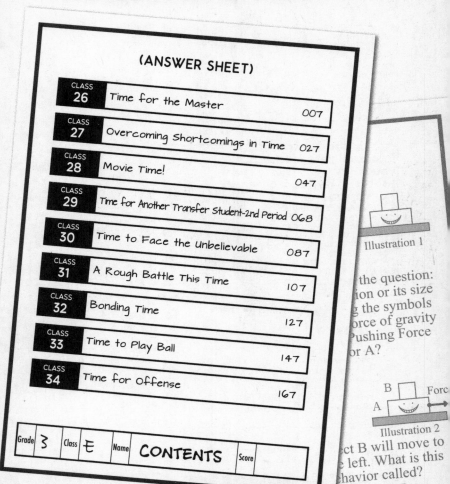

(ANSWER SHEET)

| Grade | 3 | Class | E | Name | CONTENTS | Score | |

Illustration 1

the question:
ion or its size
g the symbols
orce of gravity
Pushing Force
or A?

B   Force
A

Illustration 2

ct B will move to
e left. What is this
havior called?
nd Object B are
(5) When Object A will invariably move just like Object A.
then Object B will invariably move just like Object A.
Draw an arrow pointing at the direction of the frictional
force upon Object B on Illustration 2.

(Question 2) Answer the following question about photo
synthesis. Test tubes A through D have been prepared.
Test tubes A and B will have a waterweed cut in the
same length inside them. The test tubes are then filled
ith greenish tap water, which has been mixed with BT
vered with a rubber plug

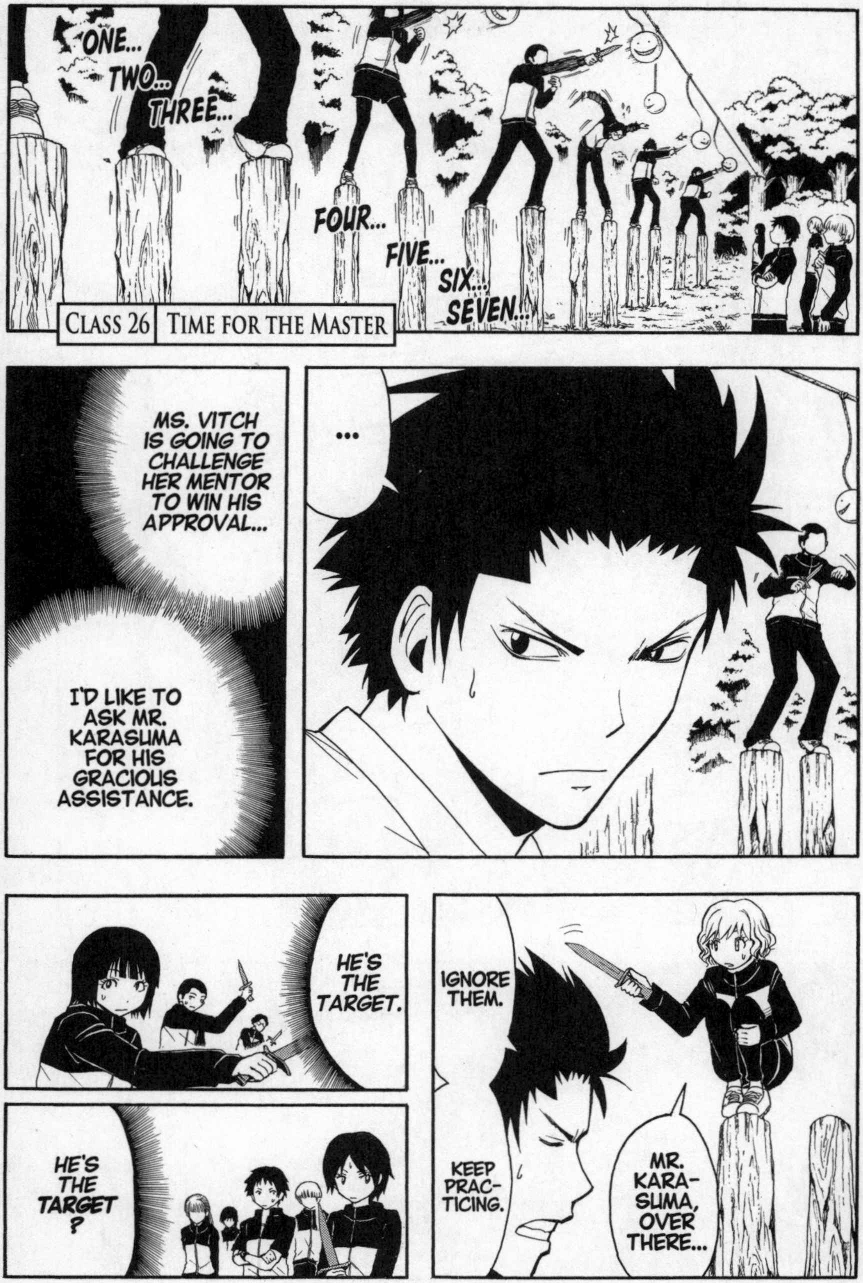
ONE...
TWO...
THREE...
FOUR...
FIVE...
SIX...
SEVEN...
Class 26 Time for the Master
...
MS. VITCH IS GOING TO CHALLENGE HER MENTOR TO WIN HIS APPROVAL...
I'D LIKE TO ASK MR. KARASUMA FOR HIS GRACIOUS ASSISTANCE.
MR. KARA-SUMA, OVER THERE...
IGNORE THEM.
KEEP PRAC-TICING.
HE'S THE TARGET.
HE'S THE TARGET?

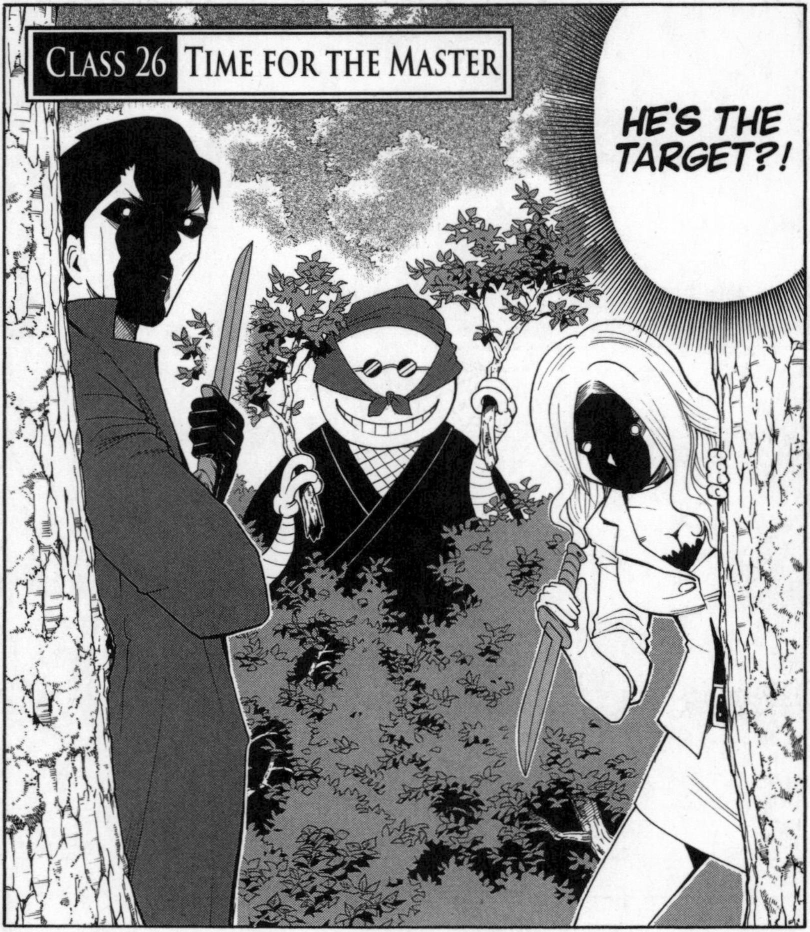
CLASS 26 TIME FOR THE MASTER
HE'S THE TARGET?!
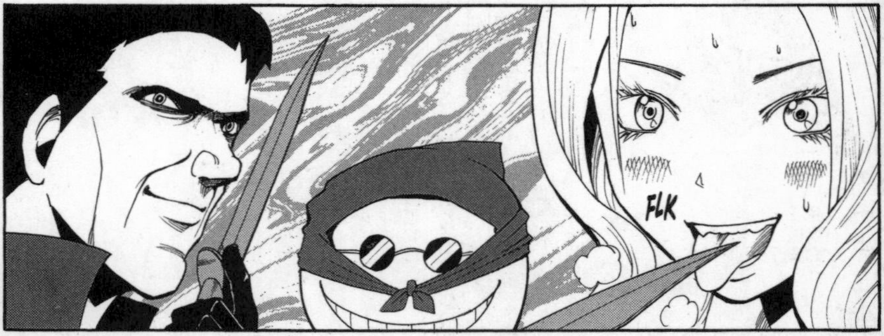
FLK

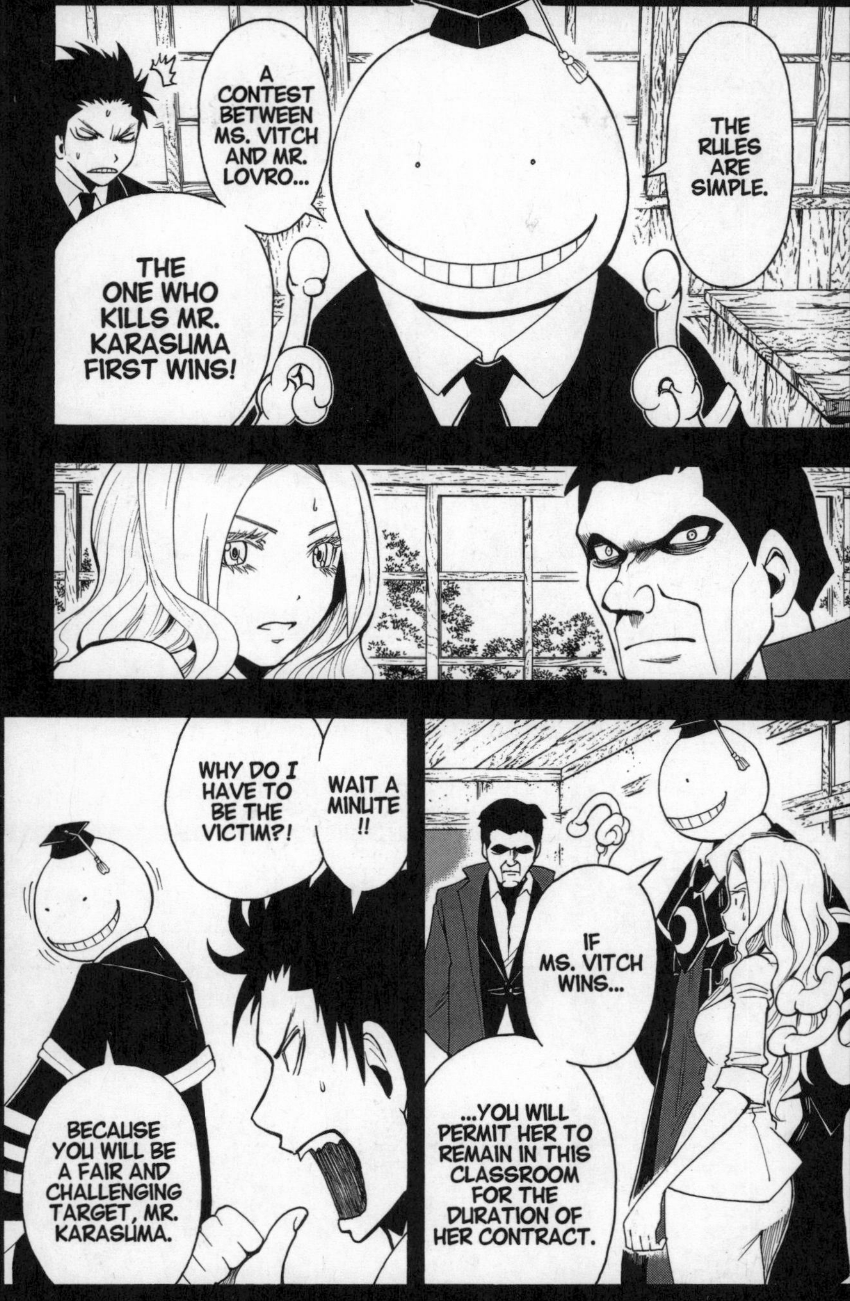
THE RULES ARE SIMPLE.
A CONTEST BETWEEN MS. VITCH AND MR. LOVRO...
THE ONE WHO KILLS MR. KARASUMA FIRST WINS!
IF MS. VITCH WINS...
...YOU WILL PERMIT HER TO REMAIN IN THIS CLASSROOM FOR THE DURATION OF HER CONTRACT.
WAIT A MINUTE !!
WHY DO I HAVE TO BE THE VICTIM?!
BECAUSE YOU WILL BE A FAIR AND CHALLENGING TARGET, MR. KARASUMA.

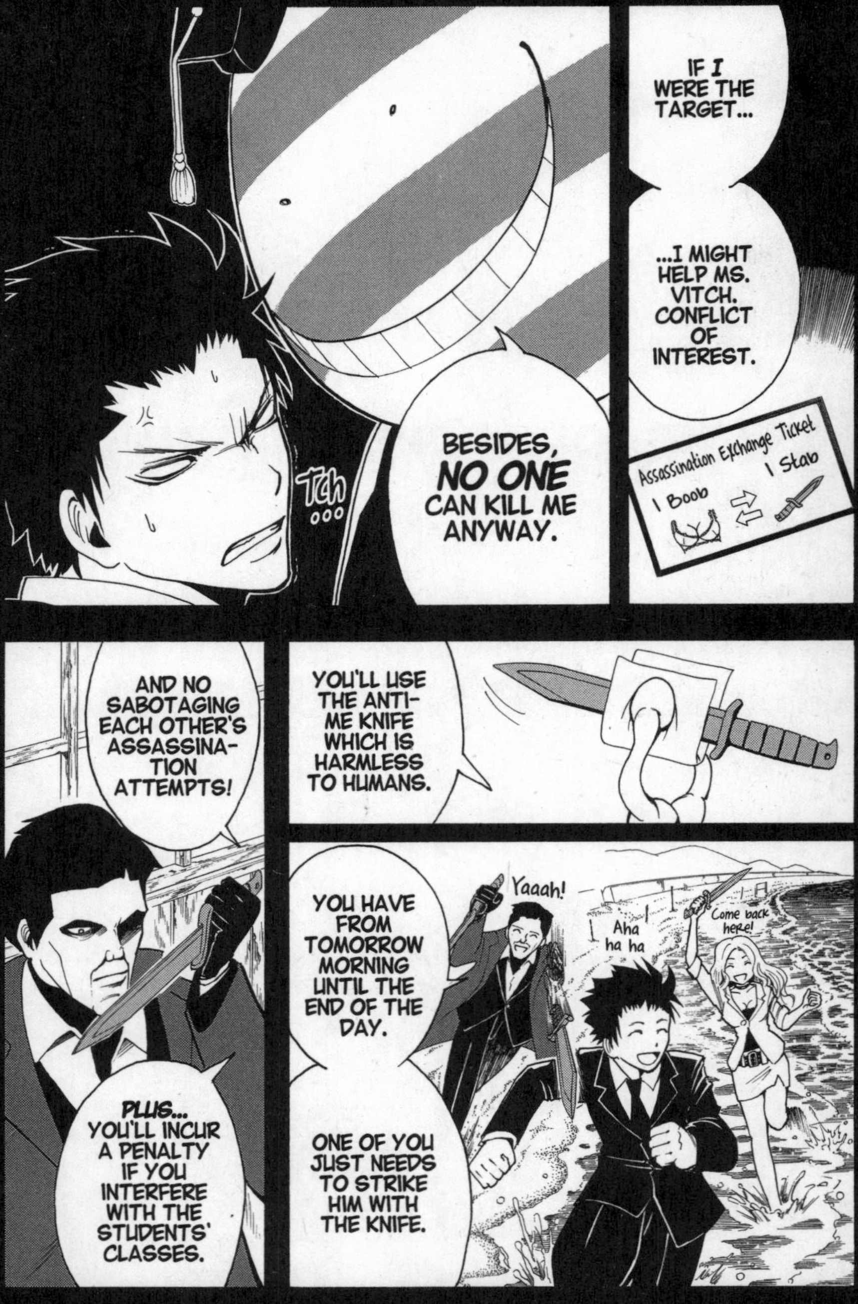
IF I WERE THE TARGET...
...I MIGHT HELP MS. VITCH. CONFLICT OF INTEREST.
Assassination Exchange Ticket
1 Boob
1 Stab
BESIDES, NO ONE CAN KILL ME ANYWAY.
Tch
YOU'LL USE THE ANTI-ME KNIFE WHICH IS HARMLESS TO HUMANS.
YOU HAVE FROM TOMORROW MORNING UNTIL THE END OF THE DAY.
Come back here!
Aha ha ha
Yaaah!
ONE OF YOU JUST NEEDS TO STRIKE HIM WITH THE KNIFE.
AND NO SABOTAGING EACH OTHER'S ASSASSINATION ATTEMPTS!
PLUS... YOU'LL INCUR A PENALTY IF YOU INTERFERE WITH THE STUDENTS' CLASSES.

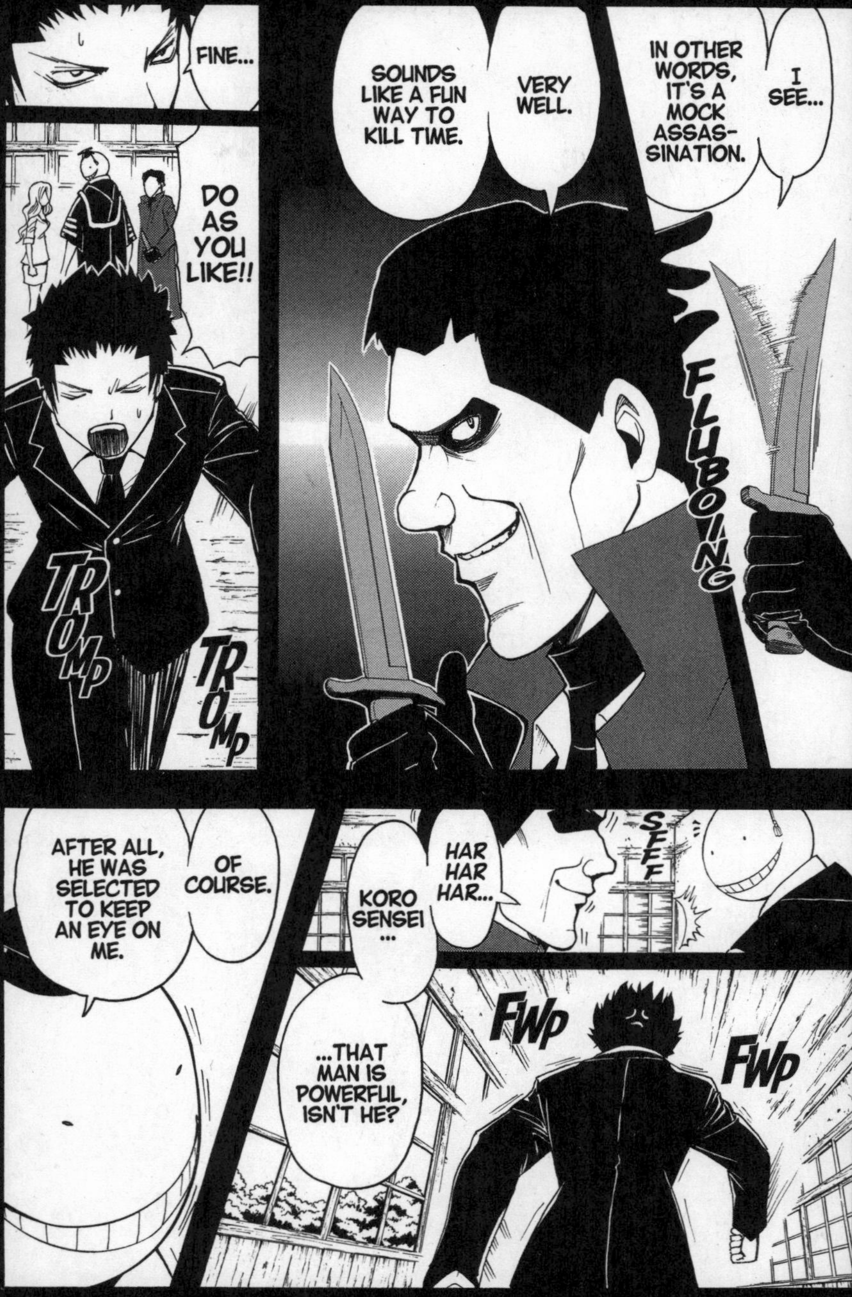
I SEE...
IN OTHER WORDS, IT'S A MOCK ASSASSINATION.
VERY WELL.
SOUNDS LIKE A FUN WAY TO KILL TIME.
FLUBOING
FINE...
DO AS YOU LIKE!!
TROMP
TROMP
SFFF
HAR HAR HAR...
KORO SENSEI ...
...THAT MAN IS POWERFUL, ISN'T HE?
FWP
FWP
OF COURSE.
AFTER ALL, HE WAS SELECTED TO KEEP AN EYE ON ME.

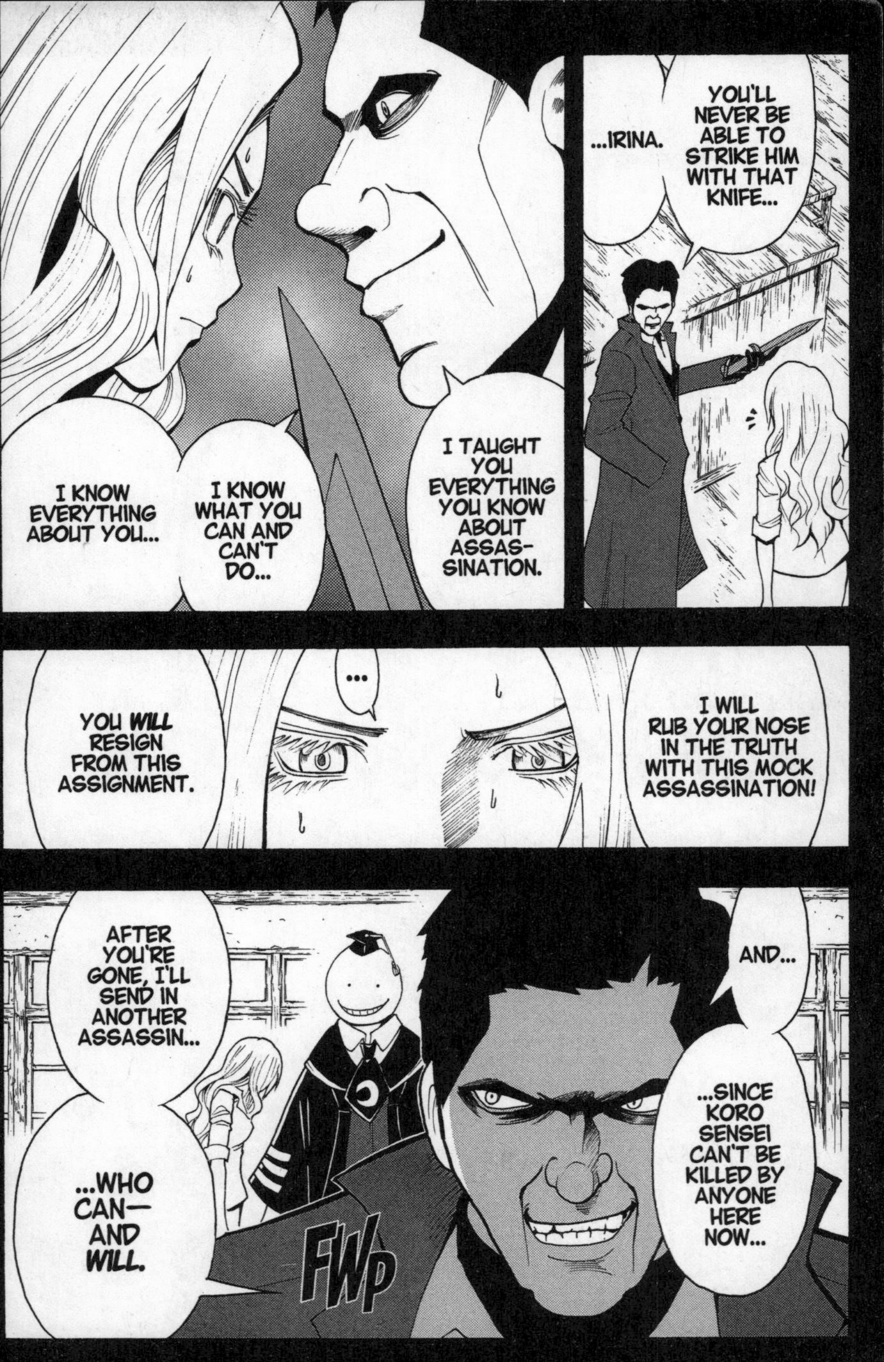
YOU'LL NEVER BE ABLE TO STRIKE HIM WITH THAT KNIFE...
...IRINA.
I TAUGHT YOU EVERYTHING YOU KNOW ABOUT ASSAS-SINATION.
I KNOW WHAT YOU CAN AND CAN'T DO...
I KNOW EVERYTHING ABOUT YOU...
I WILL RUB YOUR NOSE IN THE TRUTH WITH THIS MOCK ASSASSINATION!
...
YOU **WILL** RESIGN FROM THIS ASSIGNMENT.
AND...
...SINCE KORO SENSEI CAN'T BE KILLED BY ANYONE HERE NOW...
AFTER YOU'RE GONE, I'LL SEND IN ANOTHER ASSASSIN...
...WHO CAN— AND **WILL**.
FWP

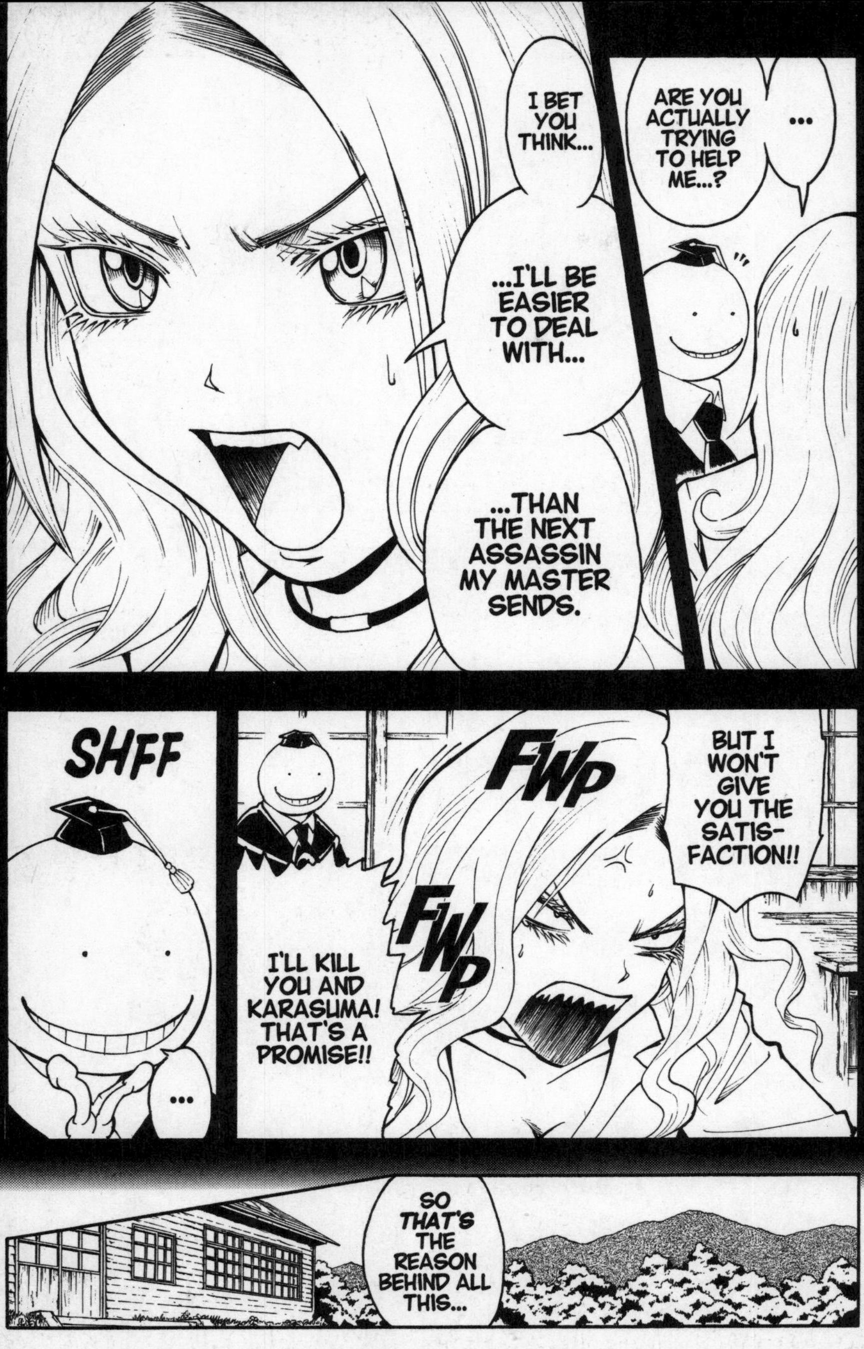
...
ARE YOU ACTUALLY TRYING TO HELP ME...?
I BET YOU THINK...
...I'LL BE EASIER TO DEAL WITH...
...THAN THE NEXT ASSASSIN MY MASTER SENDS.
FWP
BUT I WON'T GIVE YOU THE SATIS-FACTION!!
FWP
I'LL KILL YOU AND KARASUMA! THAT'S A PROMISE!!
SHFF
...
SO *THAT'S* THE REASON BEHIND ALL THIS...

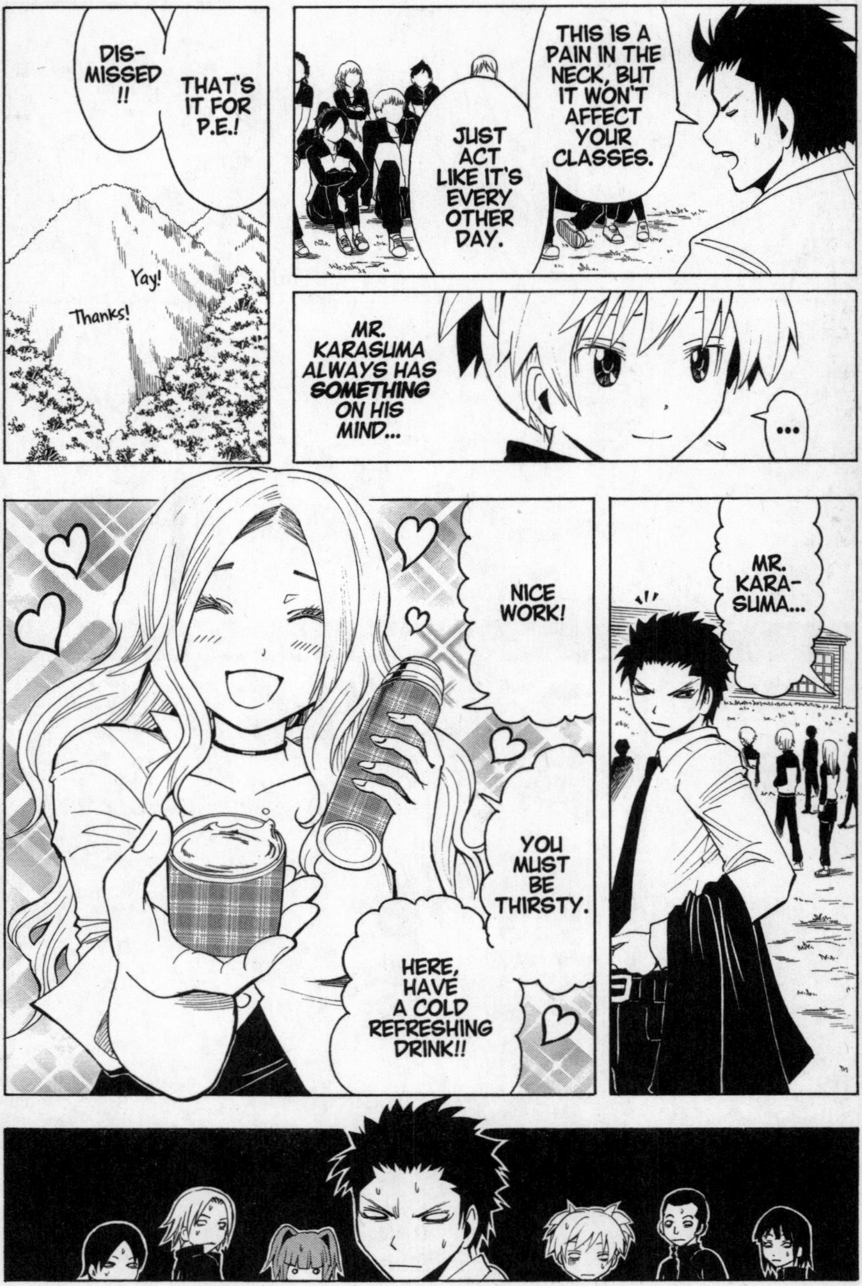
THIS IS A PAIN IN THE NECK, BUT IT WON'T AFFECT YOUR CLASSES.
JUST ACT LIKE IT'S EVERY OTHER DAY.
...
MR. KARASUMA ALWAYS HAS SOMETHING ON HIS MIND...
THAT'S IT FOR P.E.!
DIS-MISSED!!
Yay!
Thanks!
MR. KARA-SUMA...
NICE WORK!
YOU MUST BE THIRSTY.
HERE, HAVE A COLD REFRESHING DRINK!!

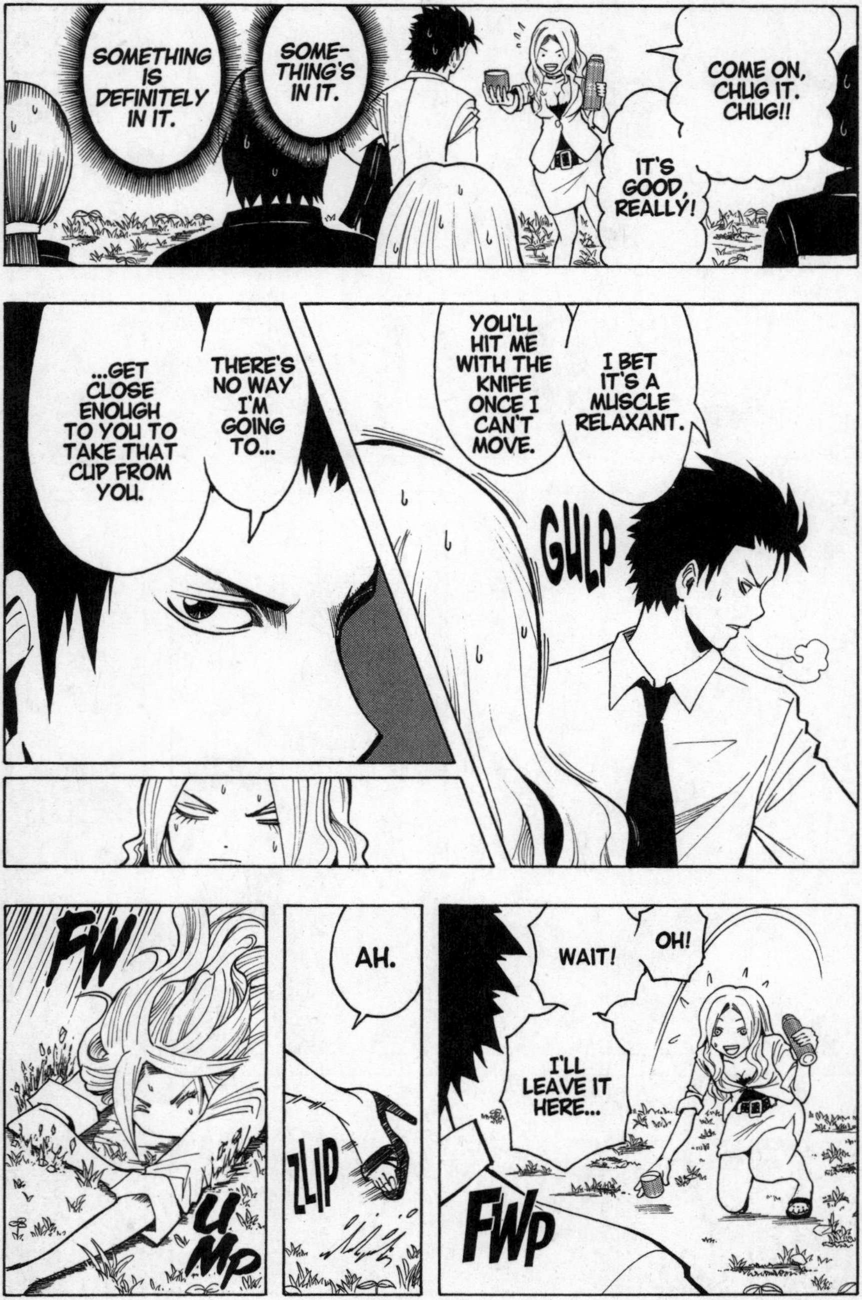
COME ON, CHUG IT. CHUG!!
IT'S GOOD, REALLY!
SOMETHING'S IN IT.
SOMETHING IS DEFINITELY IN IT.
I BET IT'S A MUSCLE RELAXANT.
YOU'LL HIT ME WITH THE KNIFE ONCE I CAN'T MOVE.
GULP
THERE'S NO WAY I'M GOING TO...
...GET CLOSE ENOUGH TO YOU TO TAKE THAT CUP FROM YOU.
OH!
WAIT!
I'LL LEAVE IT HERE...
FWP
AH.
ZLIP
FW
UMP

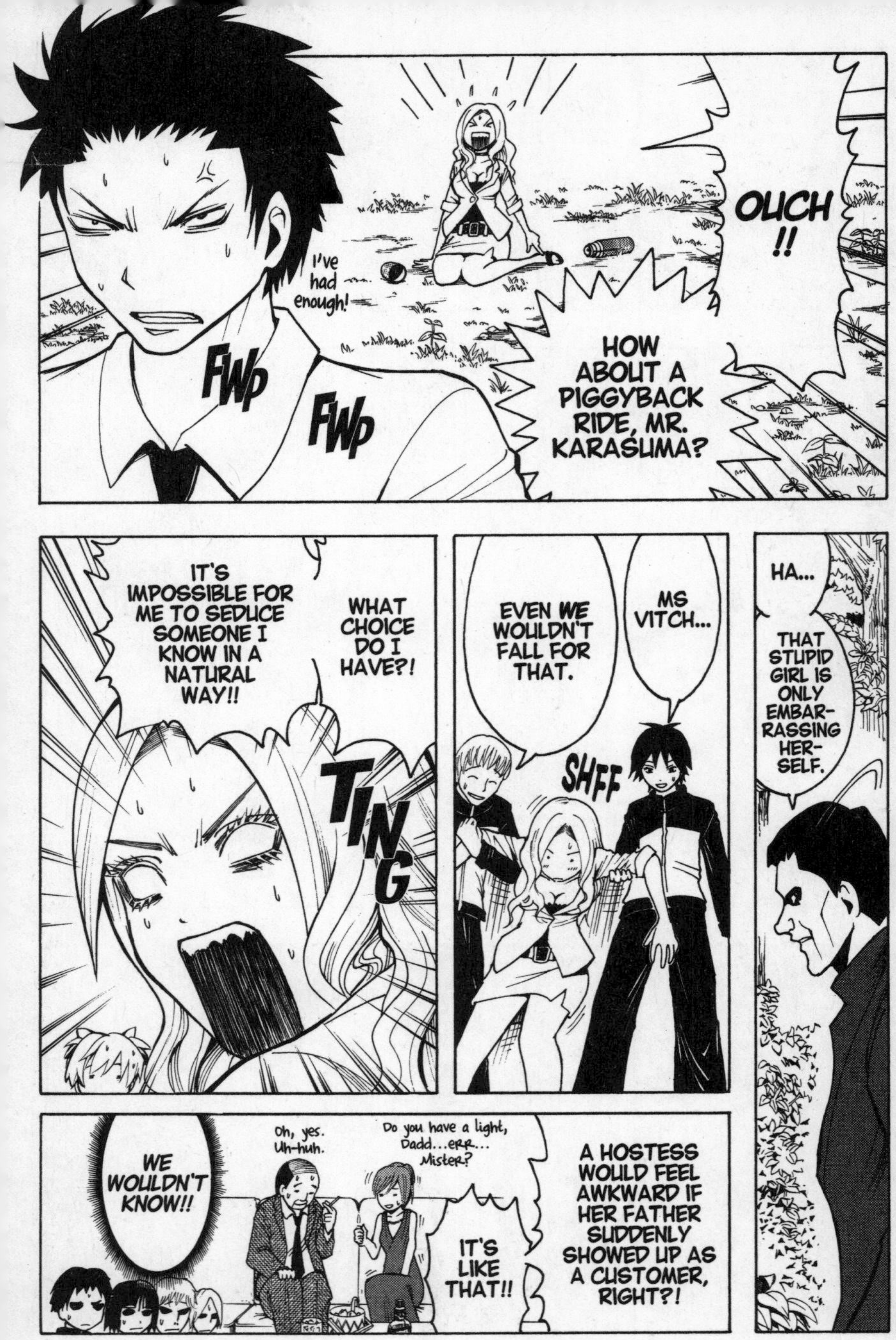
OUCH!!
HOW ABOUT A PIGGYBACK RIDE, MR. KARASUMA?
I've had enough!
FWP
FWP
HA...
THAT STUPID GIRL IS ONLY EMBARRASSING HERSELF.
MS VITCH...
EVEN WE WOULDN'T FALL FOR THAT.
SHFF
WHAT CHOICE DO I HAVE?!
IT'S IMPOSSIBLE FOR ME TO SEDUCE SOMEONE I KNOW IN A NATURAL WAY!!
TING
A HOSTESS WOULD FEEL AWKWARD IF HER FATHER SUDDENLY SHOWED UP AS A CUSTOMER, RIGHT?!
Do you have a light, Dadd…err… Mister?
Oh, yes. Uh-huh.
IT'S LIKE THAT!!
WE WOULDN'T KNOW!!

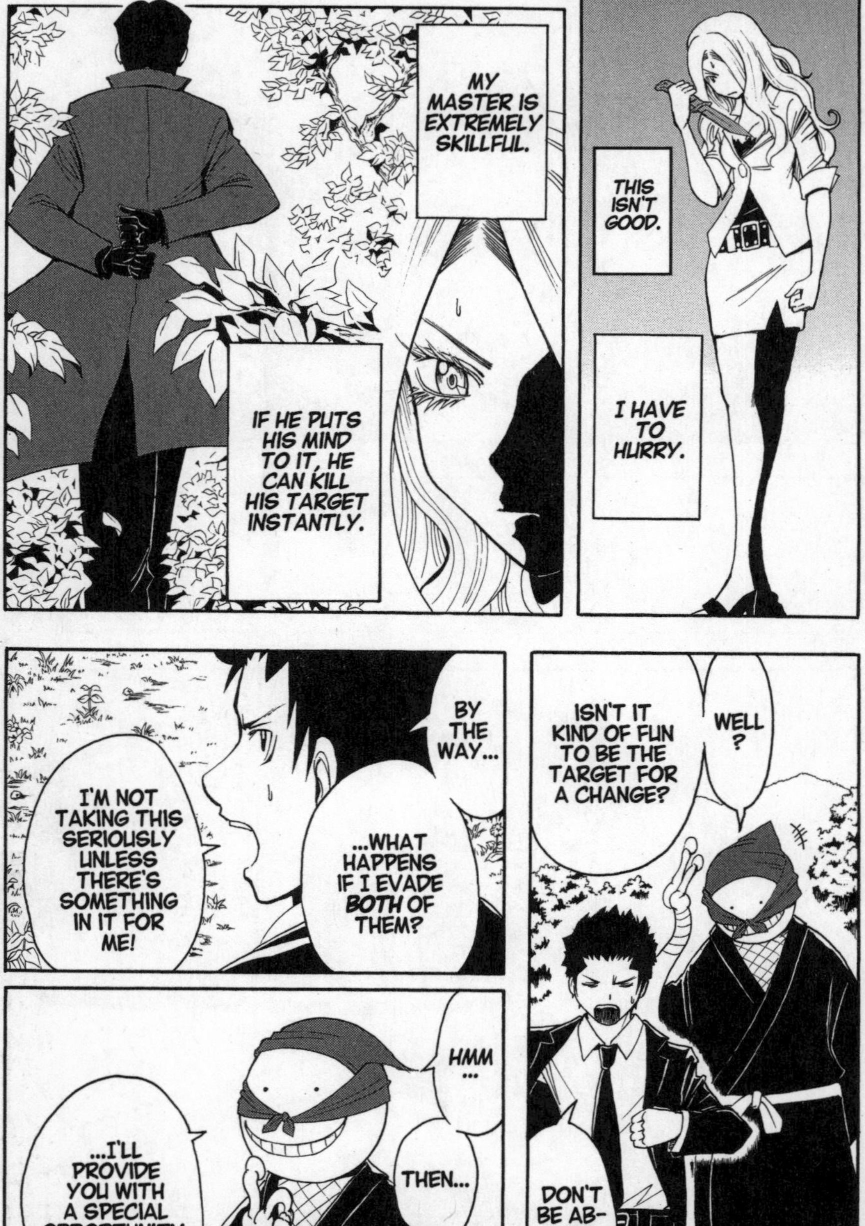
THIS ISN'T GOOD.
I HAVE TO HURRY.
MY MASTER IS EXTREMELY SKILLFUL.
IF HE PUTS HIS MIND TO IT, HE CAN KILL HIS TARGET INSTANTLY.
WELL?
ISN'T IT KIND OF FUN TO BE THE TARGET FOR A CHANGE?
DON'T BE AB-SURD.
BY THE WAY...
...WHAT HAPPENS IF I EVADE *BOTH* OF THEM?
I'M NOT TAKING THIS SERIOUSLY UNLESS THERE'S SOMETHING IN IT FOR ME!
HMM...
THEN...
...I'LL PROVIDE YOU WITH A SPECIAL OPPORTUNITY.

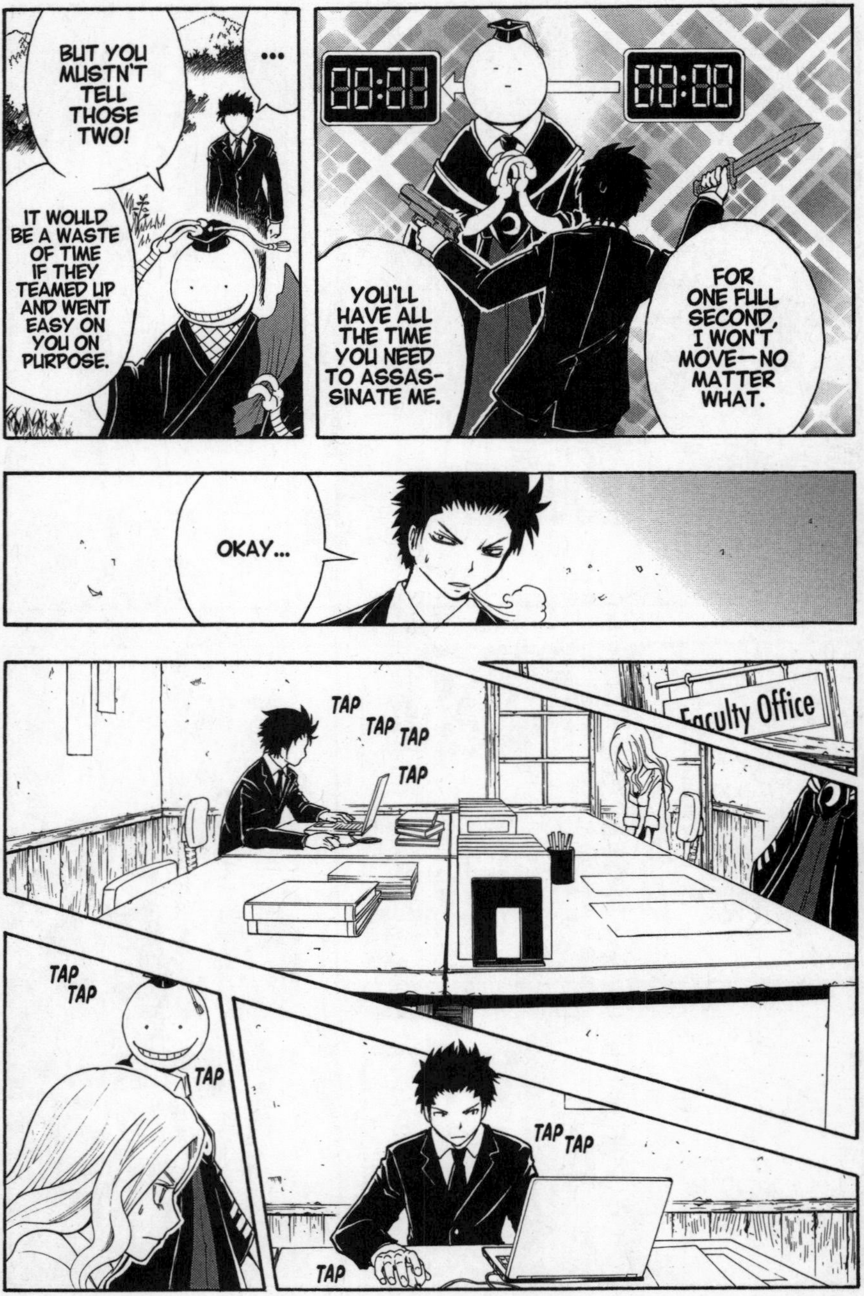
FOR ONE FULL SECOND, I WON'T MOVE—NO MATTER WHAT.
YOU'LL HAVE ALL THE TIME YOU NEED TO ASSAS-SINATE ME.
...
BUT YOU MUSTN'T TELL THOSE TWO!
IT WOULD BE A WASTE OF TIME IF THEY TEAMED UP AND WENT EASY ON YOU ON PURPOSE.
OKAY...
Faculty Office
TAP
TAP TAP
TAP
TAP TAP
TAP
TAP TAP
TAP

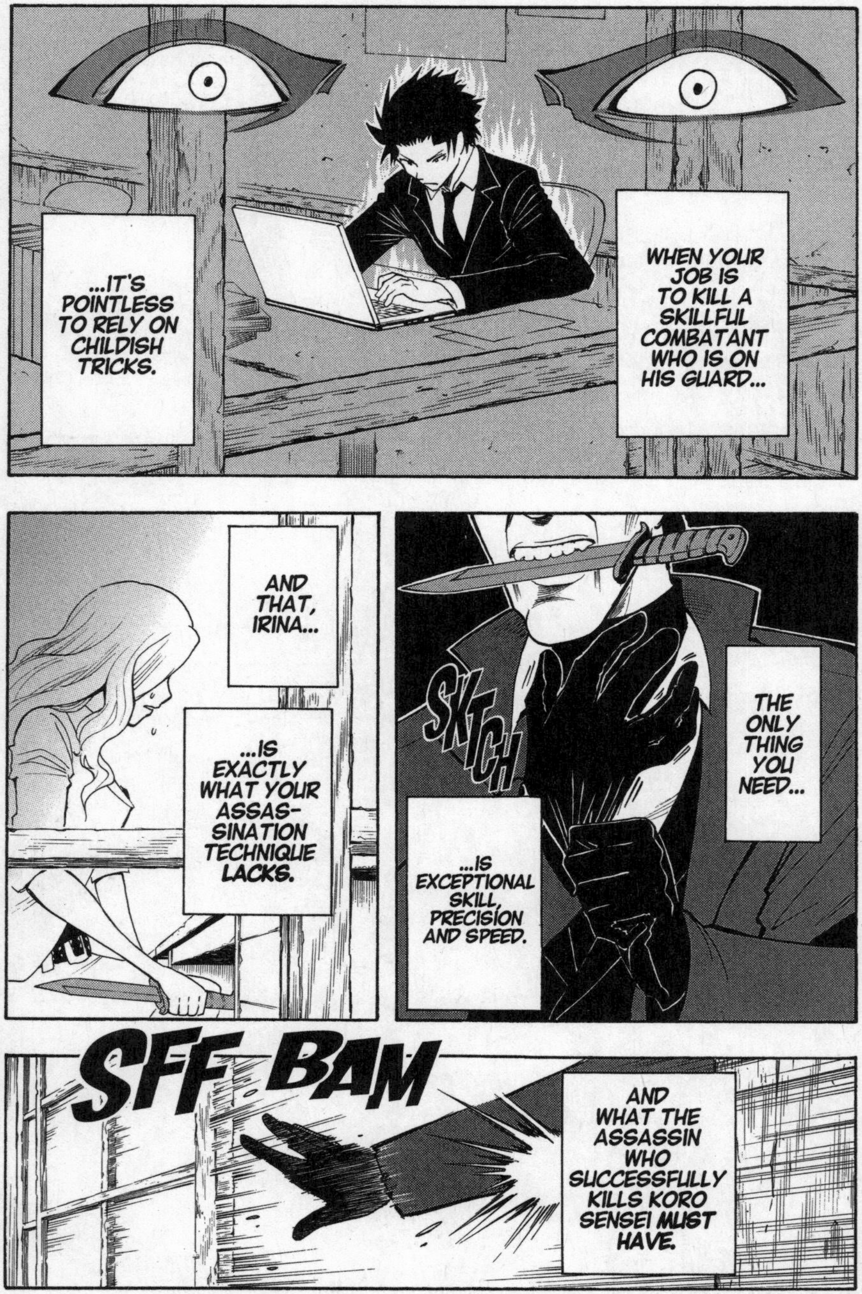
WHEN YOUR JOB IS TO KILL A SKILLFUL COMBATANT WHO IS ON HIS GUARD...
...IT'S POINTLESS TO RELY ON CHILDISH TRICKS.
THE ONLY THING YOU NEED...
SKTCH
...IS EXCEPTIONAL SKILL, PRECISION AND SPEED.
AND THAT, IRINA...
...IS EXACTLY WHAT YOUR ASSAS-SINATION TECHNIQUE LACKS.
AND WHAT THE ASSASSIN WHO SUCCESSFULLY KILLS KORO SENSEI MUST HAVE.
SFF BAM

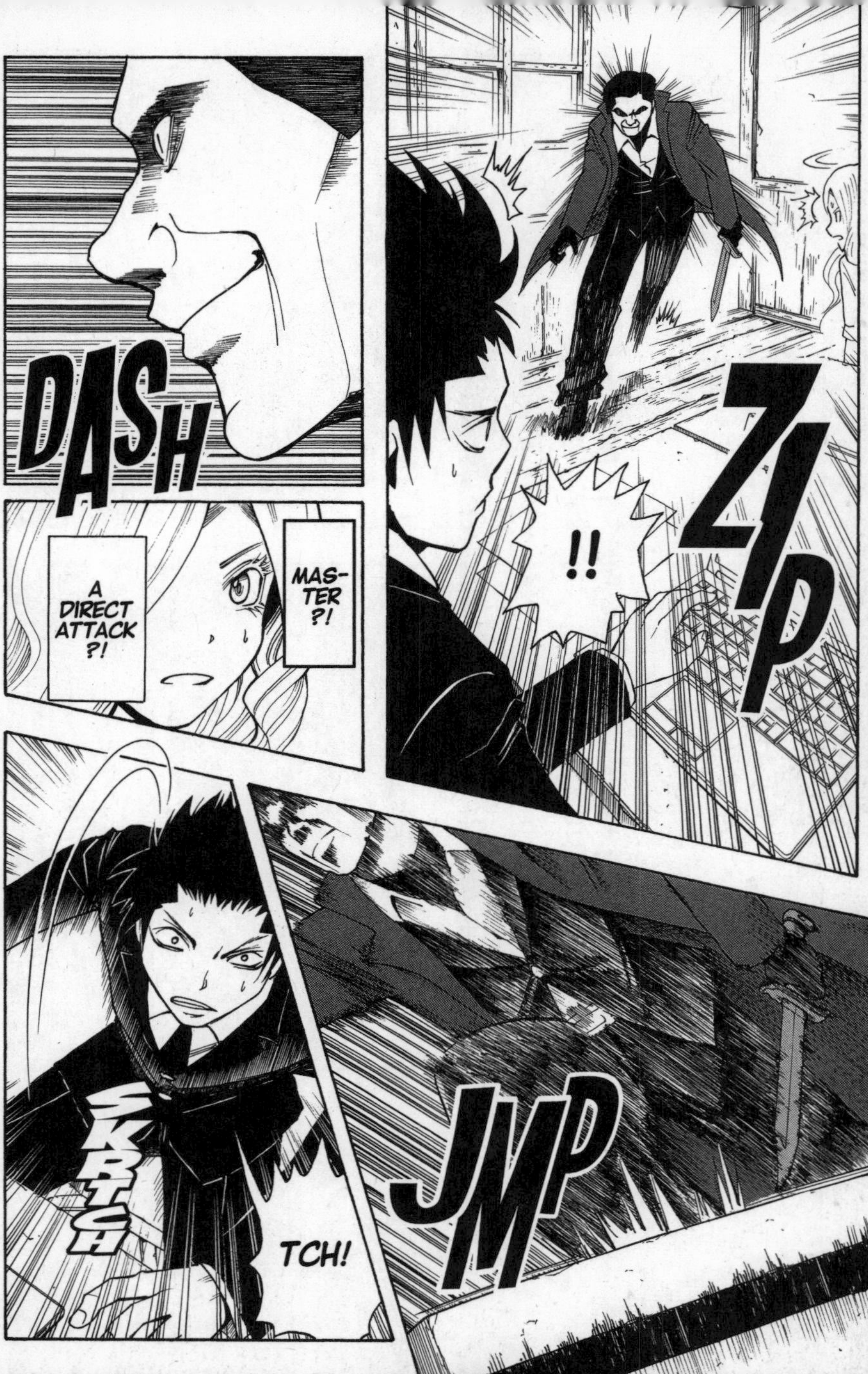
ZIP
!!
DASH
MASTER?!
A DIRECT ATTACK?!
JMP
SKRTCH
TCH!

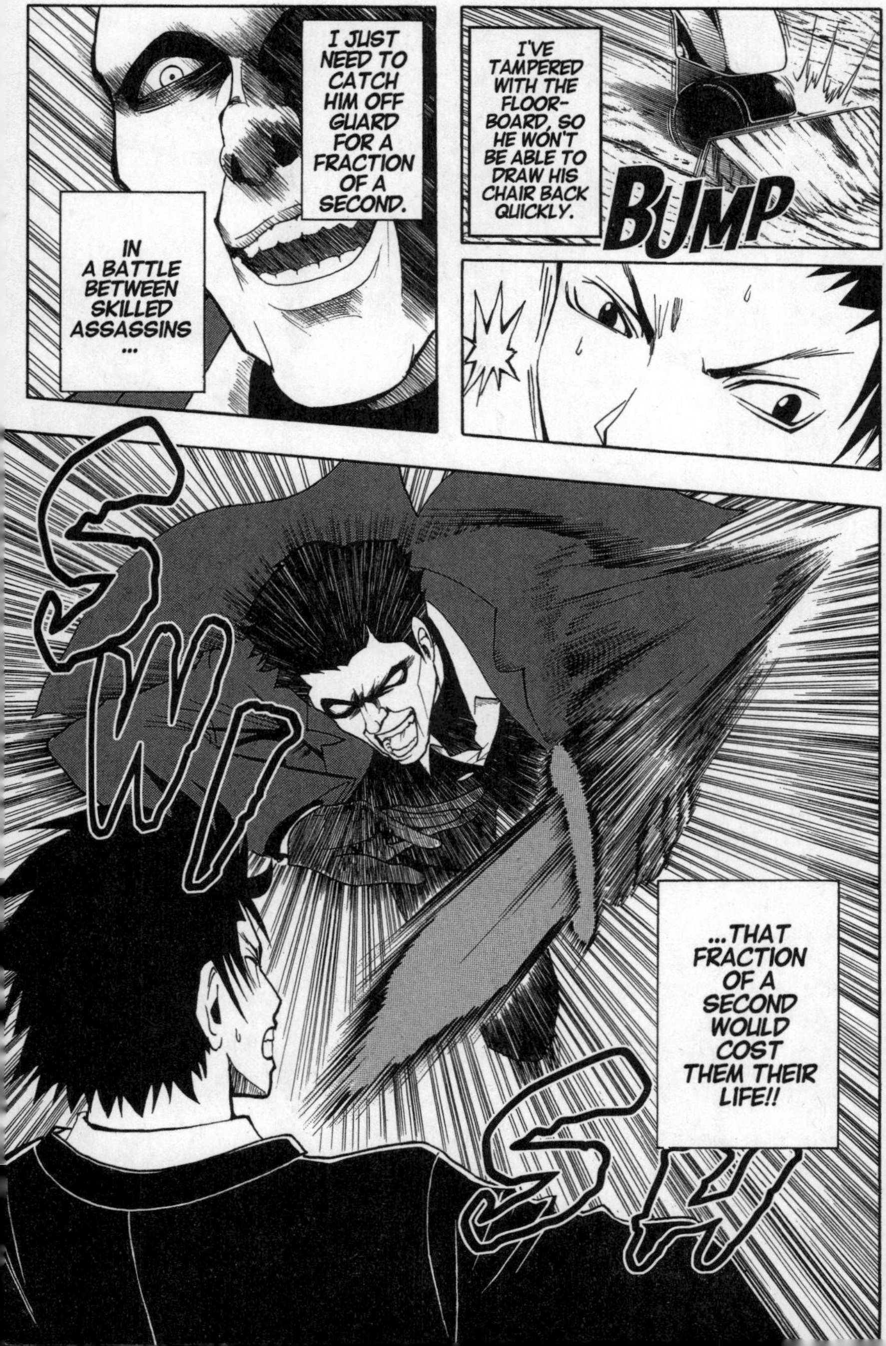
I'VE TAMPERED WITH THE FLOOR-BOARD, SO HE WON'T BE ABLE TO DRAW HIS CHAIR BACK QUICKLY.
BUMP
I JUST NEED TO CATCH HIM OFF GUARD FOR A FRACTION OF A SECOND.
IN A BATTLE BETWEEN SKILLED ASSASSINS ...
...THAT FRACTION OF A SECOND WOULD COST THEM THEIR LIFE!!
SWISH

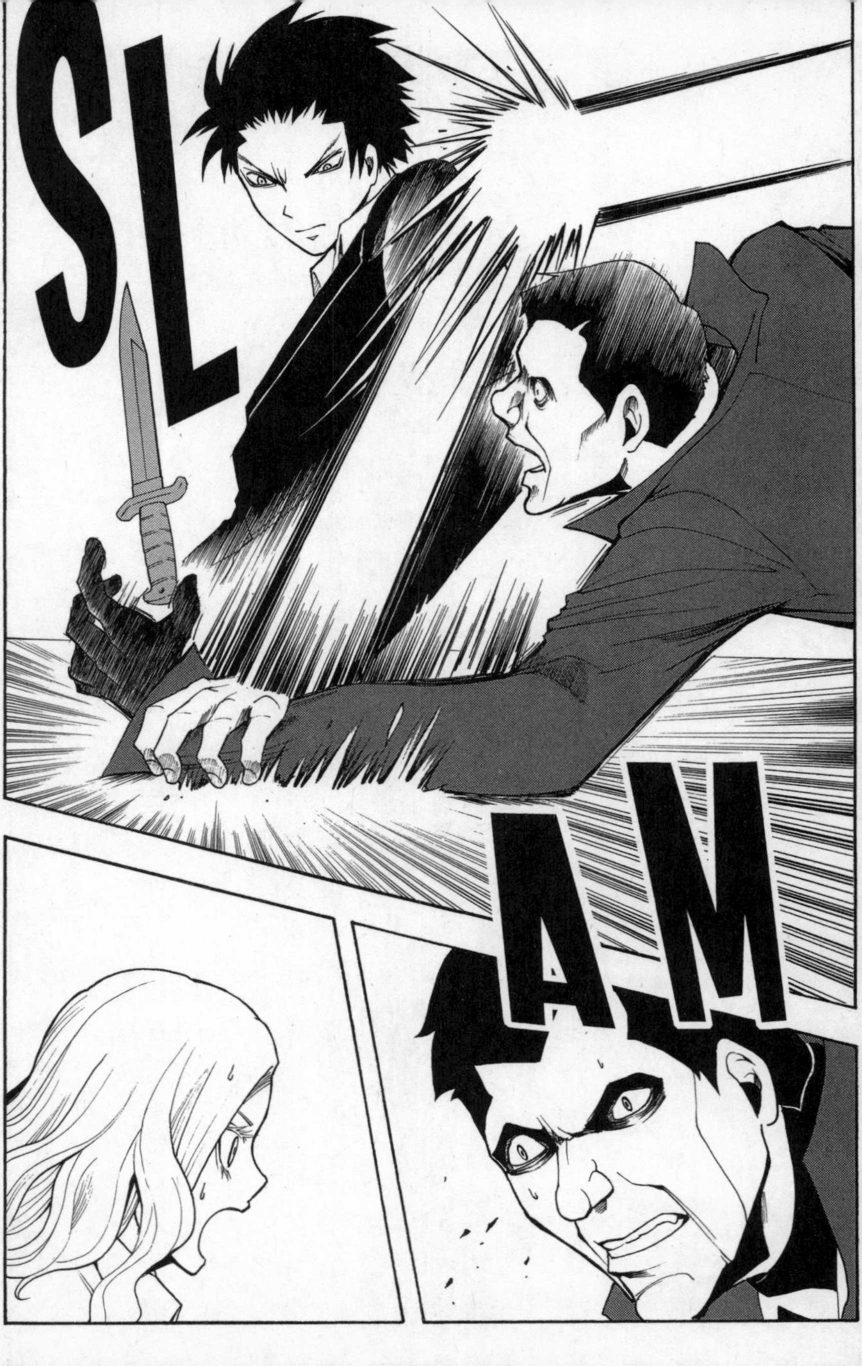
SLAM

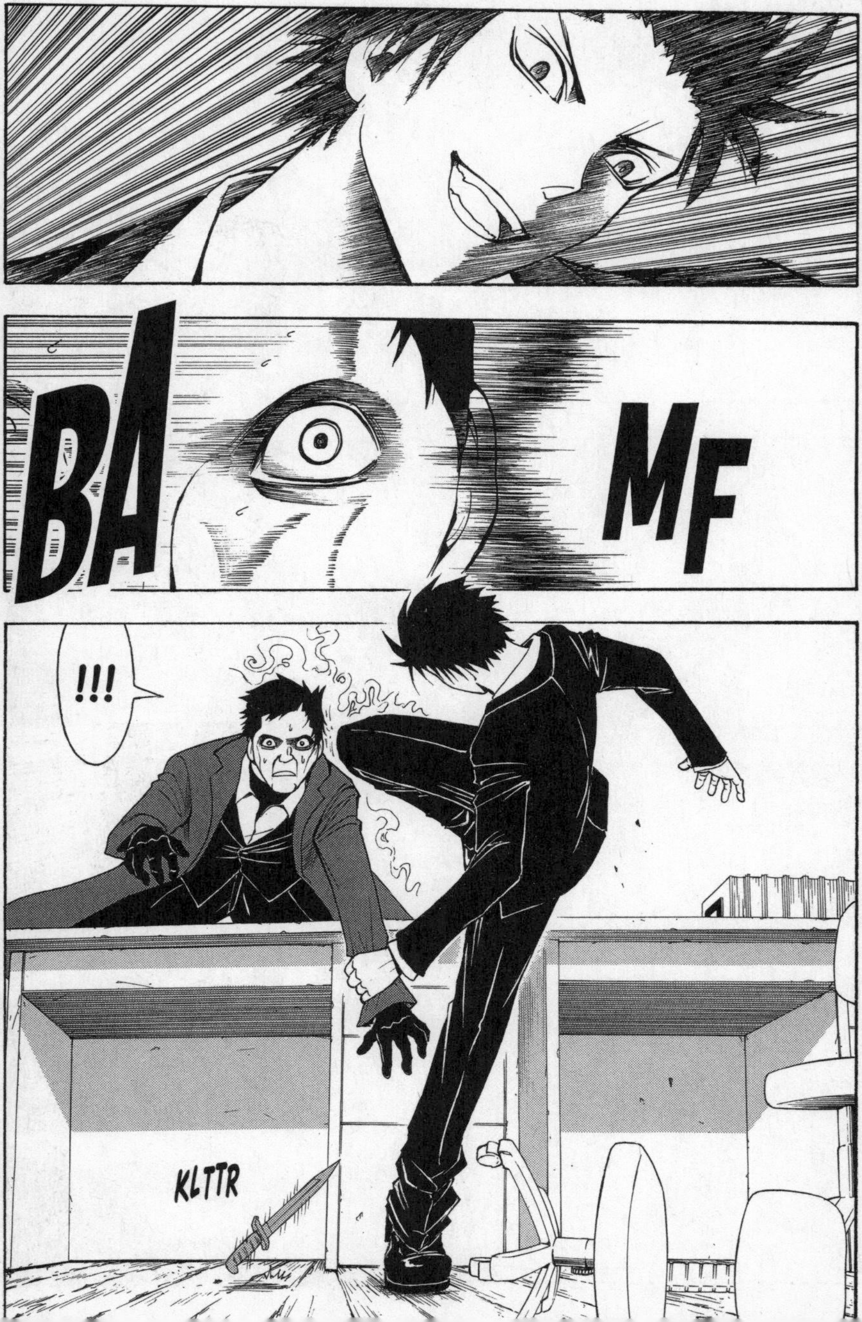
BAMF
!!!
KLTTR

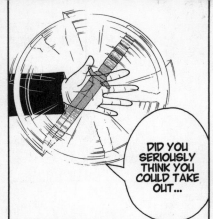

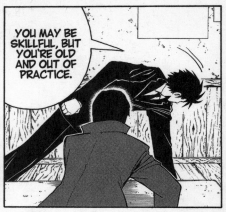

YOU MAY BE SKILLFUL, BUT YOU'RE OLD AND OUT OF PRACTICE.
DID YOU SERIOUSLY THINK YOU COULD TAKE OUT...
...SOMEONE WHO'S BEEN A MEMBER OF AN ELITE UNIT UNTIL JUST YESTERDAY?
!!
HE'S TOUGH!!
EVEN MY MASTER CAN'T KILL HIM!!
HOW CAN SOMEONE LIKE ME POSSIBLY DO WHAT HE COULDN'T BY THE END OF THE DAY?!

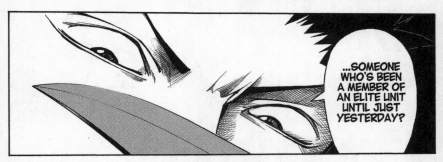

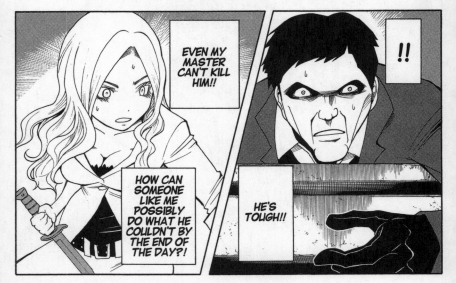

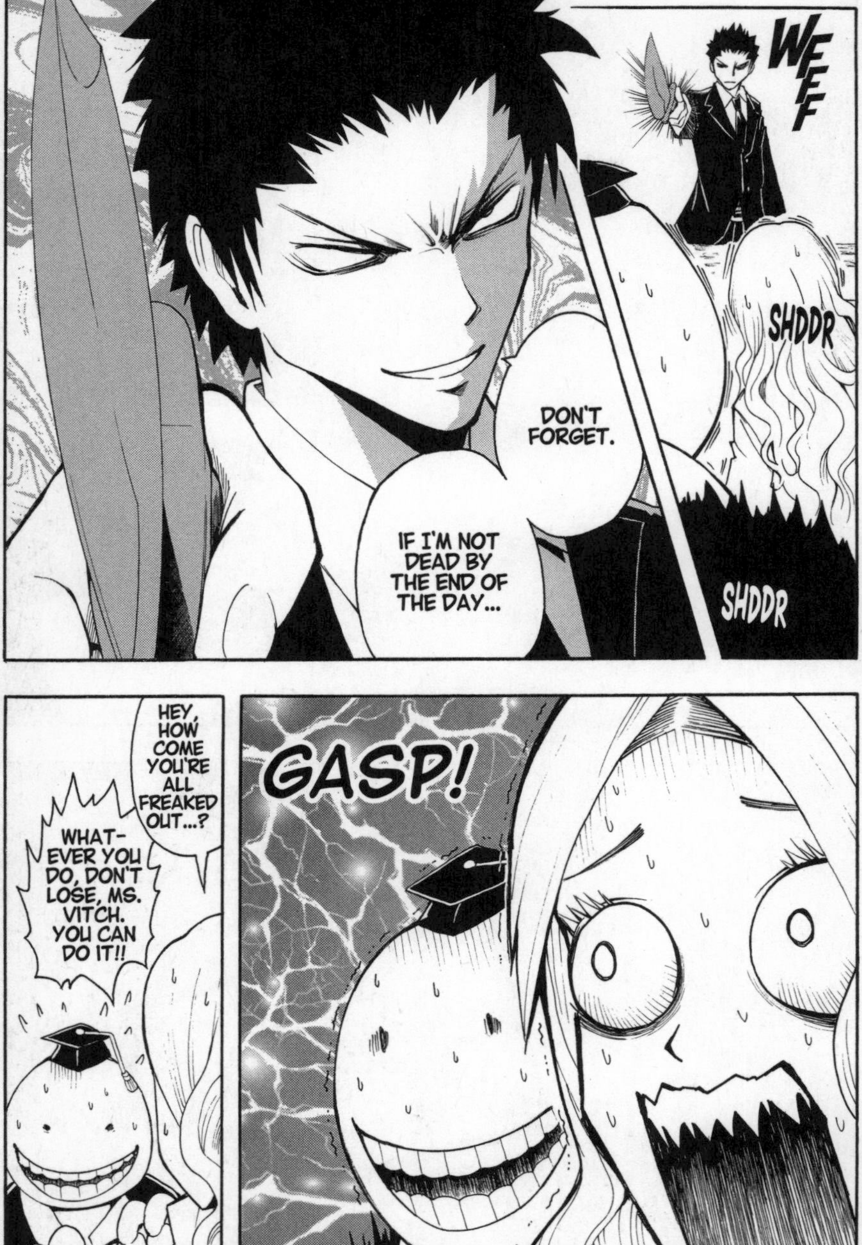
WEFF
SHDDR
DON'T FORGET.
IF I'M NOT DEAD BY THE END OF THE DAY...
SHDDR
GASP!
HEY, HOW COME YOU'RE ALL FREAKED OUT...?
WHAT-EVER YOU DO, DON'T LOSE, MS. VITCH. YOU CAN DO IT!!

For your Mother's Day gift

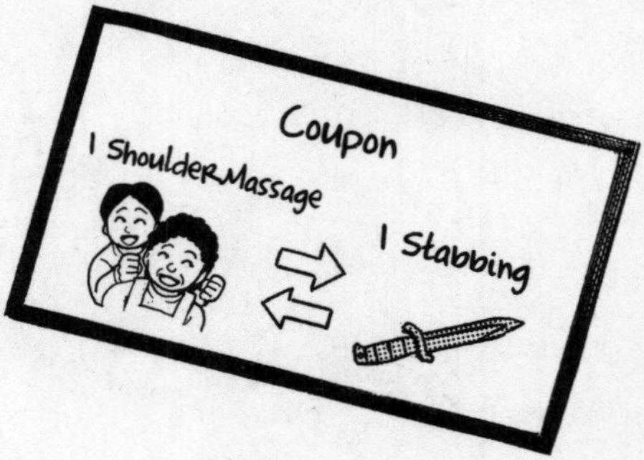
Coupon
1 Shoulder Massage
1 Stabbing

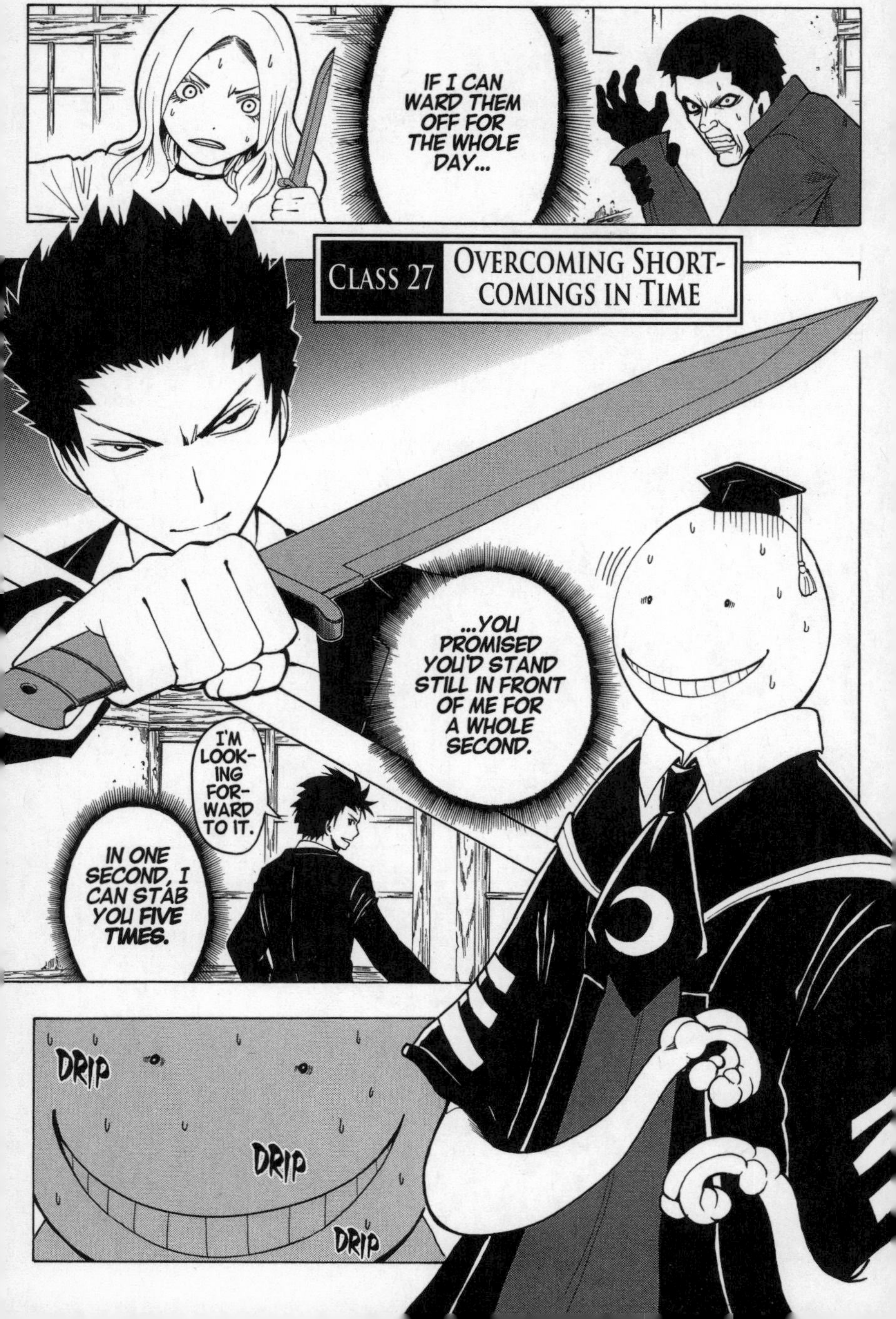
IF I CAN WARD THEM OFF FOR THE WHOLE DAY...
CLASS 27 OVERCOMING SHORT-COMINGS IN TIME
...YOU PROMISED YOU'D STAND STILL IN FRONT OF ME FOR A WHOLE SECOND.
I'M LOOK-ING FOR-WARD TO IT.
IN ONE SECOND, I CAN STAB YOU FIVE TIMES.
DRIP
DRIP
DRIP

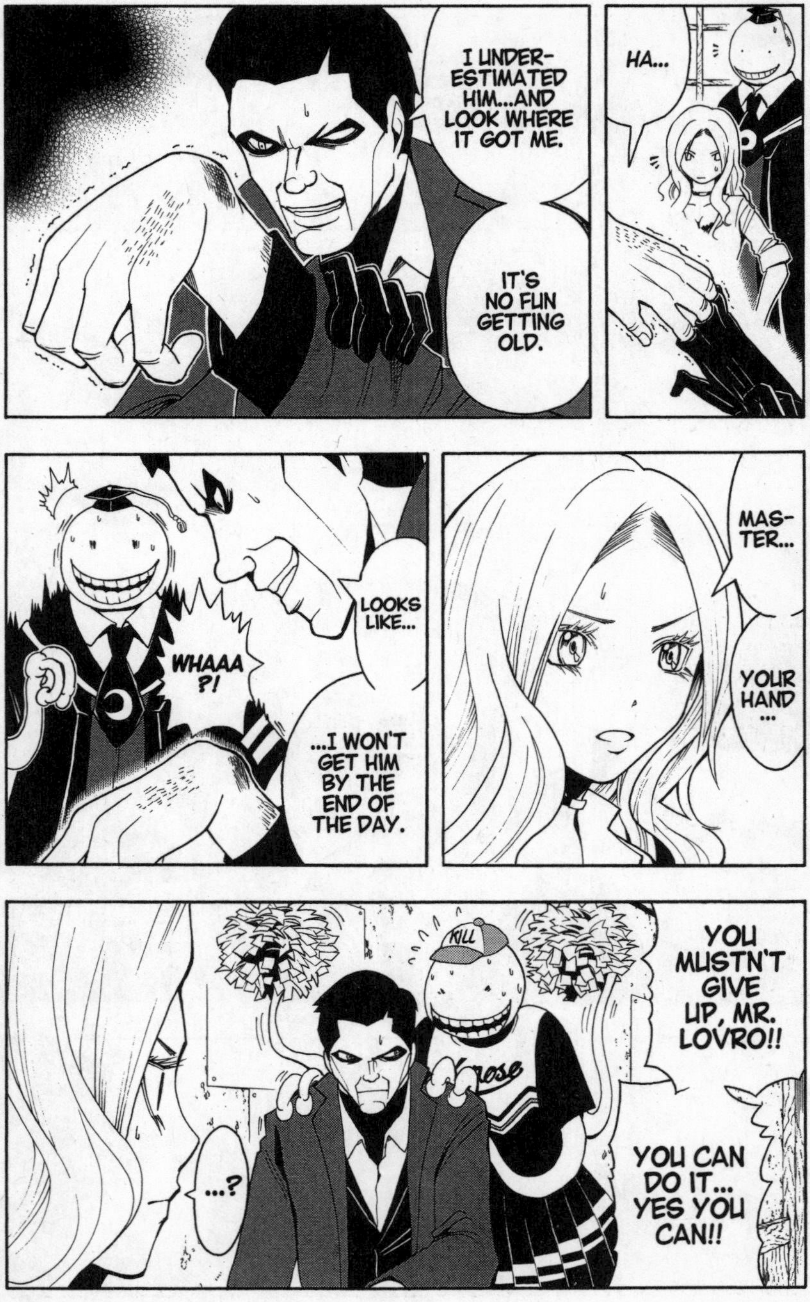
HA...
I UNDER-ESTIMATED HIM...AND LOOK WHERE IT GOT ME.
IT'S NO FUN GETTING OLD.
MAS-TER...
YOUR HAND ...
LOOKS LIKE...
...I WON'T GET HIM BY THE END OF THE DAY.
WHAAA ?!
YOU MUSTN'T GIVE UP, MR. LOVRO!!
KILL
YOU CAN DO IT... YES YOU CAN!!
...?

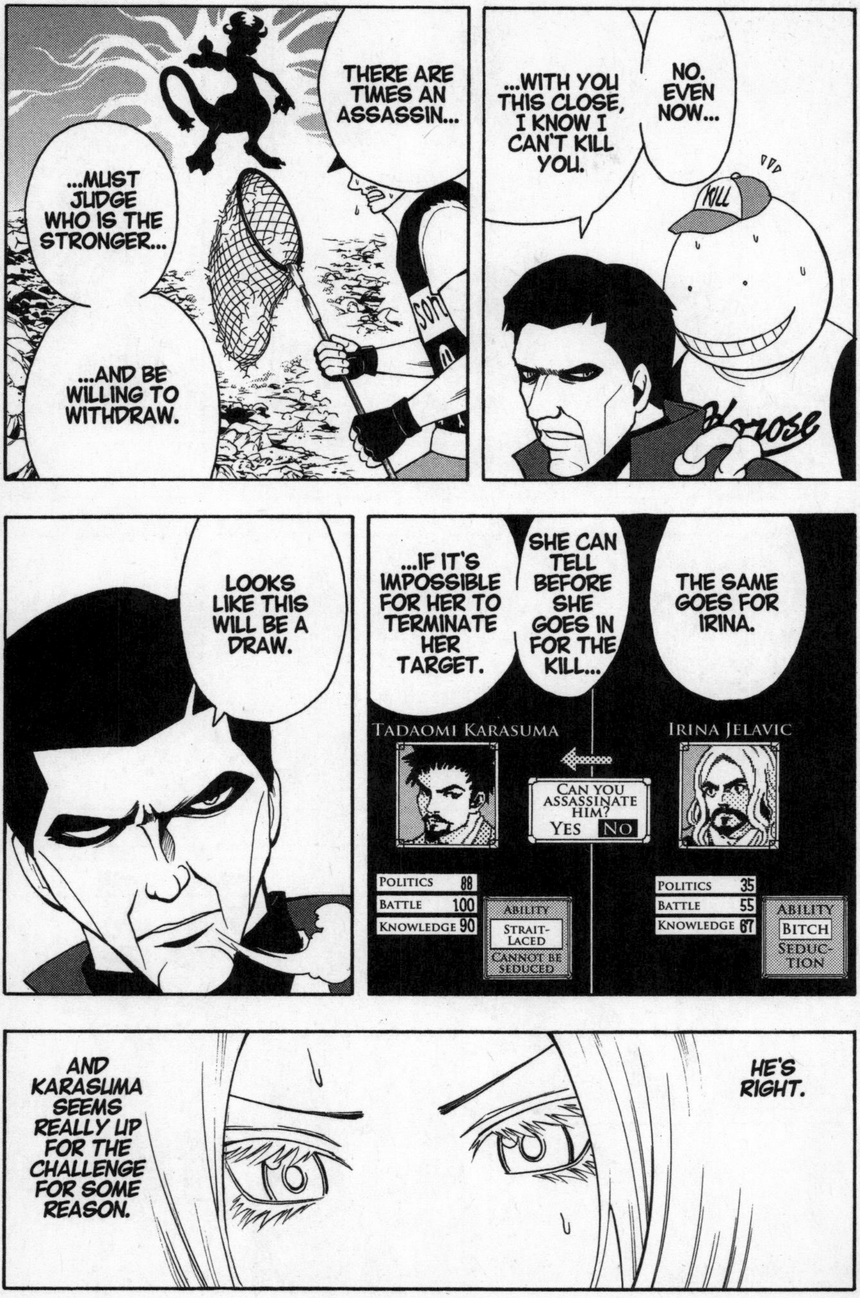
NO. EVEN NOW...
...WITH YOU THIS CLOSE, I KNOW I CAN'T KILL YOU.
KILL
Korose
THERE ARE TIMES AN ASSASSIN...
...MUST JUDGE WHO IS THE STRONGER...
...AND BE WILLING TO WITHDRAW.
THE SAME GOES FOR IRINA.
SHE CAN TELL BEFORE SHE GOES IN FOR THE KILL...
...IF IT'S IMPOSSIBLE FOR HER TO TERMINATE HER TARGET.
IRINA JELAVIC
POLITICS 35
BATTLE 55
KNOWLEDGE 67
ABILITY
BITCH
SEDUCTION
CAN YOU ASSASSINATE HIM?
YES NO
TADAOMI KARASUMA
POLITICS 88
BATTLE 100
KNOWLEDGE 90
ABILITY
STRAIT-LACED
CANNOT BE SEDUCED
LOOKS LIKE THIS WILL BE A DRAW.
HE'S RIGHT.
AND KARASUMA SEEMS REALLY UP FOR THE CHALLENGE FOR SOME REASON.

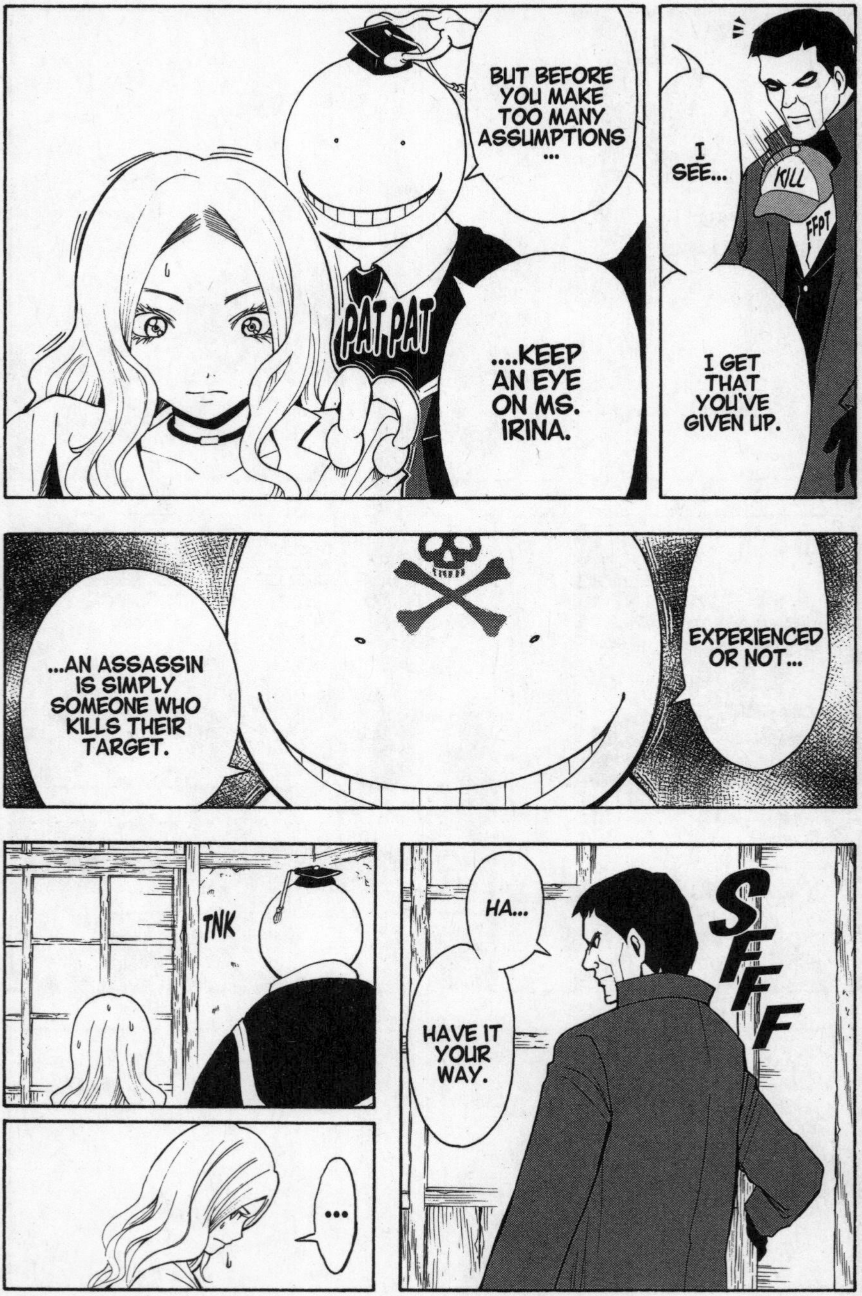
I SEE...
KILL
FFPT
I GET THAT YOU'VE GIVEN UP.
BUT BEFORE YOU MAKE TOO MANY ASSUMPTIONS ...
PAT PAT
....KEEP AN EYE ON MS. IRINA.
EXPERIENCED OR NOT...
...AN ASSASSIN IS SIMPLY SOMEONE WHO KILLS THEIR TARGET.
SFFF
HA...
HAVE IT YOUR WAY.
TNK
...

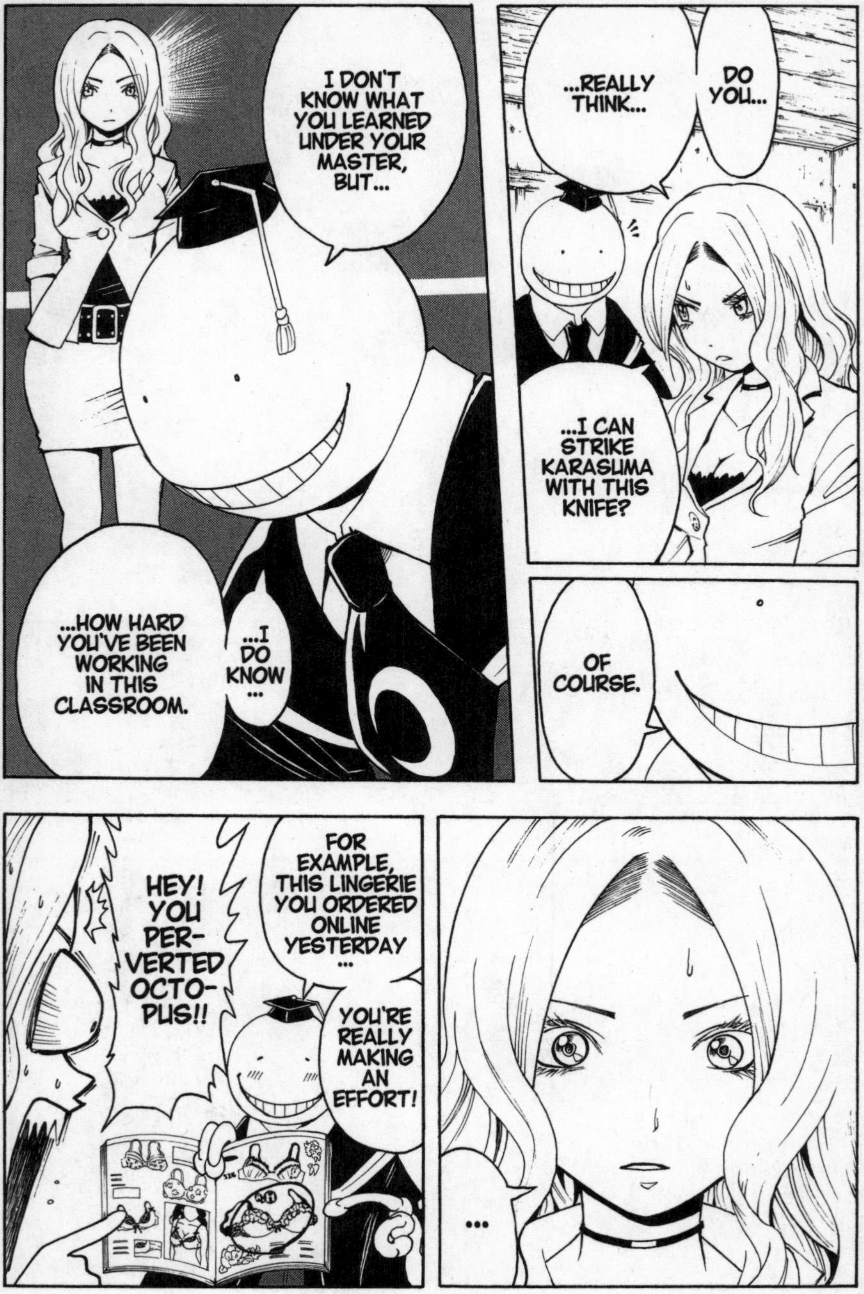
DO YOU...
...REALLY THINK...
...I CAN STRIKE KARASUMA WITH THIS KNIFE?
OF COURSE.
I DON'T KNOW WHAT YOU LEARNED UNDER YOUR MASTER, BUT...
...I DO KNOW...
...HOW HARD YOU'VE BEEN WORKING IN THIS CLASSROOM.
...
FOR EXAMPLE, THIS LINGERIE YOU ORDERED ONLINE YESTERDAY...
YOU'RE REALLY MAKING AN EFFORT!
HEY! YOU PER-VERTED OCTO-PUS!!

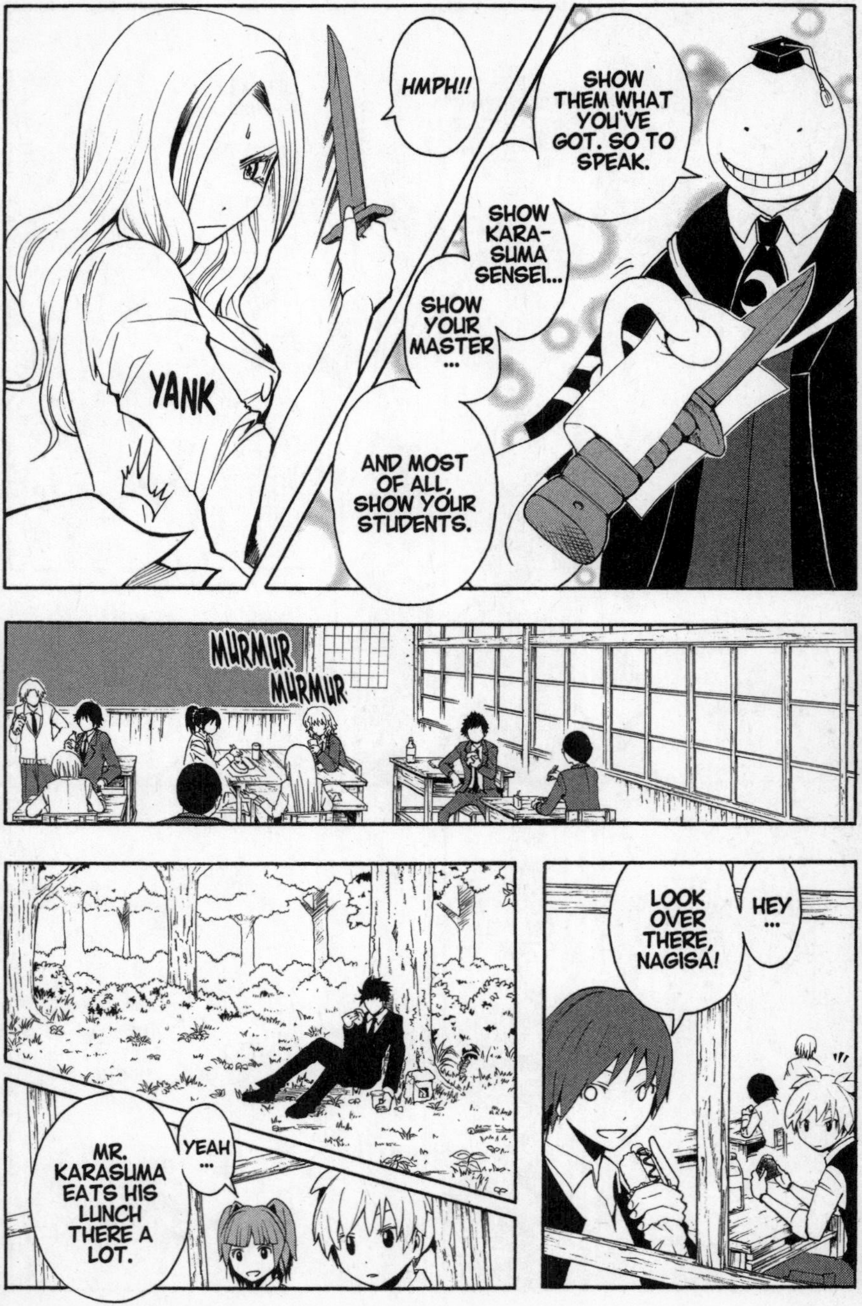
SHOW THEM WHAT YOU'VE GOT. SO TO SPEAK.
SHOW KARASUMA SENSEI...
SHOW YOUR MASTER...
AND MOST OF ALL, SHOW YOUR STUDENTS.
HMPH!!
YANK
MURMUR
MURMUR
HEY...
LOOK OVER THERE, NAGISA!
YEAH...
MR. KARASUMA EATS HIS LUNCH THERE A LOT.

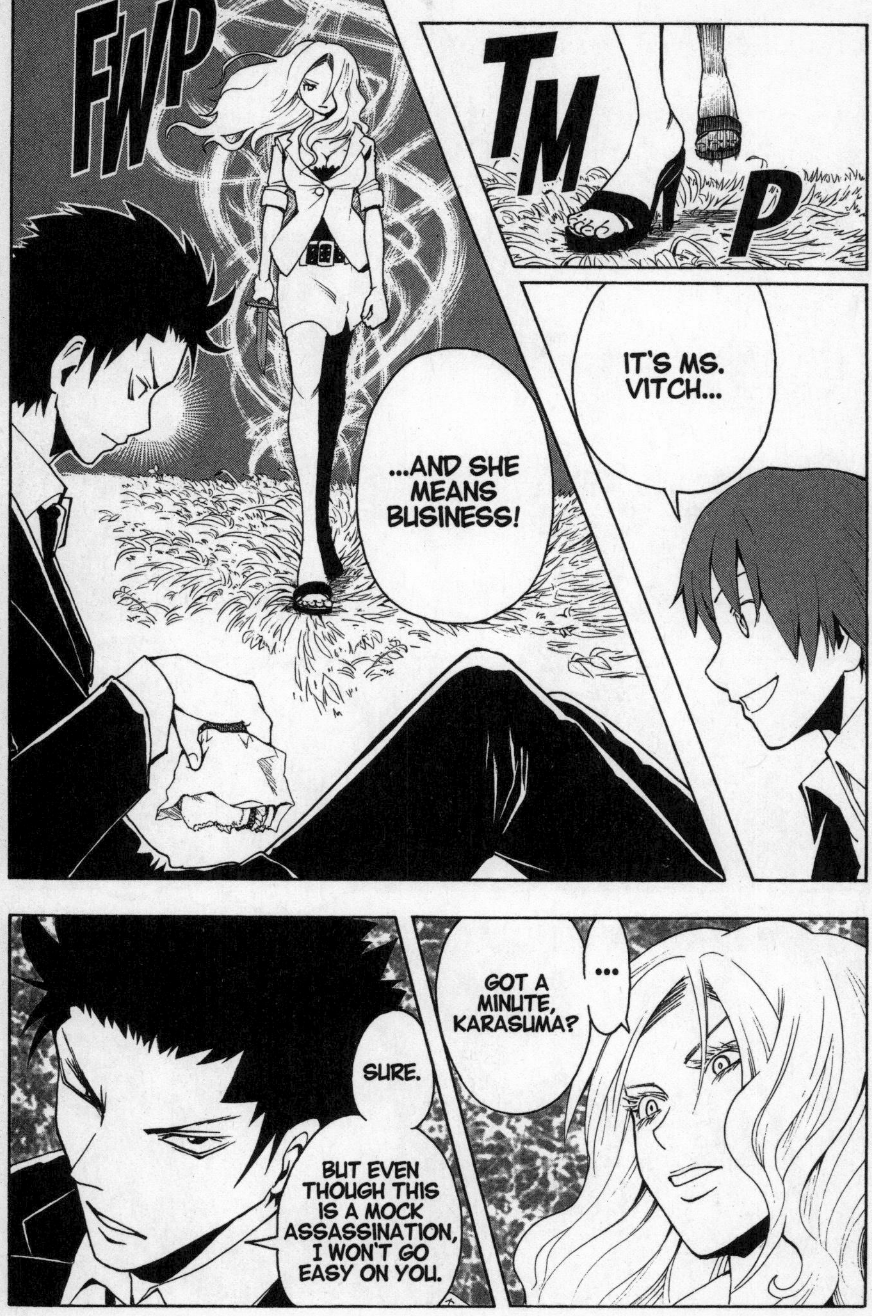
TMP
IT'S MS. VITCH...
FWP
...AND SHE MEANS BUSINESS!
...
GOT A MINUTE, KARASUMA?
SURE.
BUT EVEN THOUGH THIS IS A MOCK ASSASSINATION, I WON'T GO EASY ON YOU.

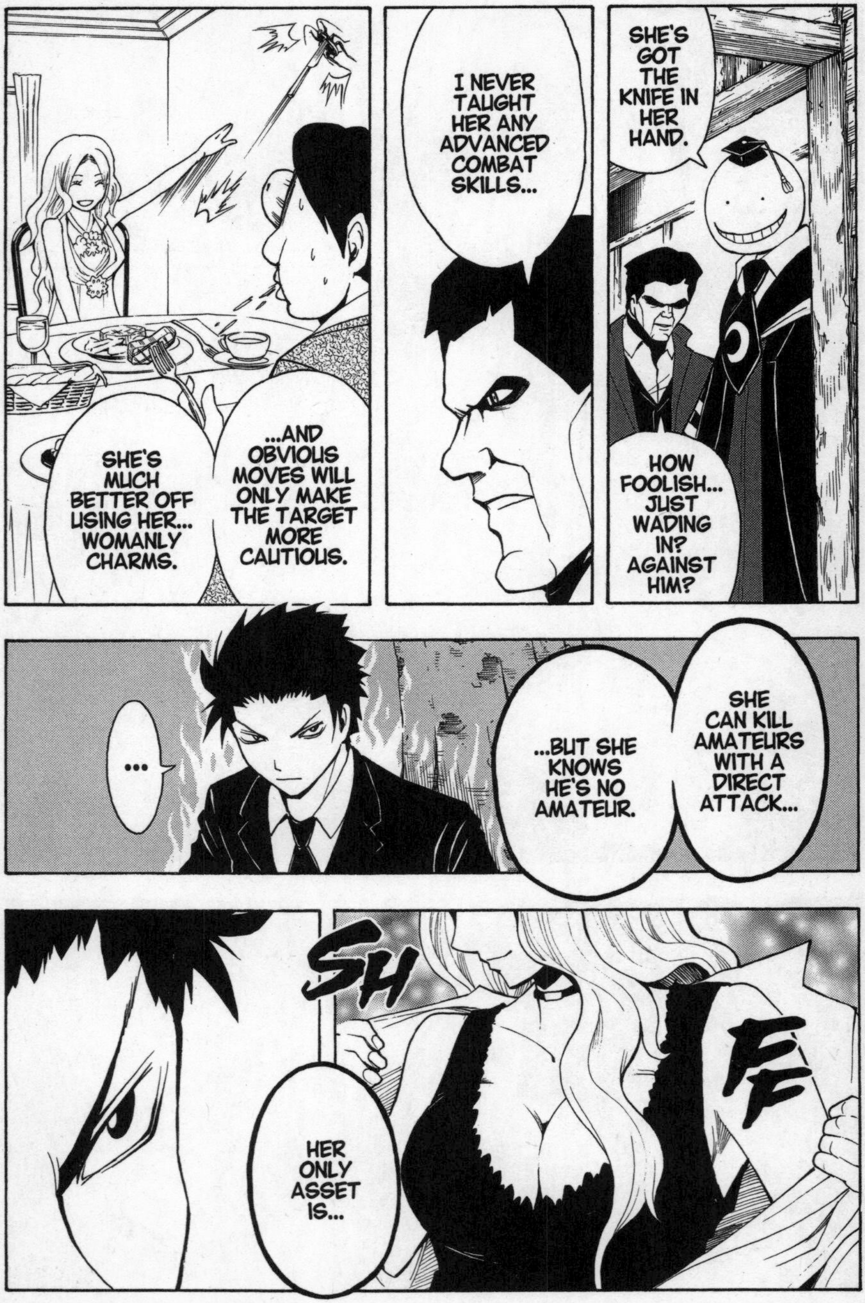
SHE'S GOT THE KNIFE IN HER HAND.
HOW FOOLISH... JUST WADING IN? AGAINST HIM?
I NEVER TAUGHT HER ANY ADVANCED COMBAT SKILLS...
...AND OBVIOUS MOVES WILL ONLY MAKE THE TARGET MORE CAUTIOUS.
SHE'S MUCH BETTER OFF USING HER... WOMANLY CHARMS.
SHE CAN KILL AMATEURS WITH A DIRECT ATTACK...
...BUT SHE KNOWS HE'S NO AMATEUR.
...
SH
FF
HER ONLY ASSET IS...

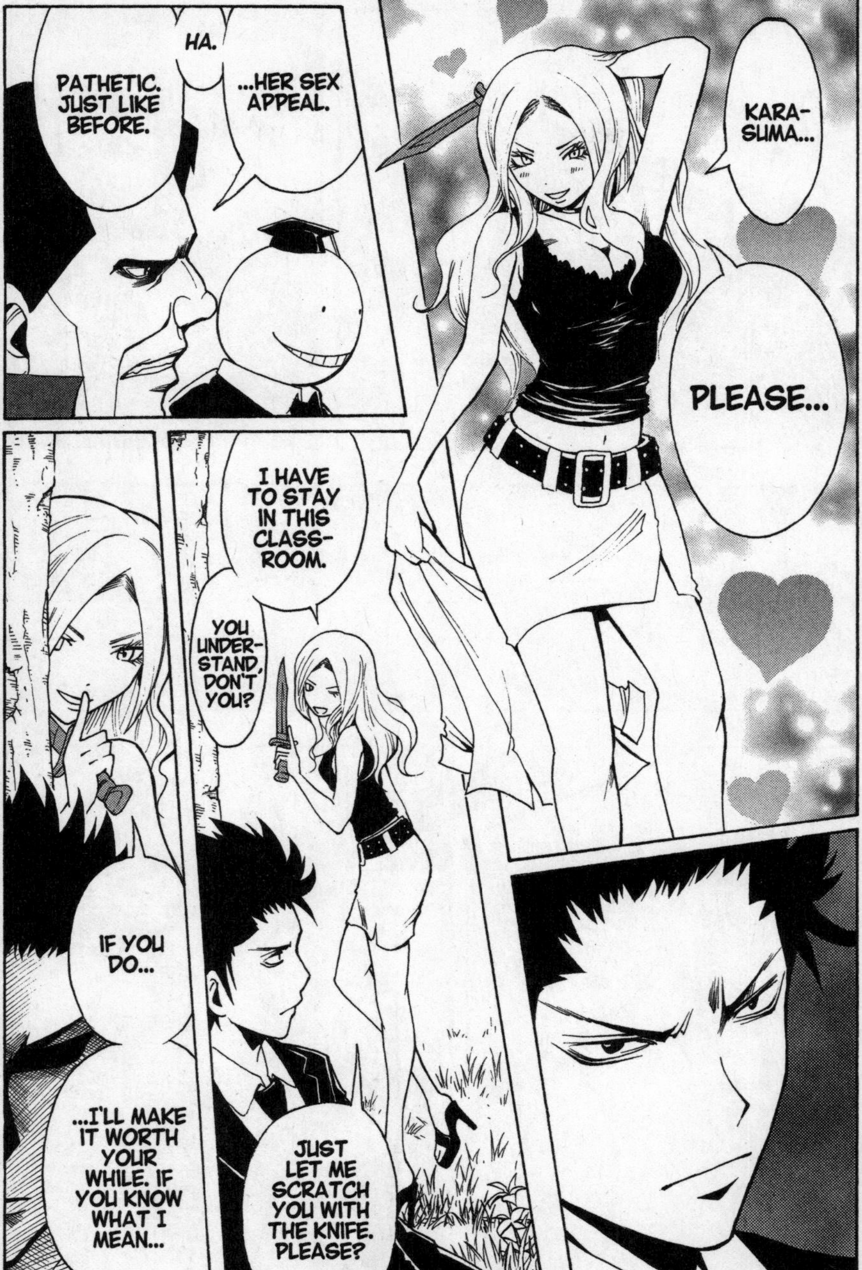
KARA-SUMA...
PLEASE...
...HER SEX APPEAL.
HA.
PATHETIC. JUST LIKE BEFORE.
I HAVE TO STAY IN THIS CLASS-ROOM.
YOU UNDER-STAND, DON'T YOU?
JUST LET ME SCRATCH YOU WITH THE KNIFE. PLEASE?
IF YOU DO...
...I'LL MAKE IT WORTH YOUR WHILE. IF YOU KNOW WHAT I MEAN...

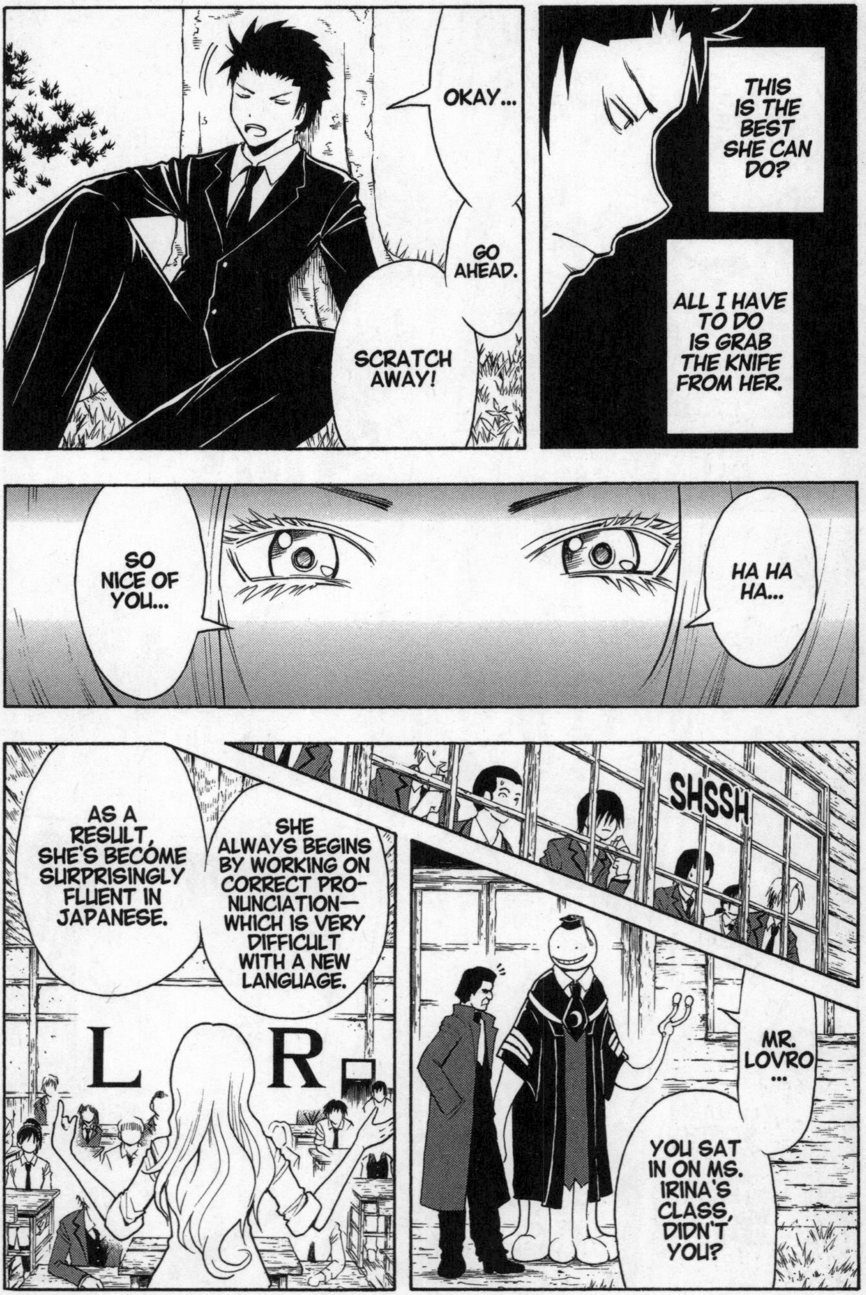
THIS IS THE BEST SHE CAN DO?
ALL I HAVE TO DO IS GRAB THE KNIFE FROM HER.
OKAY...
GO AHEAD.
SCRATCH AWAY!
HA HA HA...
SO NICE OF YOU...
SHSSH
MR. LOVRO...
YOU SAT IN ON MS. IRINA'S CLASS, DIDN'T YOU?
SHE ALWAYS BEGINS BY WORKING ON CORRECT PRO-NUNCIATION—WHICH IS VERY DIFFICULT WITH A NEW LANGUAGE.
AS A RESULT, SHE'S BECOME SURPRISINGLY FLUENT IN JAPANESE.
L
R

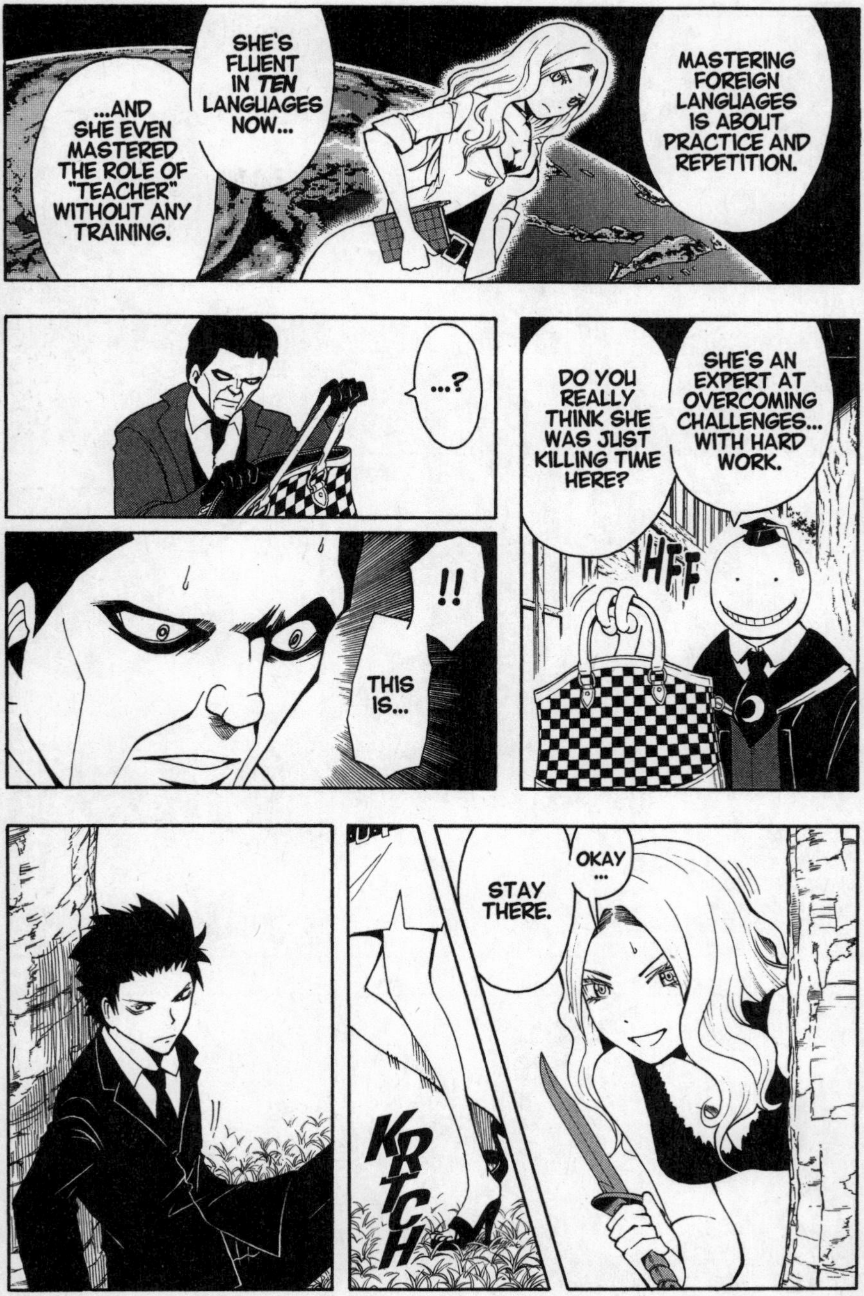
MASTERING FOREIGN LANGUAGES IS ABOUT PRACTICE AND REPETITION.
SHE'S FLUENT IN TEN LANGUAGES NOW...
...AND SHE EVEN MASTERED THE ROLE OF "TEACHER" WITHOUT ANY TRAINING.
SHE'S AN EXPERT AT OVERCOMING CHALLENGES... WITH HARD WORK.
DO YOU REALLY THINK SHE WAS JUST KILLING TIME HERE?
HFF
...?
!!
THIS IS...
OKAY ...
STAY THERE.
KRTCH

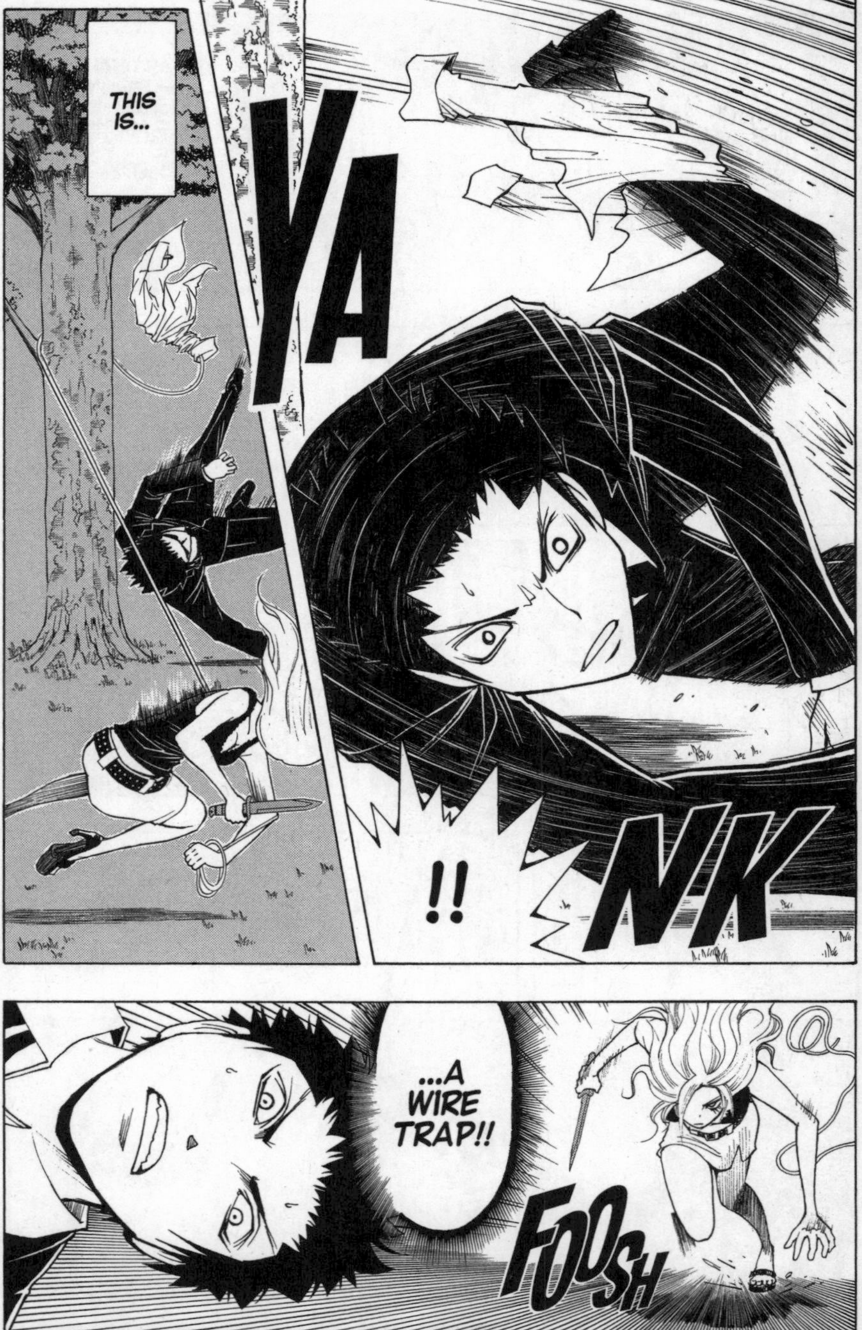

YANK
!!
THIS IS...
...A WIRE TRAP!!
FOOSH

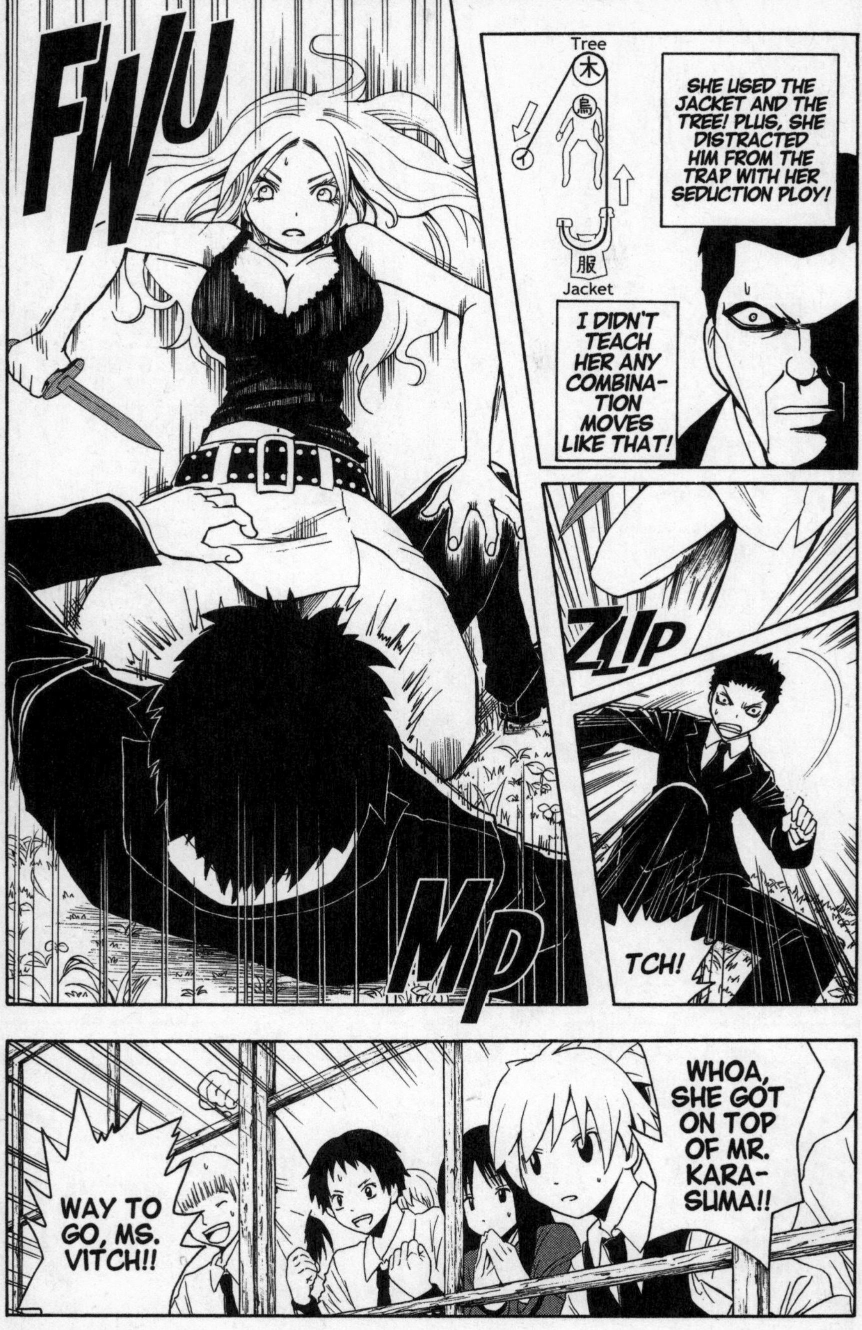
Tree
木
鳥
イ
服
Jacket
SHE USED THE JACKET AND THE TREE! PLUS, SHE DISTRACTED HIM FROM THE TRAP WITH HER SEDUCTION PLOY!
I DIDN'T TEACH HER ANY COMBINA-TION MOVES LIKE THAT!
ZLIP
TCH!
FWU
MP
WHOA, SHE GOT ON TOP OF MR. KARA-SUMA!!
WAY TO GO, MS. VITCH!!

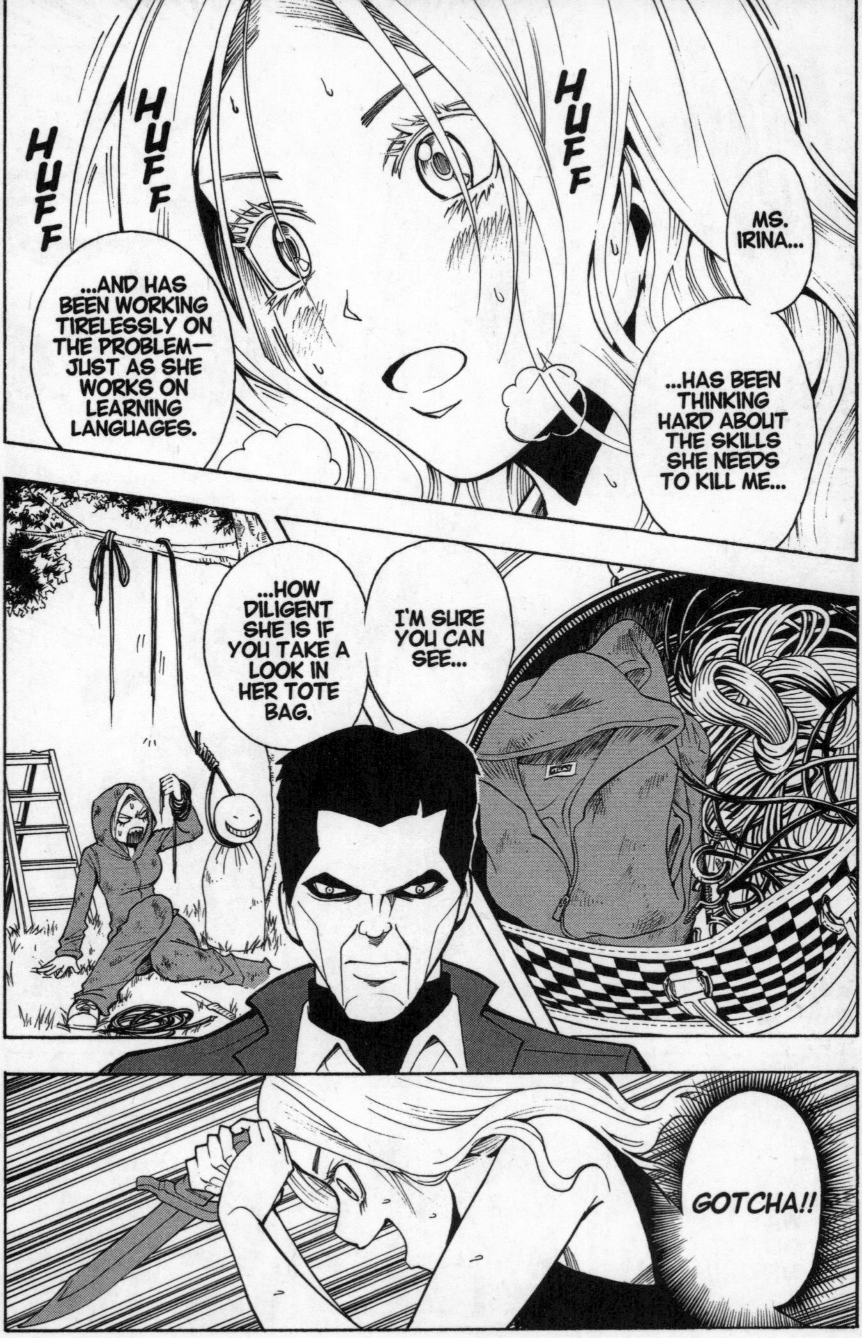
HUFF
MS. IRINA...
...HAS BEEN THINKING HARD ABOUT THE SKILLS SHE NEEDS TO KILL ME...
HUFF
HUFF
...AND HAS BEEN WORKING TIRELESSLY ON THE PROBLEM—JUST AS SHE WORKS ON LEARNING LANGUAGES.
I'M SURE YOU CAN SEE...
...HOW DILIGENT SHE IS IF YOU TAKE A LOOK IN HER TOTE BAG.
GOTCHA!!

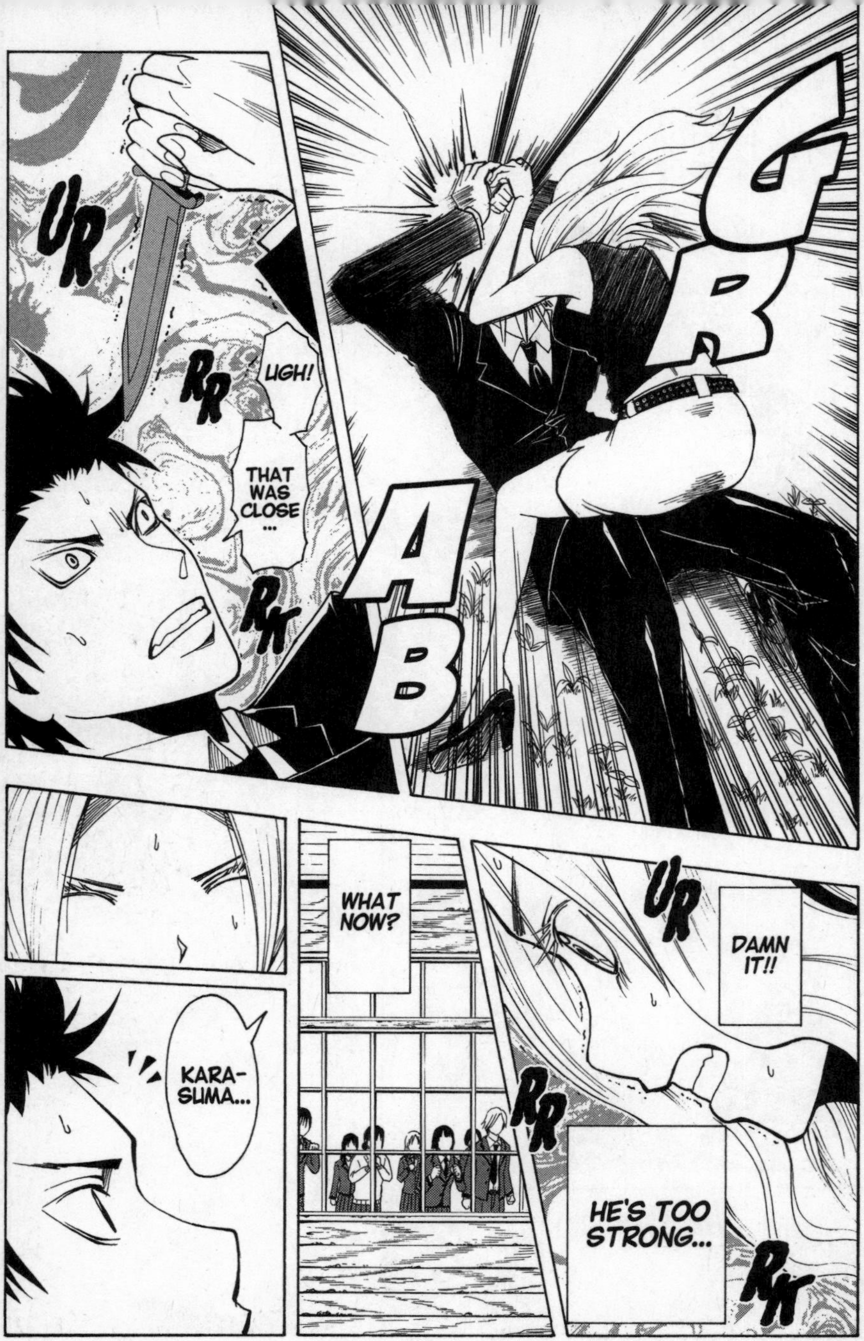
GRAB
URRRRK
UGH! THAT WAS CLOSE...
DAMN IT!!
URRRRK
HE'S TOO STRONG...
WHAT NOW?
KARA-SUMA...

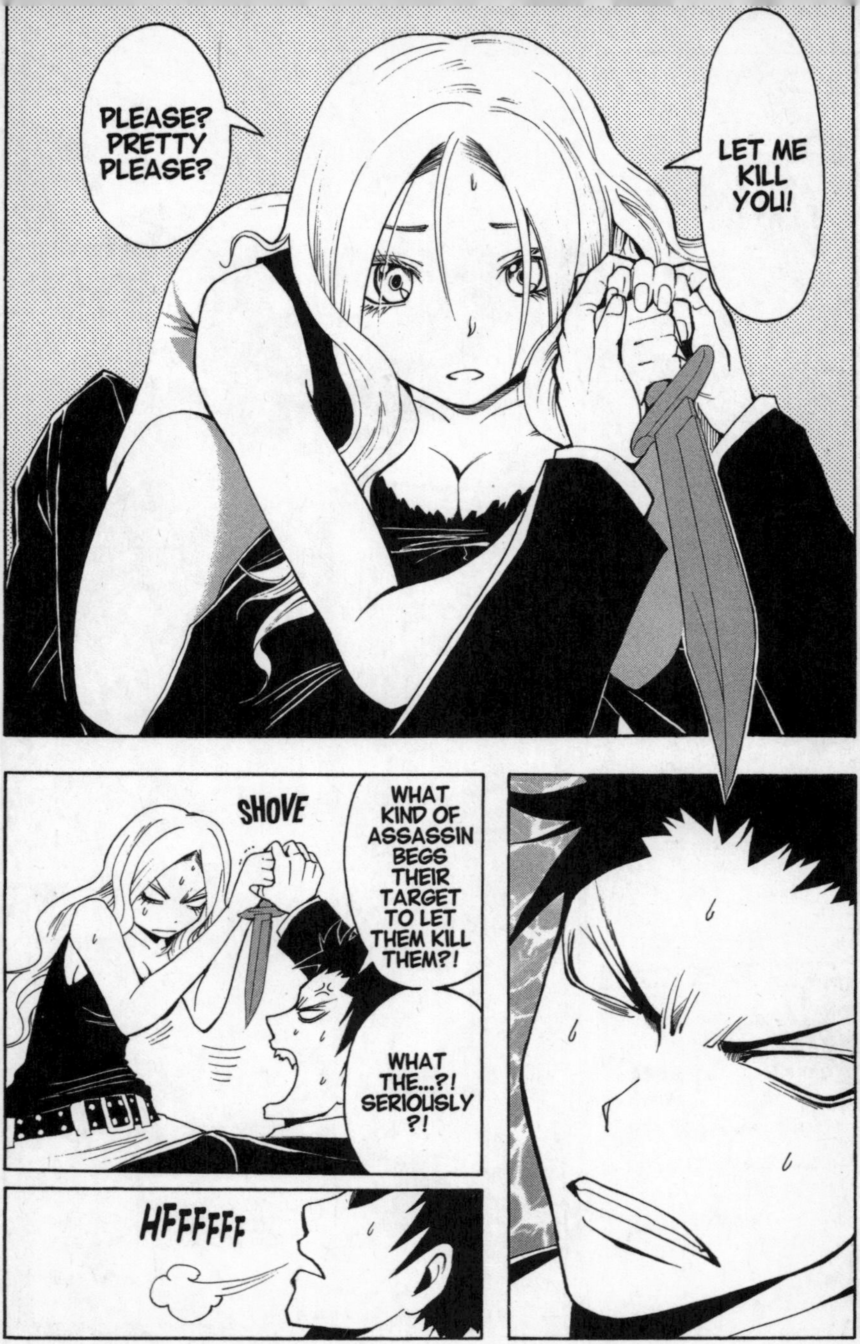
LET ME KILL YOU!
PLEASE? PRETTY PLEASE?
WHAT KIND OF ASSASSIN BEGS THEIR TARGET TO LET THEM KILL THEM?!
SHOVE
WHAT THE...?! SERIOUSLY?!
HFFFFFF

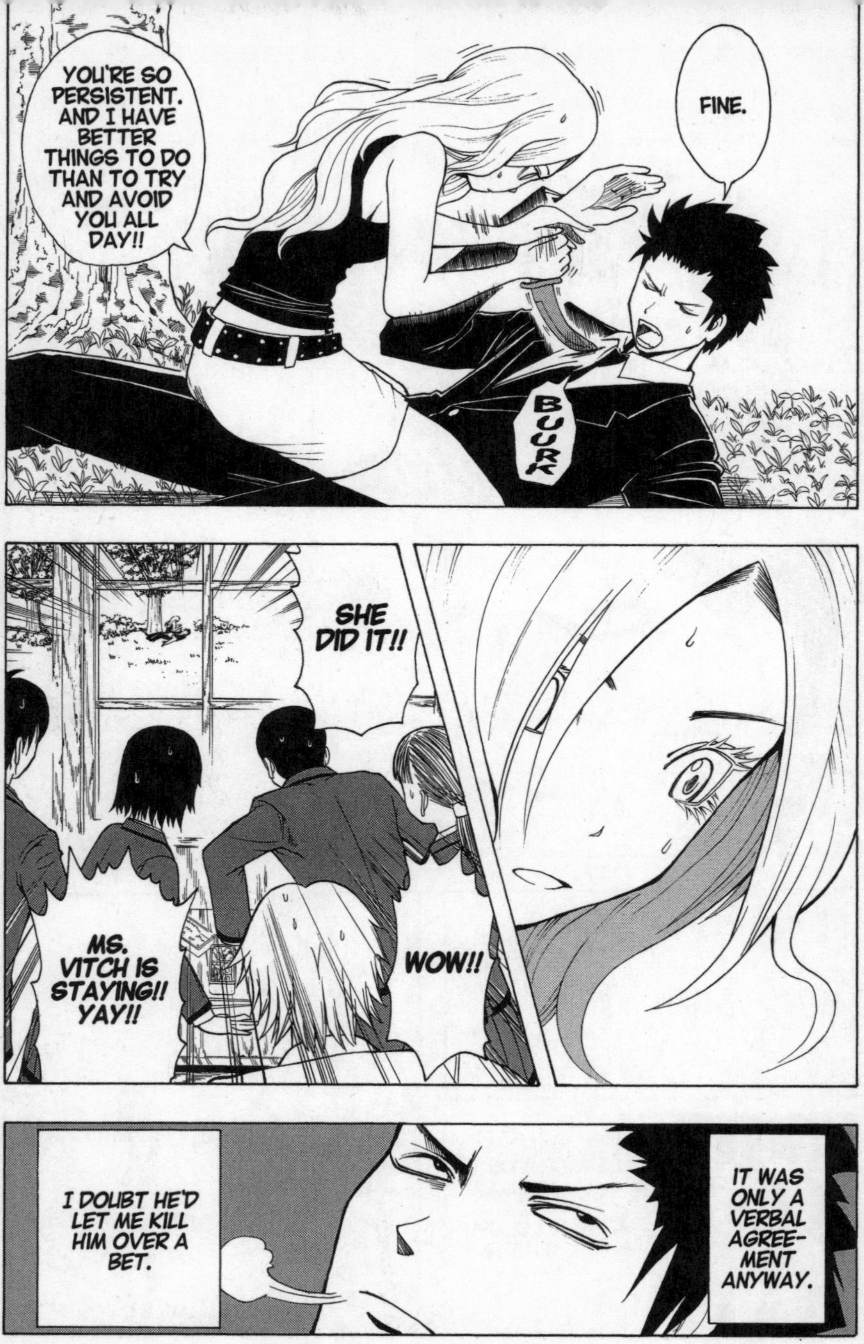
FINE.
YOU'RE SO PERSISTENT. AND I HAVE BETTER THINGS TO DO THAN TO TRY AND AVOID YOU ALL DAY!!
BUURK
SHE DID IT!!
WOW!!
MS. VITCH IS STAYING!! YAY!!
IT WAS ONLY A VERBAL AGREE-MENT ANYWAY.
I DOUBT HE'D LET ME KILL HIM OVER A BET.

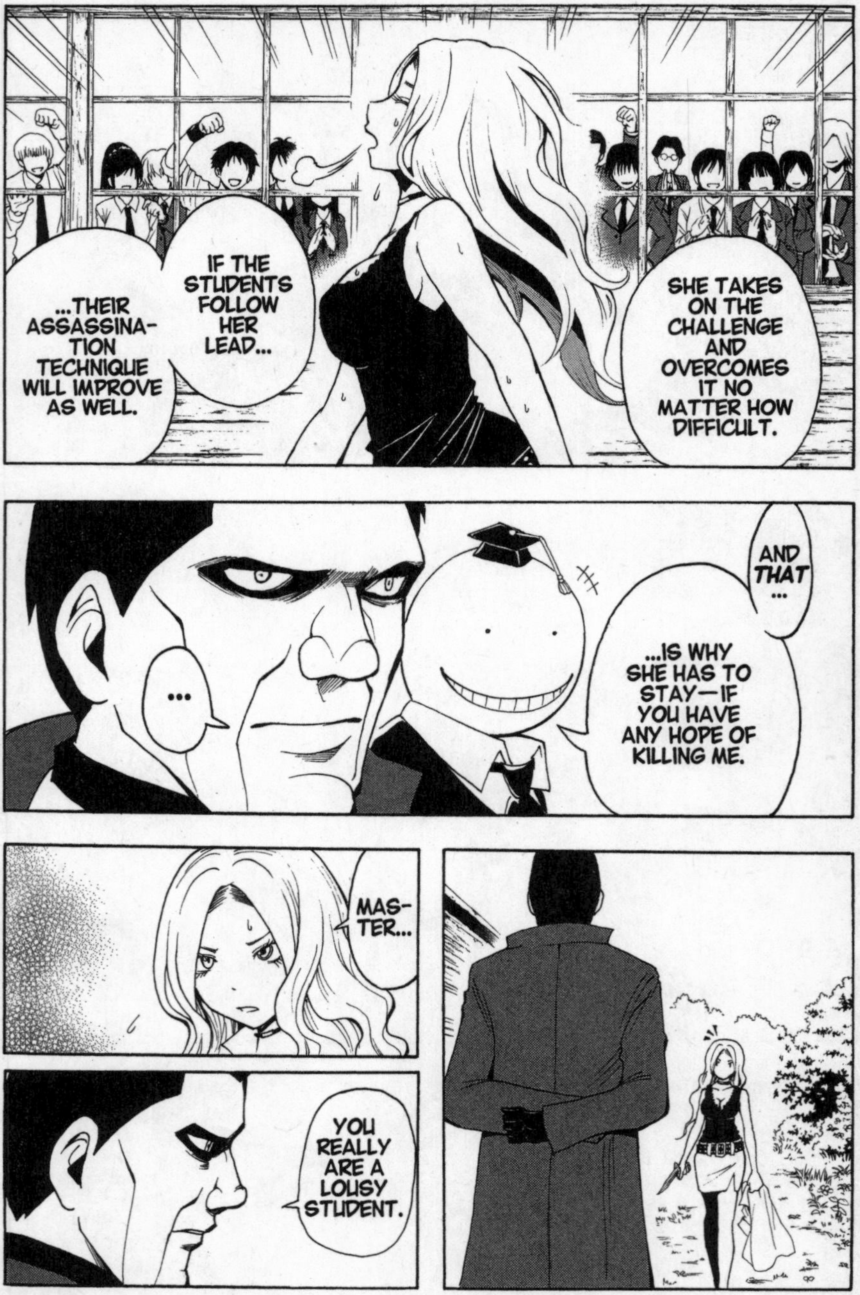
SHE TAKES ON THE CHALLENGE AND OVERCOMES IT NO MATTER HOW DIFFICULT.
IF THE STUDENTS FOLLOW HER LEAD...
...THEIR ASSASSINATION TECHNIQUE WILL IMPROVE AS WELL.
AND *THAT*...
...IS WHY SHE HAS TO STAY—IF YOU HAVE ANY HOPE OF KILLING ME.
...
MASTER...
YOU REALLY ARE A LOUSY STUDENT.

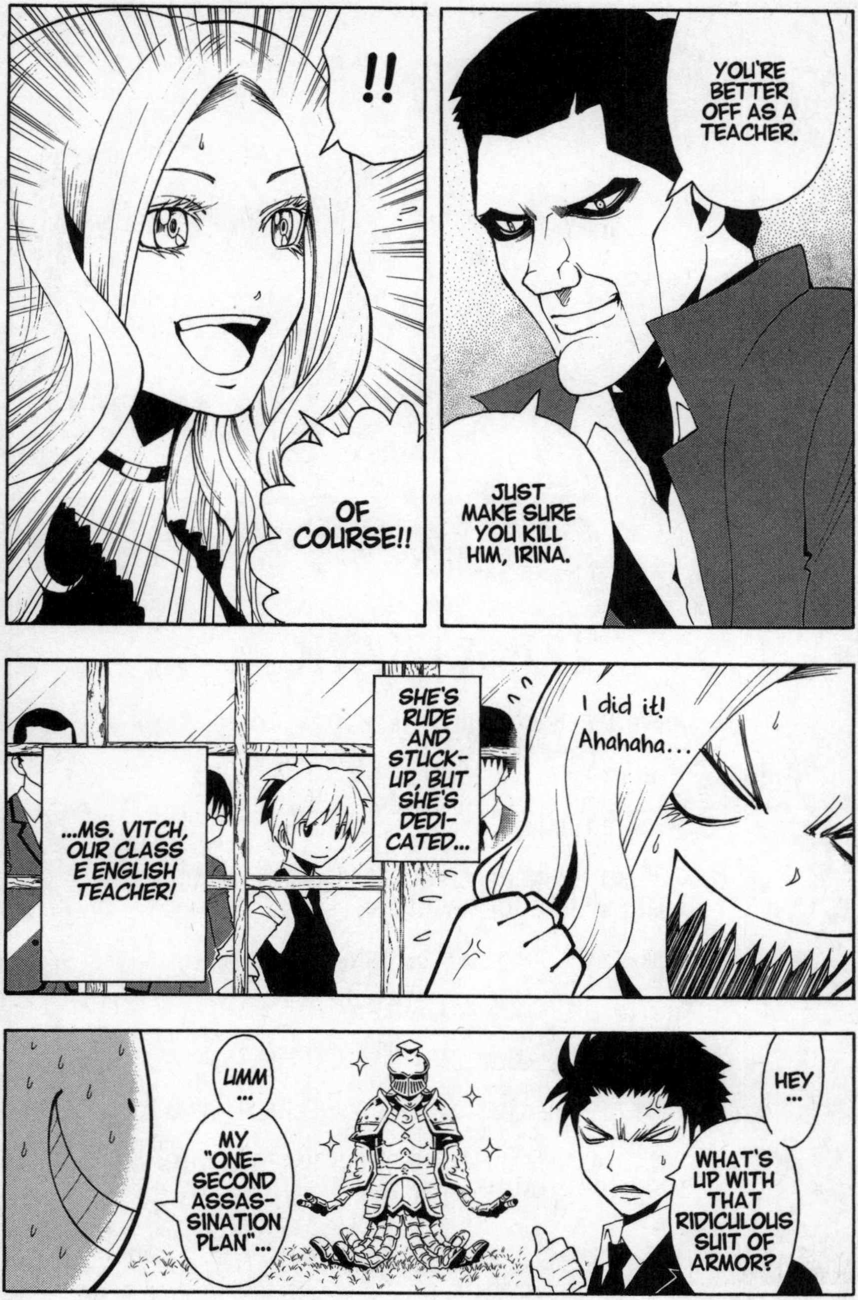
YOU'RE BETTER OFF AS A TEACHER.
JUST MAKE SURE YOU KILL HIM, IRINA.
!!
OF COURSE!!
I did it! Ahahaha...
SHE'S RUDE AND STUCK-UP, BUT SHE'S DEDICATED...
...MS. VITCH, OUR CLASS E ENGLISH TEACHER!
HEY ...
WHAT'S UP WITH THAT RIDICULOUS SUIT OF ARMOR?
UMM ...
MY "ONE-SECOND ASSASSINATION PLAN"...

IRINA JELAVIC

- 😊 BIRTHDAY: OCTOBER 10 (TWENTY YEARS OLD)

- 😊 HEIGHT: 5' 7"

- 😊 WEIGHT: 110 LBS.

- 😊 CAREER HISTORY: PROFESSIONAL ASSASSIN/CLASS E FOREIGN LANGUAGE TEACHER

- 😊 HOBBY/SKILL: ANYTHING FEMININE

- 😊 MOTTO: LIFE IS NUDITY; ADMIRE IT.

- 😊 MEASUREMENTS: BUST: 38"; WAIST: 23.6"; HIP: 35.8"

- 😊 FIRST TIME SHE ASSASSINATED A TARGET: EIGHT YEARS AGO

- 😊 FIRST TIME HER EYES POPPED OUT OF HER HEAD WHEN SHE SHOUTED AT SOMEONE: THIS YEAR

Class 28 | Movie Time!

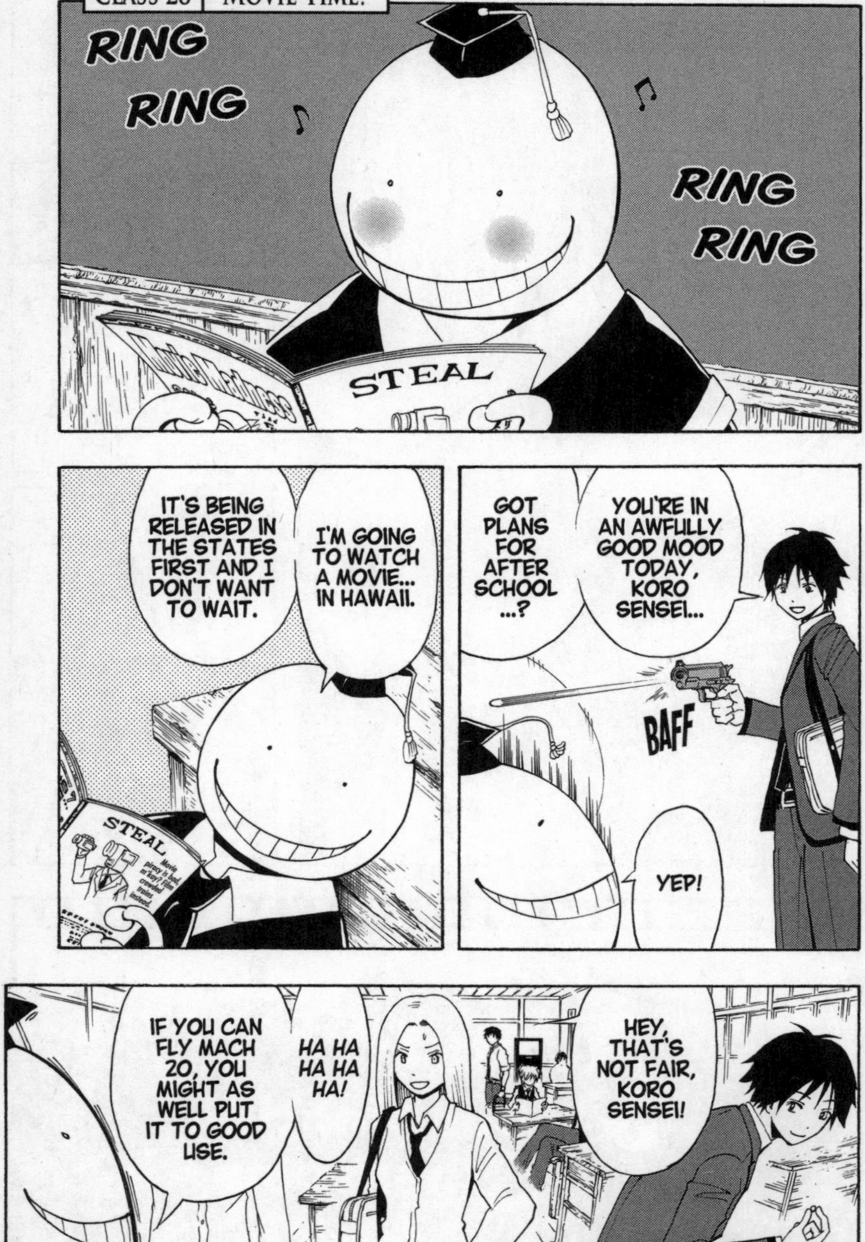
RING RING
RING RING
STEAL
YOU'RE IN AN AWFULLY GOOD MOOD TODAY, KORO SENSEI...
GOT PLANS FOR AFTER SCHOOL ...?
BAFF
YEP!
I'M GOING TO WATCH A MOVIE... IN HAWAII.
IT'S BEING RELEASED IN THE STATES FIRST AND I DON'T WANT TO WAIT.
STEAL
Movie piracy is bad, m'kay? Film crowded trains instead.
HEY, THAT'S NOT FAIR, KORO SENSEI!
HA HA HA HA HA!
IF YOU CAN FLY MACH 20, YOU MIGHT AS WELL PUT IT TO GOOD USE.

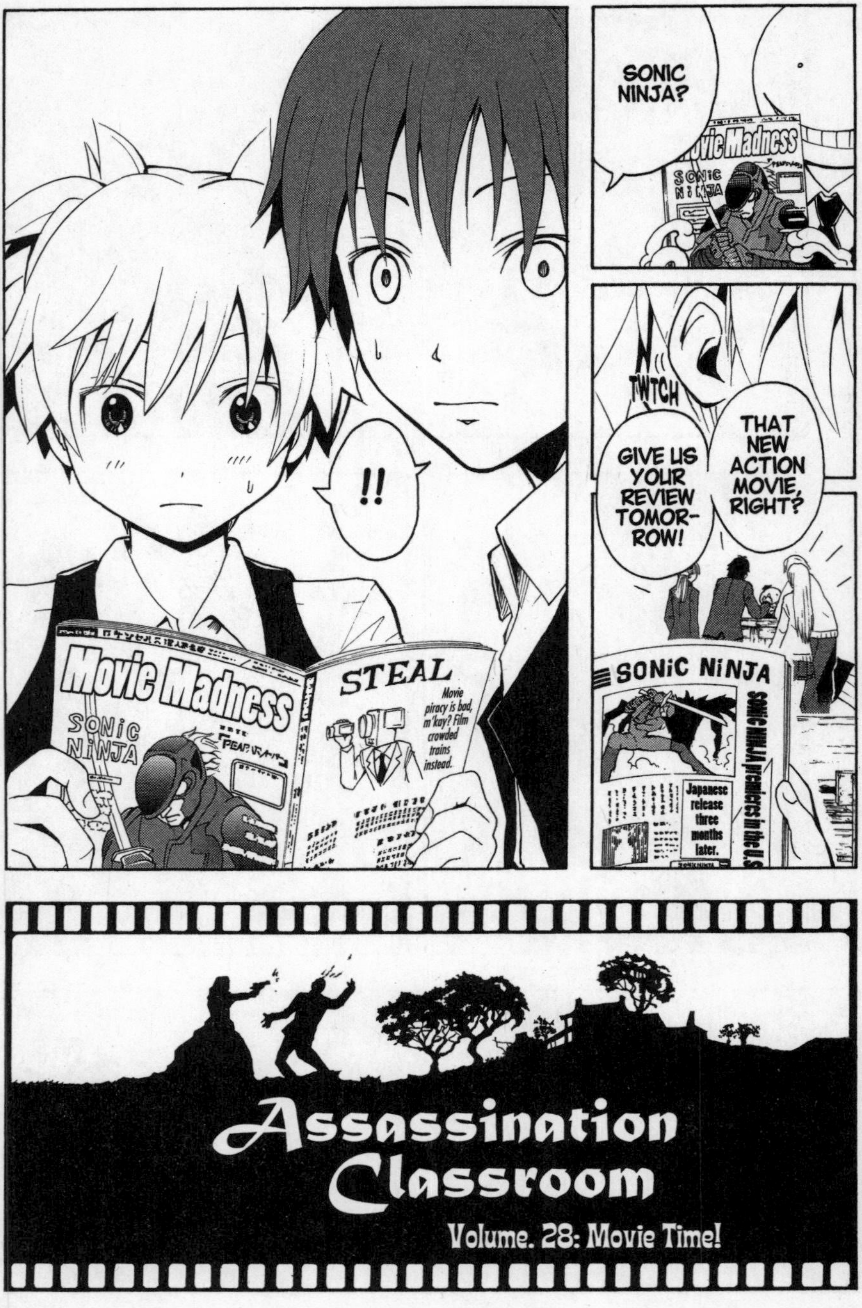
SONIC NINJA?
Movie Madness
SONIC NINJA
TWTCH
THAT NEW ACTION MOVIE, RIGHT?
GIVE US YOUR REVIEW TOMORROW!
SONIC NINJA
SONIC NINJA premieres in the U.S.
Japanese release three months later.
!!
Movie Madness
SONIC NINJA
STEAL
Movie piracy is bad, m'kay? Film crowded trains instead.
Assassination Classroom
Volume. 28: Movie Time!

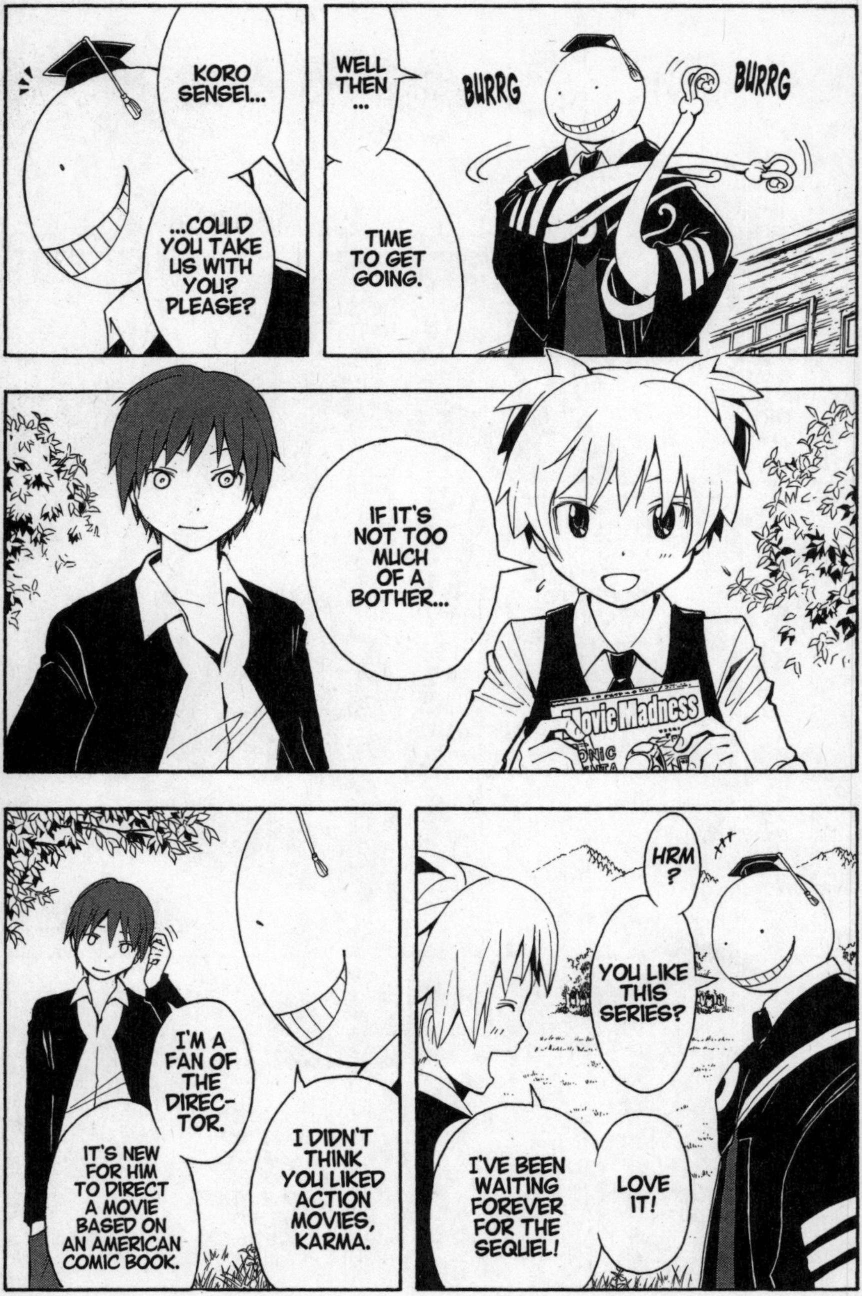
WELL THEN ...
BURRG
BURRG
TIME TO GET GOING.
KORO SENSEI...
...COULD YOU TAKE US WITH YOU? PLEASE?
IF IT'S NOT TOO MUCH OF A BOTHER...
Movie Madness
HRM?
YOU LIKE THIS SERIES?
LOVE IT!
I'VE BEEN WAITING FOREVER FOR THE SEQUEL!
I DIDN'T THINK YOU LIKED ACTION MOVIES, KARMA.
I'M A FAN OF THE DIREC- TOR.
IT'S NEW FOR HIM TO DIRECT A MOVIE BASED ON AN AMERICAN COMIC BOOK.

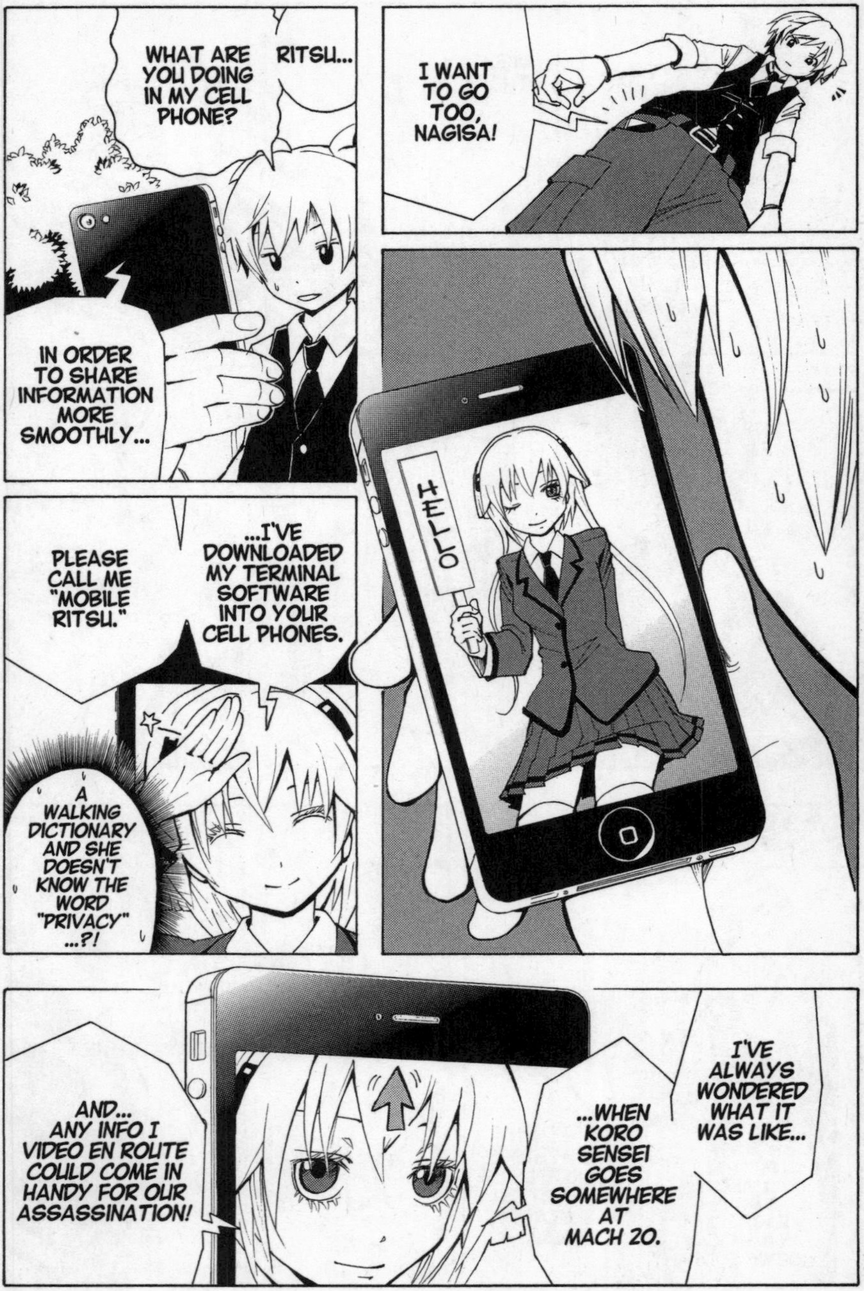
I WANT TO GO TOO, NAGISA!
RITSU...
WHAT ARE YOU DOING IN MY CELL PHONE?
IN ORDER TO SHARE INFORMATION MORE SMOOTHLY...
HELLO
...I'VE DOWNLOADED MY TERMINAL SOFTWARE INTO YOUR CELL PHONES.
PLEASE CALL ME "MOBILE RITSU."
A WALKING DICTIONARY AND SHE DOESN'T KNOW THE WORD "PRIVACY" ...?!
I'VE ALWAYS WONDERED WHAT IT WAS LIKE...
...WHEN KORO SENSEI GOES SOMEWHERE AT MACH 20.
AND... ANY INFO I VIDEO EN ROUTE COULD COME IN HANDY FOR OUR ASSASSINATION!

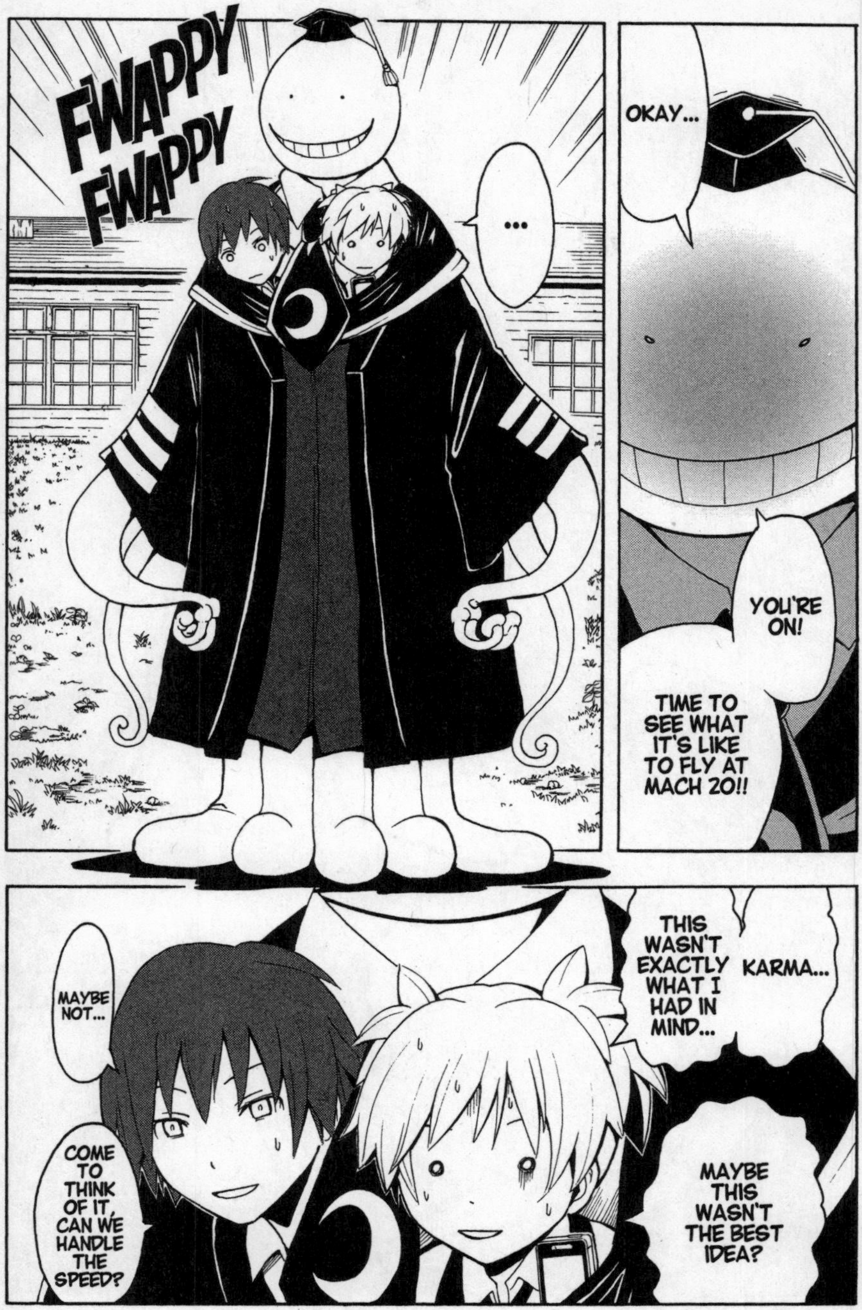
OKAY...
YOU'RE ON!
TIME TO SEE WHAT IT'S LIKE TO FLY AT MACH 20!!
FWAPPY FWAPPY
...
KARMA...
THIS WASN'T EXACTLY WHAT I HAD IN MIND...
MAYBE THIS WASN'T THE BEST IDEA?
MAYBE NOT...
COME TO THINK OF IT, CAN WE HANDLE THE SPEED?

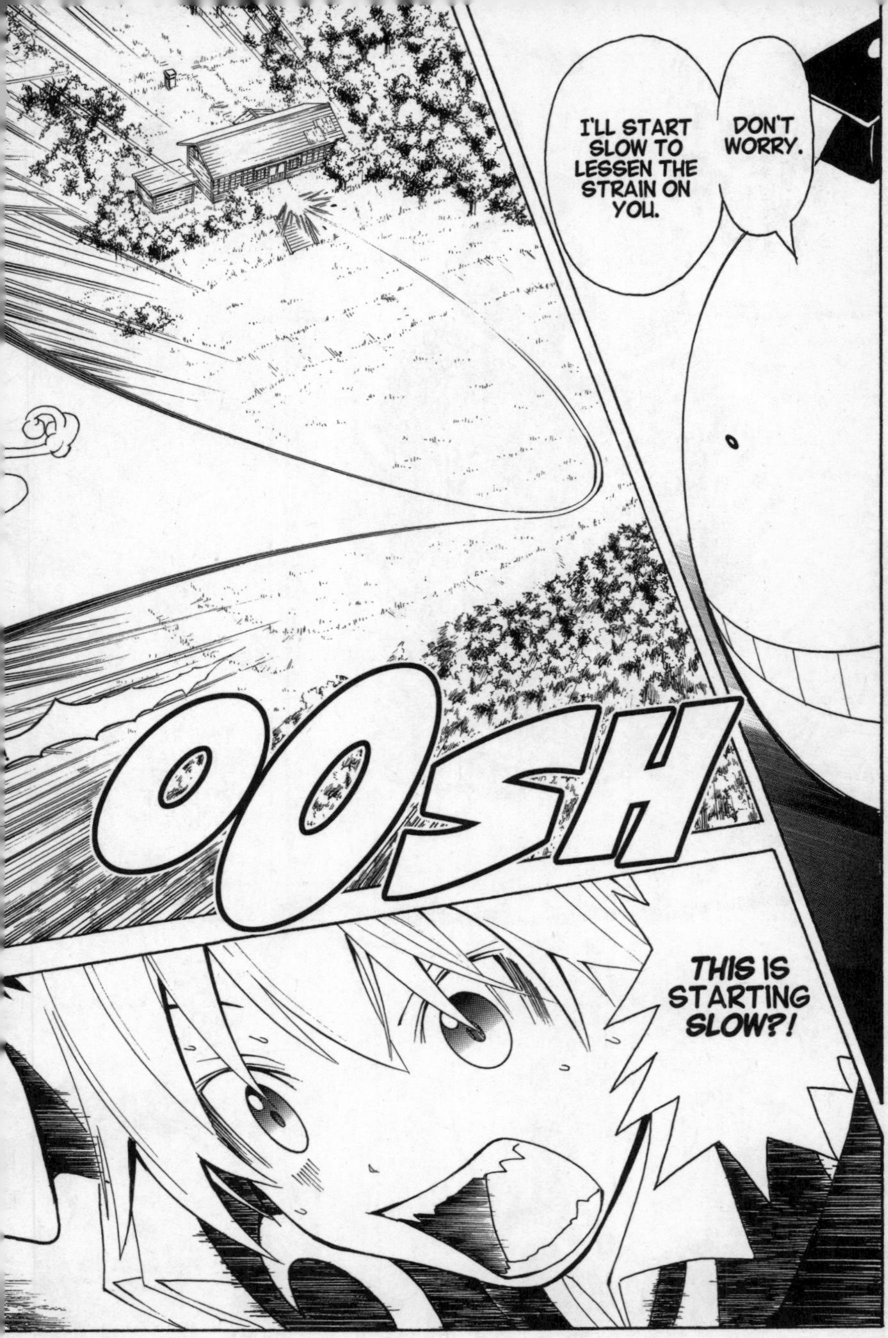
DON'T WORRY.
I'LL START SLOW TO LESSEN THE STRAIN ON YOU.
OOSH
THIS IS STARTING SLOW?!

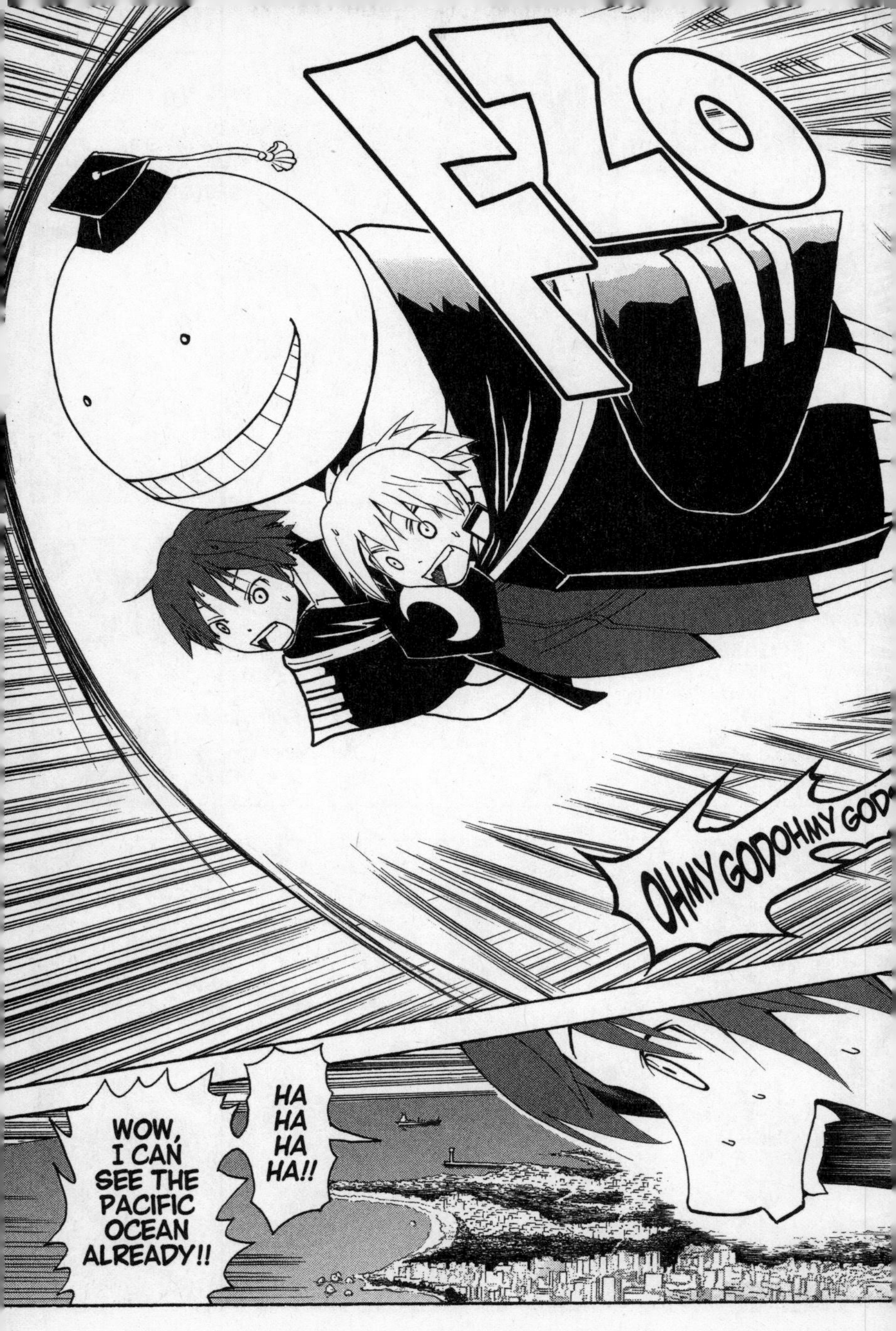
OHMY GODOHMY GOD
HA HA HA HA!!
WOW, I CAN SEE THE PACIFIC OCEAN ALREADY!!

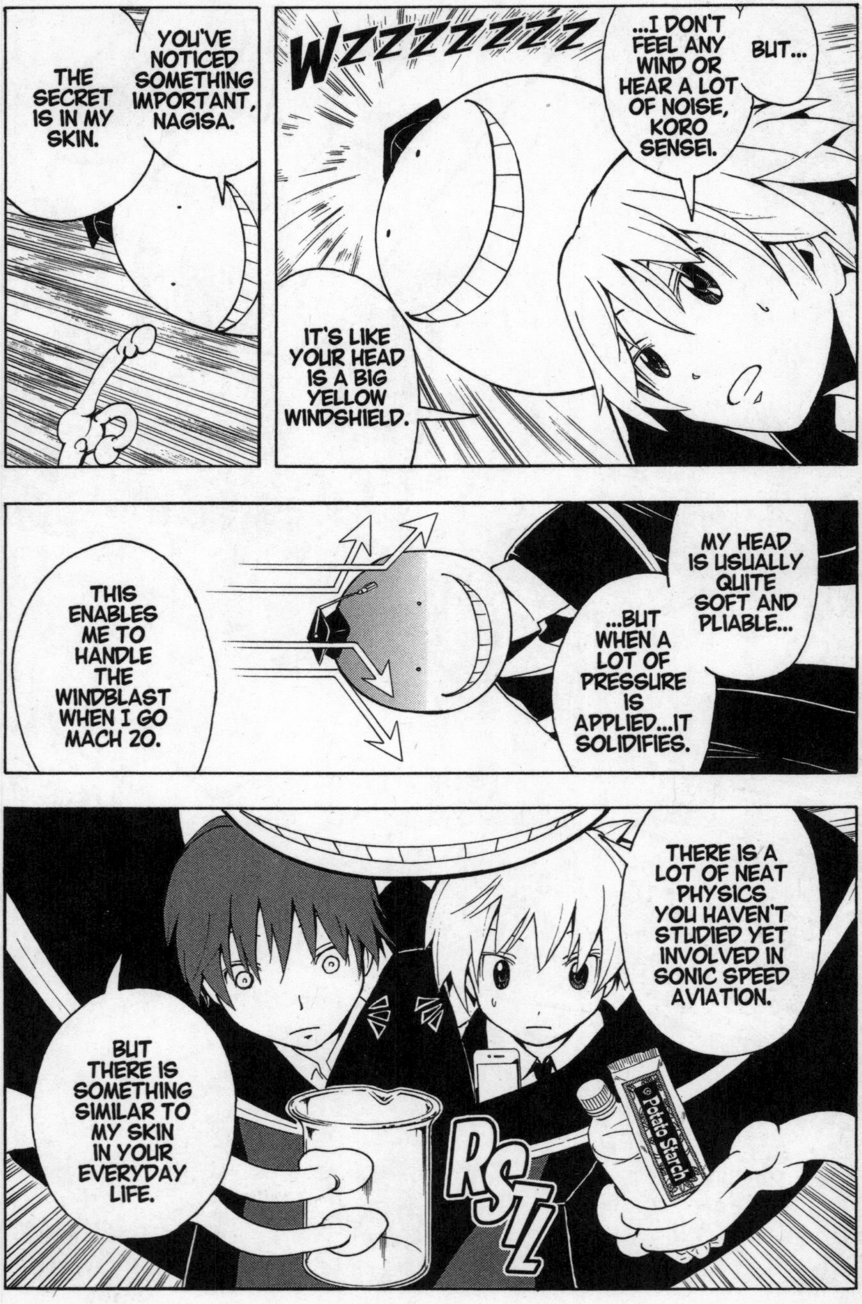
BUT...
...I DON'T FEEL ANY WIND OR HEAR A LOT OF NOISE, KORO SENSEI.
WZZZZZZZ
IT'S LIKE YOUR HEAD IS A BIG YELLOW WINDSHIELD.
YOU'VE NOTICED SOMETHING IMPORTANT, NAGISA.
THE SECRET IS IN MY SKIN.
MY HEAD IS USUALLY QUITE SOFT AND PLIABLE...
...BUT WHEN A LOT OF PRESSURE IS APPLIED...IT SOLIDIFIES.
THIS ENABLES ME TO HANDLE THE WINDBLAST WHEN I GO MACH 20.
THERE IS A LOT OF NEAT PHYSICS YOU HAVEN'T STUDIED YET INVOLVED IN SONIC SPEED AVIATION.
Potato Starch
RSTL
BUT THERE IS SOMETHING SIMILAR TO MY SKIN IN YOUR EVERYDAY LIFE.

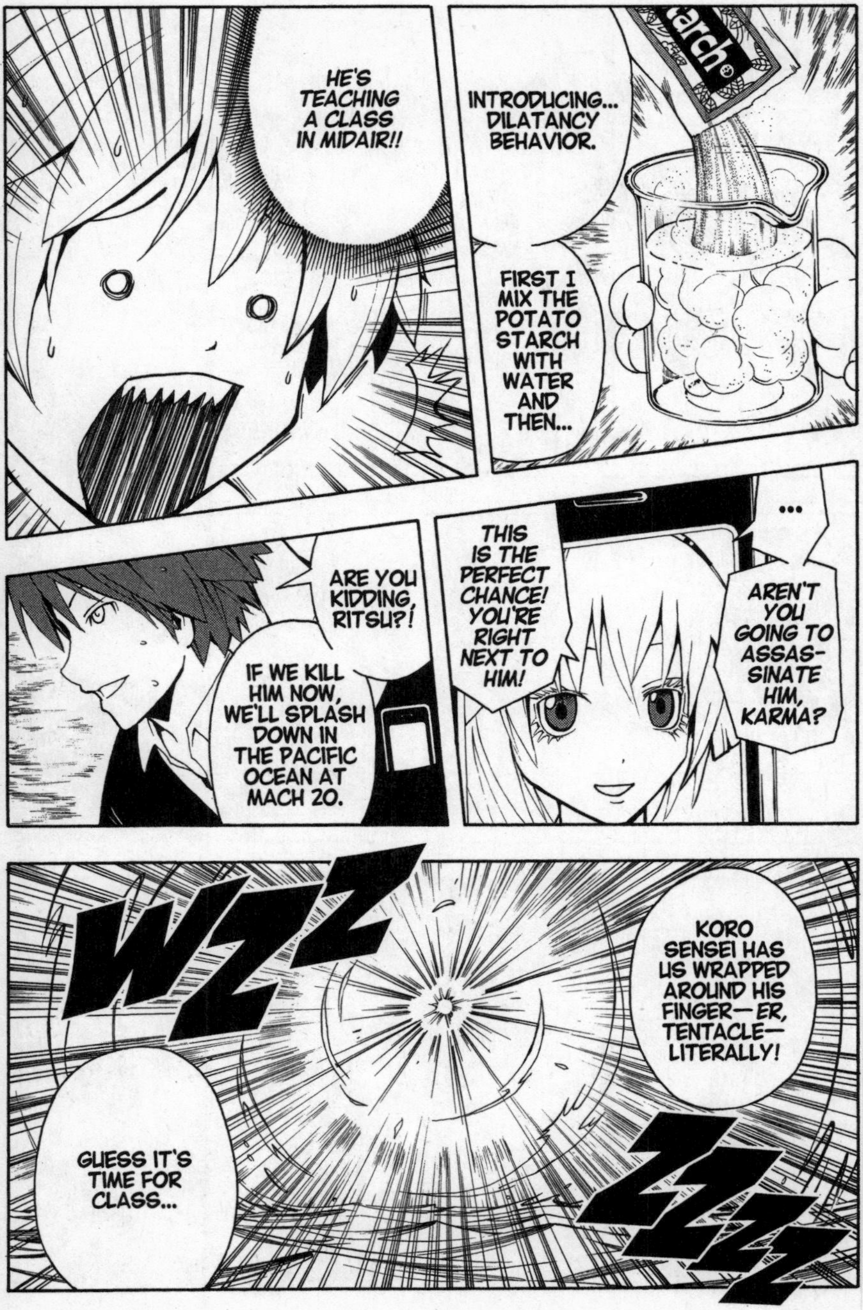
INTRODUCING... DILATANCY BEHAVIOR.
FIRST I MIX THE POTATO STARCH WITH WATER AND THEN...
HE'S TEACHING A CLASS IN MIDAIR!!
...
AREN'T YOU GOING TO ASSAS-SINATE HIM, KARMA?
THIS IS THE PERFECT CHANCE! YOU'RE RIGHT NEXT TO HIM!
ARE YOU KIDDING, RITSU?!
IF WE KILL HIM NOW, WE'LL SPLASH DOWN IN THE PACIFIC OCEAN AT MACH 20.
KORO SENSEI HAS US WRAPPED AROUND HIS FINGER—ER, TENTACLE—LITERALLY!
ZZZZ
WZZ
GUESS IT'S TIME FOR CLASS...

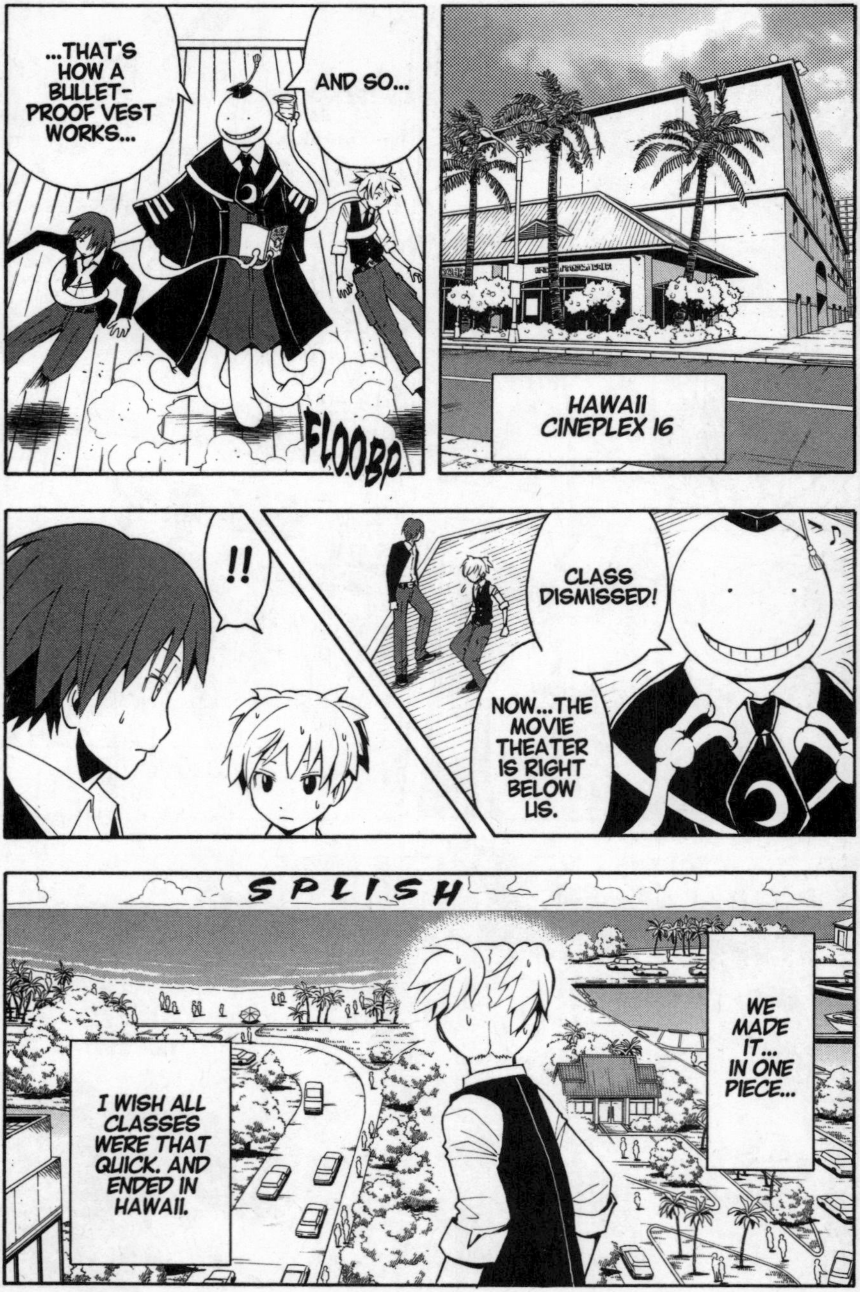
HAWAII CINEPLEX 16
AND SO...
...THAT'S HOW A BULLET-PROOF VEST WORKS...
FLOOBP
CLASS DISMISSED!
NOW...THE MOVIE THEATER IS RIGHT BELOW US.
!!
SPLISH
WE MADE IT... IN ONE PIECE...
I WISH ALL CLASSES WERE THAT QUICK. AND ENDED IN HAWAII.

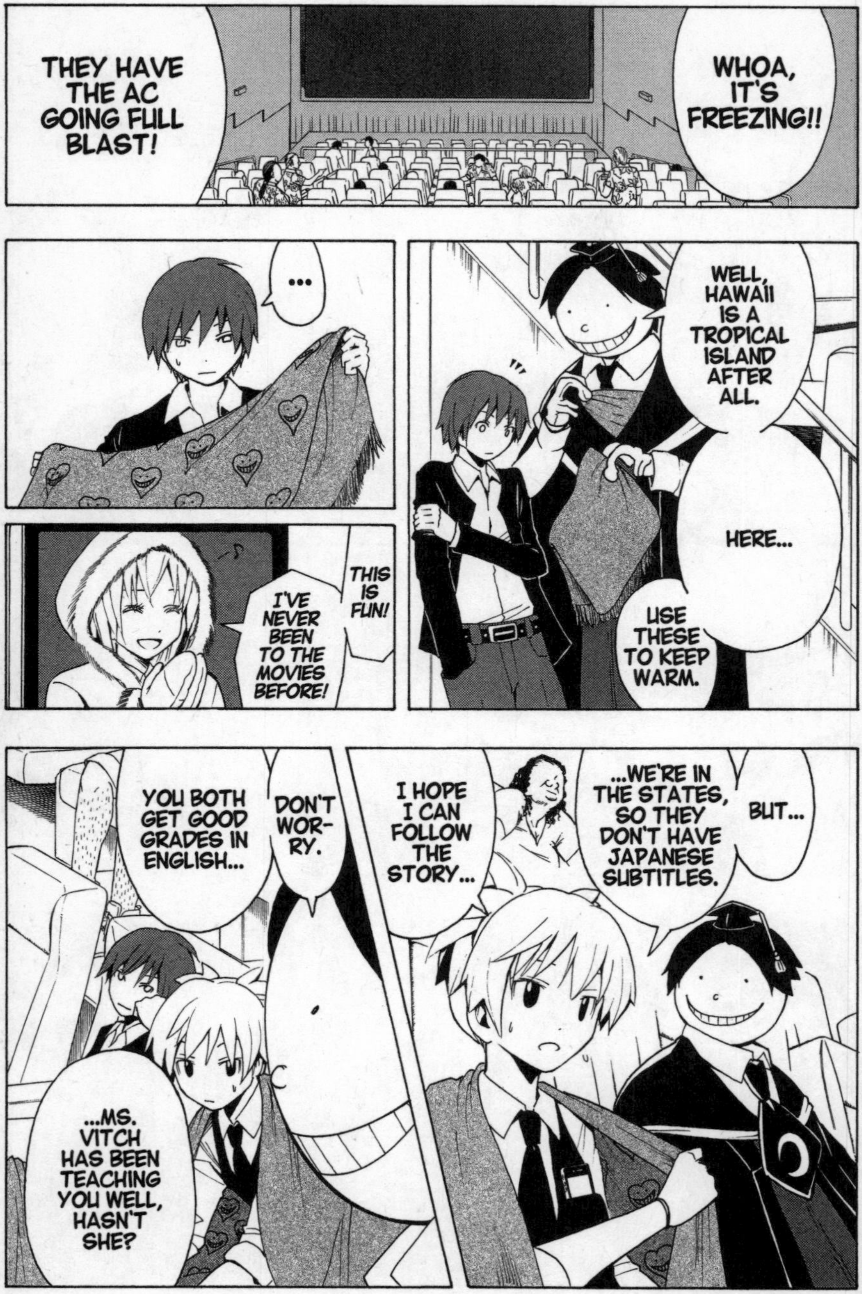
WHOA, IT'S FREEZING!!
THEY HAVE THE AC GOING FULL BLAST!
WELL, HAWAII IS A TROPICAL ISLAND AFTER ALL.
HERE...
USE THESE TO KEEP WARM.
...
THIS IS FUN!
I'VE NEVER BEEN TO THE MOVIES BEFORE!
BUT...
...WE'RE IN THE STATES, SO THEY DON'T HAVE JAPANESE SUBTITLES.
I HOPE I CAN FOLLOW THE STORY...
DON'T WORRY.
YOU BOTH GET GOOD GRADES IN ENGLISH...
...MS. VITCH HAS BEEN TEACHING YOU WELL, HASN'T SHE?

・・・

THANKS...

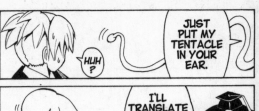

JUST PUT MY TENTACLE IN YOUR EAR.

HUH?

I'LL TRANSLATE THE WORDS YOU HAVEN'T STUDIED YET.

AS FOR THE REST, SIT BACK, LISTEN CLOSELY AND ENJOY THE SHOW.

AND HERE... WHAT'S A MOVIE WITHOUT POPCORN AND SODA?

THIS IS REALLY FUN!!

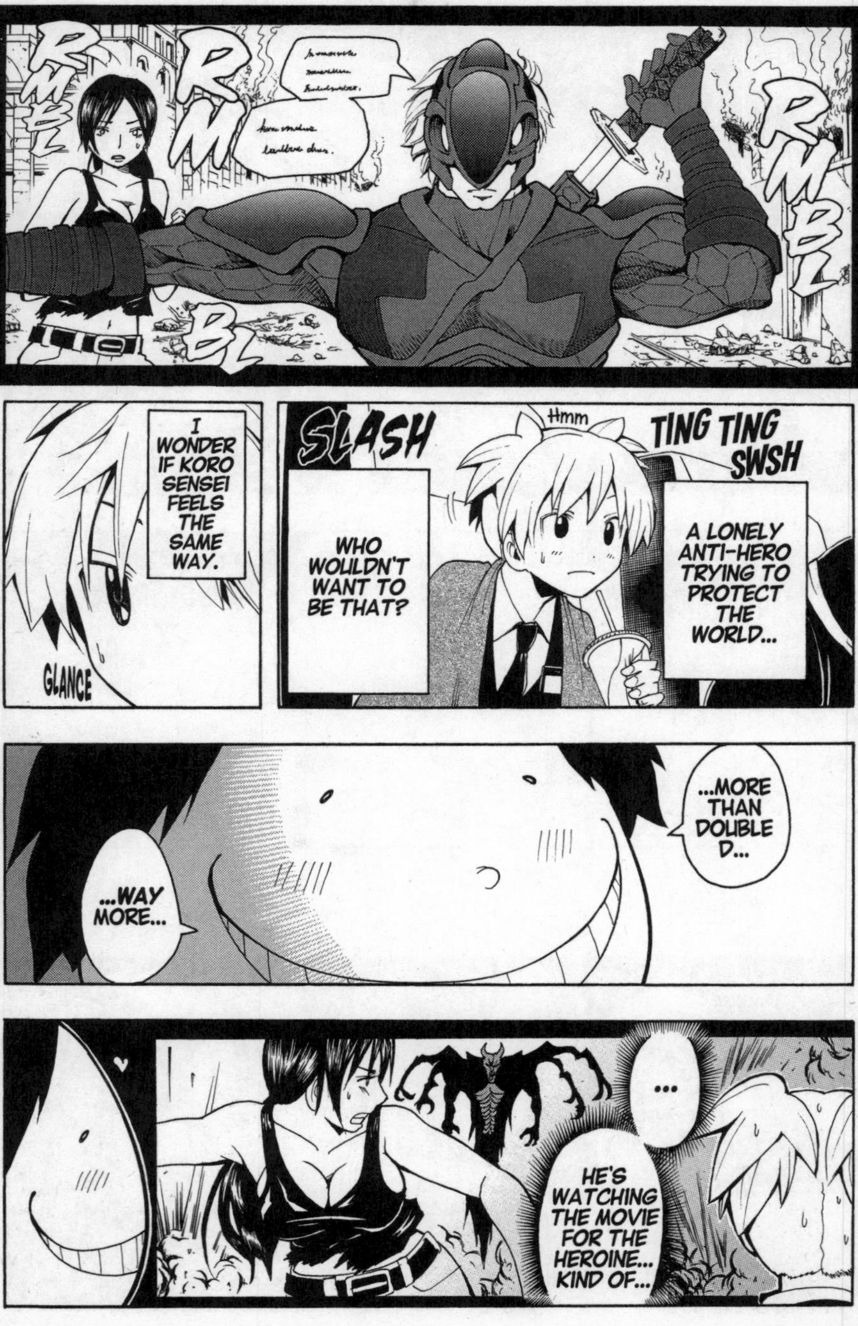
RMBL
RMBL
RMBL
TING TING
SWSH
A LONELY ANTI-HERO TRYING TO PROTECT THE WORLD...
Hmm
SLASH
WHO WOULDN'T WANT TO BE THAT?
I WONDER IF KORO SENSEI FEELS THE SAME WAY.
GLANCE
...MORE THAN DOUBLE D...
...WAY MORE...
...
HE'S WATCHING THE MOVIE FOR THE HEROINE... KIND OF...

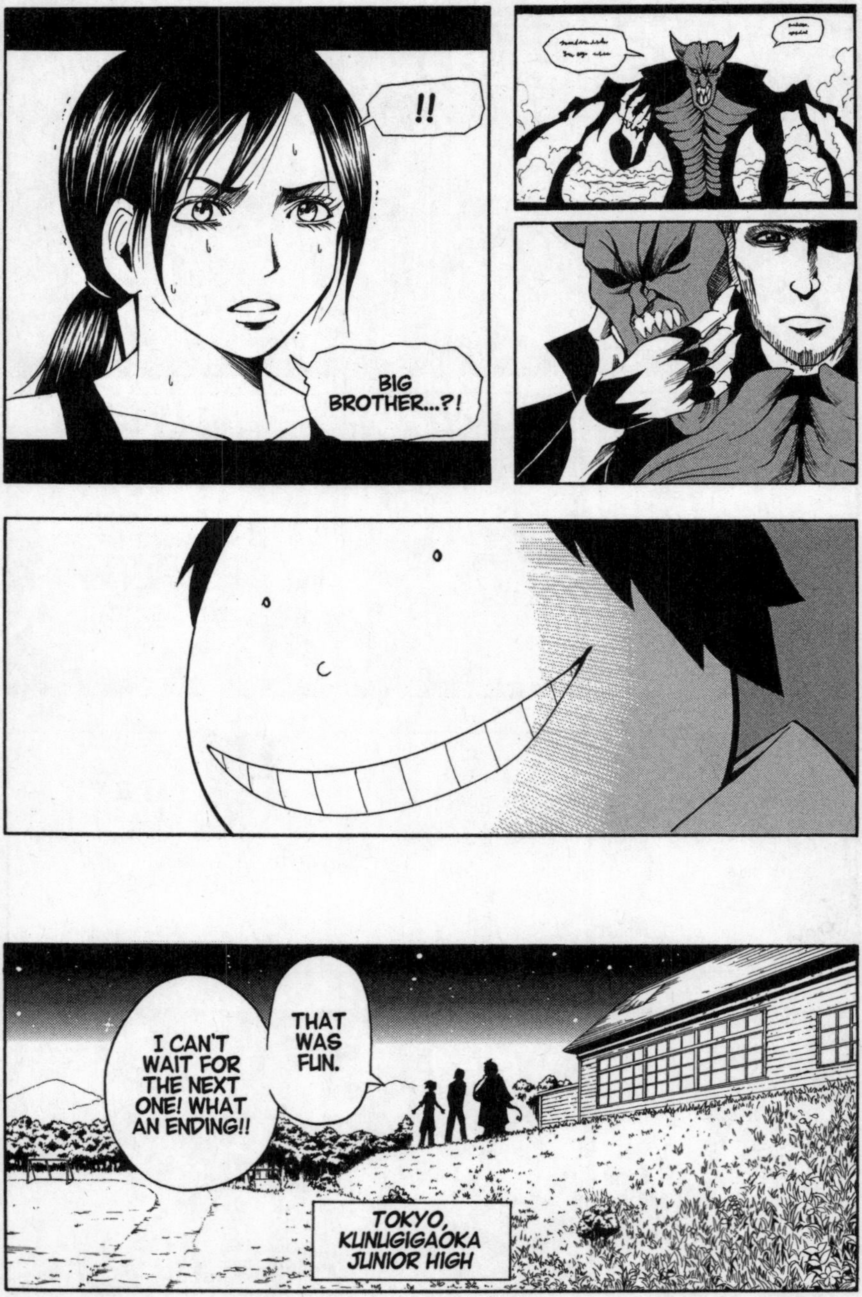
!!
BIG BROTHER...?!
THAT WAS FUN.
I CAN'T WAIT FOR THE NEXT ONE! WHAT AN ENDING!!
TOKYO, KUNUGIGAOKA JUNIOR HIGH

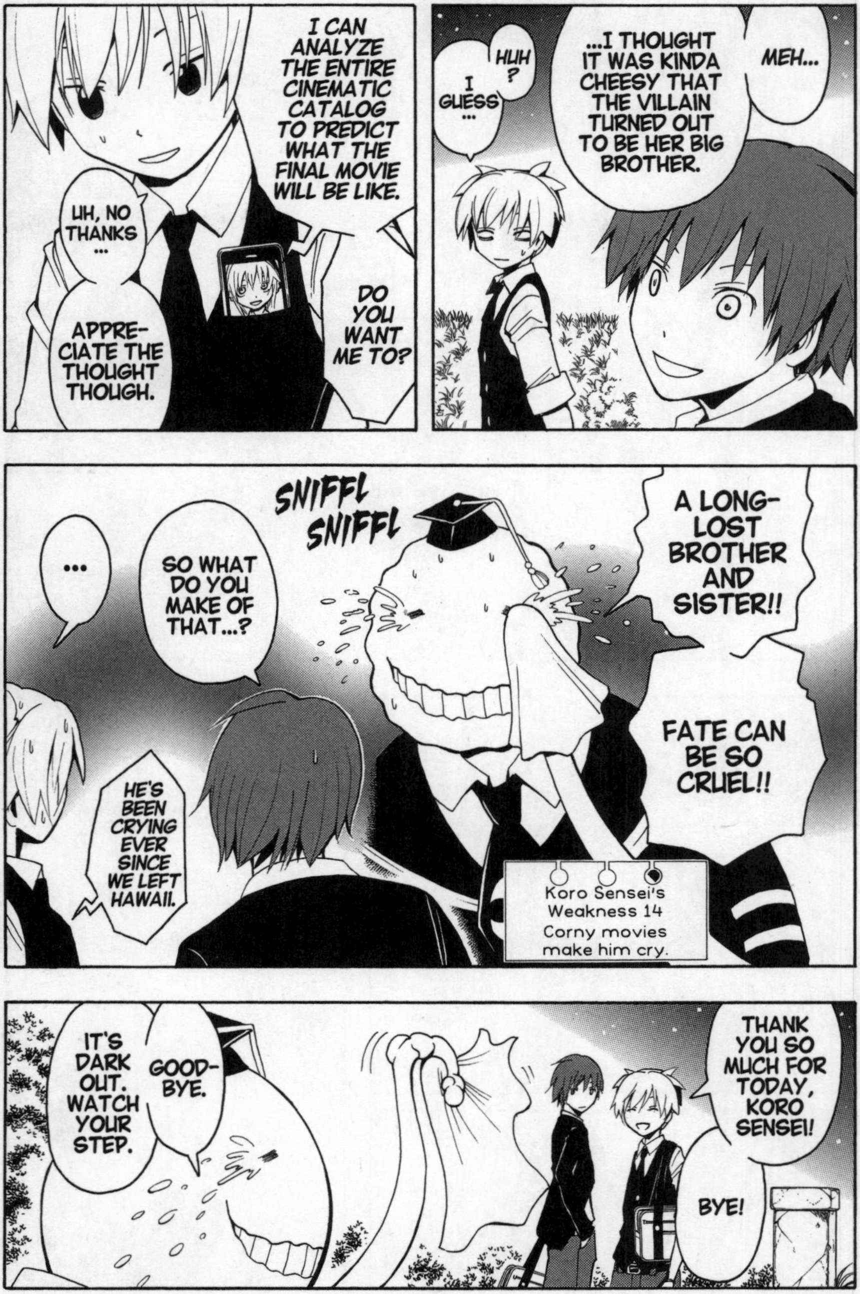
MEH...
...I THOUGHT IT WAS KINDA CHEESY THAT THE VILLAIN TURNED OUT TO BE HER BIG BROTHER.
HUH?
I GUESS...
I CAN ANALYZE THE ENTIRE CINEMATIC CATALOG TO PREDICT WHAT THE FINAL MOVIE WILL BE LIKE.
DO YOU WANT ME TO?
UH, NO THANKS...
APPRECIATE THE THOUGHT THOUGH.
A LONG-LOST BROTHER AND SISTER!!
SNIFFL SNIFFL
FATE CAN BE SO CRUEL!!
SO WHAT DO YOU MAKE OF THAT...?
...
HE'S BEEN CRYING EVER SINCE WE LEFT HAWAII.
Koro Sensei's Weakness 14
Corny movies make him cry.
THANK YOU SO MUCH FOR TODAY, KORO SENSEI!
BYE!
GOOD-BYE.
IT'S DARK OUT. WATCH YOUR STEP.

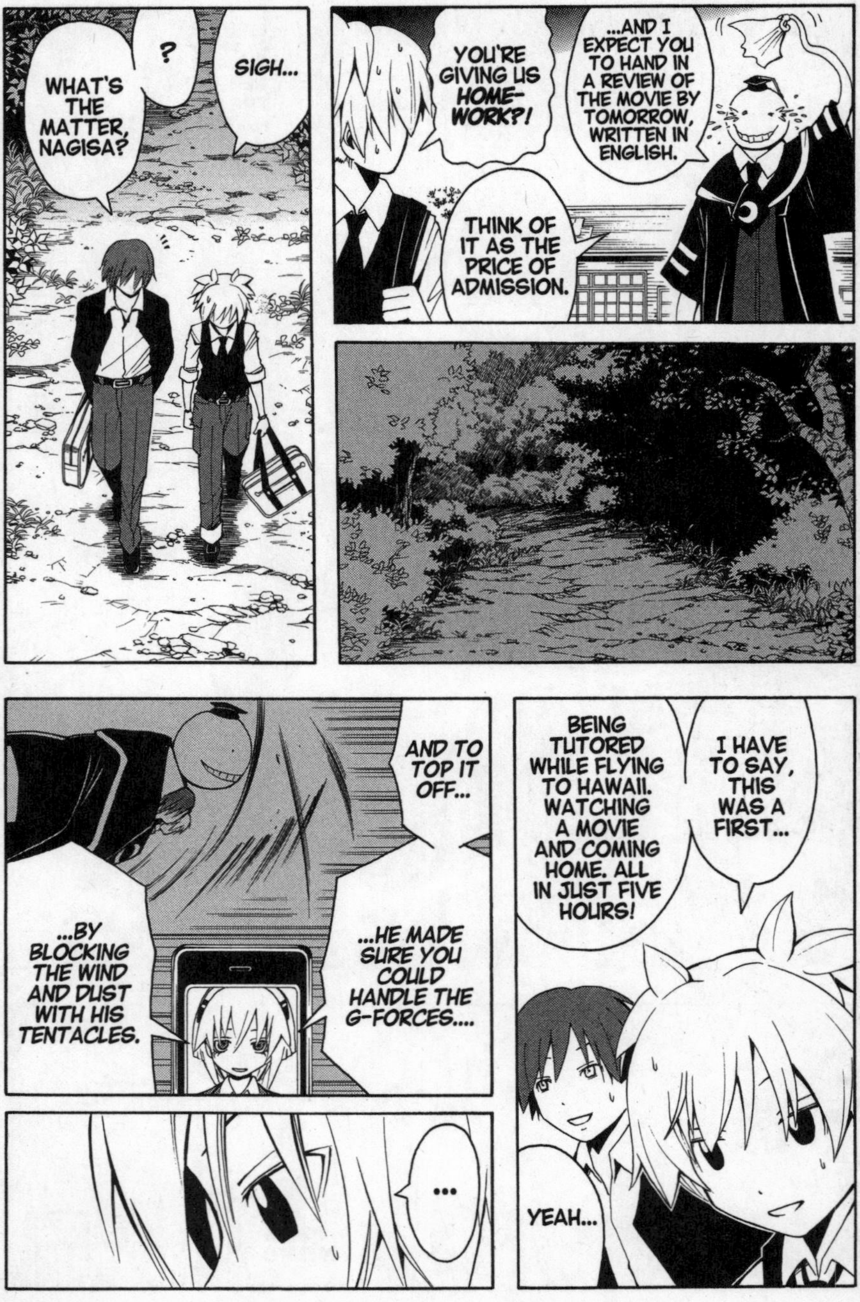
...AND I EXPECT YOU TO HAND IN A REVIEW OF THE MOVIE BY TOMORROW, WRITTEN IN ENGLISH.
YOU'RE GIVING US HOMEWORK?!
THINK OF IT AS THE PRICE OF ADMISSION.
SIGH...
?
WHAT'S THE MATTER, NAGISA?
I HAVE TO SAY, THIS WAS A FIRST...
BEING TUTORED WHILE FLYING TO HAWAII. WATCHING A MOVIE AND COMING HOME. ALL IN JUST FIVE HOURS!
YEAH...
AND TO TOP IT OFF...
...HE MADE SURE YOU COULD HANDLE THE G-FORCES....
...BY BLOCKING THE WIND AND DUST WITH HIS TENTACLES.
...

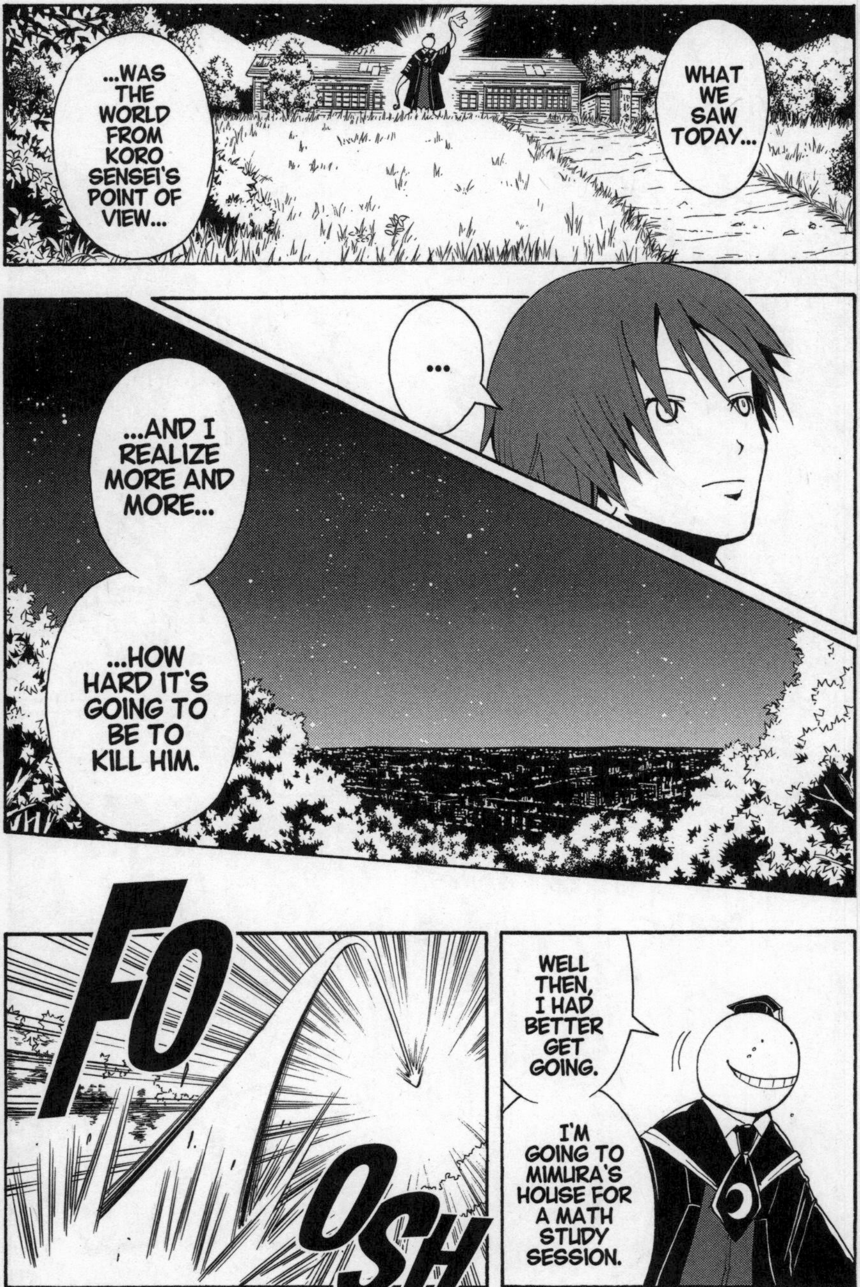
WHAT WE SAW TODAY...
...WAS THE WORLD FROM KORO SENSEI'S POINT OF VIEW...
...
...AND I REALIZE MORE AND MORE...
...HOW HARD IT'S GOING TO BE TO KILL HIM.
WELL THEN, I HAD BETTER GET GOING.
I'M GOING TO MIMURA'S HOUSE FOR A MATH STUDY SESSION.
FOOSH

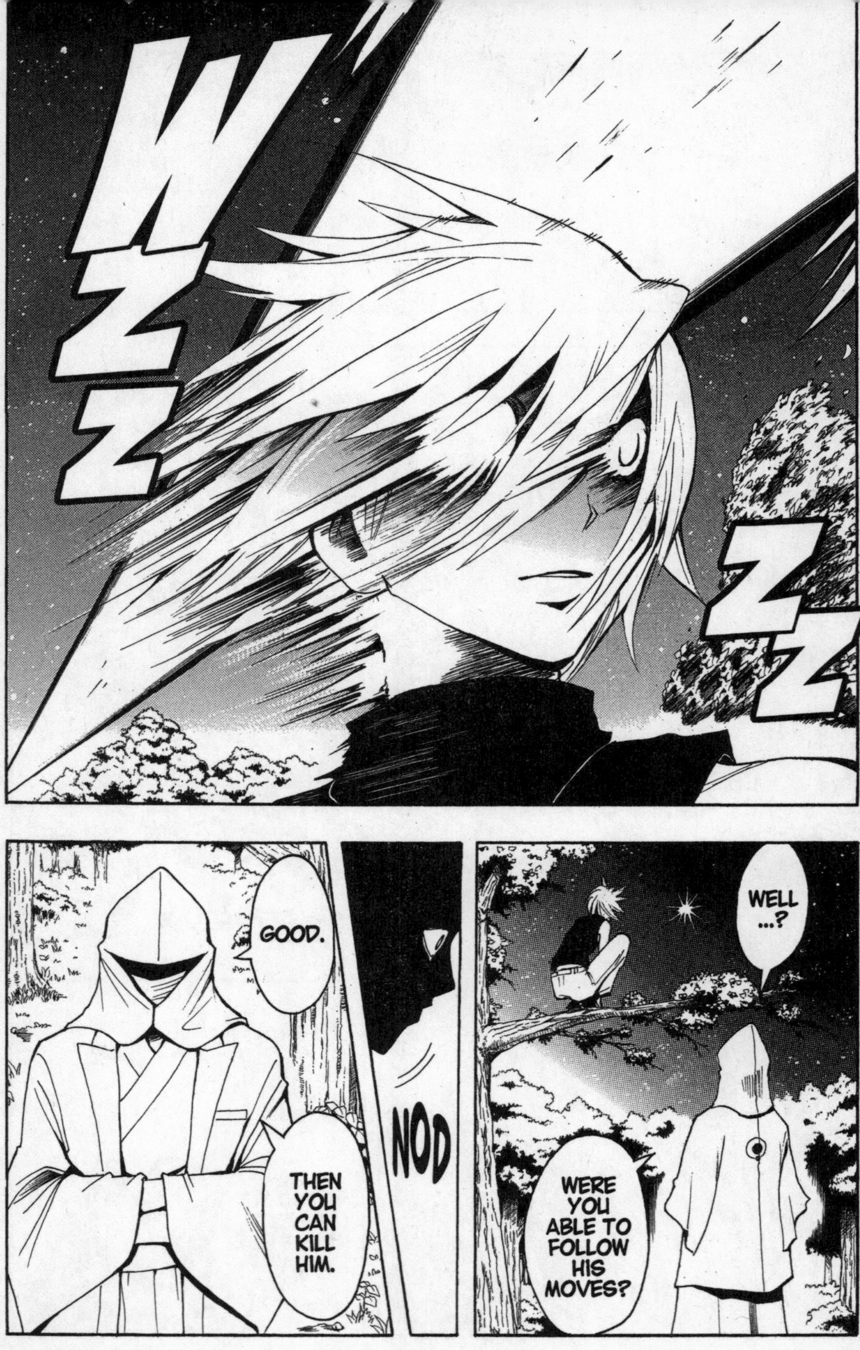
WZZZ
ZZ
WELL ...?
WERE YOU ABLE TO FOLLOW HIS MOVES?
NOD
GOOD.
THEN YOU CAN KILL HIM.

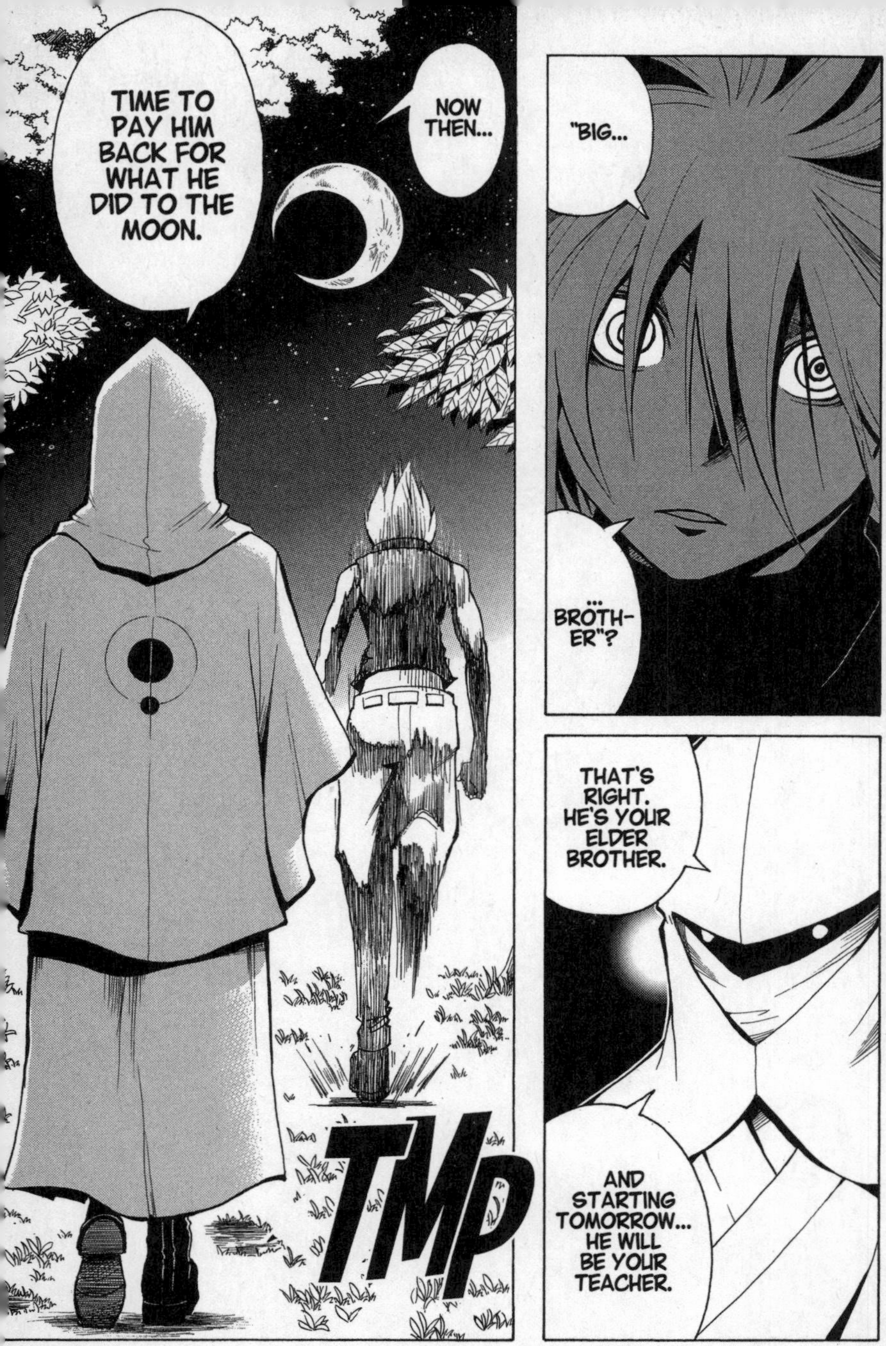
"BIG...
... BRÖTH-ER"?
THAT'S RIGHT. HE'S YOUR ELDER BROTHER.
AND STARTING TOMORROW... HE WILL BE YOUR TEACHER.
NOW THEN...
TIME TO PAY HIM BACK FOR WHAT HE DID TO THE MOON.
TMP

STORY

OUR HERO CONTINUES TO FIGHT FOR MANKIND, AGAINST ALL ODDS! BUT HIS ENEMY, ADAM, DRAWS HIM INTO A WORLD OF CORRUPTION TO LURE HIM BACK TO THE DARK SIDE. CAN OUR HERO KEEP FROM SLIPPING BACK INTO THE VOID?

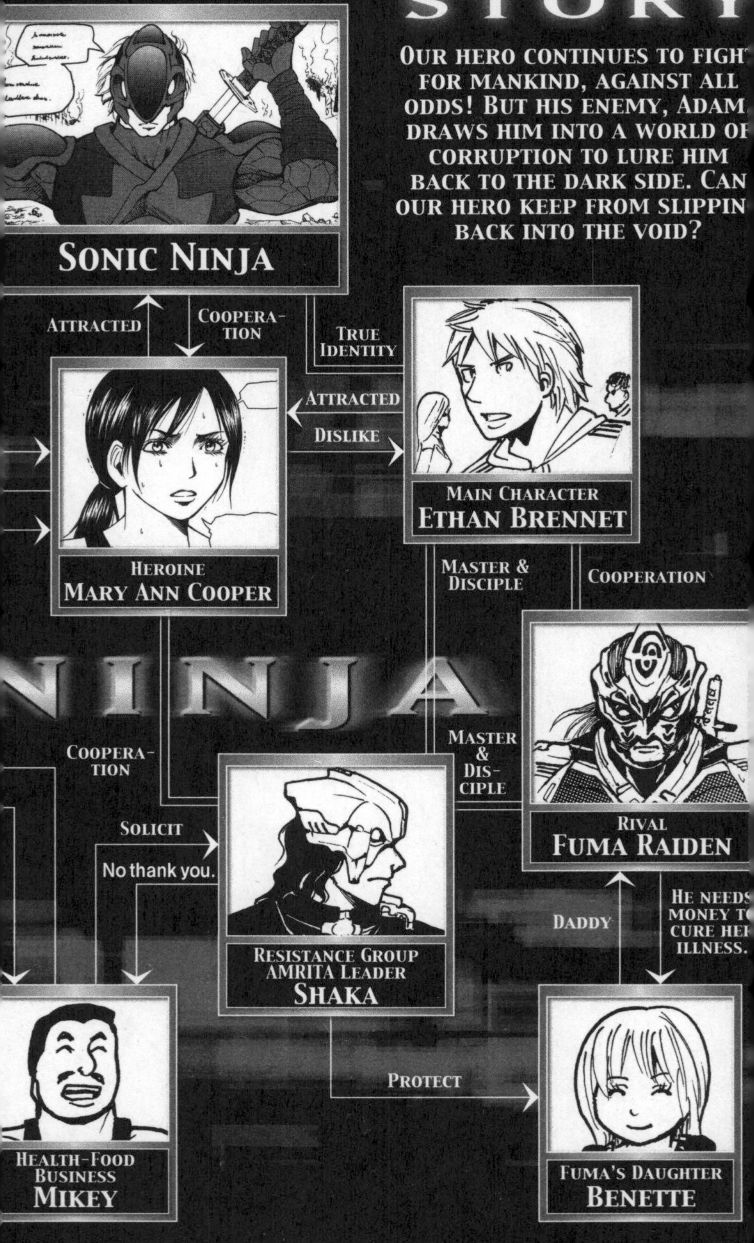

SONIC NINJA
ATTRACTED
COOPERATION
TRUE IDENTITY
ATTRACTED
DISLIKE
MAIN CHARACTER
ETHAN BRENNET
HEROINE
MARY ANN COOPER
MASTER & DISCIPLE
COOPERATION
NINJA
RIVAL
FUMA RAIDEN
MASTER & DISCIPLE
COOPERATION
SOLICIT
No thank you.
RESISTANCE GROUP AMRITA LEADER
SHAKA
DADDY
HE NEEDS MONEY TO CURE HER ILLNESS.
PROTECT
HEALTH-FOOD BUSINESS
MIKEY
FUMA'S DAUGHTER
BENETTE

PERSUADE
ENEMY
FUTURE MAFIA ZAP LEADER
ADAM
ARCH-
ENEMY
PERSUADE
TRUE IDENTITY
MAFIA "BAD" LEADER
GABLE
PERSUADE
LONG-LOST
ELDER BROTHER
PERSUADE
PERSUADE
PERSUADE
DANNY COOPER
SONIC
PER-
SUADE
REQUEST FOR
BROCHURES
PERSUADE
SOLICIT
JUST FOR
ONE MONTH...
PERSUADE
NEWS
SOLICIT
PRETENDED
TO BE OUT
MYSTERIOUS MAN
KANYUSAI
TAKEDA
NEWSPAPER DELIVERY
JONES

Class 29 Time for Another Transfer Student—2nd Period

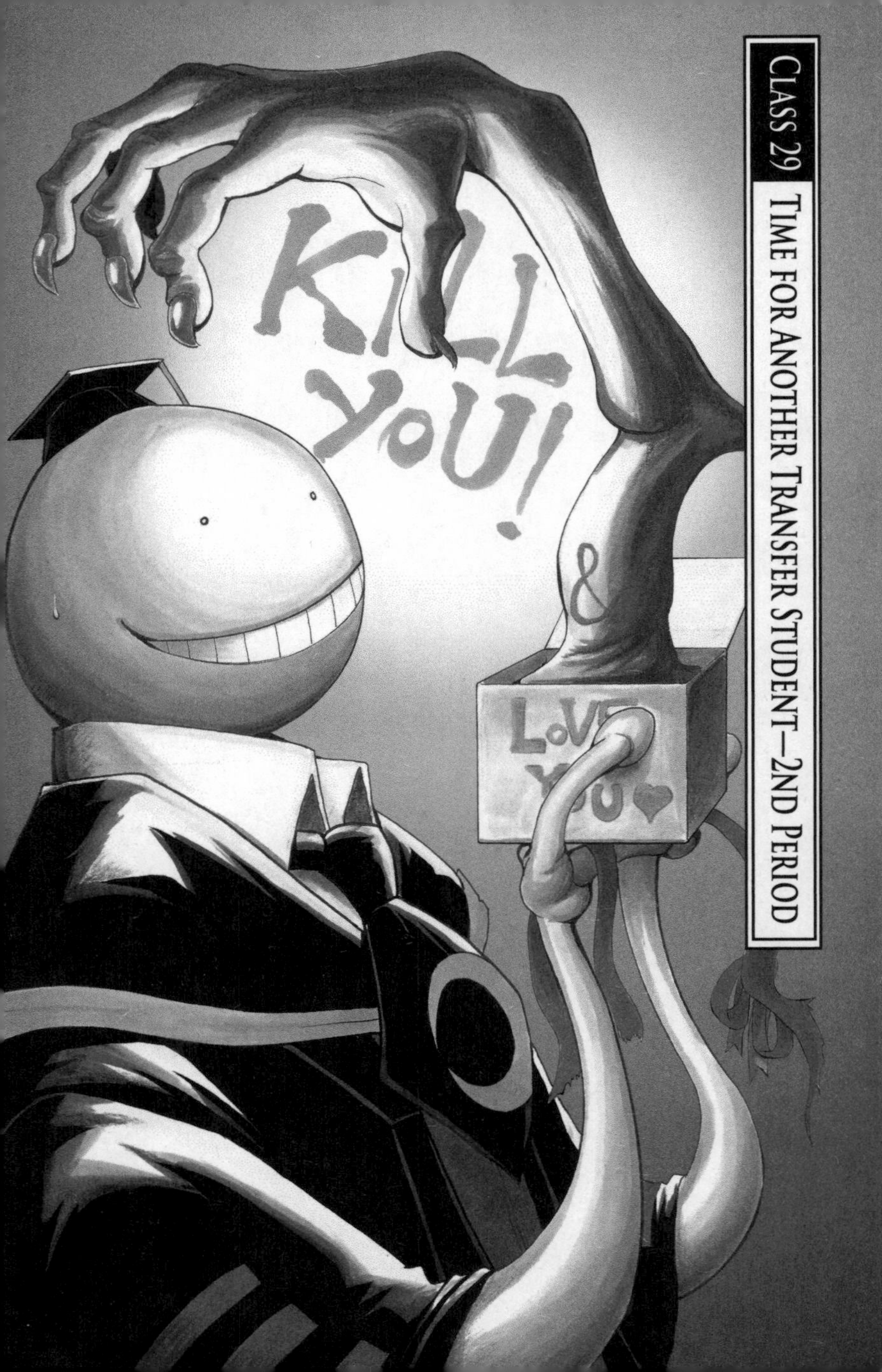
KILL YOU!
&
LOVE YOU

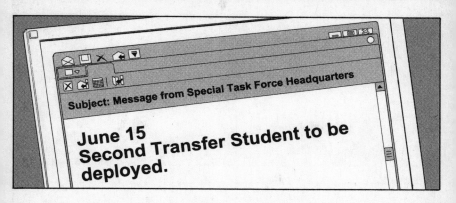

Subject: Message from Special Task Force Headquarters

June 15
Second Transfer Student to be deployed.

The much-awaited real deal.

Further preparation not needed.
Just follow the escort's orders.

KLCK

...

Understood.

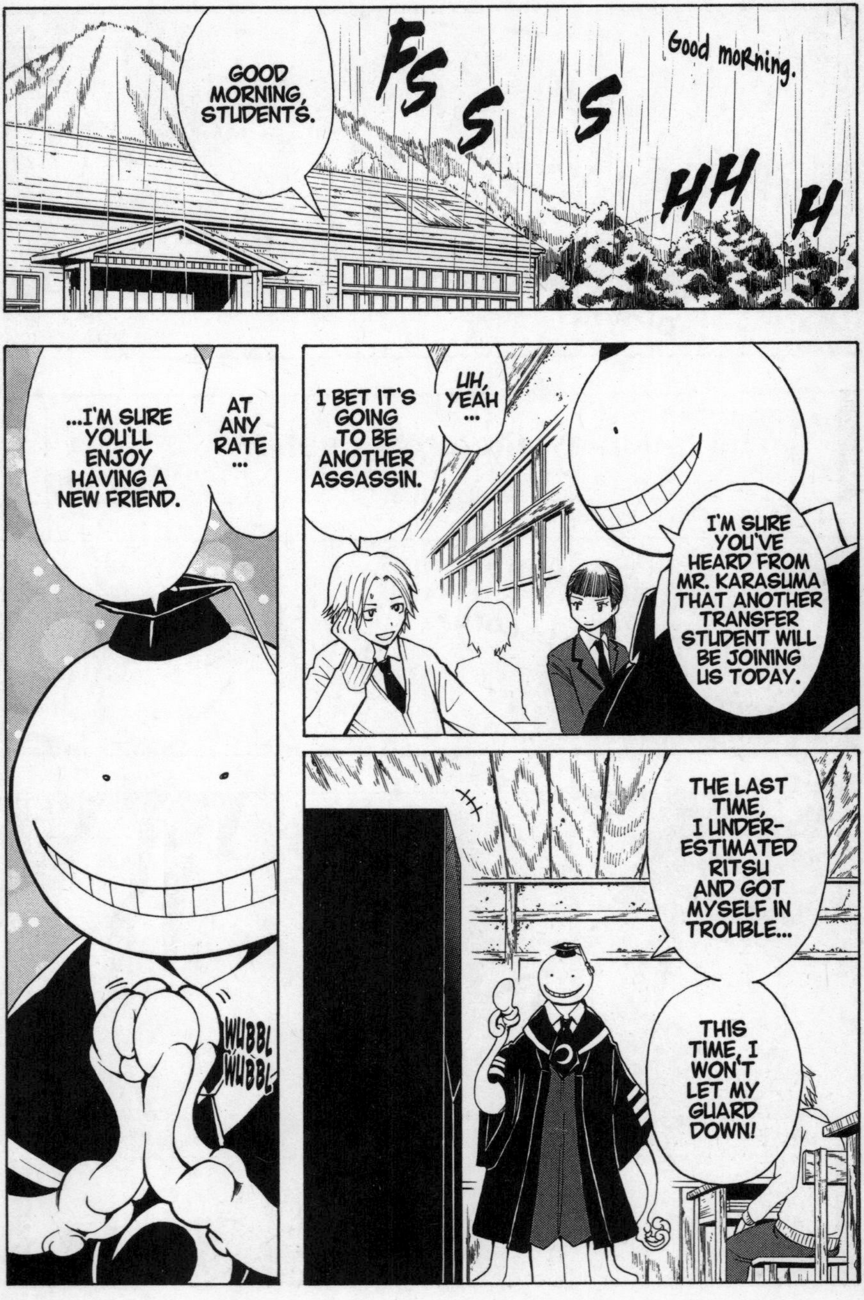
Good morning.
FSSSHHH
GOOD MORNING, STUDENTS.
I'M SURE YOU'VE HEARD FROM MR. KARASUMA THAT ANOTHER TRANSFER STUDENT WILL BE JOINING US TODAY.
UH, YEAH ...
I BET IT'S GOING TO BE ANOTHER ASSASSIN.
THE LAST TIME, I UNDER-ESTIMATED RITSU AND GOT MYSELF IN TROUBLE...
THIS TIME, I WON'T LET MY GUARD DOWN!
AT ANY RATE ...
...I'M SURE YOU'LL ENJOY HAVING A NEW FRIEND.
WUBBL WUBBL

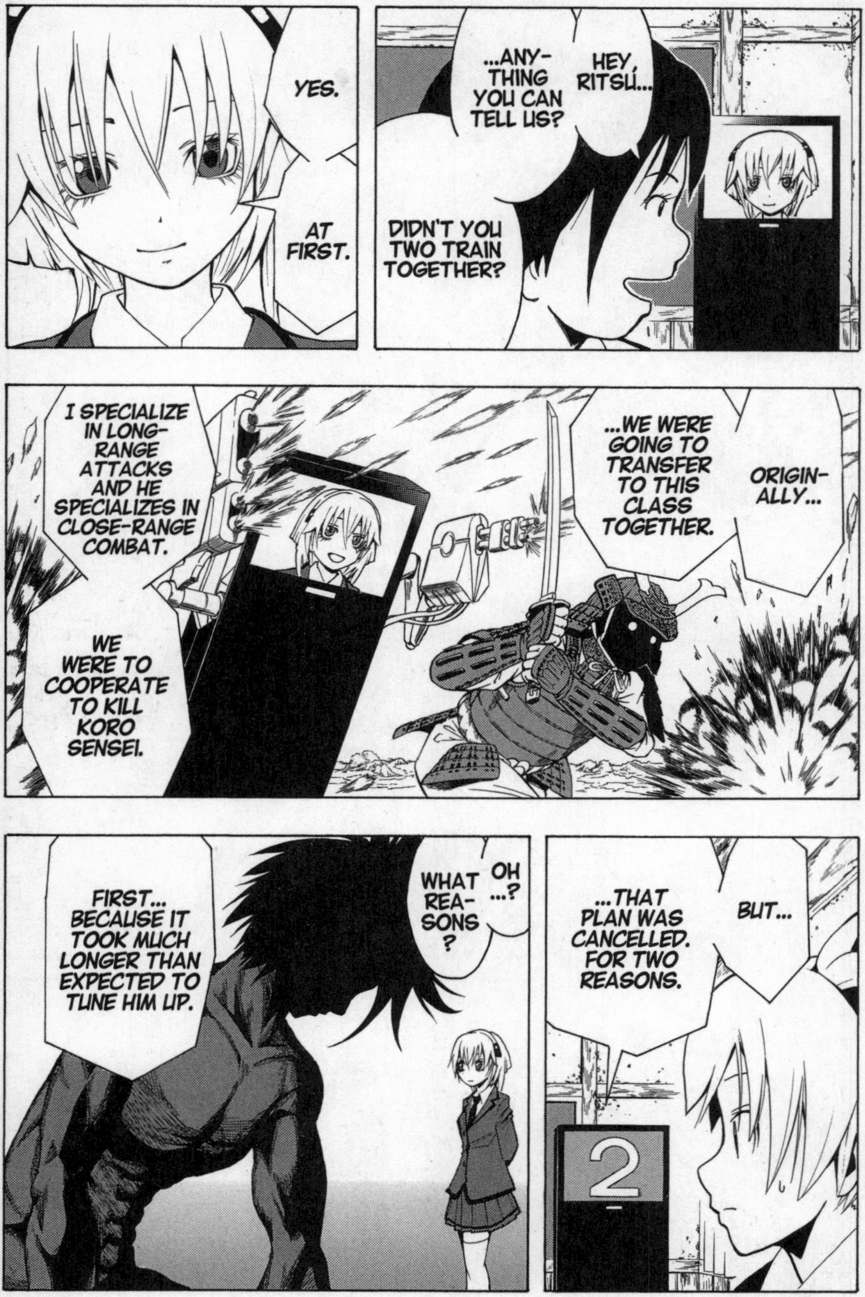
HEY, RITSU...
...ANY-THING YOU CAN TELL US?
DIDN'T YOU TWO TRAIN TOGETHER?
YES.
AT FIRST.
ORIGIN-ALLY...
...WE WERE GOING TO TRANSFER TO THIS CLASS TOGETHER.
I SPECIALIZE IN LONG-RANGE ATTACKS AND HE SPECIALIZES IN CLOSE-RANGE COMBAT.
WE WERE TO COOPERATE TO KILL KORO SENSEI.
BUT...
...THAT PLAN WAS CANCELLED. FOR TWO REASONS.
2
OH ...?
WHAT REA-SONS ?
FIRST... BECAUSE IT TOOK MUCH LONGER THAN EXPECTED TO TUNE HIM UP.

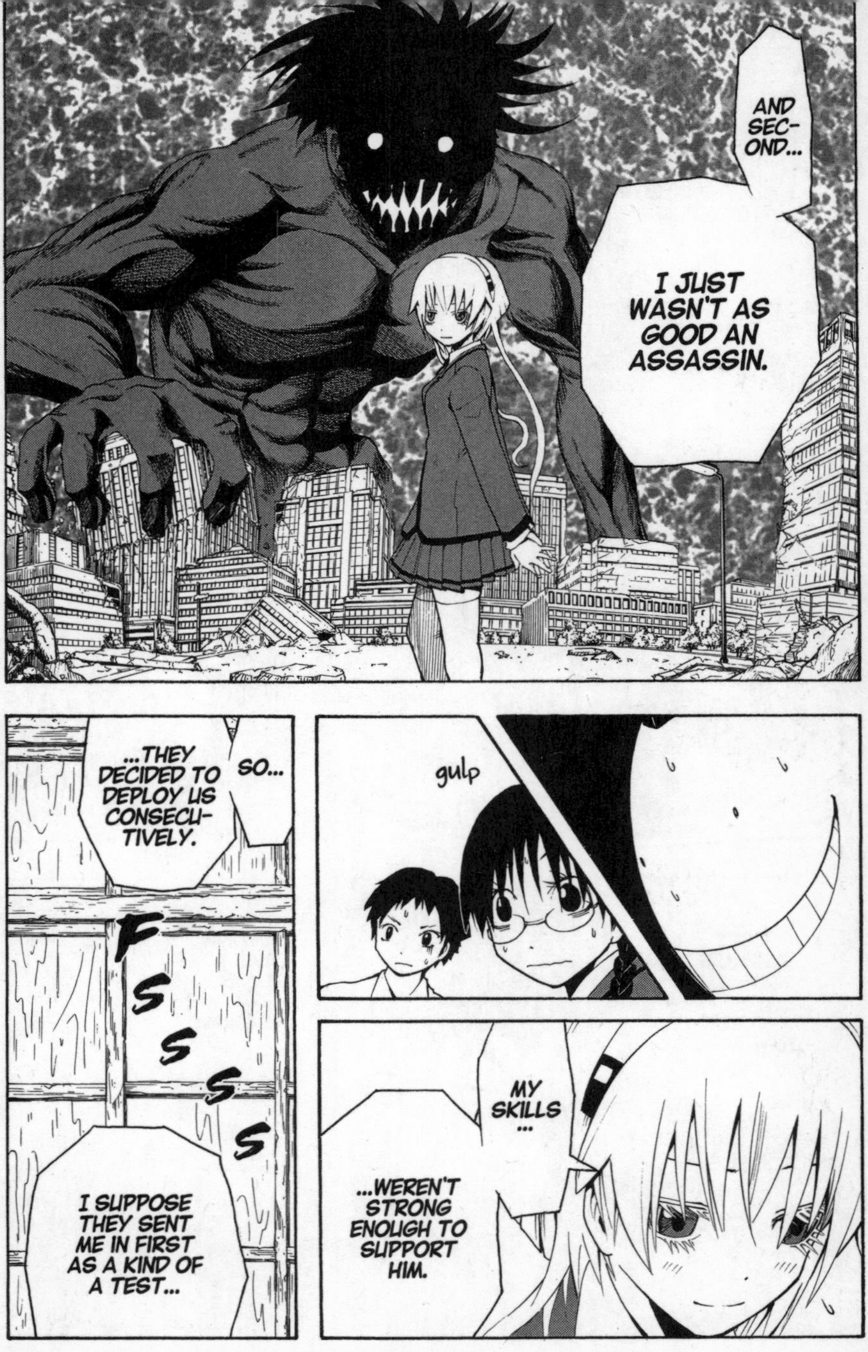
AND SEC-
OND...
I JUST WASN'T AS GOOD AN ASSASSIN.
gulp
MY SKILLS ...
...WEREN'T STRONG ENOUGH TO SUPPORT HIM.
SO...
...THEY DECIDED TO DEPLOY US CONSECU-TIVELY.
FSSSSS
I SUPPOSE THEY SENT ME IN FIRST AS A KIND OF A TEST...

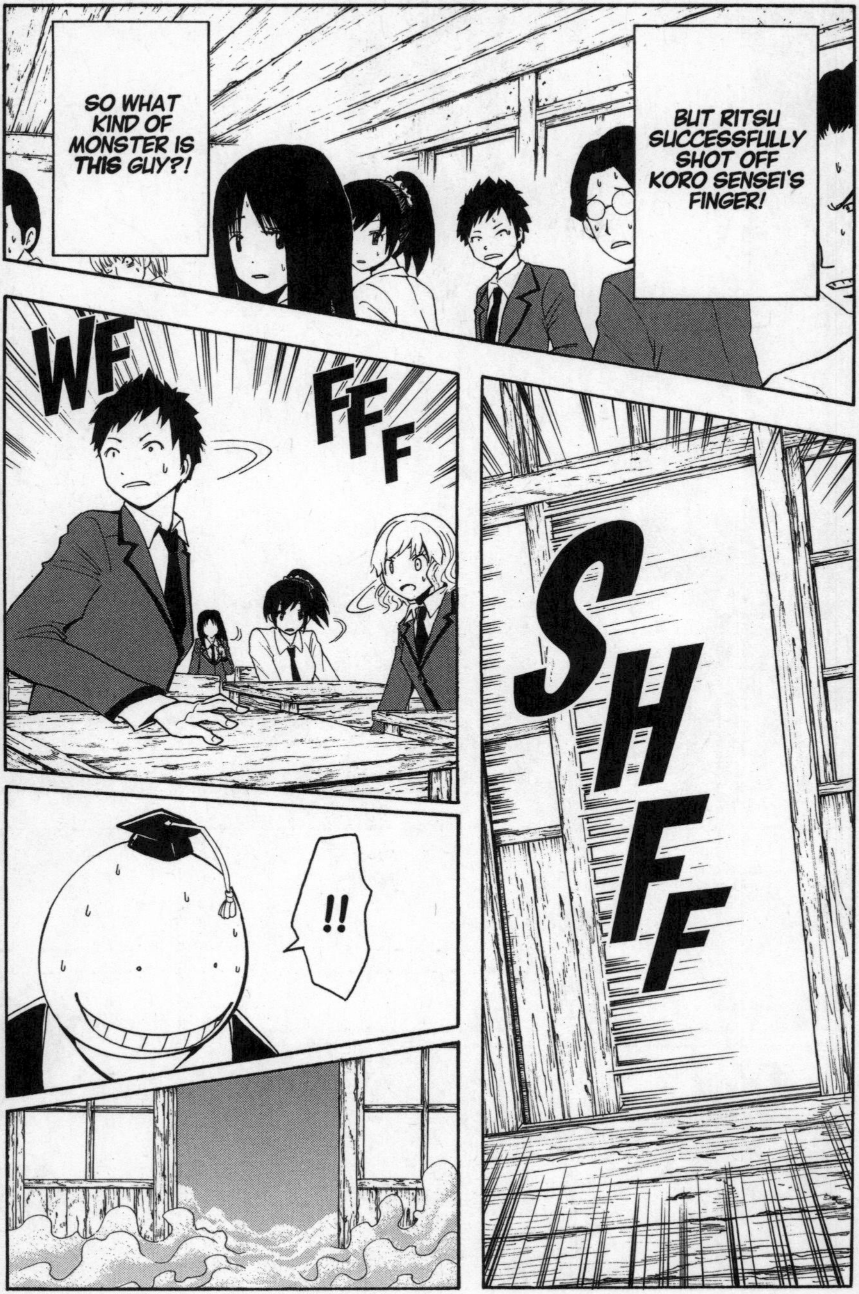
BUT RITSU SUCCESSFULLY SHOT OFF KORO SENSEI'S FINGER!
SO WHAT KIND OF MONSTER IS THIS GUY?!
SHFFF
WF FFF
!!

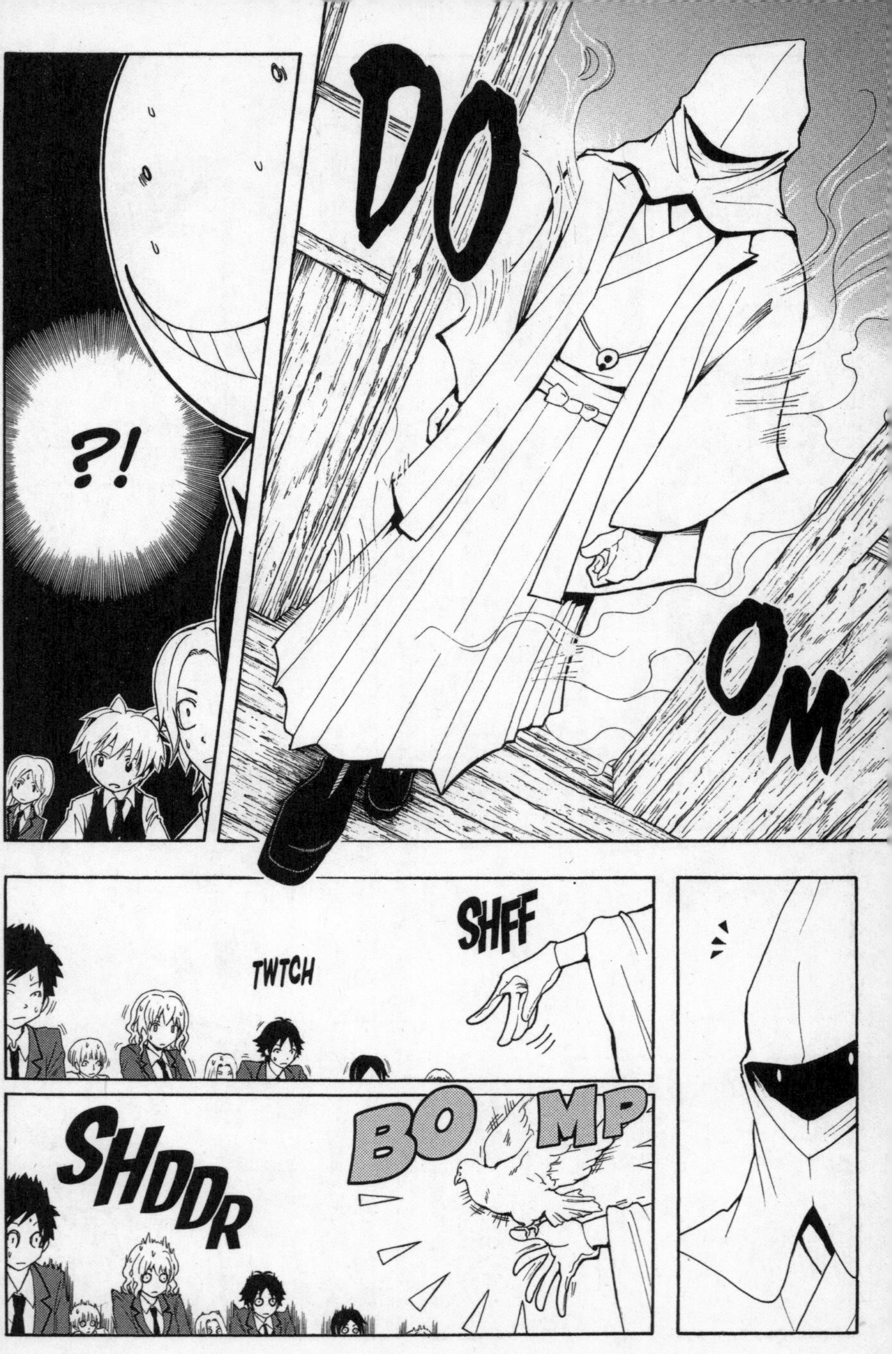
DO
OM
?!
SHFF
TWTCH
BO
MP
SHDDR

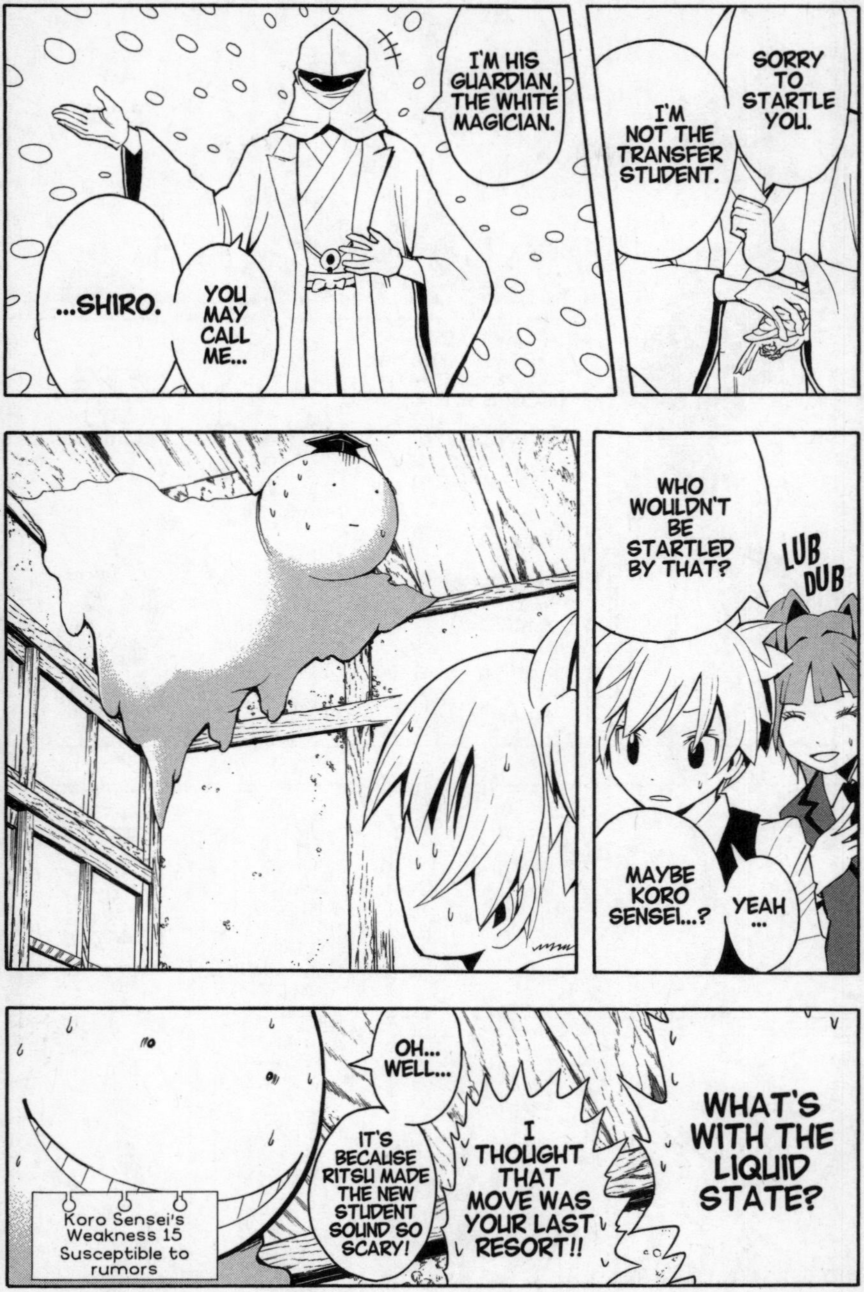
SORRY TO STARTLE YOU.
I'M NOT THE TRANSFER STUDENT.
I'M HIS GUARDIAN, THE WHITE MAGICIAN.
YOU MAY CALL ME...
...SHIRO.
WHO WOULDN'T BE STARTLED BY THAT?
LUB DUB
YEAH ...
MAYBE KORO SENSEI...?
WHAT'S WITH THE LIQUID STATE?
I THOUGHT THAT MOVE WAS YOUR LAST RESORT!!
OH... WELL...
IT'S BECAUSE RITSU MADE THE NEW STUDENT SOUND SO SCARY!
Koro Sensei's Weakness 15 Susceptible to rumors

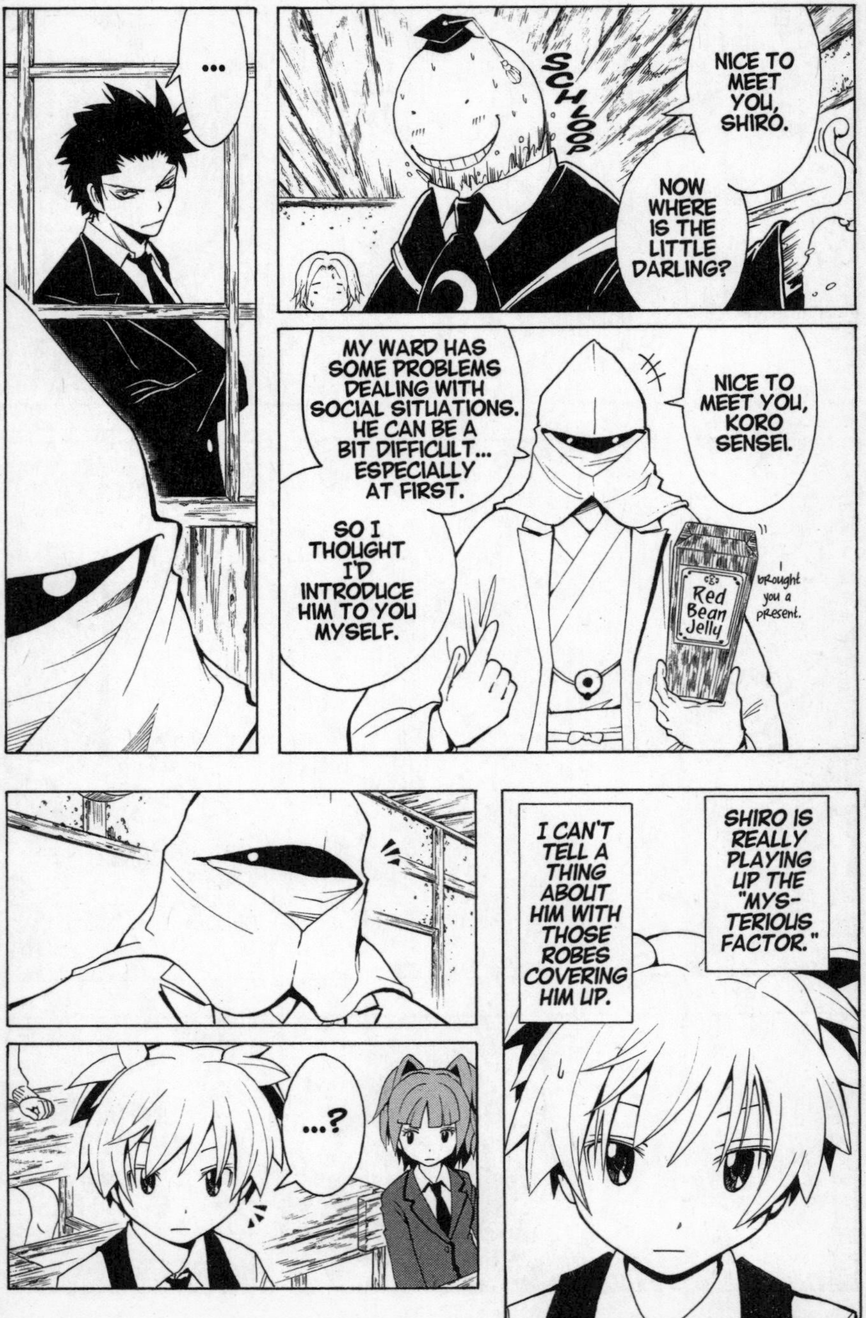
SCHLOOP
NICE TO MEET YOU, SHIRO.
NOW WHERE IS THE LITTLE DARLING?
NICE TO MEET YOU, KORO SENSEI.
I brought you a present.
Red Bean Jelly
MY WARD HAS SOME PROBLEMS DEALING WITH SOCIAL SITUATIONS. HE CAN BE A BIT DIFFICULT... ESPECIALLY AT FIRST.
SO I THOUGHT I'D INTRODUCE HIM TO YOU MYSELF.
...
SHIRO IS REALLY PLAYING UP THE "MYS-TERIOUS FACTOR."
I CAN'T TELL A THING ABOUT HIM WITH THOSE ROBES COVERING HIM UP.
...?

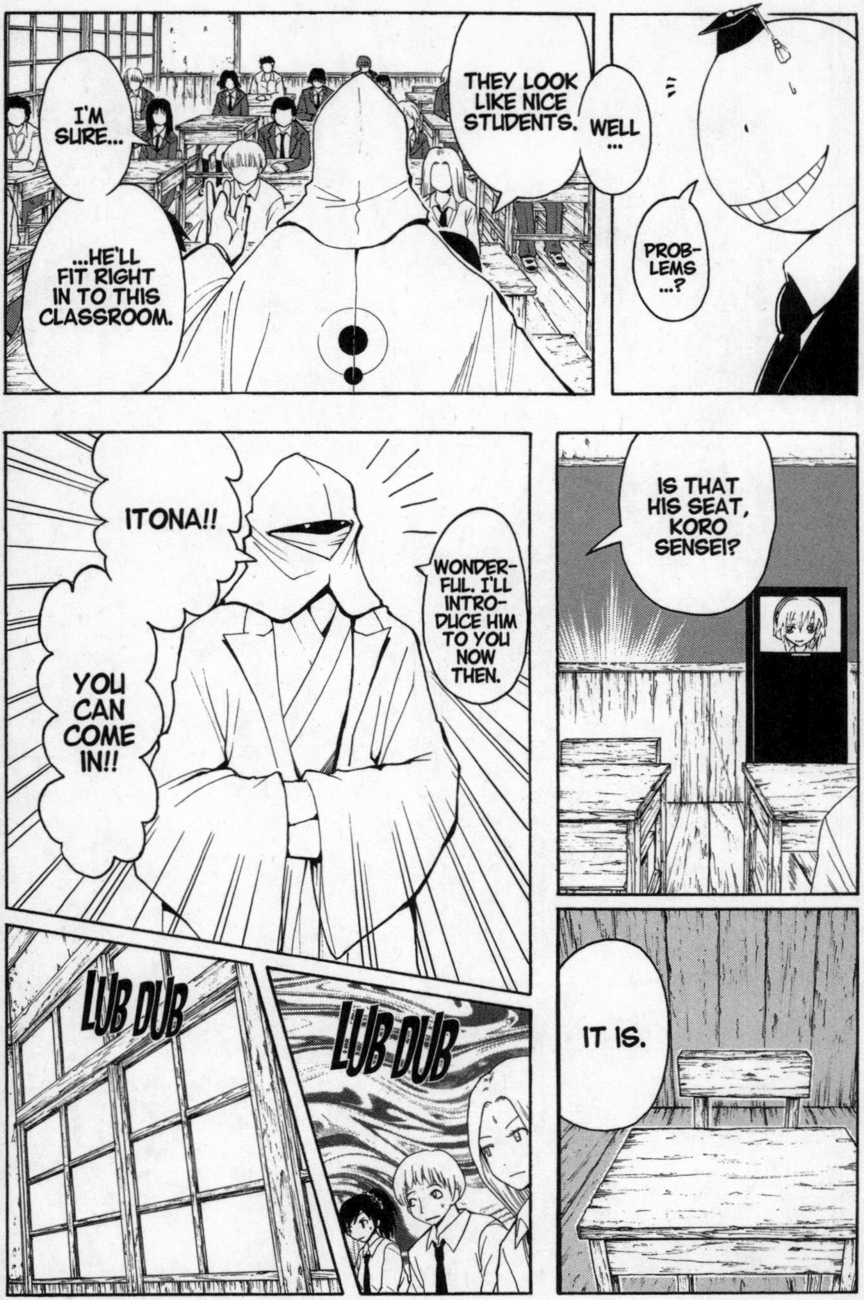

WELL ...
PROBLEMS ...?
THEY LOOK LIKE NICE STUDENTS.
I'M SURE...
...HE'LL FIT RIGHT IN TO THIS CLASSROOM.
IS THAT HIS SEAT, KORO SENSEI?
IT IS.
WONDERFUL. I'LL INTRODUCE HIM TO YOU NOW THEN.
ITONA!!
YOU CAN COME IN!!
LUB DUB
LUB DUB

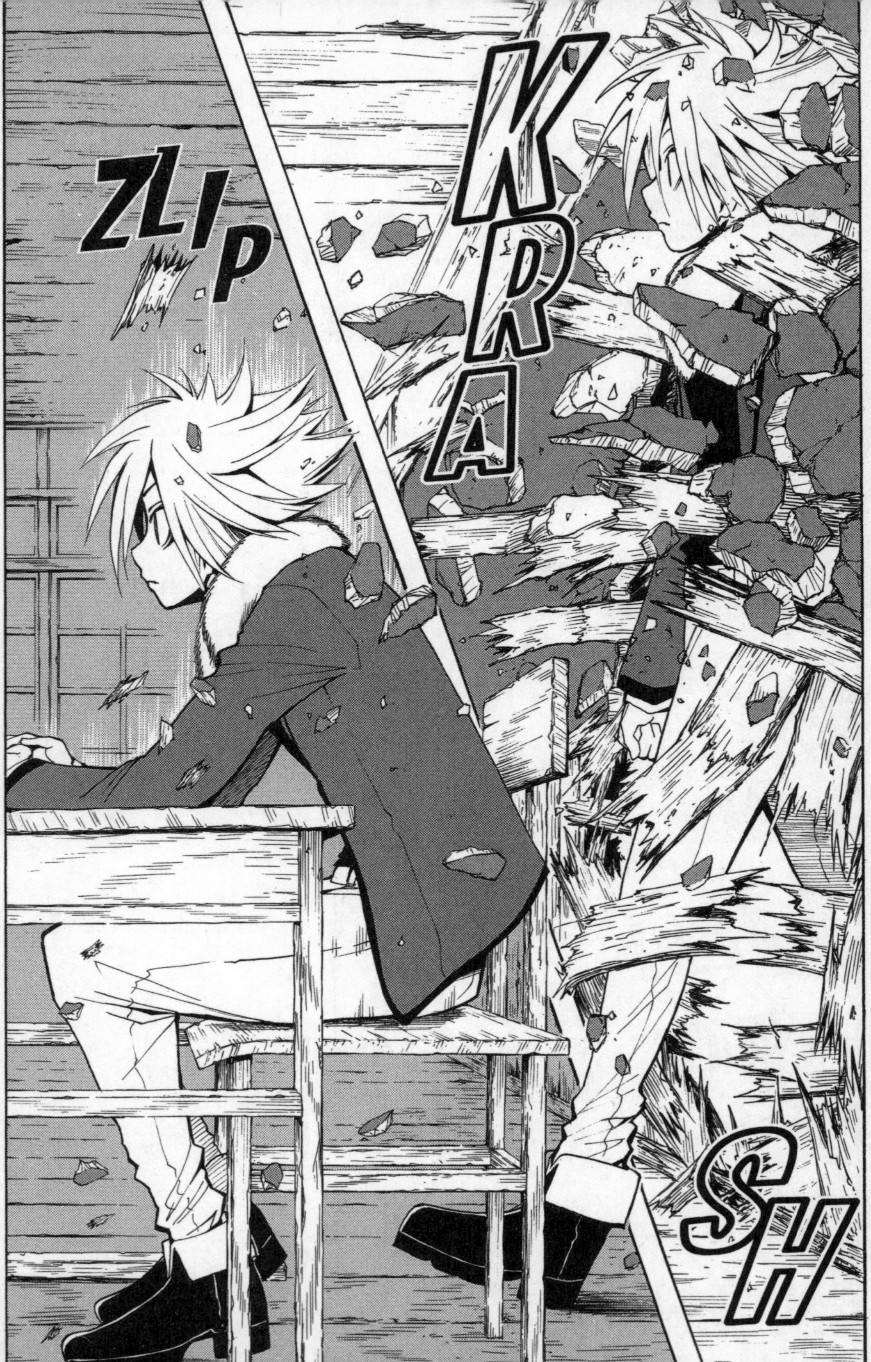
KRA
ZLIP
SH

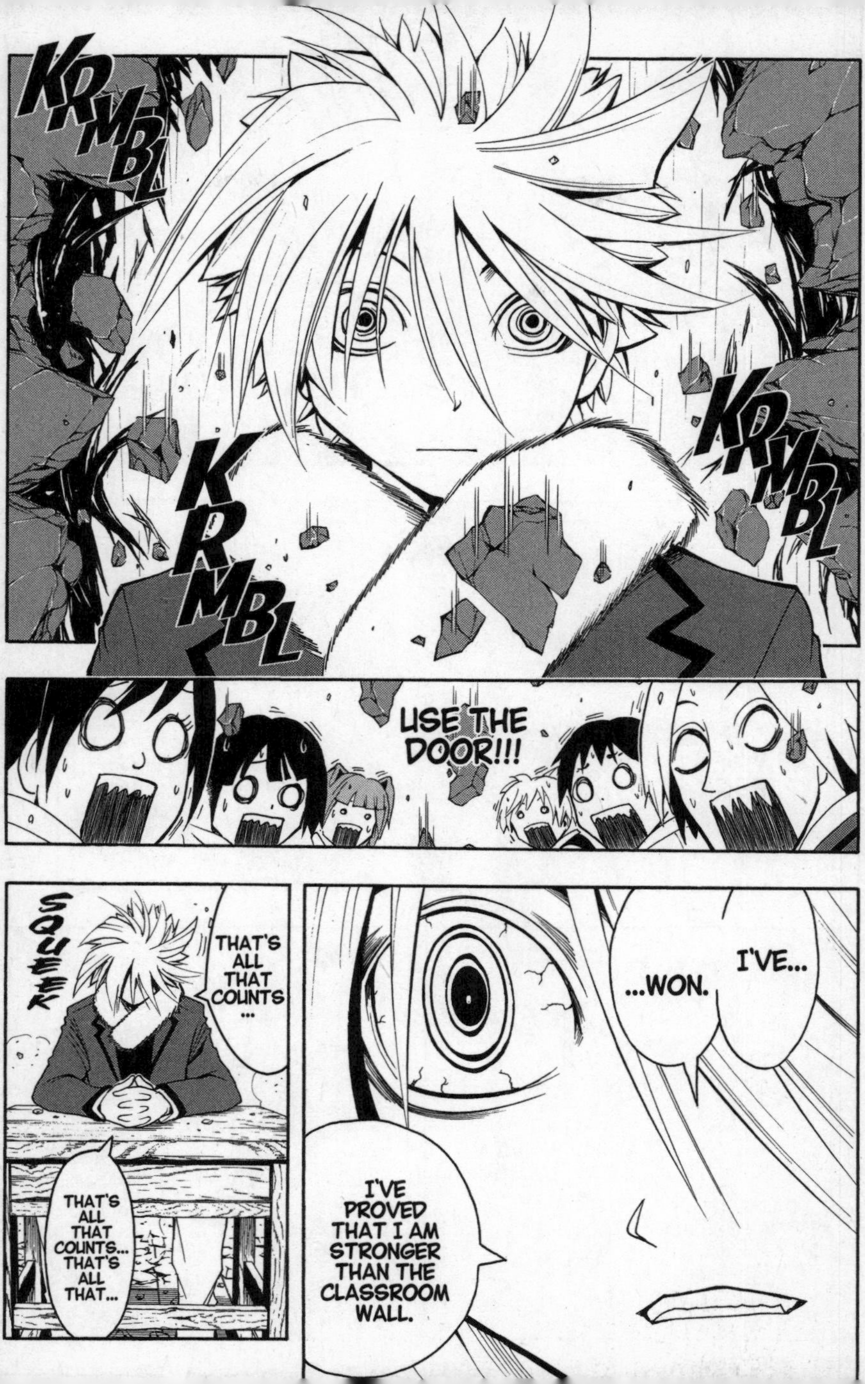
KRMBL
KRMBL
KRMBL
USE THE DOOR!!!
I'VE...
...WON.
I'VE PROVED THAT I AM STRONGER THAN THE CLASSROOM WALL.
SQUEEK
THAT'S ALL THAT COUNTS...
THAT'S ALL THAT COUNTS... THAT'S ALL THAT...

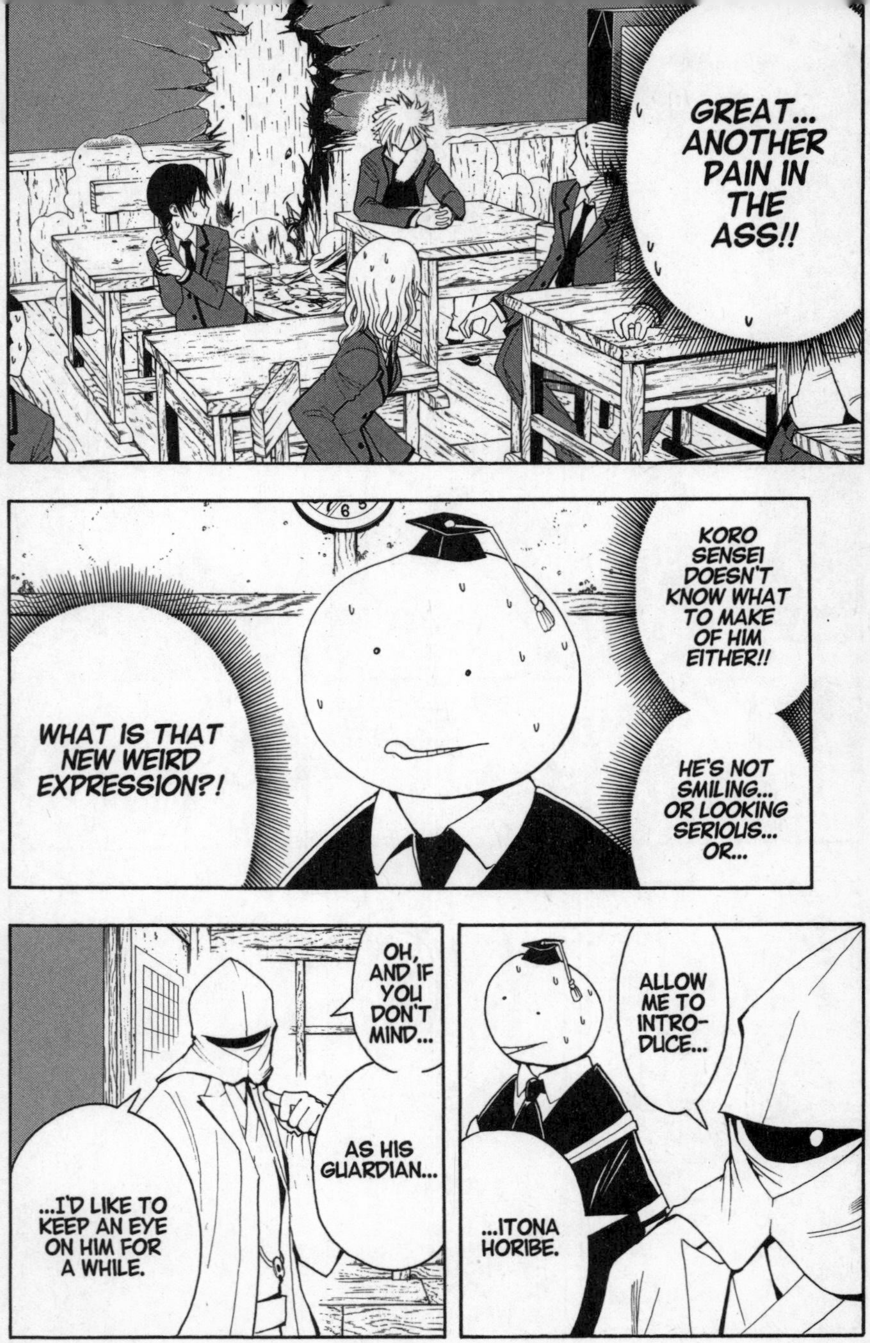
GREAT... ANOTHER PAIN IN THE ASS!!
KORO SENSEI DOESN'T KNOW WHAT TO MAKE OF HIM EITHER!!
HE'S NOT SMILING... OR LOOKING SERIOUS... OR...
WHAT IS THAT NEW WEIRD EXPRESSION?!
ALLOW ME TO INTRO-DUCE...
...ITONA HORIBE.
OH, AND IF YOU DON'T MIND...
AS HIS GUARDIAN...
...I'D LIKE TO KEEP AN EYE ON HIM FOR A WHILE.

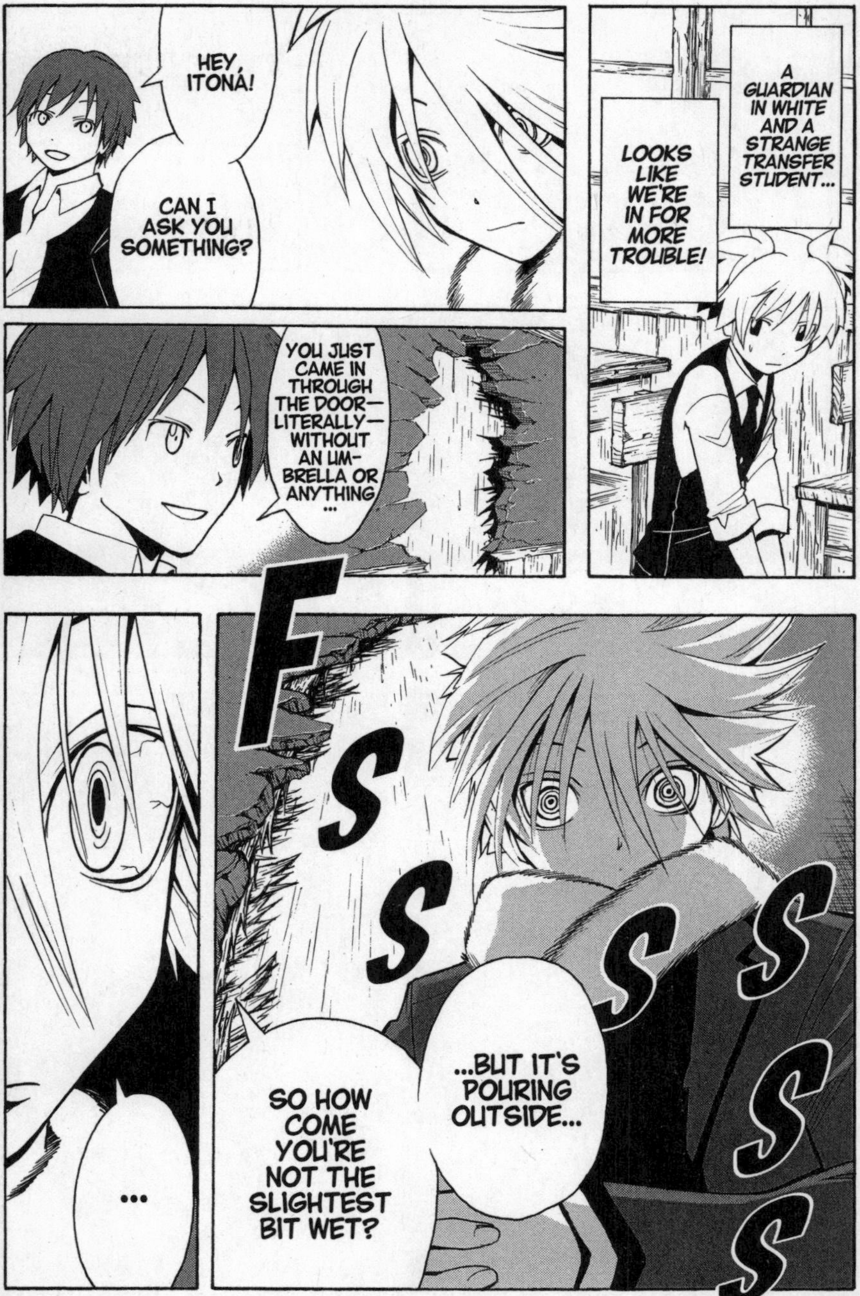
A GUARDIAN IN WHITE AND A STRANGE TRANSFER STUDENT...
LOOKS LIKE WE'RE IN FOR MORE TROUBLE!
HEY, ITONA!
CAN I ASK YOU SOMETHING?
YOU JUST CAME IN THROUGH THE DOOR— LITERALLY— WITHOUT AN UMBRELLA OR ANYTHING...
FSSSSSSSS
...BUT IT'S POURING OUTSIDE...
SO HOW COME YOU'RE NOT THE SLIGHTEST BIT WET?
...

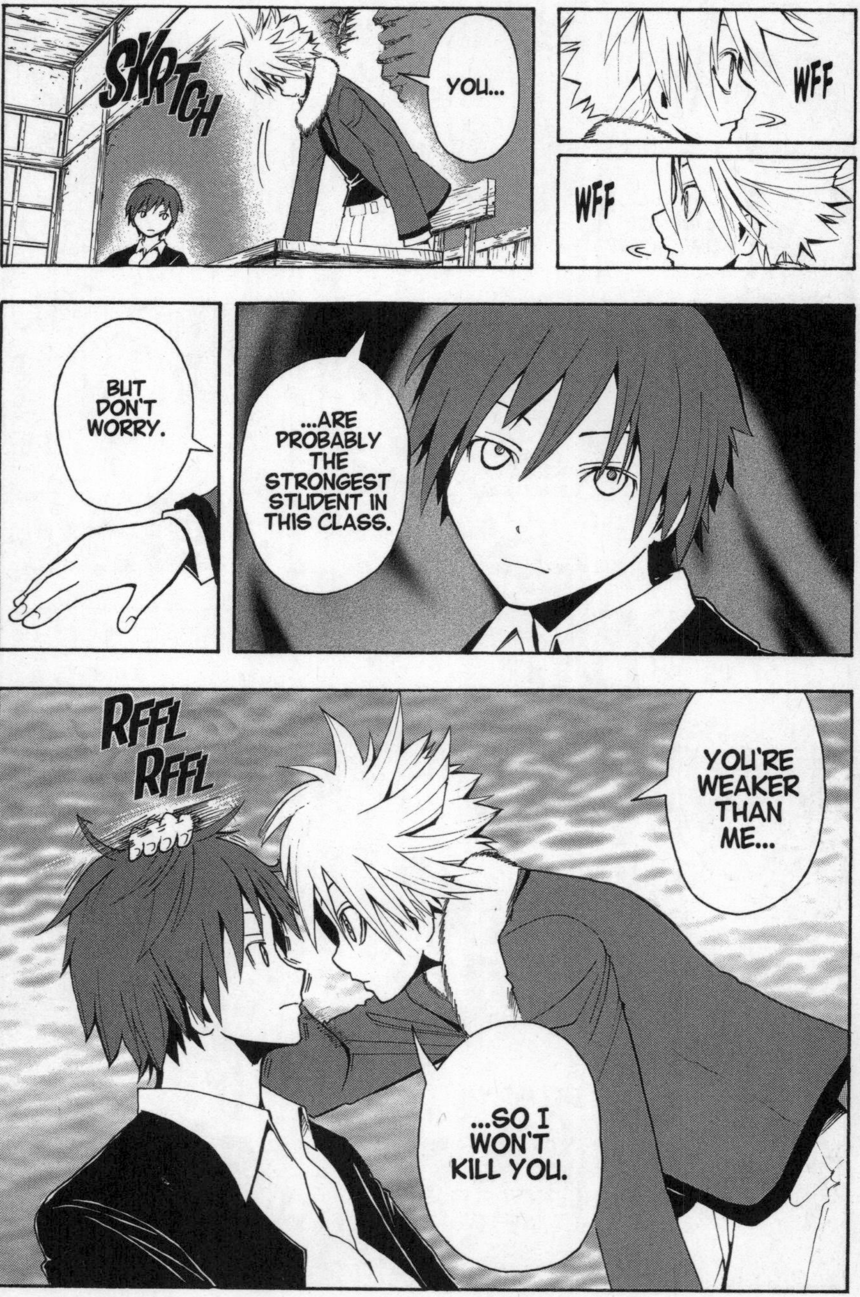
WFF
WFF
SKRTCH
YOU...
...ARE PROBABLY THE STRONGEST STUDENT IN THIS CLASS.
BUT DON'T WORRY.
RFFL RFFL
YOU'RE WEAKER THAN ME...
...SO I WON'T KILL YOU.

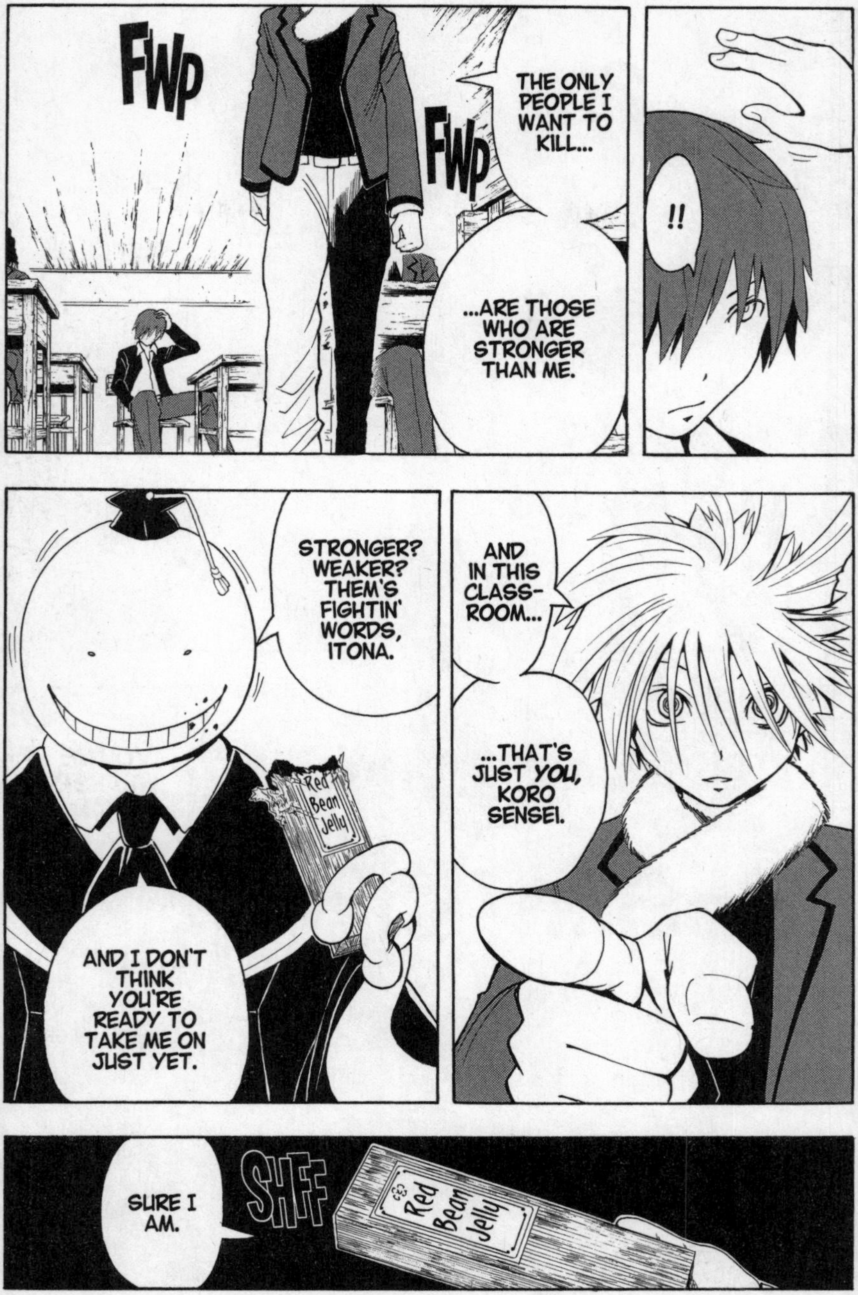
!!
THE ONLY PEOPLE I WANT TO KILL...
FWP
FWP
...ARE THOSE WHO ARE STRONGER THAN ME.
AND IN THIS CLASS-ROOM...
...THAT'S JUST *YOU*, KORO SENSEI.
STRONGER? WEAKER? THEM'S FIGHTIN' WORDS, ITONA.
Red Bean Jelly
AND I DON'T THINK YOU'RE READY TO TAKE ME ON JUST YET.
Red Bean Jelly
SHFF
SURE I AM.

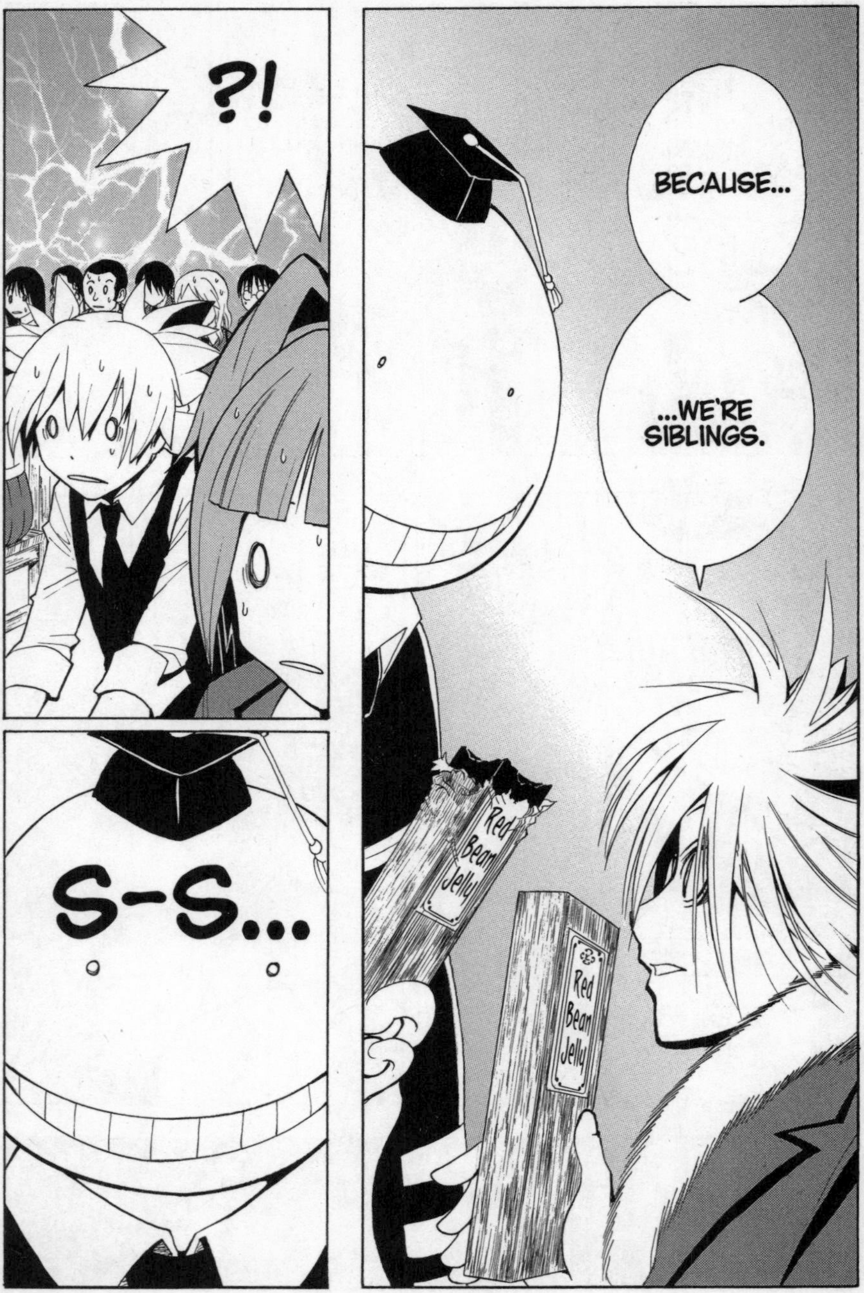
BECAUSE...
...WE'RE SIBLINGS.
Red Bean Jelly
Red Bean Jelly
?!
S-S...

SIBLINGS
?!

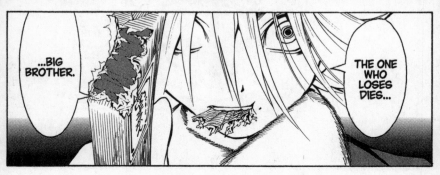

...BIG
BROTHER.

THE ONE
WHO
LOSES
DIES...

THERE IS NO SUCH THING AS A YOUNGER BROTHER WHO IS SUPERIOR TO HIS ELDER BROTHER!!*

*FIST OF THE NORTH STAR

CLASS 30 TIME TO FACE THE UNBELIEVABLE

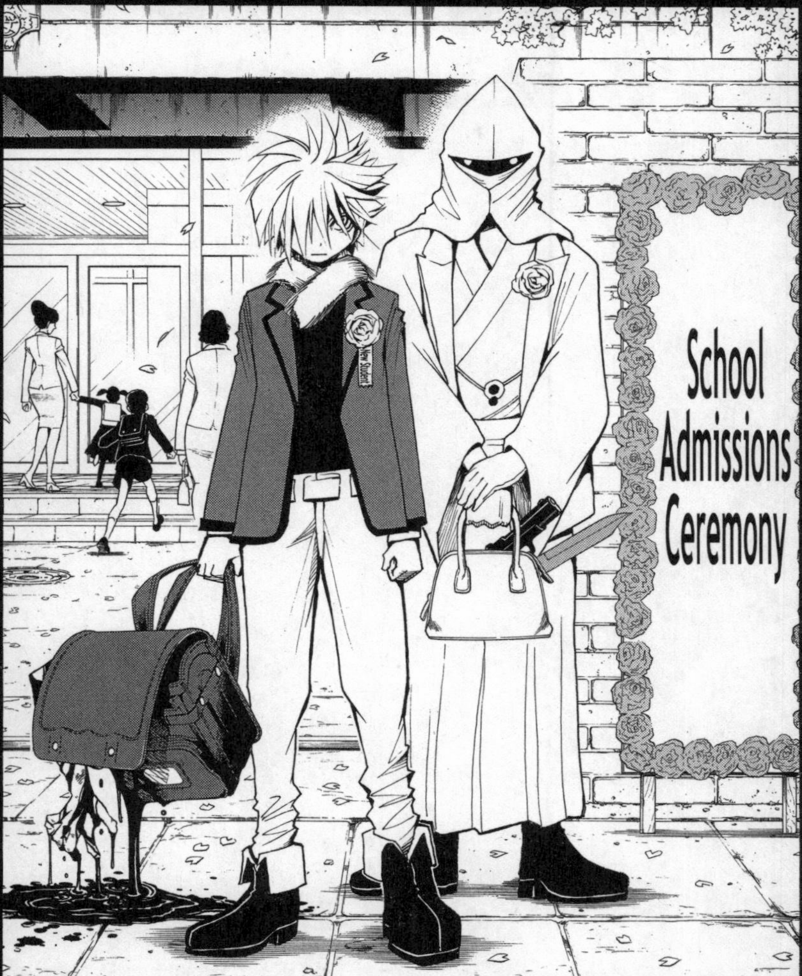
New Student
School Admissions Ceremony

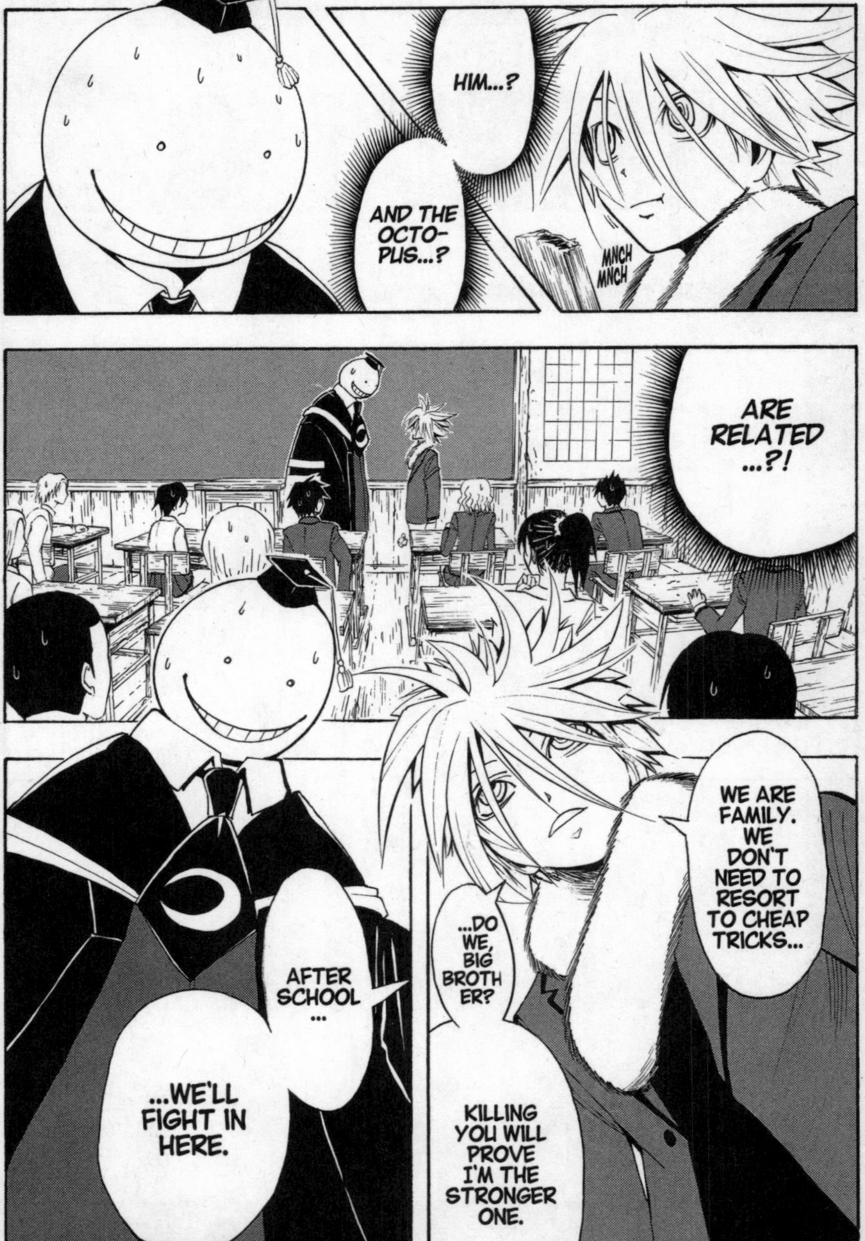
HIM...?
AND THE OCTO-PUS...?
MNCH MNCH
ARE RELATED ...?!
WE ARE FAMILY. WE DON'T NEED TO RESORT TO CHEAP TRICKS...
...DO WE, BIG BROTHER?
KILLING YOU WILL PROVE I'M THE STRONGER ONE.
AFTER SCHOOL ...
...WE'LL FIGHT IN HERE.

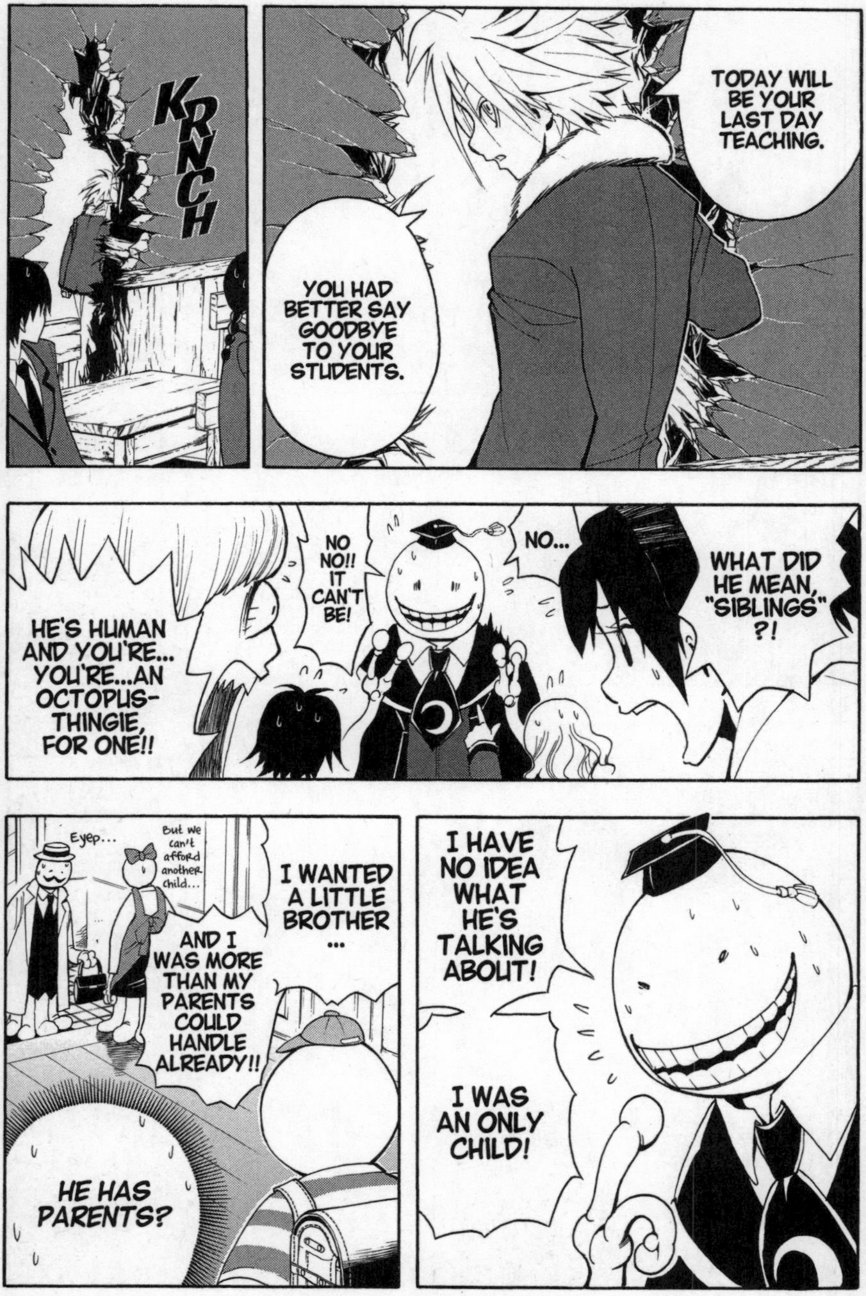
TODAY WILL BE YOUR LAST DAY TEACHING.
YOU HAD BETTER SAY GOODBYE TO YOUR STUDENTS.
KRNCH
WHAT DID HE MEAN, "SIBLINGS"?!
NO...
NO NO!! IT CAN'T BE!
HE'S HUMAN AND YOU'RE... YOU'RE...AN OCTOPUS-THINGIE, FOR ONE!!
I HAVE NO IDEA WHAT HE'S TALKING ABOUT!
I WAS AN ONLY CHILD!
I WANTED A LITTLE BROTHER...
AND I WAS MORE THAN MY PARENTS COULD HANDLE ALREADY!!
But we can't afford another child...
Eyep...
HE HAS PARENTS?

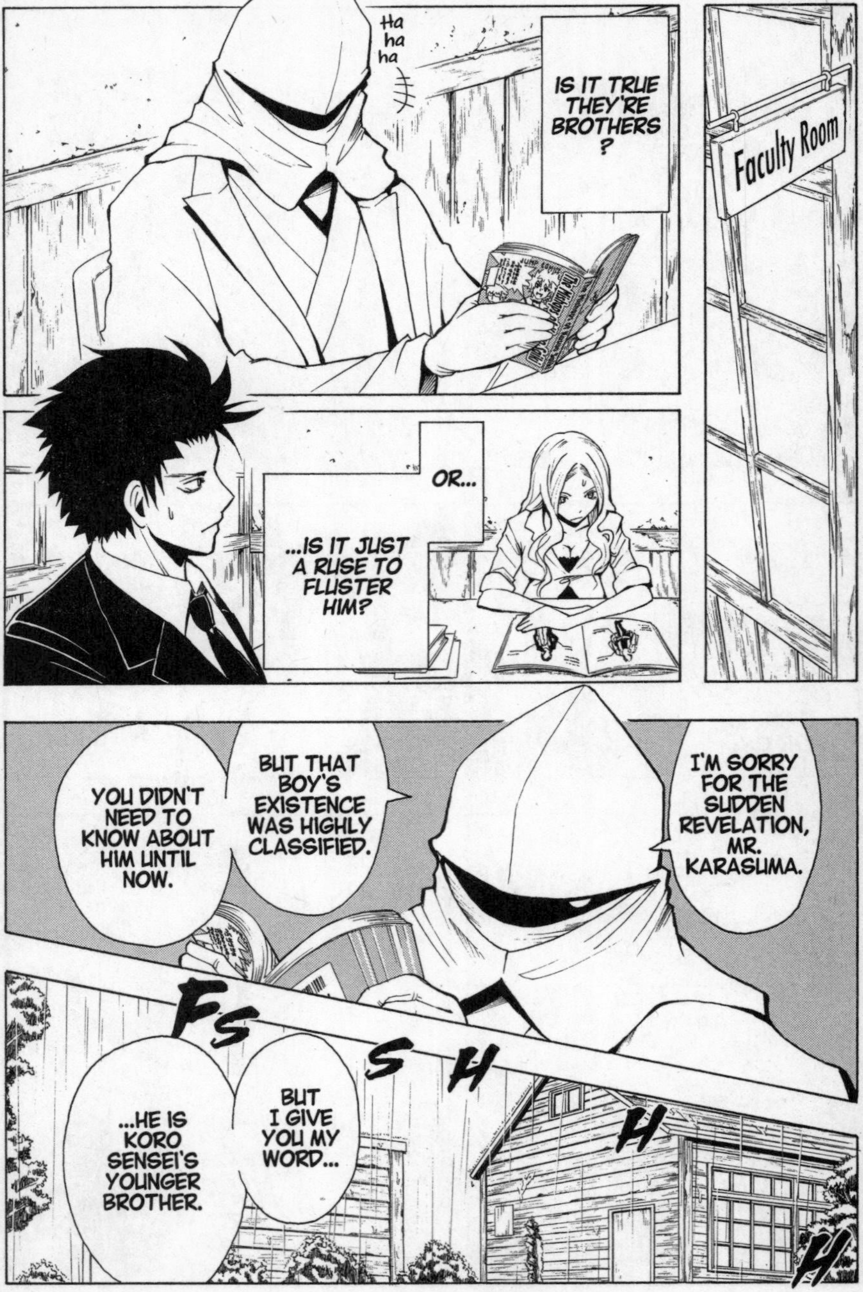
Faculty Room
IS IT TRUE THEY'RE BROTHERS?
Ha ha ha
OR...
...IS IT JUST A RUSE TO FLUSTER HIM?
I'M SORRY FOR THE SUDDEN REVELATION, MR. KARASUMA.
BUT THAT BOY'S EXISTENCE WAS HIGHLY CLASSIFIED.
YOU DIDN'T NEED TO KNOW ABOUT HIM UNTIL NOW.
FSSHHH
BUT I GIVE YOU MY WORD...
...HE IS KORO SENSEI'S YOUNGER BROTHER.

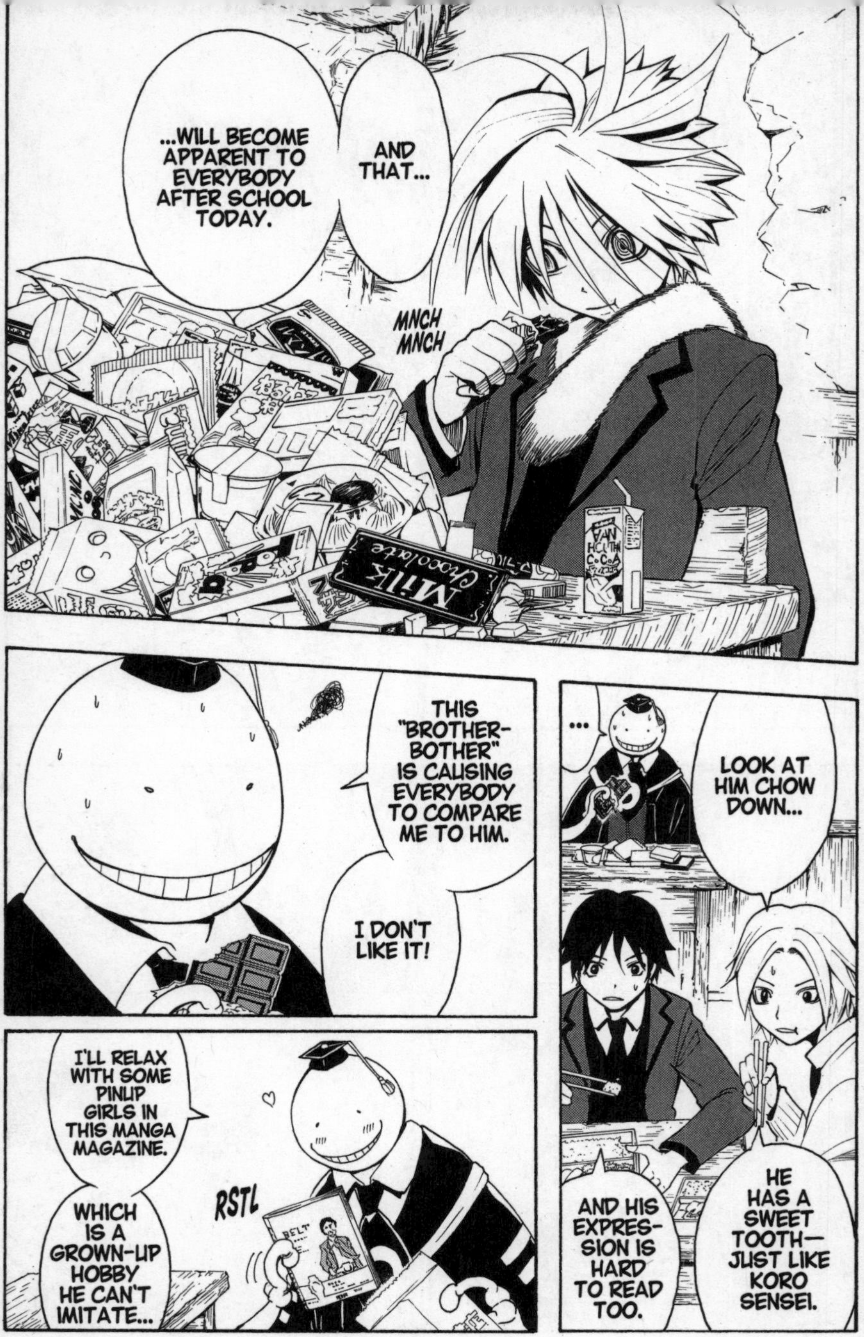
AND THAT...
...WILL BECOME APPARENT TO EVERYBODY AFTER SCHOOL TODAY.
MNCH MNCH
Milk Chocolate
...
LOOK AT HIM CHOW DOWN...
HE HAS A SWEET TOOTH—JUST LIKE KORO SENSEI.
AND HIS EXPRESSION IS HARD TO READ TOO.
THIS "BROTHER-BOTHER" IS CAUSING EVERYBODY TO COMPARE ME TO HIM.
I DON'T LIKE IT!
I'LL RELAX WITH SOME PINUP GIRLS IN THIS MANGA MAGAZINE.
WHICH IS A GROWN-UP HOBBY HE CAN'T IMITATE...
RSTL

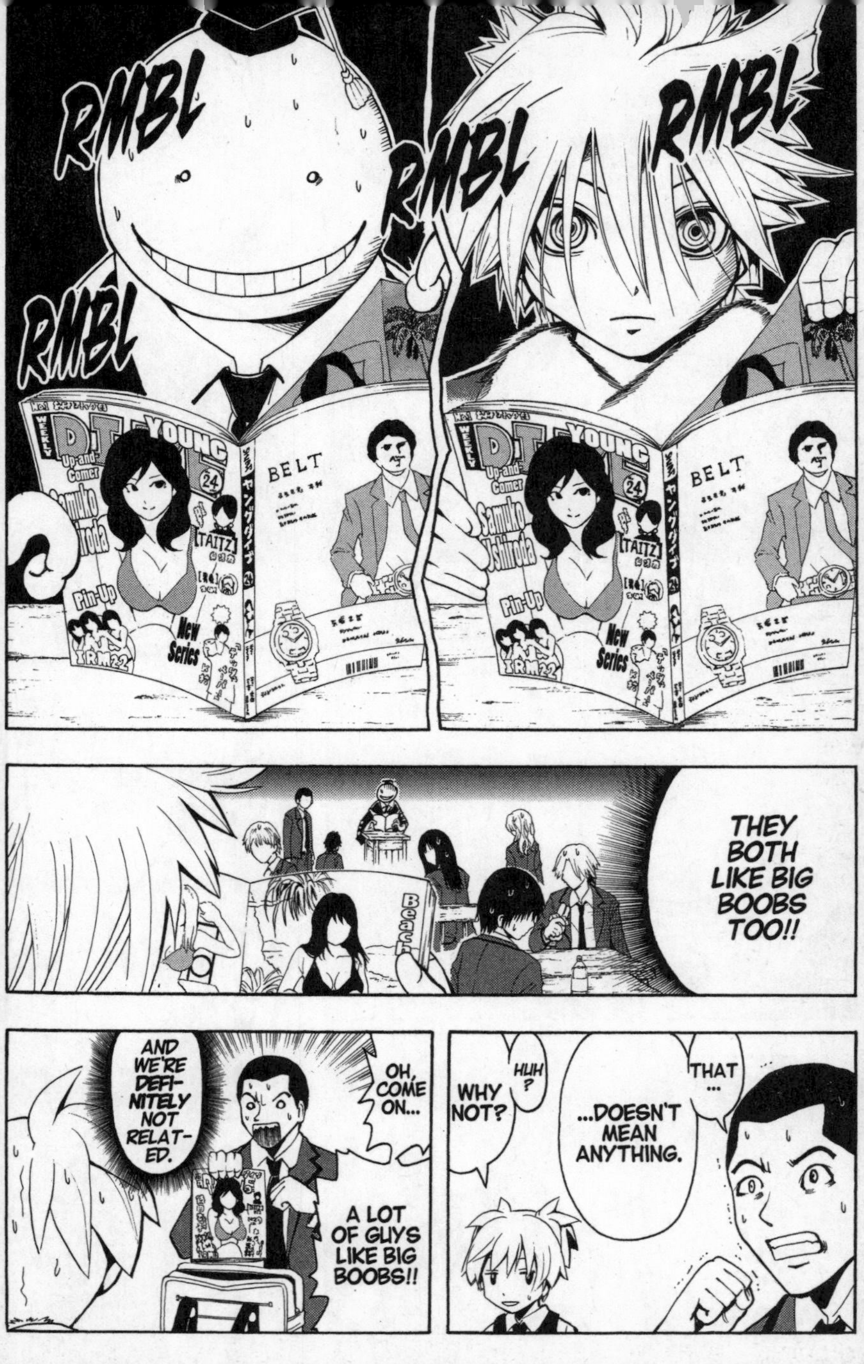
RMBL
RMBL
WEEKLY
YOUNG
Up-and-Comer
24
Samuko Ushiroda
TAITZ
Pin-Up
IRM22
New Series
BELT
RMBL
RMBL
WEEKLY
YOUNG
Up-and-Comer
24
Samuko Ushiroda
TAITZ
Pin-Up
IRM22
New Series
BELT
THEY BOTH LIKE BIG BOOBS TOO!!
Beach
...
THAT ...
HUH?
...DOESN'T MEAN ANYTHING.
WHY NOT?
OH, COME ON...
AND WE'RE DEFI-NITELY NOT RELAT-ED.
A LOT OF GUYS LIKE BIG BOOBS!!

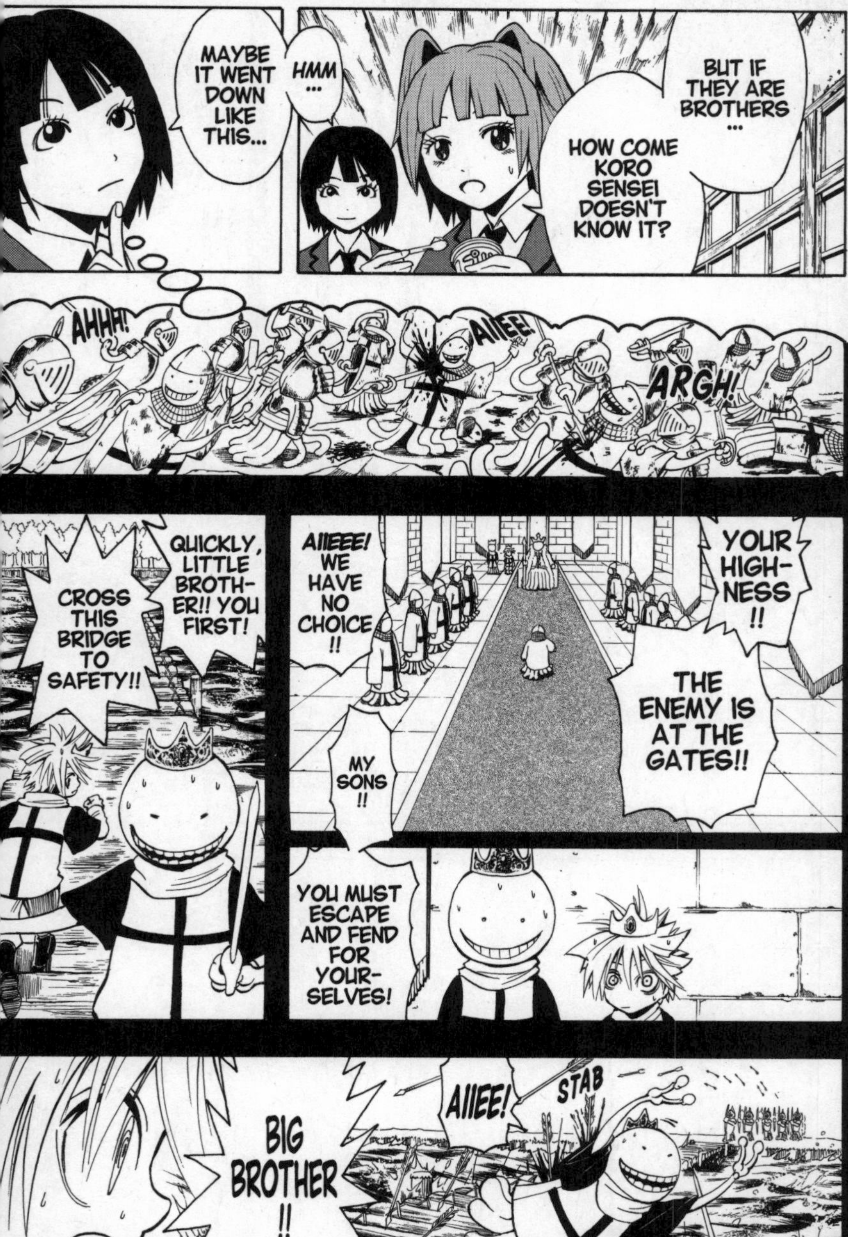
BUT IF THEY ARE BROTHERS...
HOW COME KORO SENSEI DOESN'T KNOW IT?
HMM...
MAYBE IT WENT DOWN LIKE THIS...
ARGH!
AIIEE!
AHHH!
YOUR HIGHNESS!!
THE ENEMY IS AT THE GATES!!
AIIEEE! WE HAVE NO CHOICE!!
MY SONS!!
YOU MUST ESCAPE AND FEND FOR YOURSELVES!
QUICKLY, LITTLE BROTHER!! YOU FIRST!
CROSS THIS BRIDGE TO SAFETY!!
STAB
AIIEE!
BIG BROTHER!!

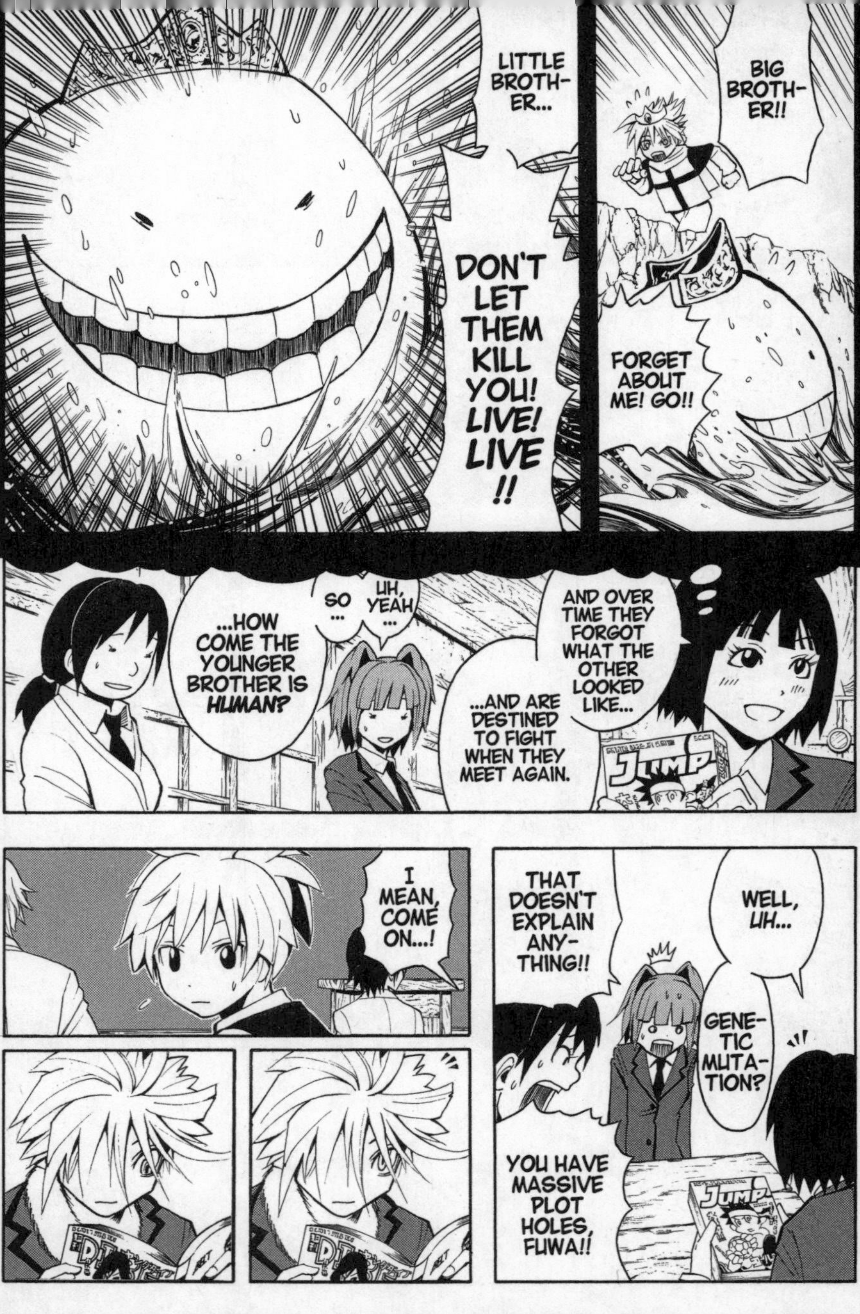
BIG BROTH-ER!!
FORGET ABOUT ME! GO!!
LITTLE BROTH-ER...
DON'T LET THEM KILL YOU! LIVE! LIVE!!
AND OVER TIME THEY FORGOT WHAT THE OTHER LOOKED LIKE...
...AND ARE DESTINED TO FIGHT WHEN THEY MEET AGAIN.
UH, YEAH ...
SO ...
...HOW COME THE YOUNGER BROTHER IS HUMAN?
WELL, UH...
THAT DOESN'T EXPLAIN ANY-THING!!
GENE-TIC MUTA-TION?
YOU HAVE MASSIVE PLOT HOLES, FUWA!!
I MEAN, COME ON...!

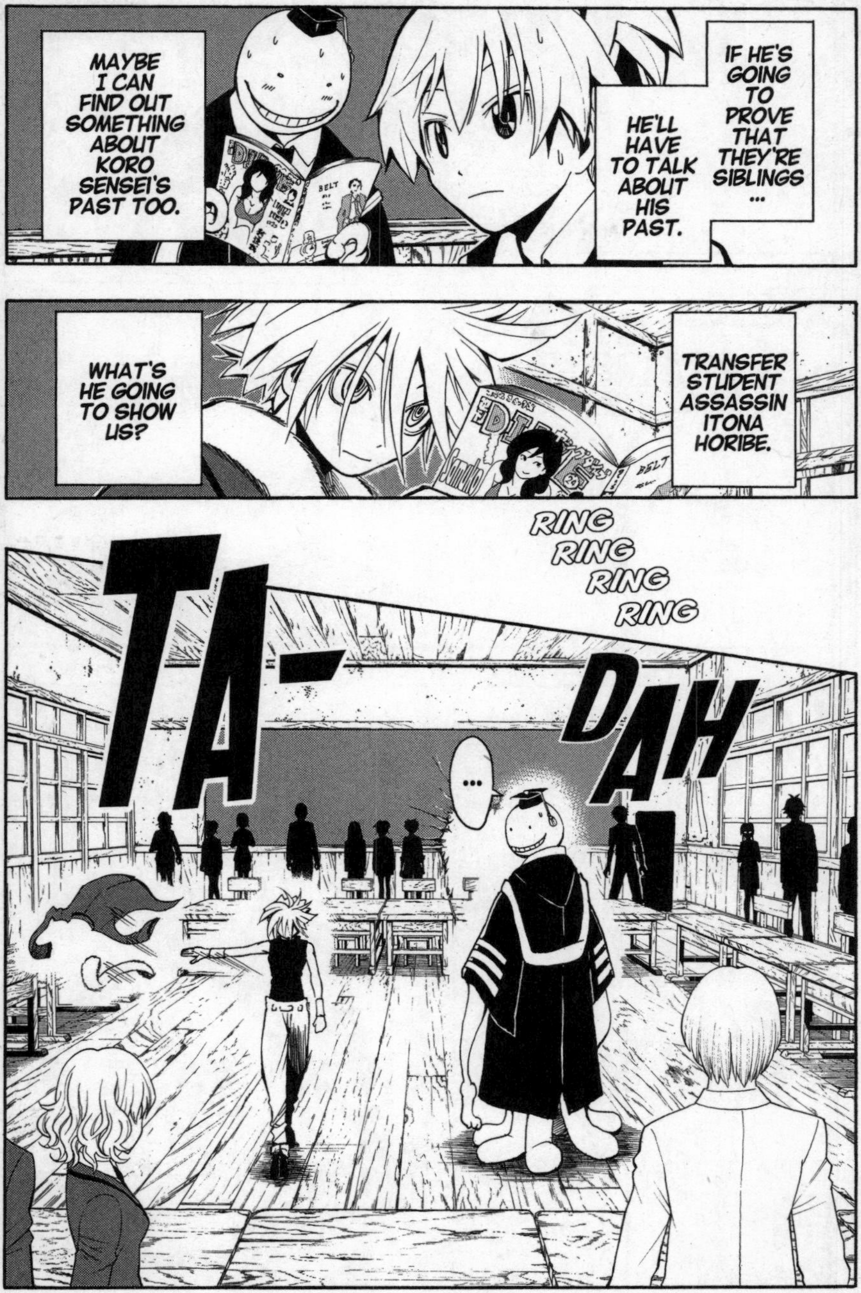
IF HE'S GOING TO PROVE THAT THEY'RE SIBLINGS...
HE'LL HAVE TO TALK ABOUT HIS PAST.
MAYBE I CAN FIND OUT SOMETHING ABOUT KORO SENSEI'S PAST TOO.
TRANSFER STUDENT ASSASSIN ITONA HORIBE.
WHAT'S HE GOING TO SHOW US?
RING RING RING RING
TA-DAH
...

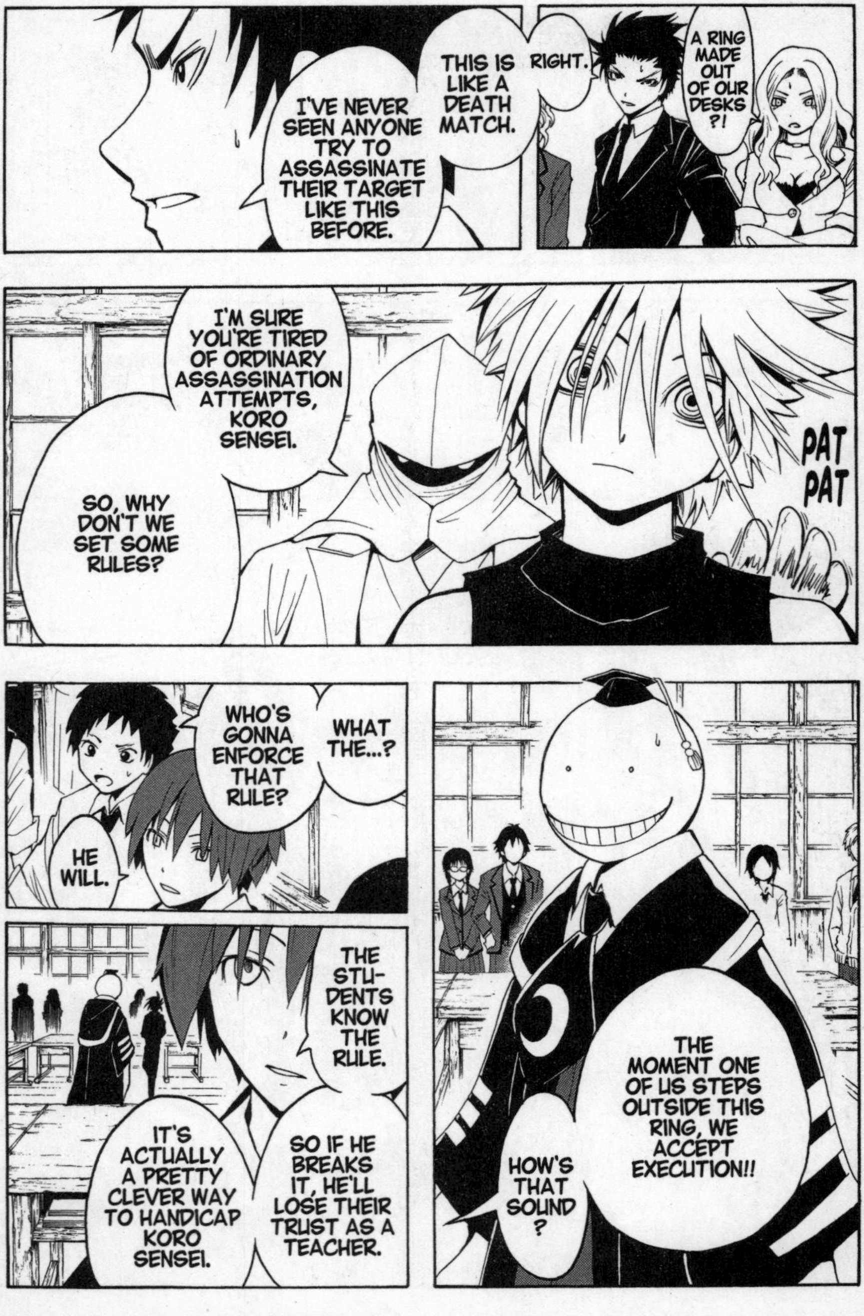
A RING MADE OUT OF OUR DESKS ?!
RIGHT.
THIS IS LIKE A DEATH MATCH.
I'VE NEVER SEEN ANYONE TRY TO ASSASSINATE THEIR TARGET LIKE THIS BEFORE.
PAT PAT
I'M SURE YOU'RE TIRED OF ORDINARY ASSASSINATION ATTEMPTS, KORO SENSEI.
SO, WHY DON'T WE SET SOME RULES?
THE MOMENT ONE OF US STEPS OUTSIDE THIS RING, WE ACCEPT EXECUTION!!
HOW'S THAT SOUND ?
WHAT THE...?
WHO'S GONNA ENFORCE THAT RULE?
HE WILL.
THE STU-DENTS KNOW THE RULE.
SO IF HE BREAKS IT, HE'LL LOSE THEIR TRUST AS A TEACHER.
IT'S ACTUALLY A PRETTY CLEVER WAY TO HANDICAP KORO SENSEI.

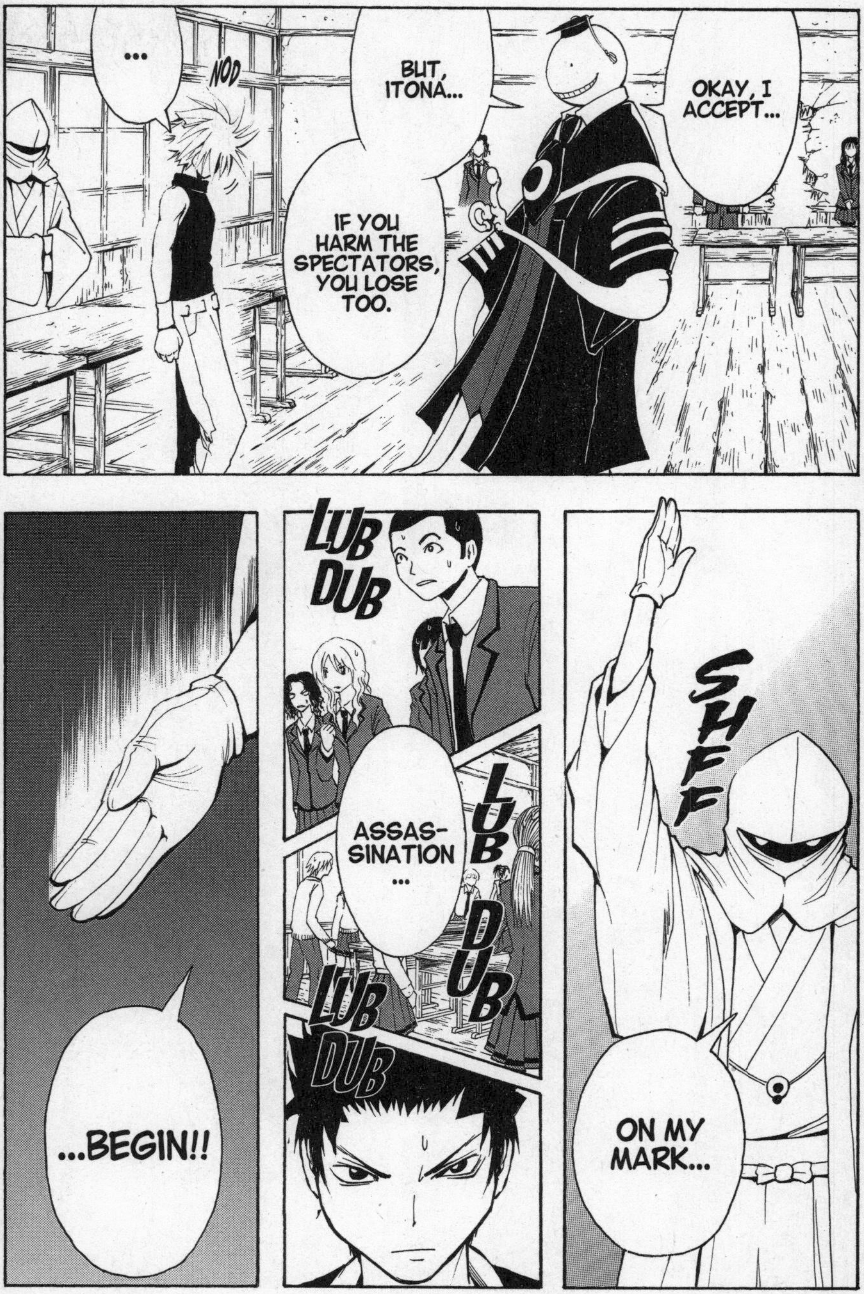

OKAY, I ACCEPT...
BUT, ITONA...
IF YOU HARM THE SPECTATORS, YOU LOSE TOO.
NOD
...
SHFF
ON MY MARK...
LUB DUB
ASSAS-SINATION ...
LUB DUB
LUB DUB
...BEGIN!!

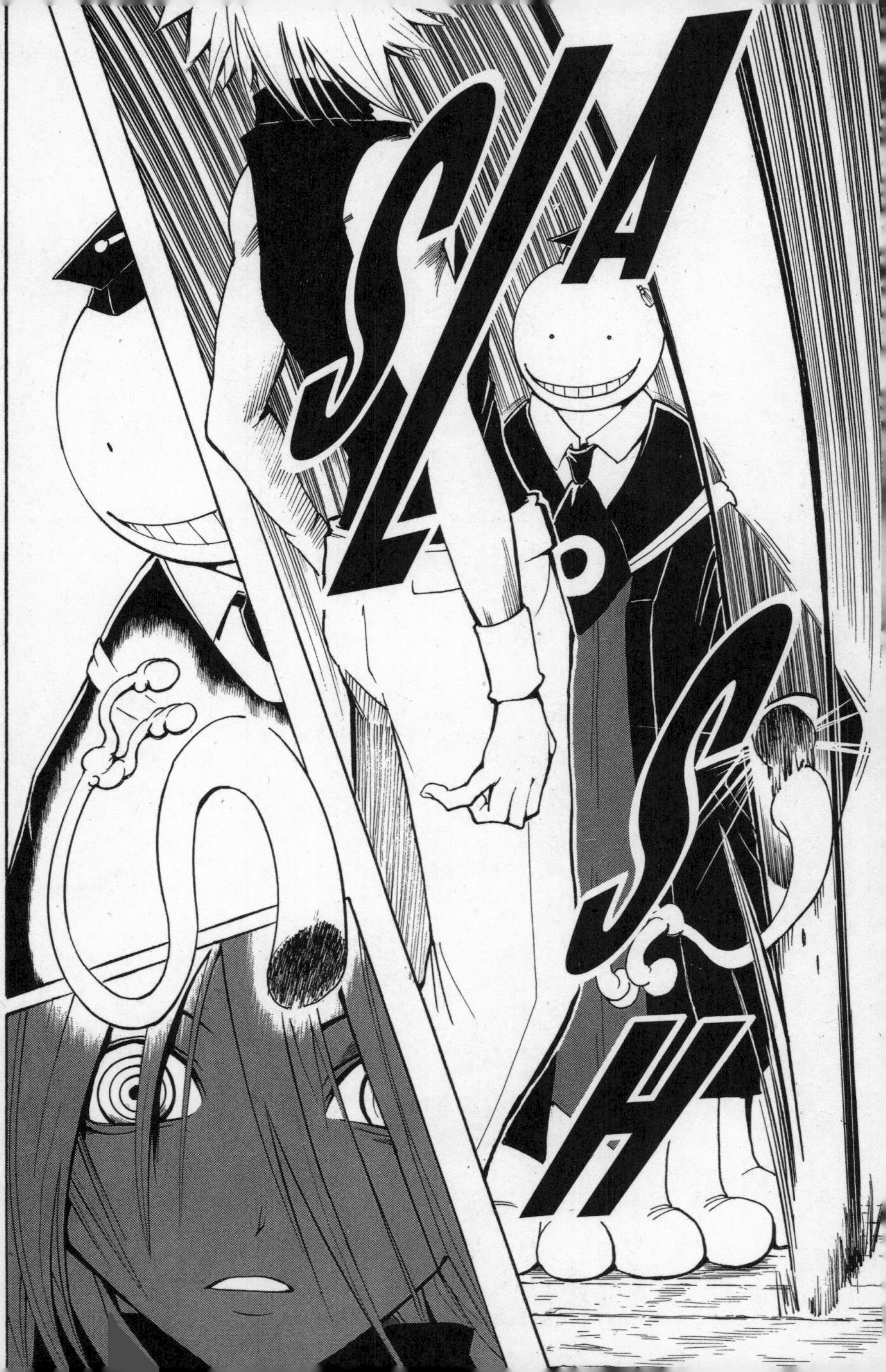

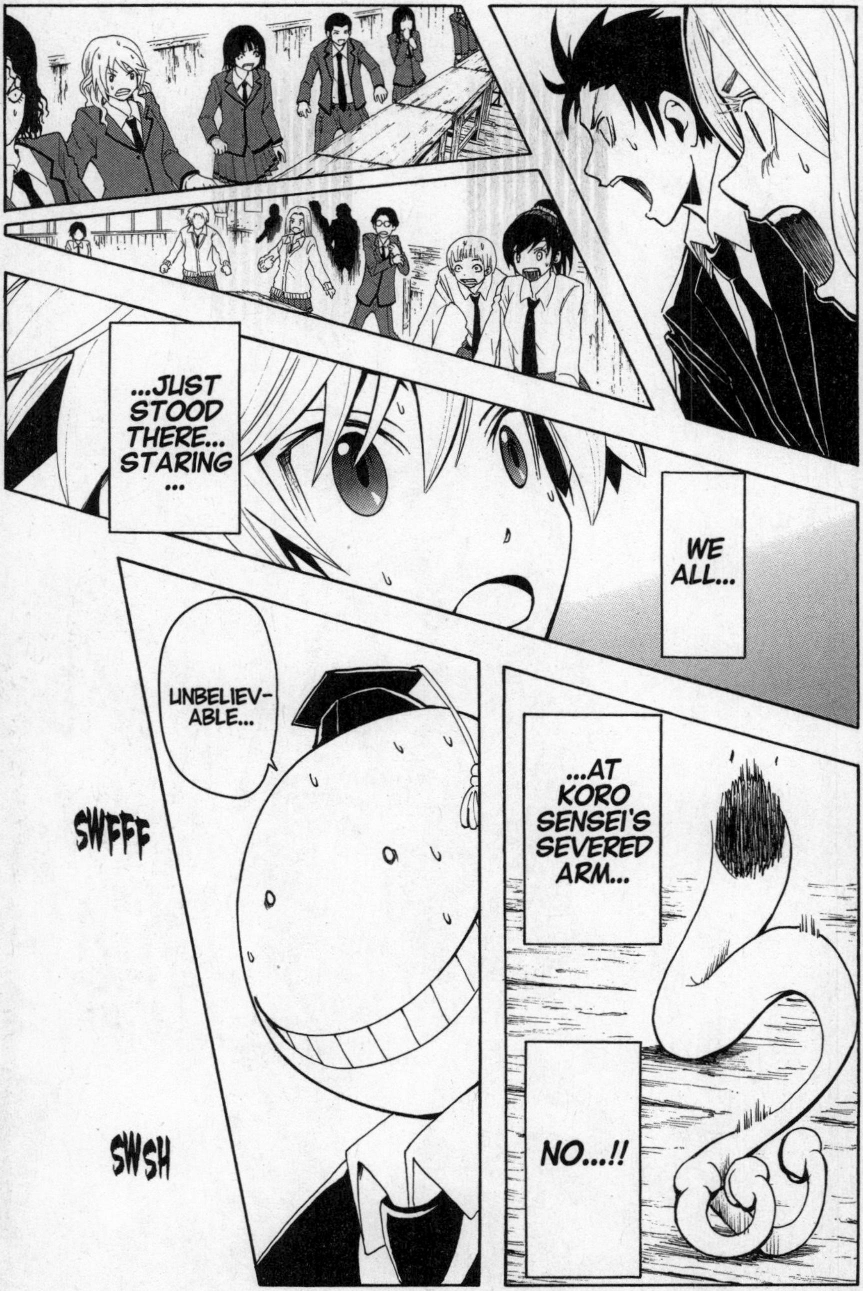
WE ALL...
...JUST STOOD THERE... STARING...
...AT KORO SENSEI'S SEVERED ARM...
NO...!!
UNBELIEVABLE...
SWFFF
SWSH

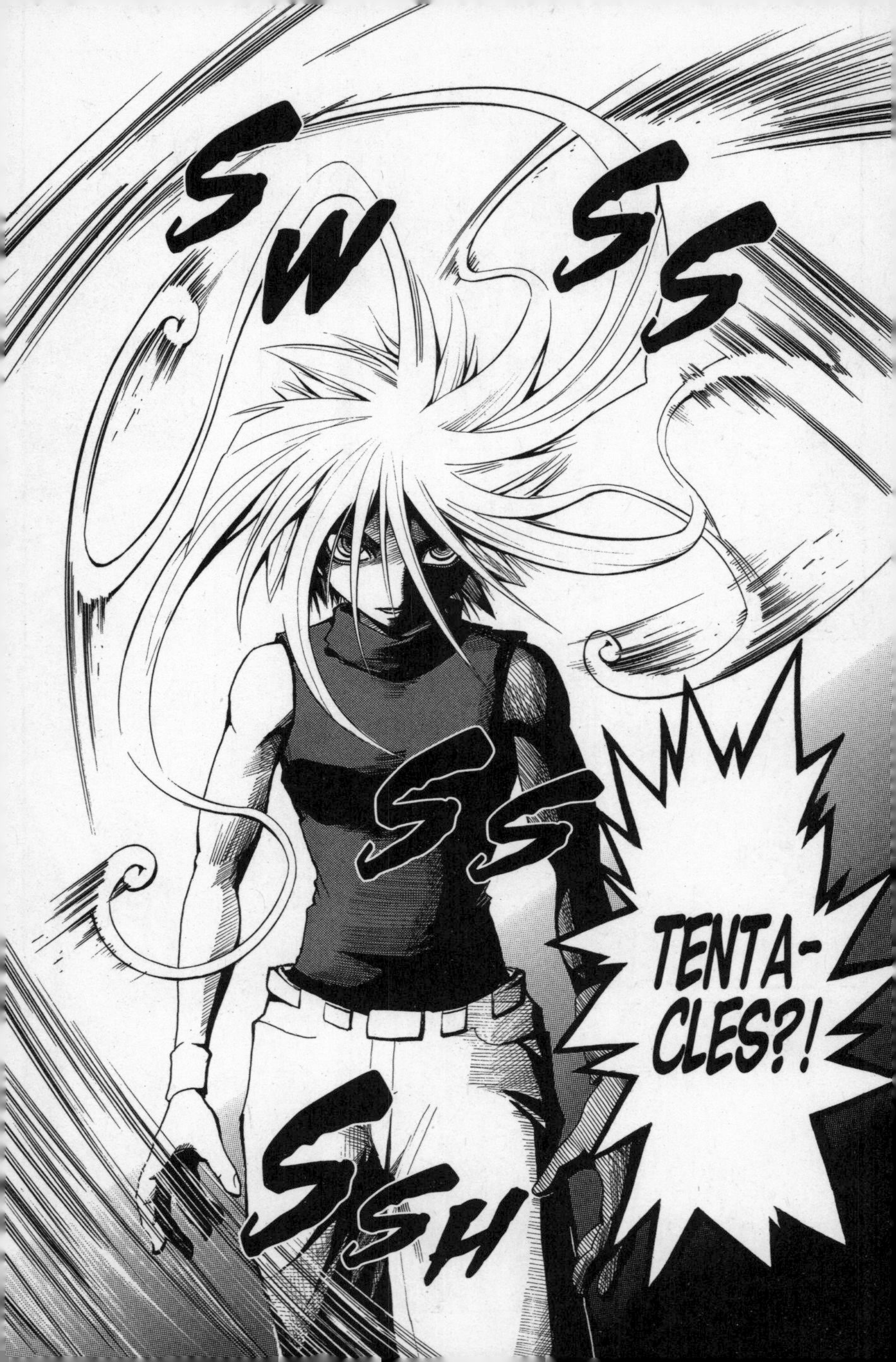
SWSSS
TENTA-CLES?!
SSS
SSSH

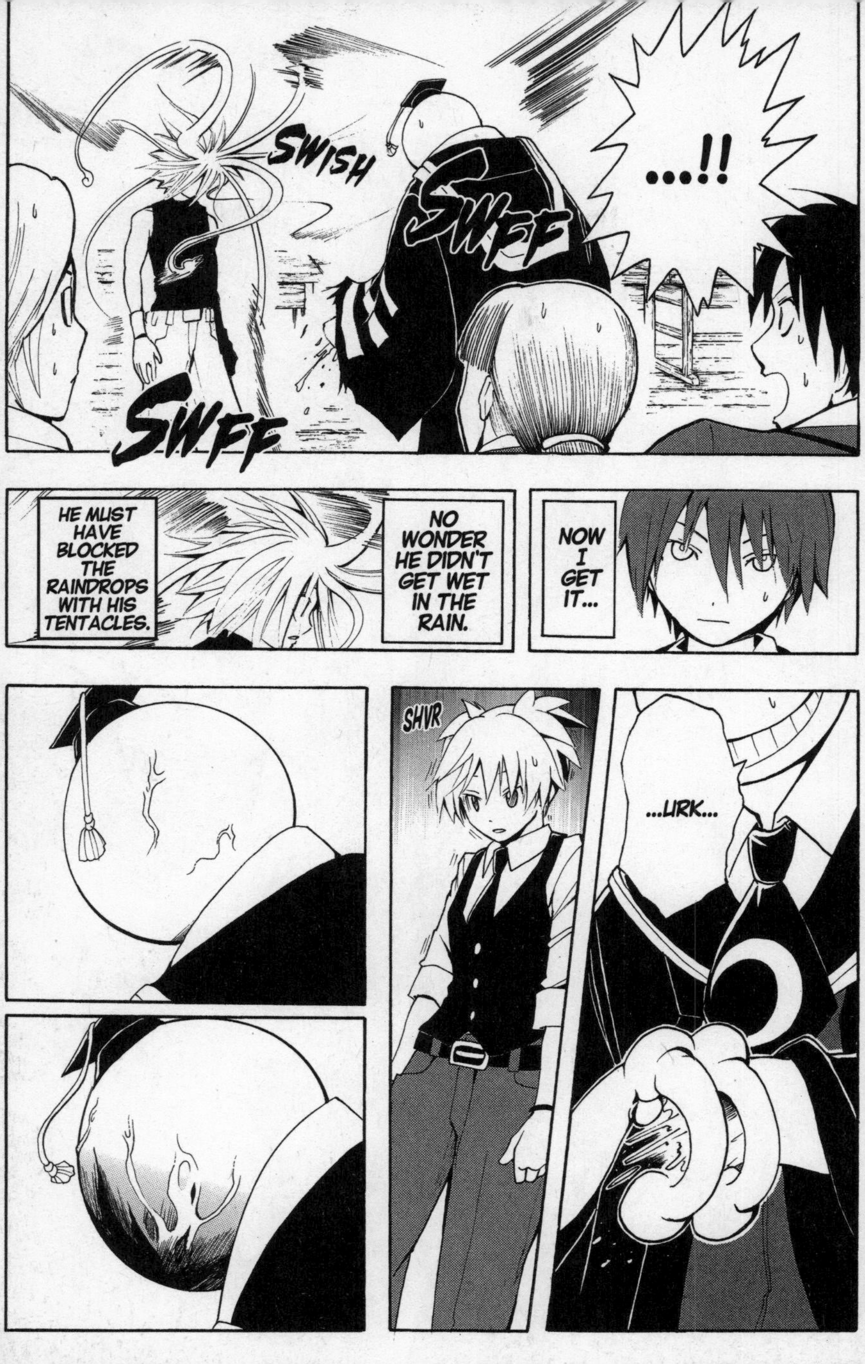
...!!
SWFF
SWISH
SWFF
NOW I GET IT...
NO WONDER HE DIDN'T GET WET IN THE RAIN.
HE MUST HAVE BLOCKED THE RAINDROPS WITH HIS TENTACLES.
...URK...
SHVR

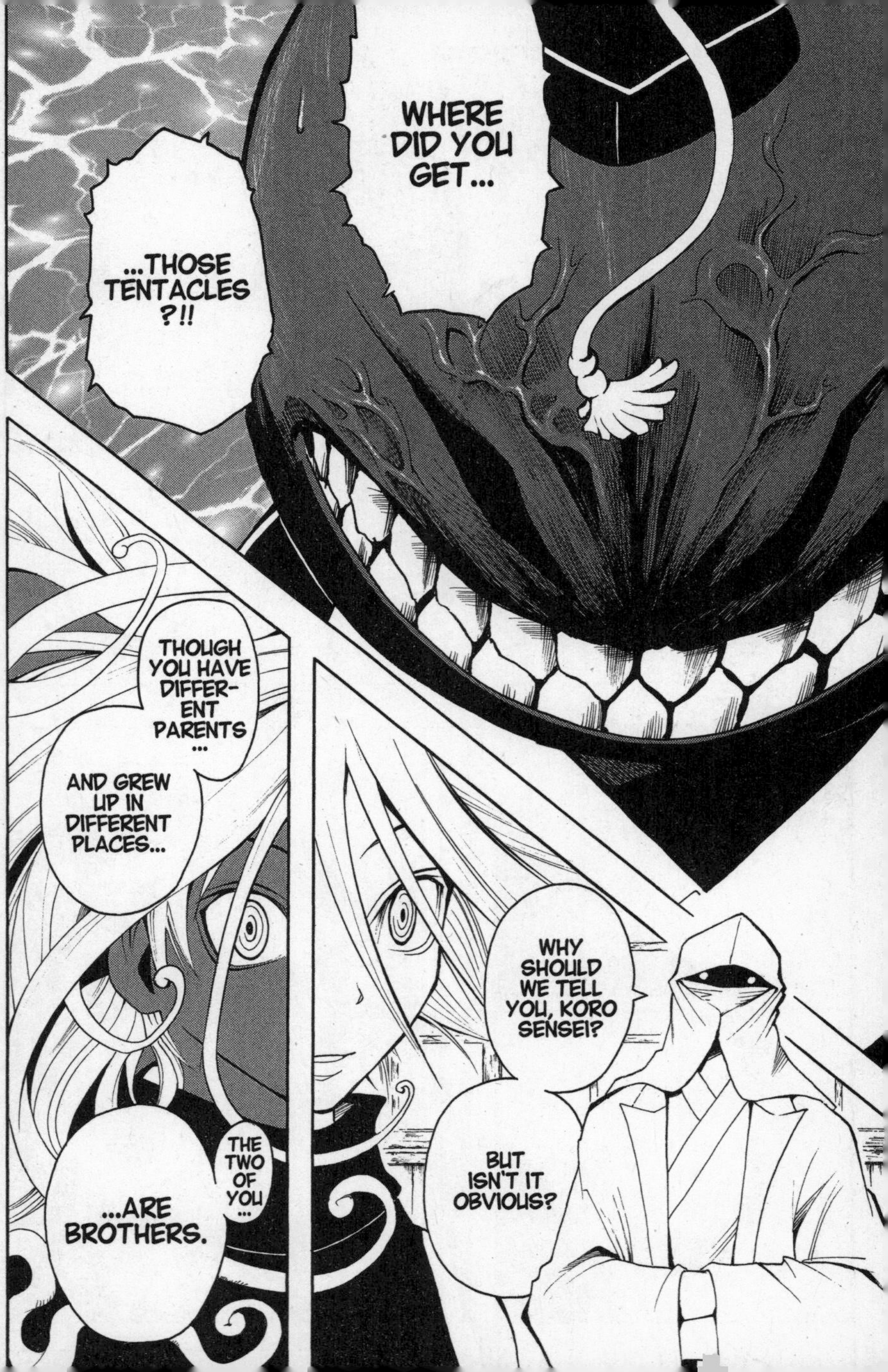
WHERE DID YOU GET...
...THOSE TENTACLES?!!
WHY SHOULD WE TELL YOU, KORO SENSEI?
BUT ISN'T IT OBVIOUS?
THOUGH YOU HAVE DIFFERENT PARENTS...
AND GREW UP IN DIFFERENT PLACES...
THE TWO OF YOU...
...ARE BROTHERS.

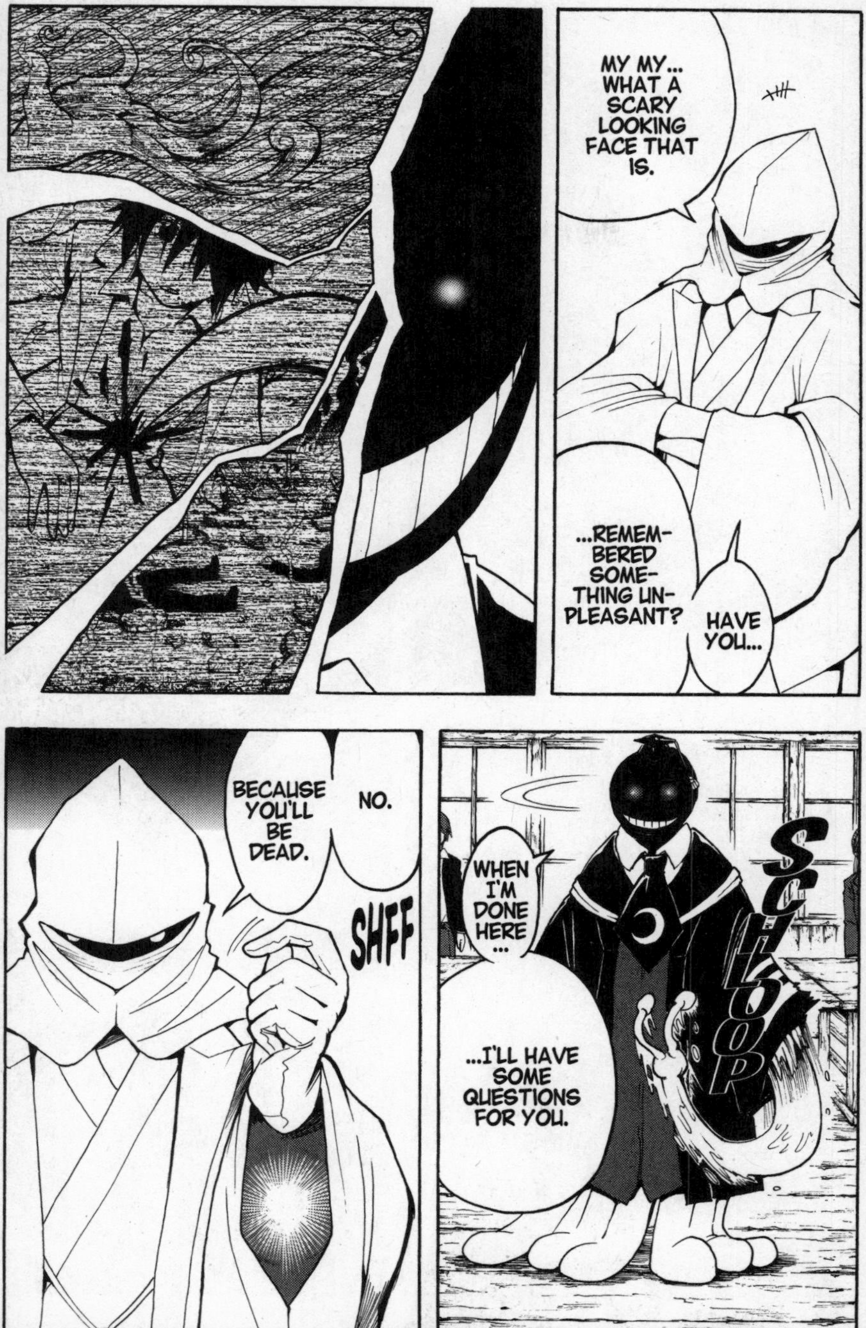
MY MY... WHAT A SCARY LOOKING FACE THAT IS.
HAVE YOU...
...REMEMBERED SOMETHING UNPLEASANT?
WHEN I'M DONE HERE...
...I'LL HAVE SOME QUESTIONS FOR YOU.
SCHLOOP
NO.
BECAUSE YOU'LL BE DEAD.
SHFF

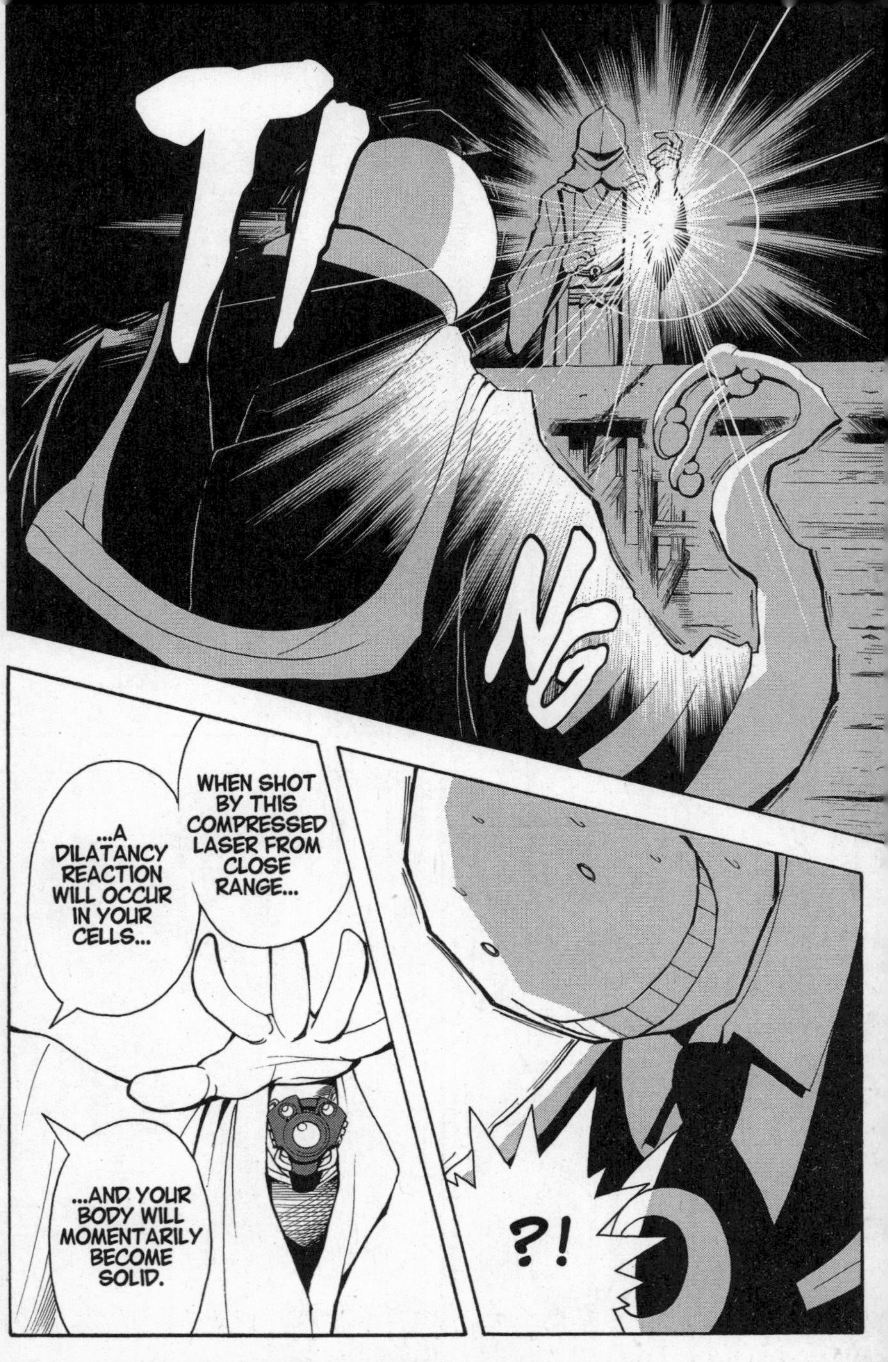
TING
?!
WHEN SHOT BY THIS COMPRESSED LASER FROM CLOSE RANGE...
...A DILATANCY REACTION WILL OCCUR IN YOUR CELLS...
...AND YOUR BODY WILL MOMENTARILY BECOME SOLID.

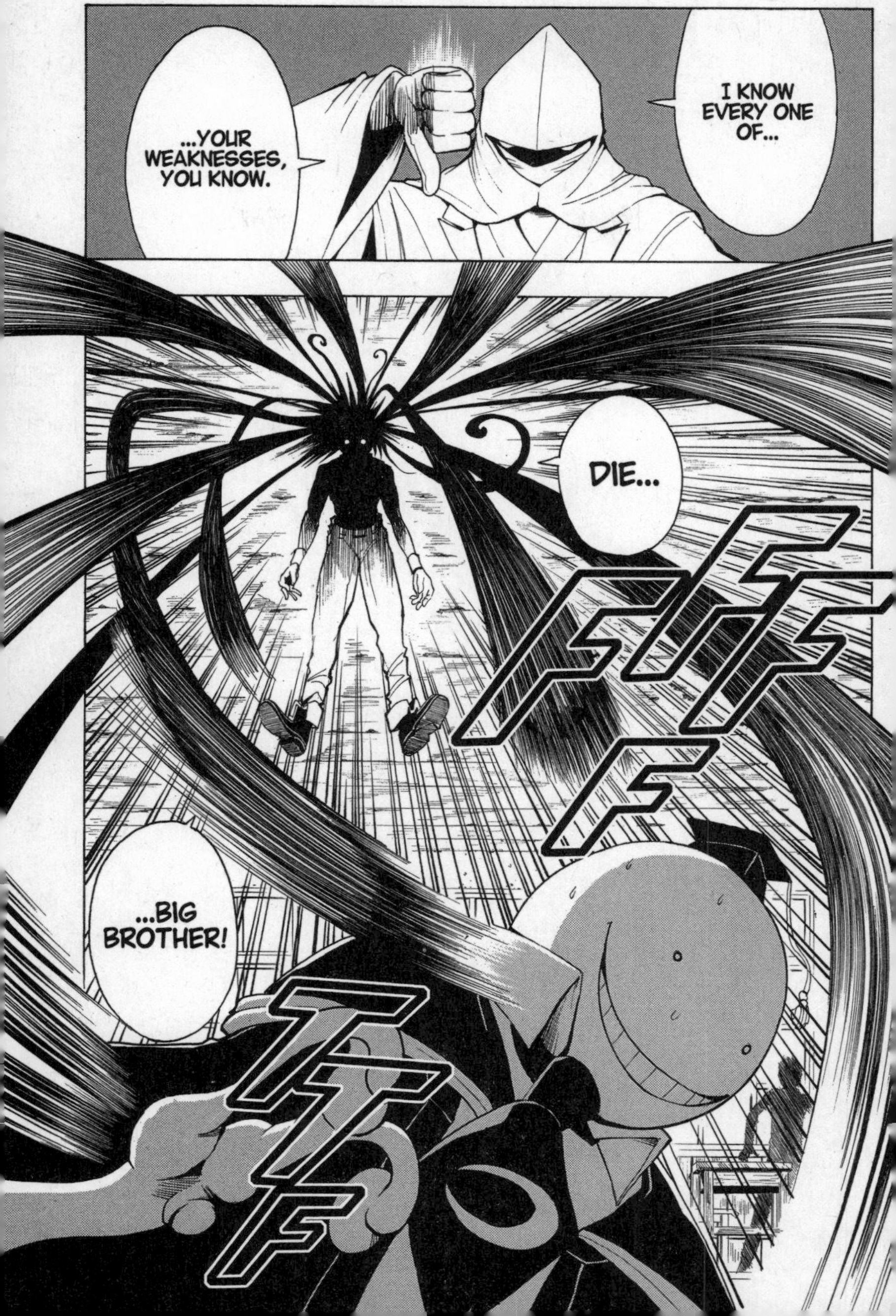
I KNOW EVERY ONE OF...
...YOUR WEAKNESSES, YOU KNOW.
DIE...
...BIG BROTHER!

E-2 YUMA ISOGAI

- 😊 BIRTHDAY: NOVEMBER 13
- 😊 HEIGHT: 5' 8"
- 😊 WEIGHT: 125.7 LBS.
- 😊 FAVORITE SUBJECT: GEOGRAPHY
- 😊 LEAST FAVORITE SUBJECT: BIOLOGY
- 😊 HOBBY/SKILL: TENNIS
- 😊 FUTURE GOAL: FAIR TRADE BUSINESS
- 😊 CLASSMATE'S OPINION OF HIM:
  - IT'S ANNOYING THAT HE'S GOOD-LOOKING.
  - IT'S ANNOYING THAT HE'S GOOD AT EVERYTHING.
  - IT'S ANNOYING THAT HE ISN'T CONCEITED ABOUT THOSE TRAITS.

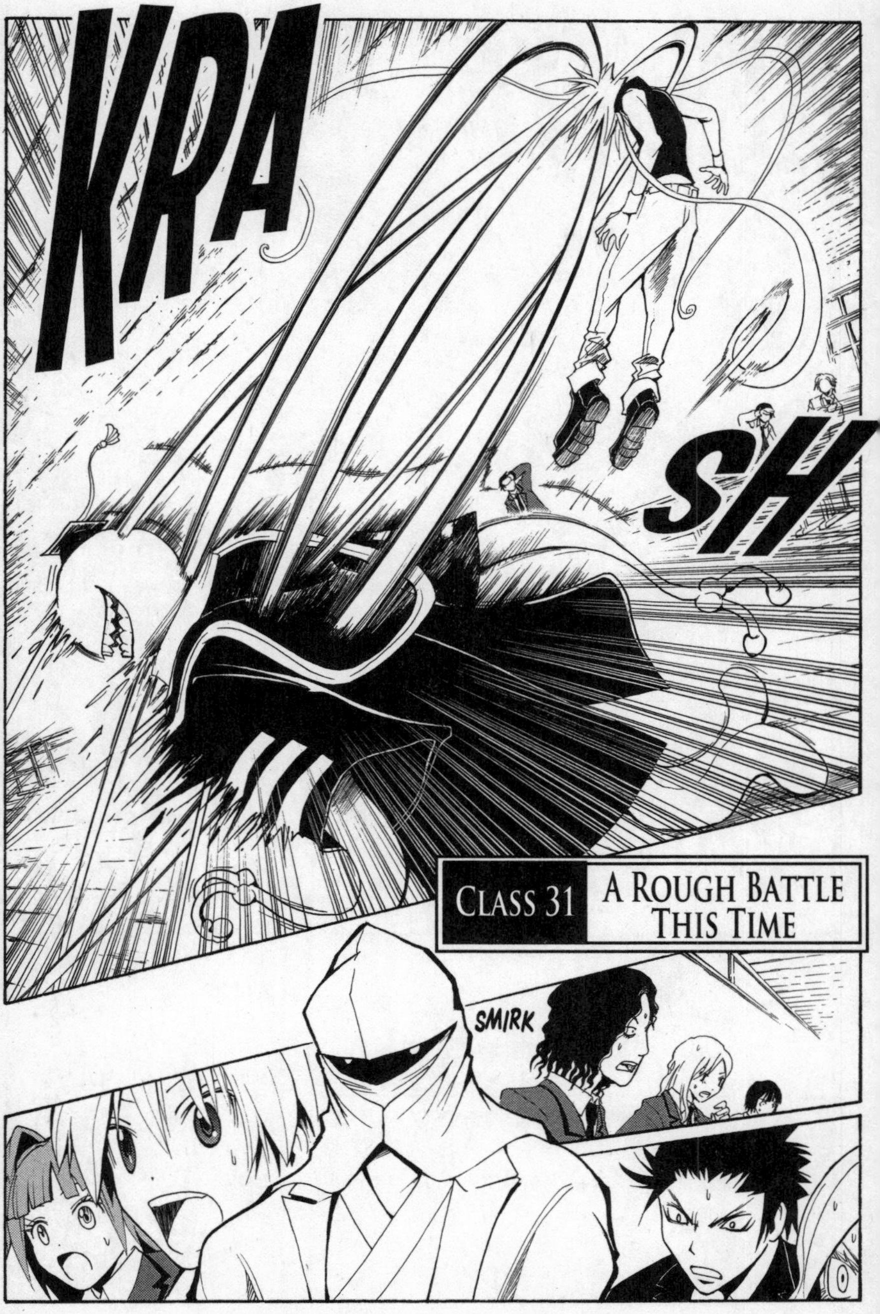
KRA
SH
CLASS 31
A ROUGH BATTLE THIS TIME
SMIRK

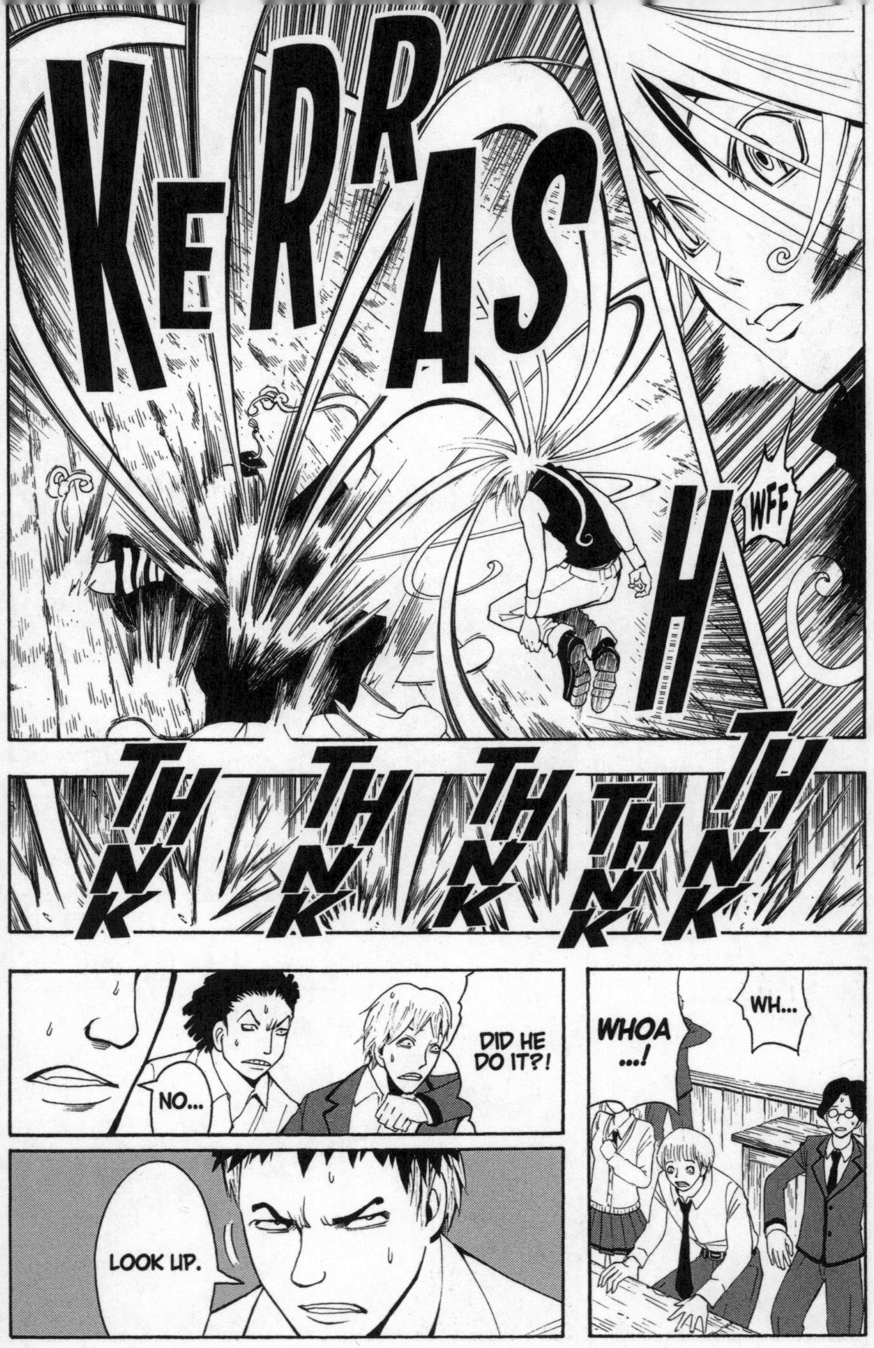
KERRASH
WFF
THNK
THNK
THNK
THNK
THNK
WH...
WHOA ...!
DID HE DO IT?!
NO...
LOOK UP.

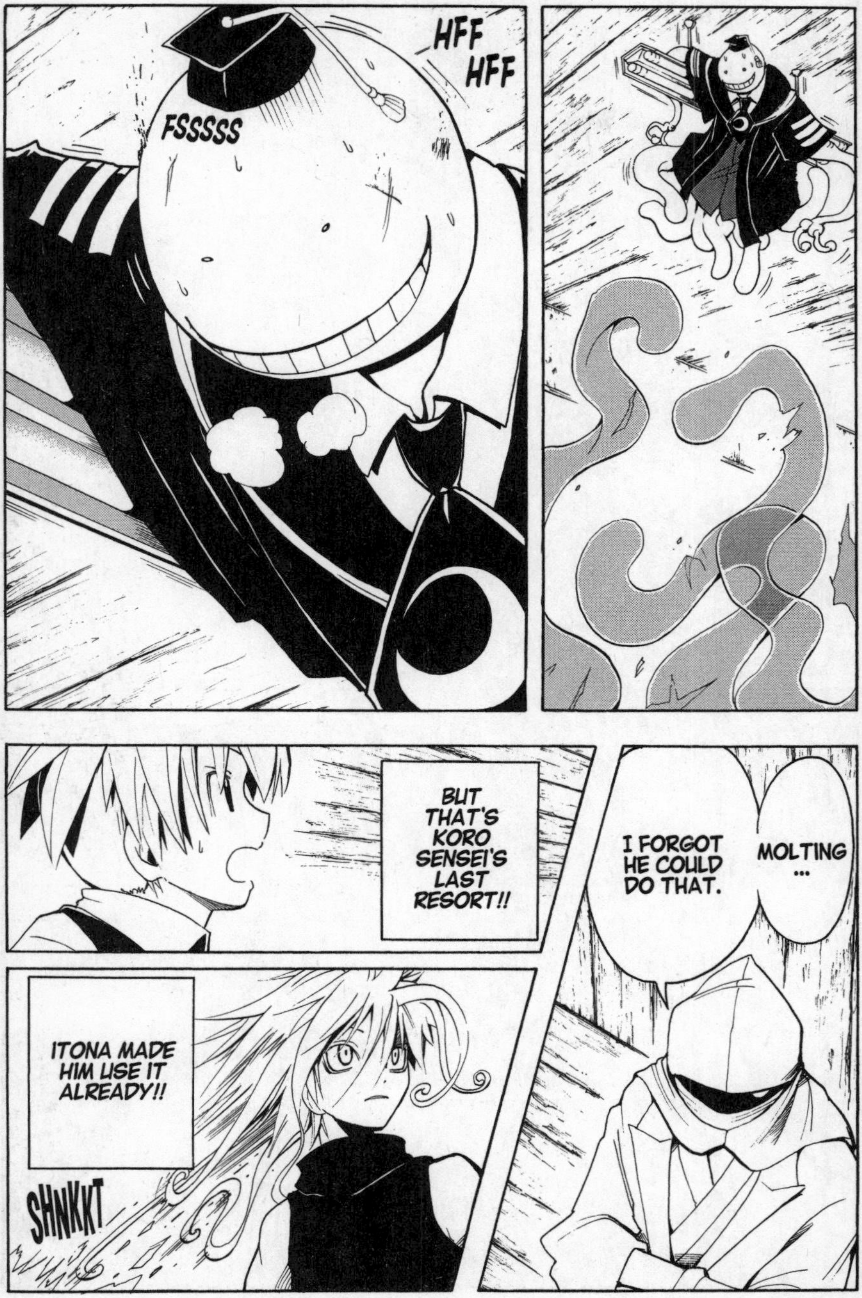
HFF HFF
FSSSSS
MOLTING...
I FORGOT HE COULD DO THAT.
BUT THAT'S KORO SENSEI'S LAST RESORT!!
ITONA MADE HIM USE IT ALREADY!!
SHNKKT

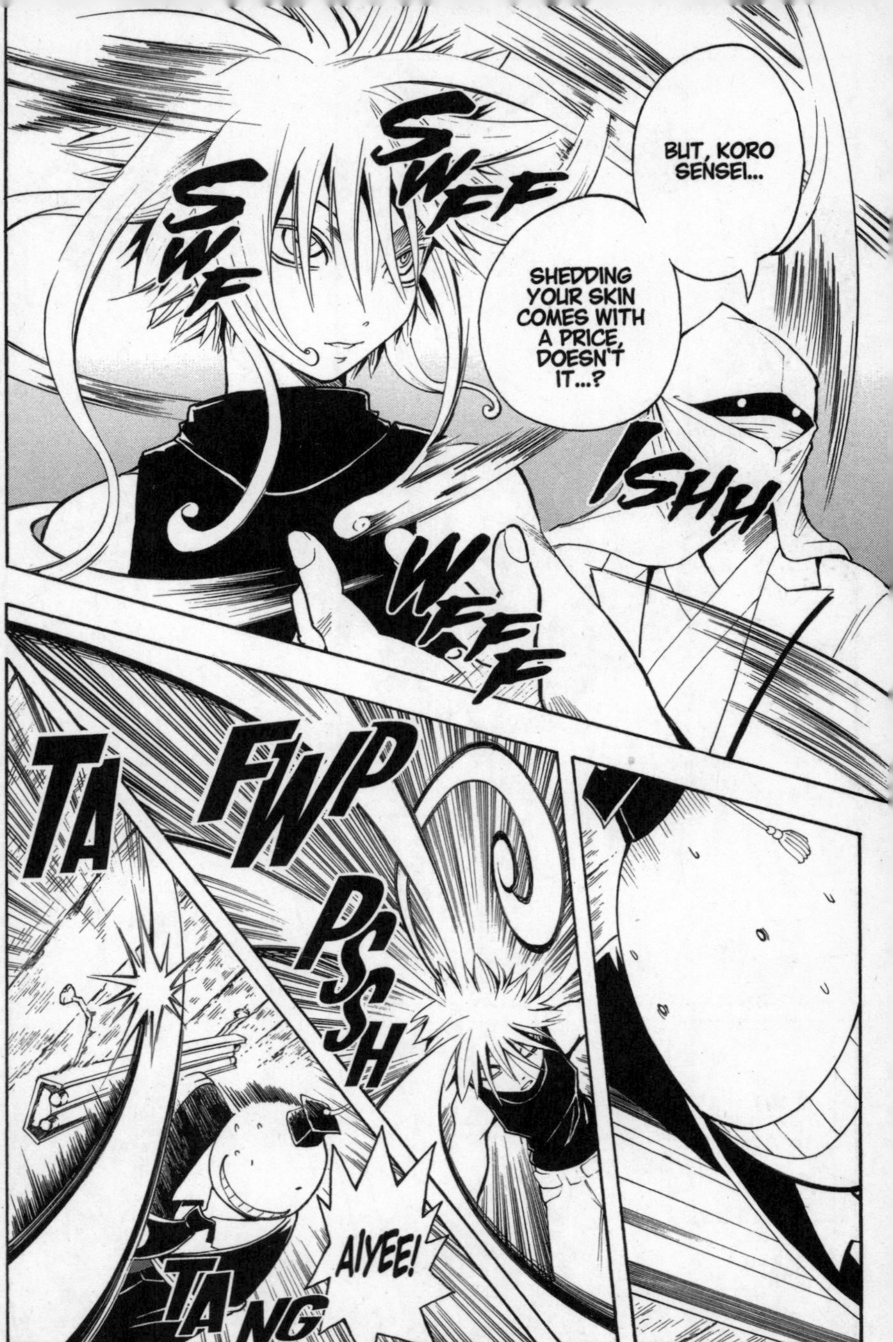
BUT, KORO SENSEI...
SHEDDING YOUR SKIN COMES WITH A PRICE, DOESN'T IT...?
SWFF
SWF
SHH
WFFF
FWP
PSSH
TA
AIYEE!
TA TANG

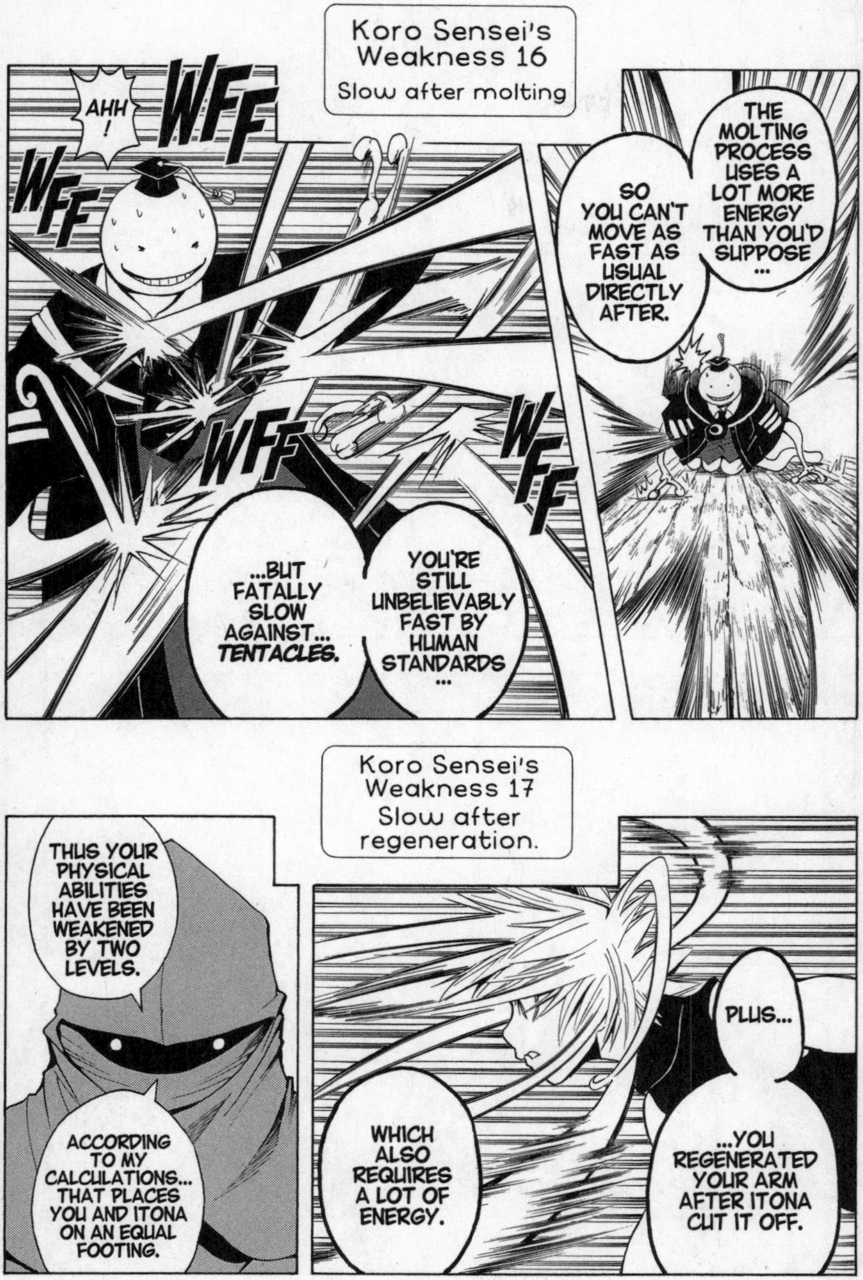
Koro Sensei's Weakness 16
Slow after molting
THE MOLTING PROCESS USES A LOT MORE ENERGY THAN YOU'D SUPPOSE...
SO YOU CAN'T MOVE AS FAST AS USUAL DIRECTLY AFTER.
AHH!
WFF
WFF
WFF
WFF
YOU'RE STILL UNBELIEVABLY FAST BY HUMAN STANDARDS...
...BUT FATALLY SLOW AGAINST... *TENTACLES.*
Koro Sensei's Weakness 17
Slow after regeneration.
PLUS...
...YOU REGENERATED YOUR ARM AFTER ITONA CUT IT OFF.
WHICH ALSO REQUIRES A LOT OF ENERGY.
THUS YOUR PHYSICAL ABILITIES HAVE BEEN WEAKENED BY TWO LEVELS.
ACCORDING TO MY CALCULATIONS... THAT PLACES YOU AND ITONA ON AN EQUAL FOOTING.

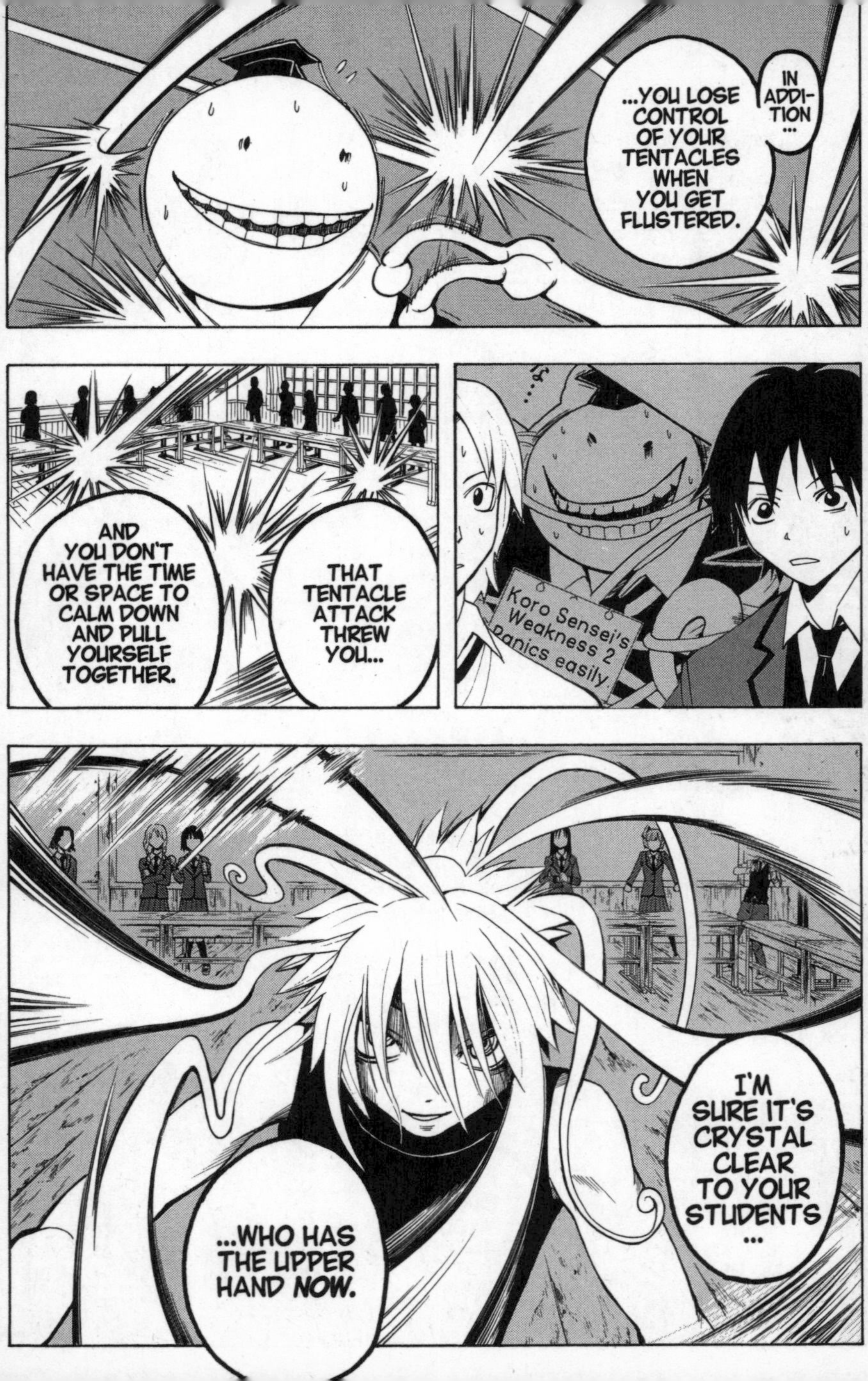
IN ADDITION...
...YOU LOSE CONTROL OF YOUR TENTACLES WHEN YOU GET FLUSTERED.
Koro Sensei's Weakness 2 panics easily
THAT TENTACLE ATTACK THREW YOU...
AND YOU DON'T HAVE THE TIME OR SPACE TO CALM DOWN AND PULL YOURSELF TOGETHER.
I'M SURE IT'S CRYSTAL CLEAR TO YOUR STUDENTS...
...WHO HAS THE UPPER HAND NOW.

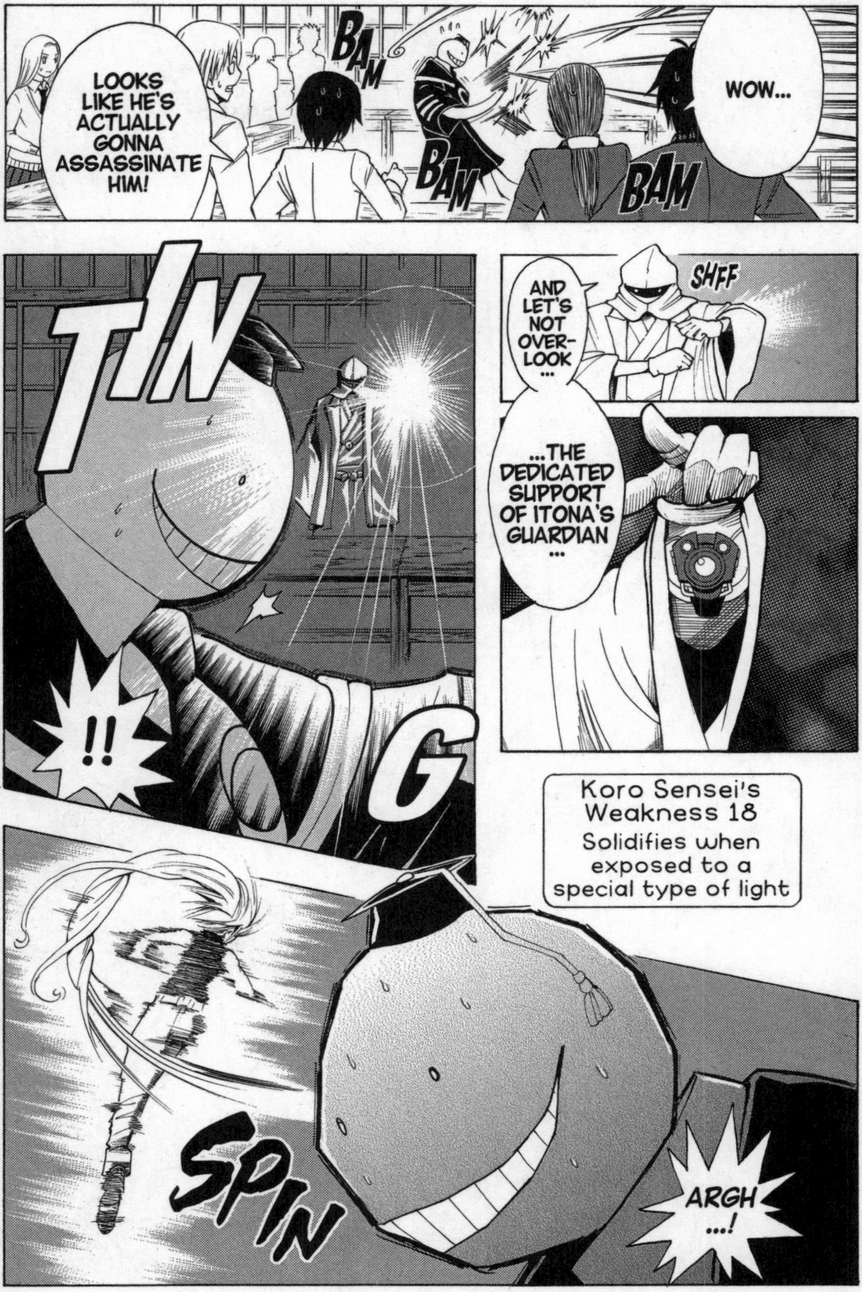

WOW...
BAM
BAM
BAM
LOOKS LIKE HE'S ACTUALLY GONNA ASSASSINATE HIM!
SHFF
AND LET'S NOT OVER-LOOK...
...THE DEDICATED SUPPORT OF ITONA'S GUARDIAN...
TING
!!
Koro Sensei's Weakness 18
Solidifies when exposed to a special type of light
ARGH...!
SPIN

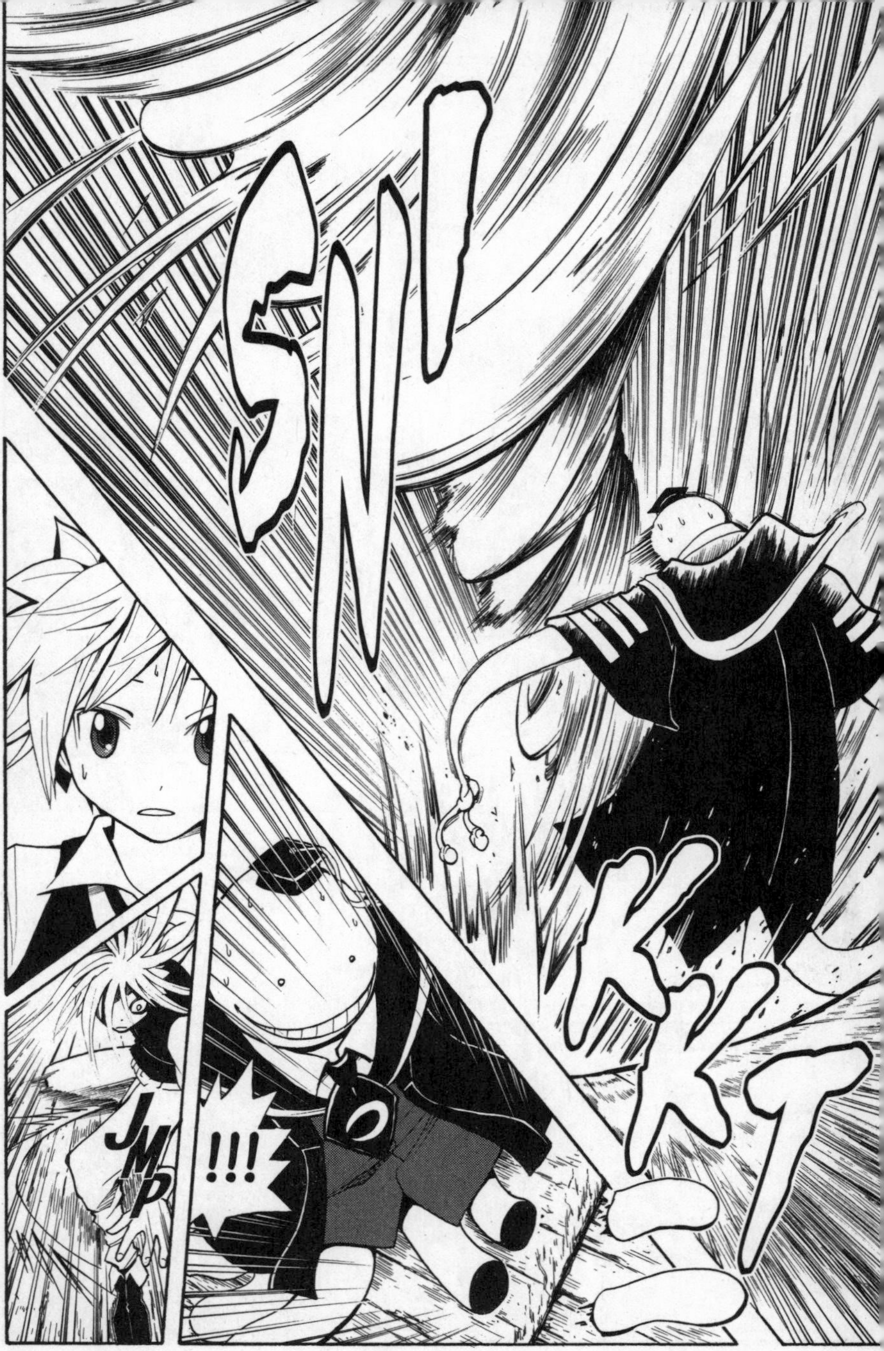
SNI
KYT
!!!
JMP

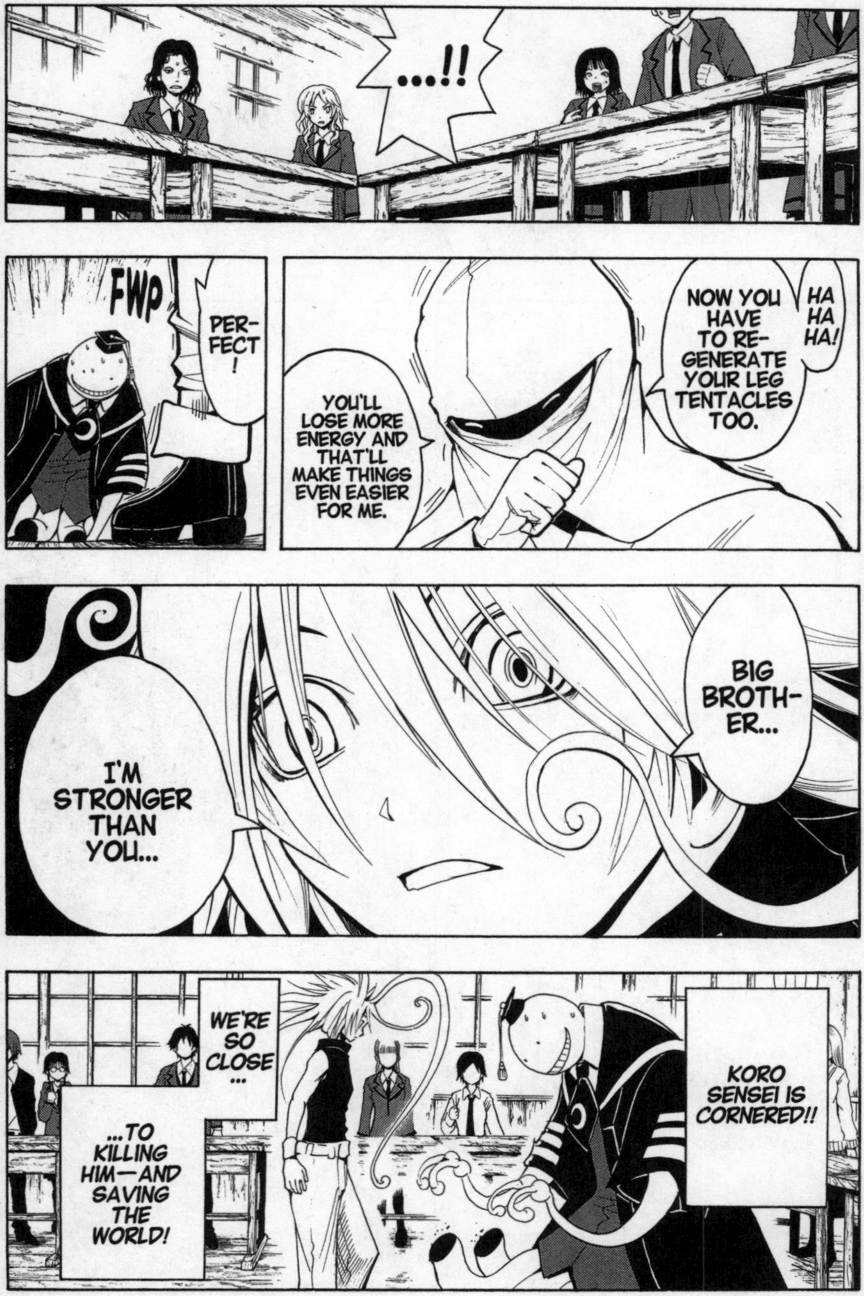
...!!
HA HA HA!
NOW YOU HAVE TO REGENERATE YOUR LEG TENTACLES TOO.
YOU'LL LOSE MORE ENERGY AND THAT'LL MAKE THINGS EVEN EASIER FOR ME.
PERFECT!
FWP
BIG BROTHER...
I'M STRONGER THAN YOU...
KORO SENSEI IS CORNERED!!
WE'RE SO CLOSE...
...TO KILLING HIM—AND SAVING THE WORLD!

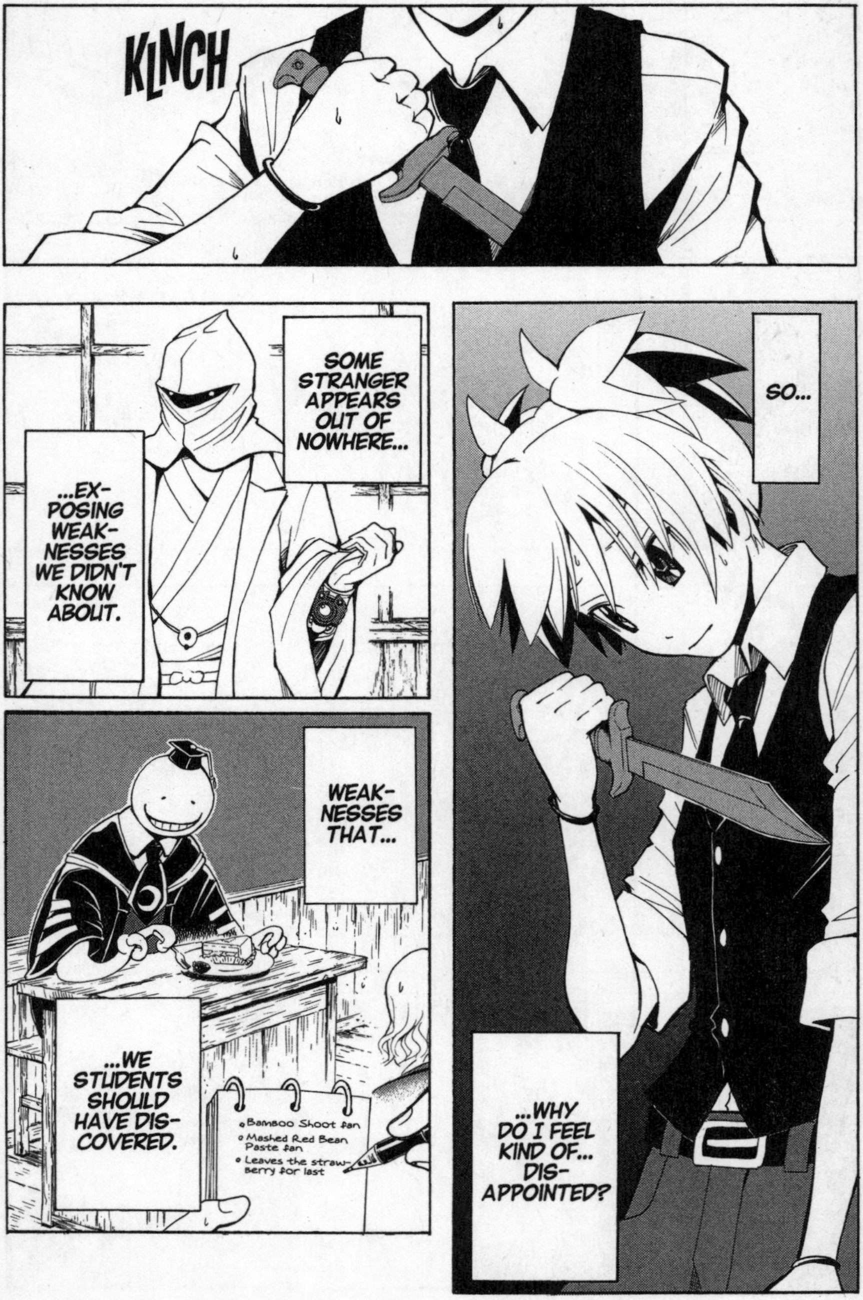
KLNCH
SO...
...WHY DO I FEEL KIND OF... DIS-APPOINTED?
SOME STRANGER APPEARS OUT OF NOWHERE...
...EX-POSING WEAK-NESSES WE DIDN'T KNOW ABOUT.
WEAK-NESSES THAT...
...WE STUDENTS SHOULD HAVE DIS-COVERED.
Bamboo Shoot fan
Mashed Red Bean Paste fan
Leaves the straw-berry for last

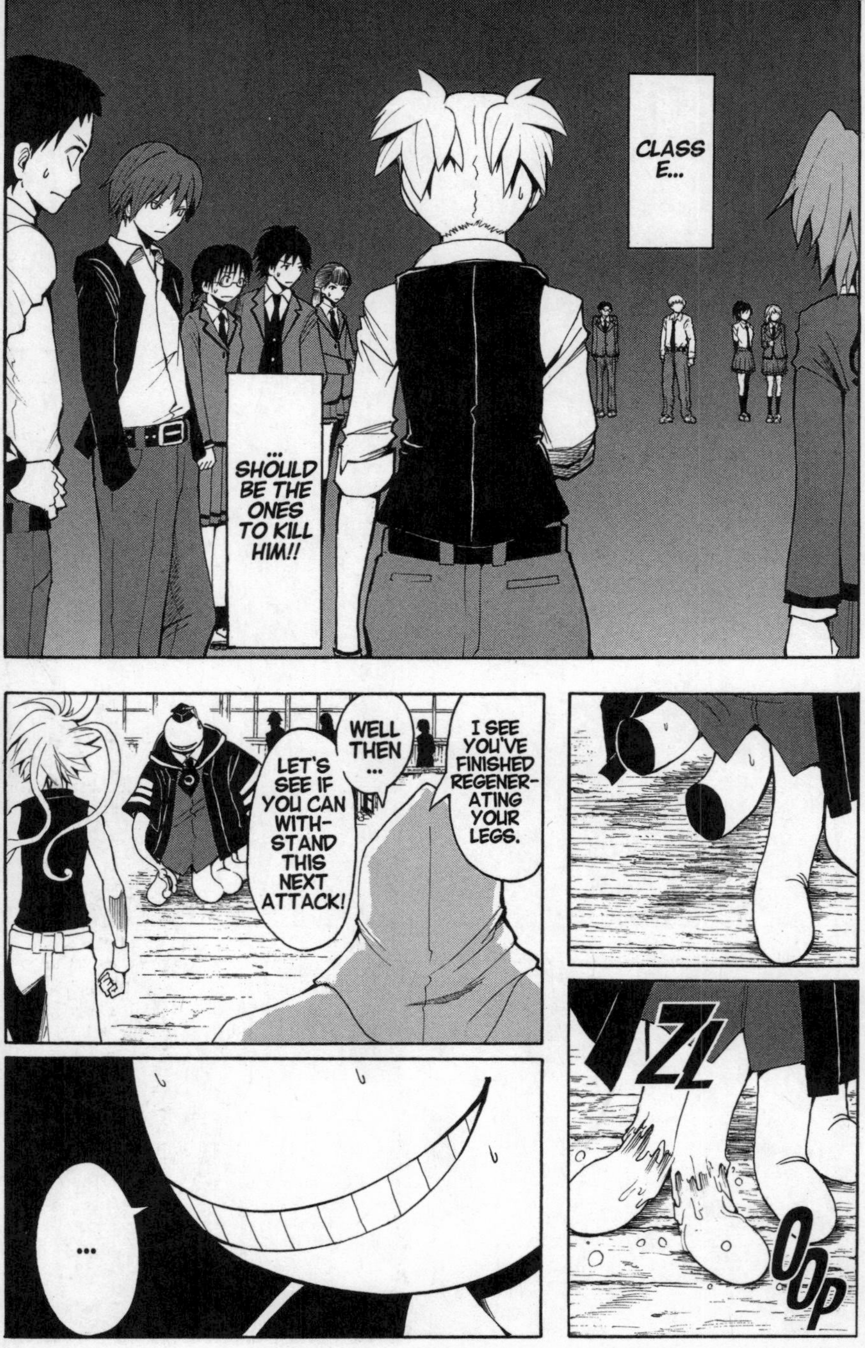
CLASS E...
...SHOULD BE THE ONES TO KILL HIM!!
ZZOOP
I SEE YOU'VE FINISHED REGENER-ATING YOUR LEGS.
WELL THEN...
LET'S SEE IF YOU CAN WITH-STAND THIS NEXT ATTACK!
...

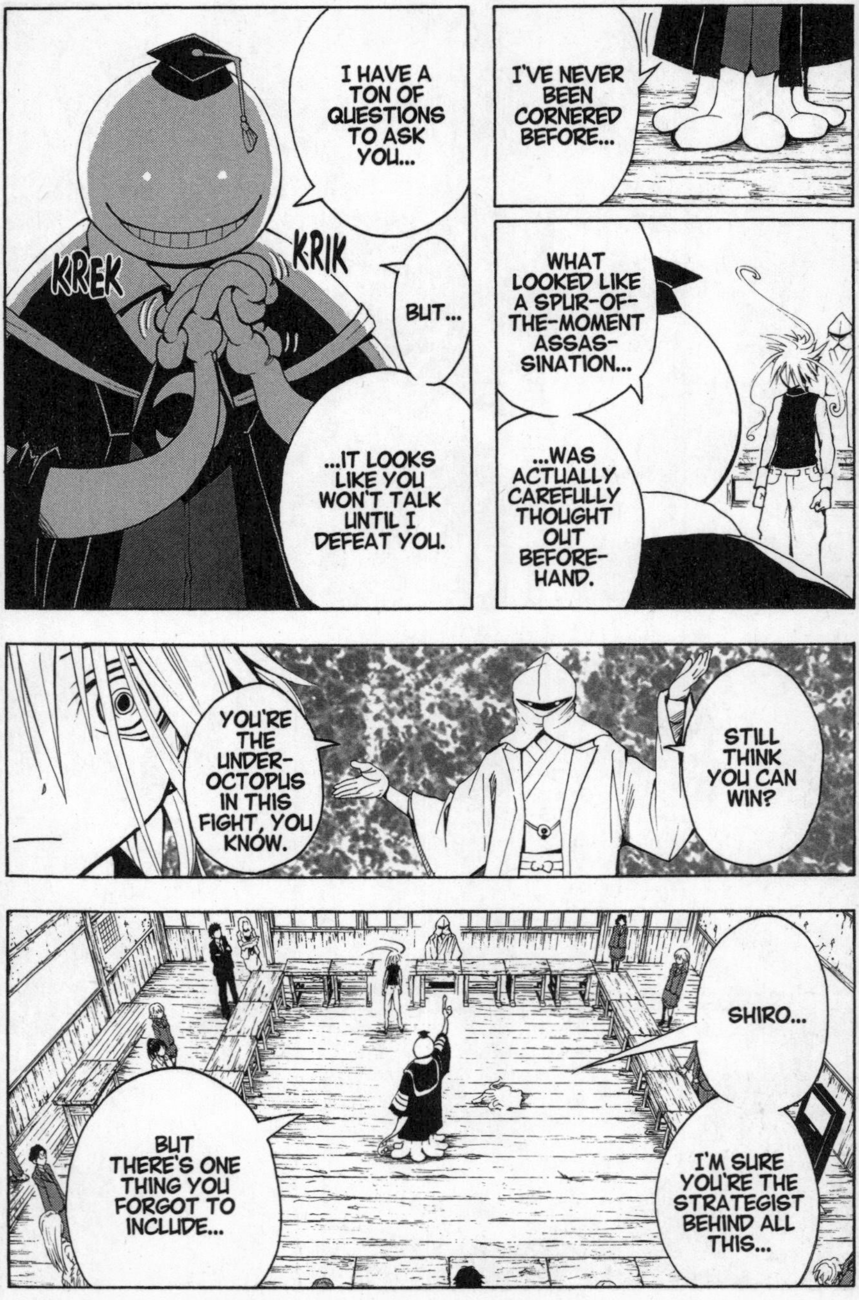
I'VE NEVER BEEN CORNERED BEFORE...
WHAT LOOKED LIKE A SPUR-OF-THE-MOMENT ASSAS-SINATION...
...WAS ACTUALLY CAREFULLY THOUGHT OUT BEFORE-HAND.
I HAVE A TON OF QUESTIONS TO ASK YOU...
K-RIK
KREK
BUT...
...IT LOOKS LIKE YOU WON'T TALK UNTIL I DEFEAT YOU.
STILL THINK YOU CAN WIN?
YOU'RE THE UNDER-OCTOPUS IN THIS FIGHT, YOU KNOW.
SHIRO...
I'M SURE YOU'RE THE STRATEGIST BEHIND ALL THIS...
BUT THERE'S ONE THING YOU FORGOT TO INCLUDE...

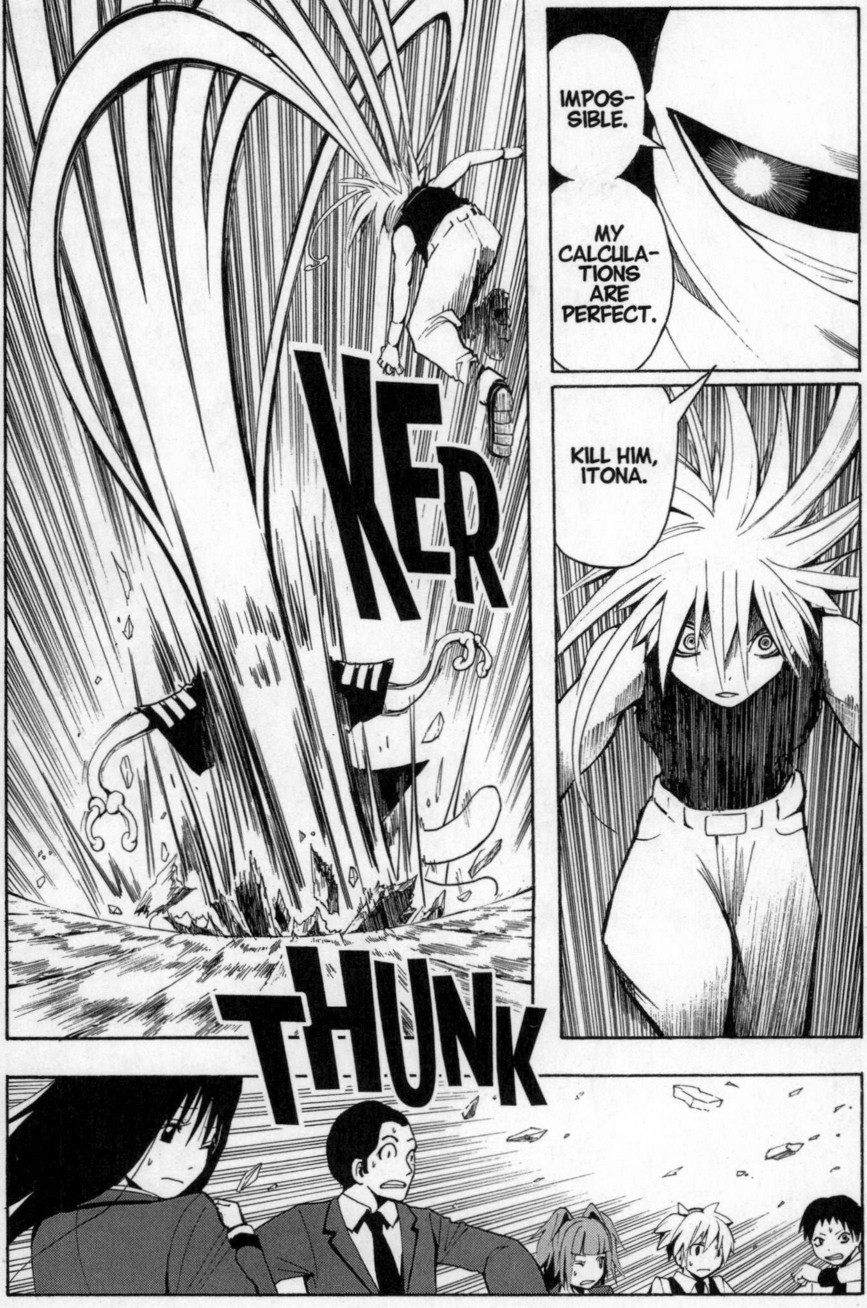
IMPOSSIBLE.
MY CALCULATIONS ARE PERFECT.
KILL HIM, ITONA.
KER
THUNK

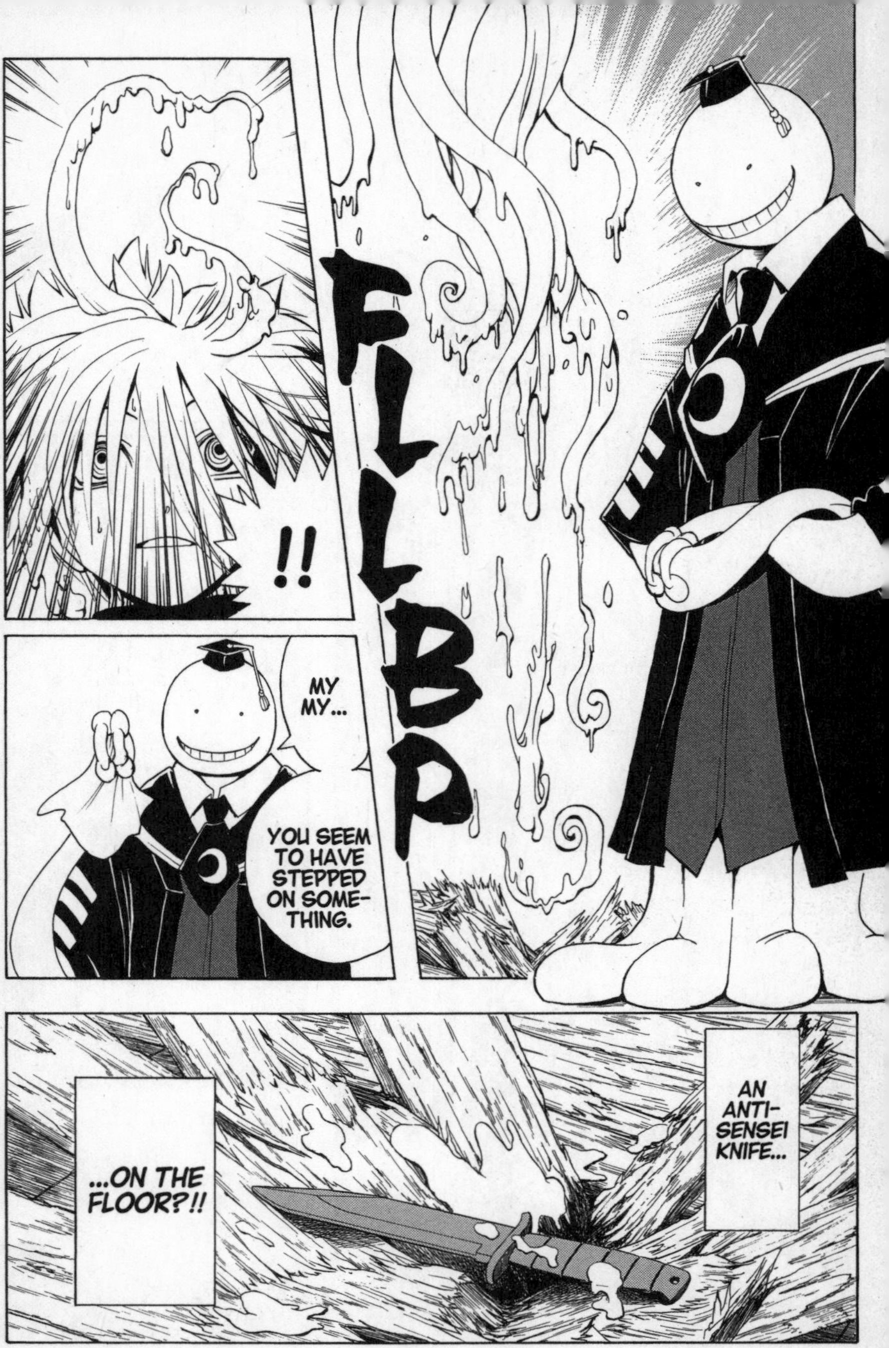
FLLBP
!!
MY MY...
YOU SEEM TO HAVE STEPPED ON SOMETHING.
AN ANTI-SENSEI KNIFE...
...ON THE FLOOR?!!

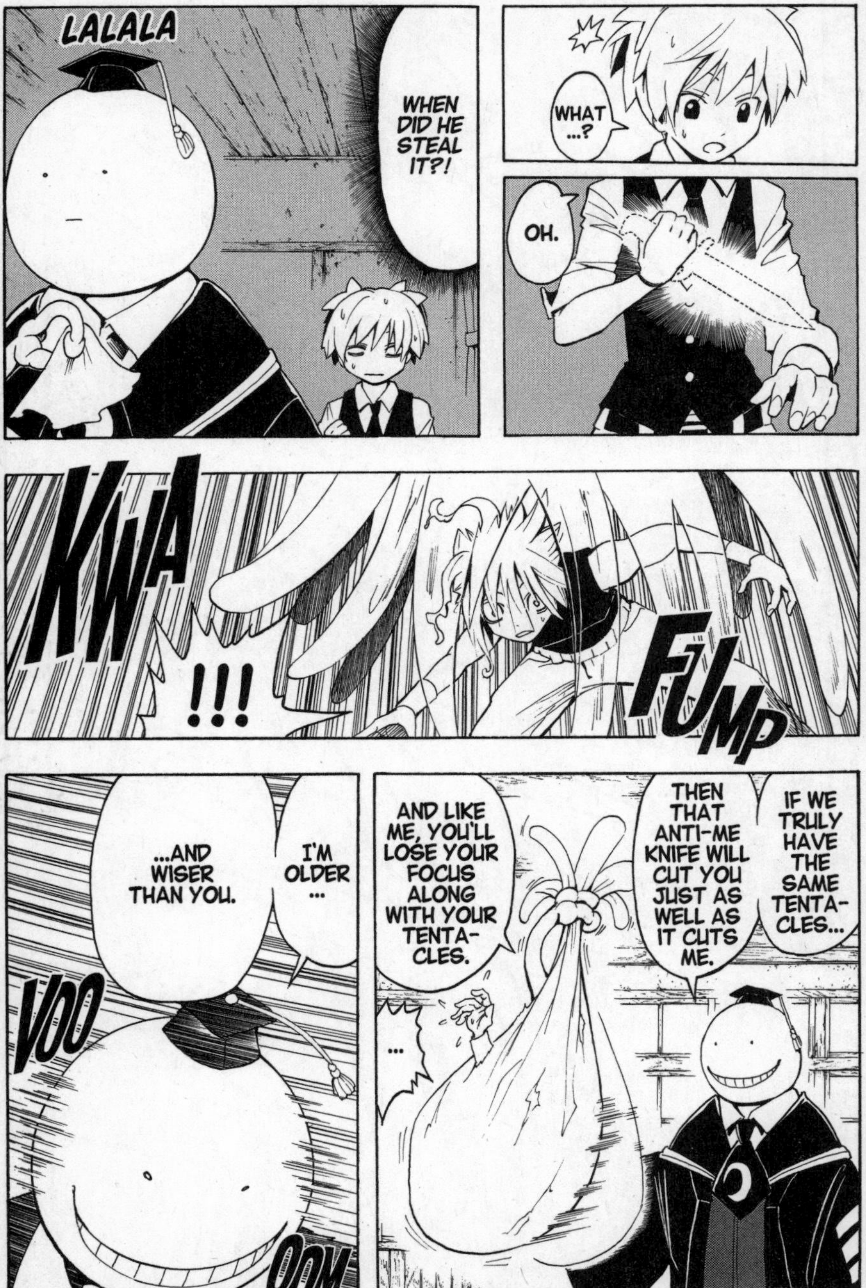
WHAT ...?
OH.
WHEN DID HE STEAL IT?!
LALALA
FUMP
KWA
!!!
IF WE TRULY HAVE THE SAME TENTA-CLES...
THEN THAT ANTI-ME KNIFE WILL CUT YOU JUST AS WELL AS IT CUTS ME.
AND LIKE ME, YOU'LL LOSE YOUR FOCUS ALONG WITH YOUR TENTA-CLES.
...
I'M OLDER ...
...AND WISER THAN YOU.
VOO
OOM

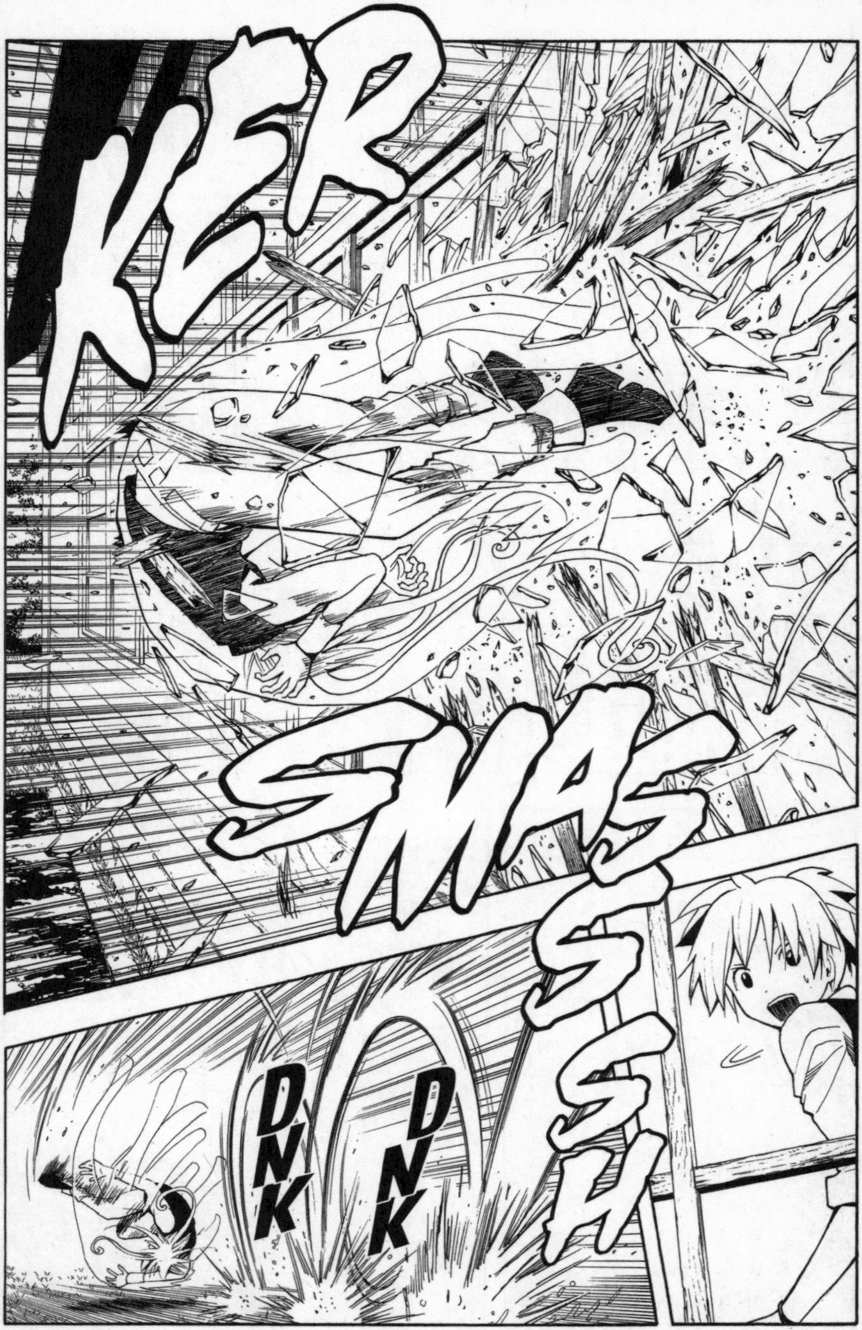
KER
SMASSSH
DNK DNK

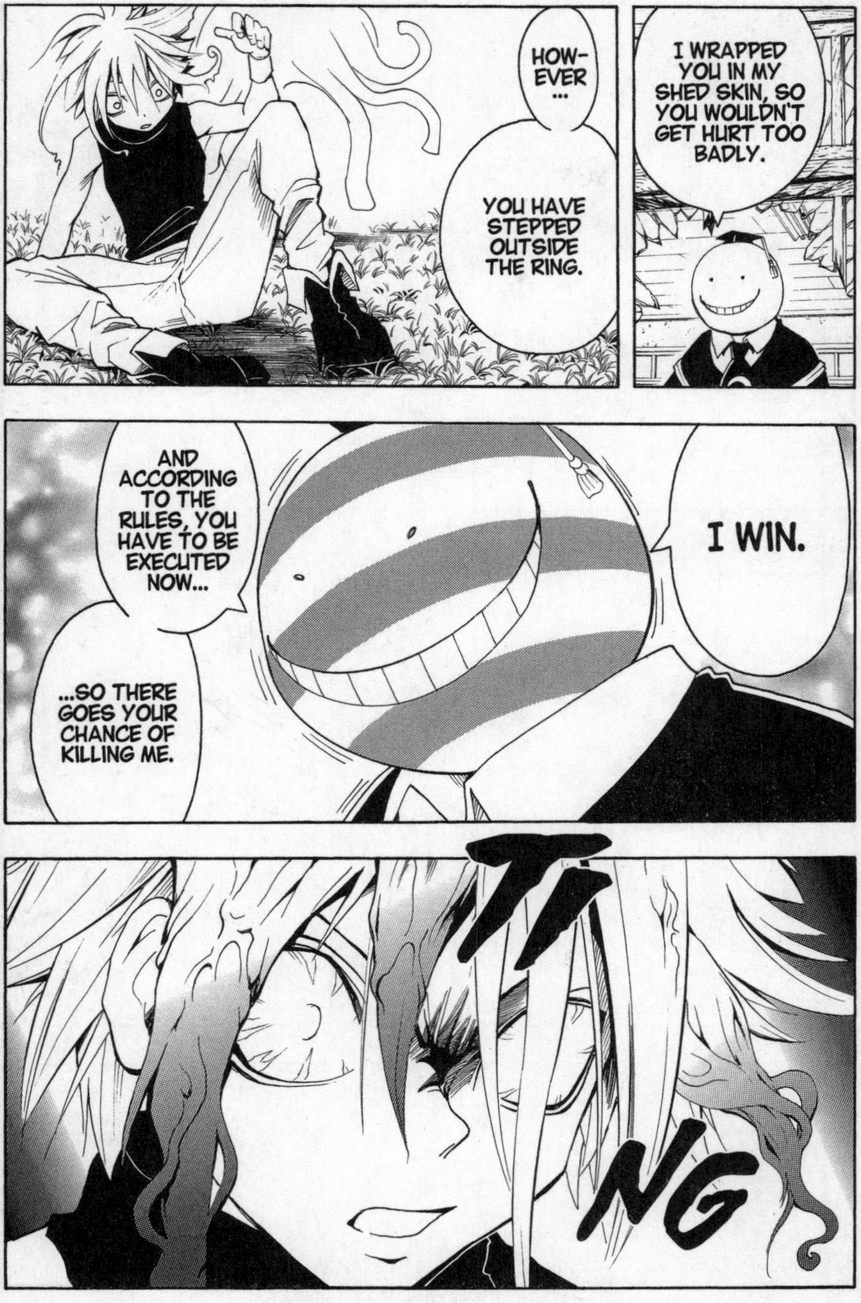
I WRAPPED YOU IN MY SHED SKIN, SO YOU WOULDN'T GET HURT TOO BADLY.
HOW-EVER ...
YOU HAVE STEPPED OUTSIDE THE RING.
I WIN.
AND ACCORDING TO THE RULES, YOU HAVE TO BE EXECUTED NOW...
...SO THERE GOES YOUR CHANCE OF KILLING ME.
TING

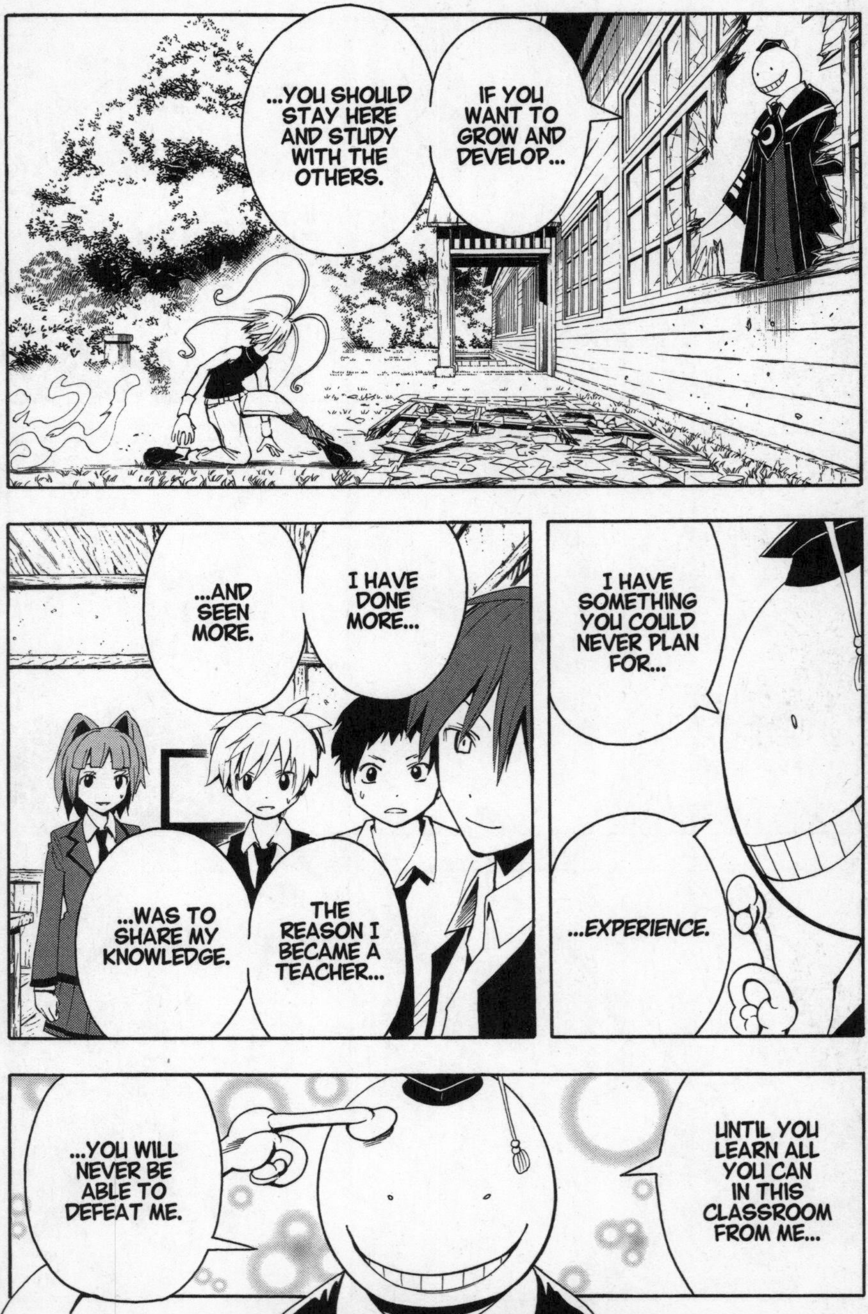
IF YOU WANT TO GROW AND DEVELOP...
...YOU SHOULD STAY HERE AND STUDY WITH THE OTHERS.
I HAVE SOMETHING YOU COULD NEVER PLAN FOR...
...EXPERIENCE.
I HAVE DONE MORE...
...AND SEEN MORE.
THE REASON I BECAME A TEACHER...
...WAS TO SHARE MY KNOWLEDGE.
UNTIL YOU LEARN ALL YOU CAN IN THIS CLASSROOM FROM ME...
...YOU WILL NEVER BE ABLE TO DEFEAT ME.

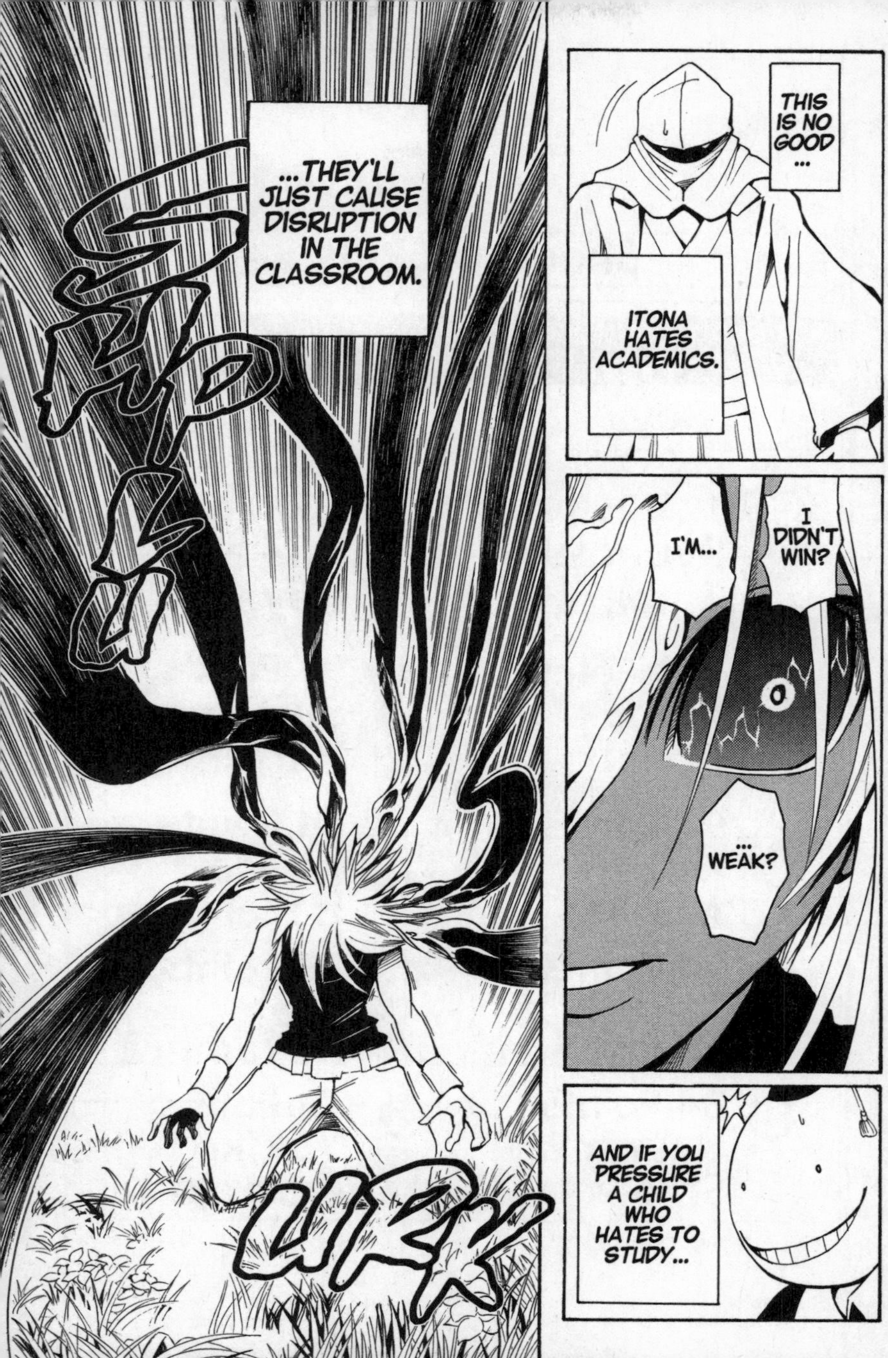
THIS IS NO GOOD ...
ITONA HATES ACADEMICS.
I DIDN'T WIN?
I'M...
... WEAK?
AND IF YOU PRESSURE A CHILD WHO HATES TO STUDY...
...THEY'LL JUST CAUSE DISRUPTION IN THE CLASSROOM.

Class 3-E

Best 5

Shooting Skills

Scores of the Outdoor Shooting Test in June (Out of 200 points)

Boys	Girls
1 122 Points **Ryunosuke Chiba**	**1** 101 Points **Rinka Hayami**
2 103 Points **Yuma Isogai**	**2** 91 Points **Sumire Hara**
3 97 Points **Karma Akabane**	**3** 84 Points **Kirara Hazama**
4 90 Points **Takuya Muramatsu**	**4** 79 Points **Rio Nakamura**
5 84 Points **Nagisa Shiota**	**5** 73 Points **Yukiko Kanzaki**

Class 32 Bonding Time

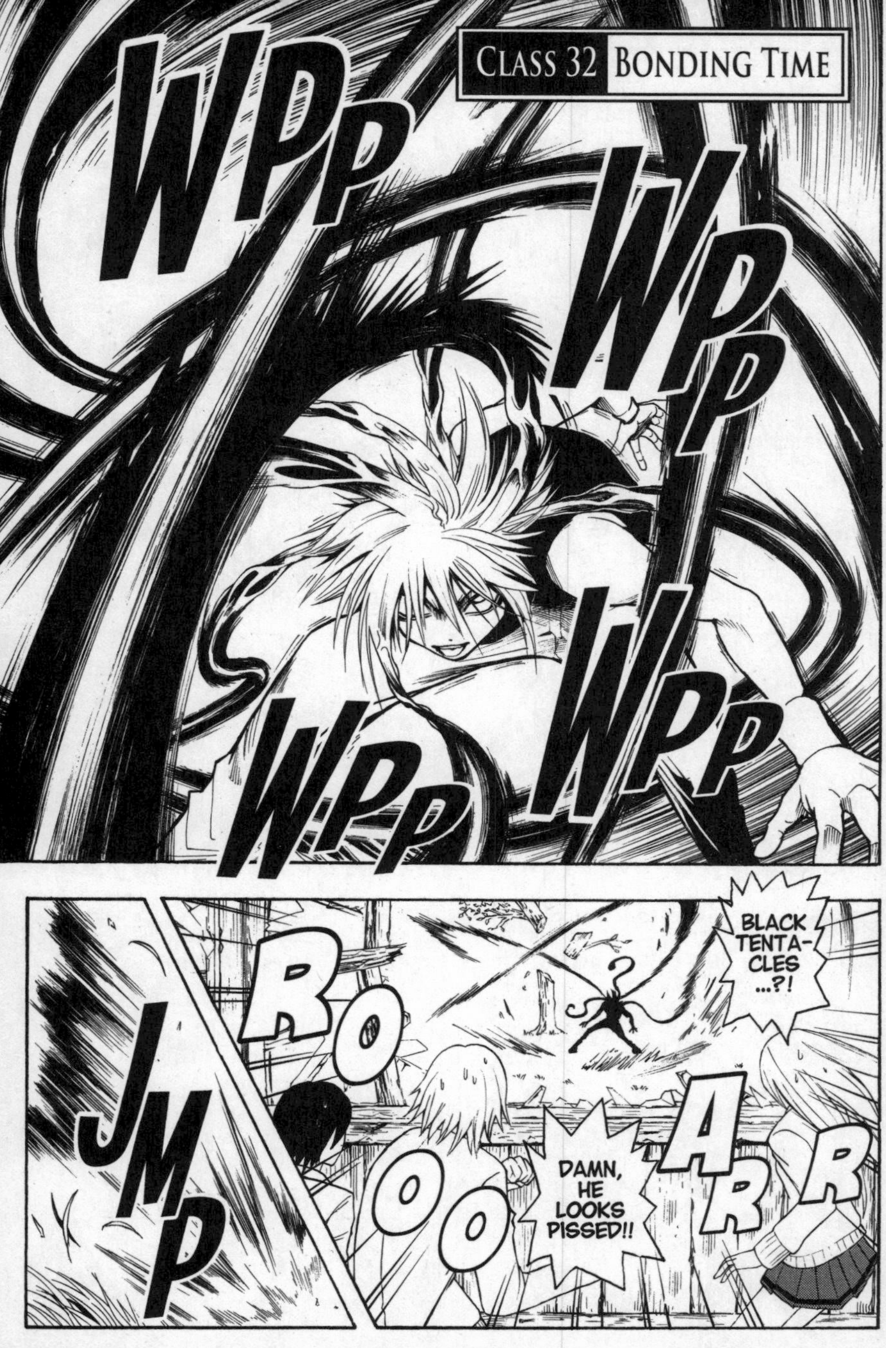
WPP
WPP
WPP
WPP
BLACK TENTACLES ...?!
ROOOOAR
DAMN, HE LOOKS PISSED!!
JMP

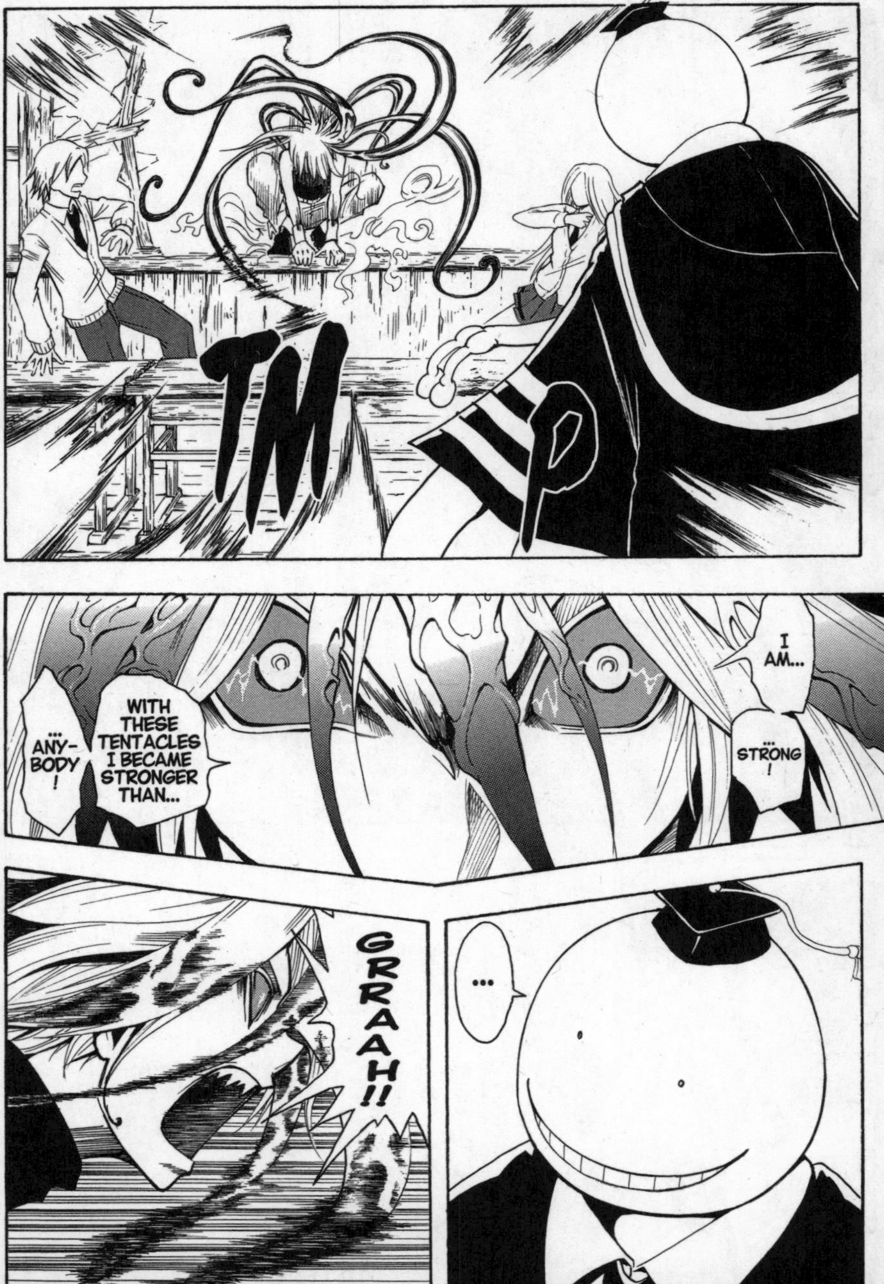
TMP
I AM...
...STRONG!
WITH THESE TENTACLES I BECAME STRONGER THAN...
...ANYBODY!
...
GRRAAH!!

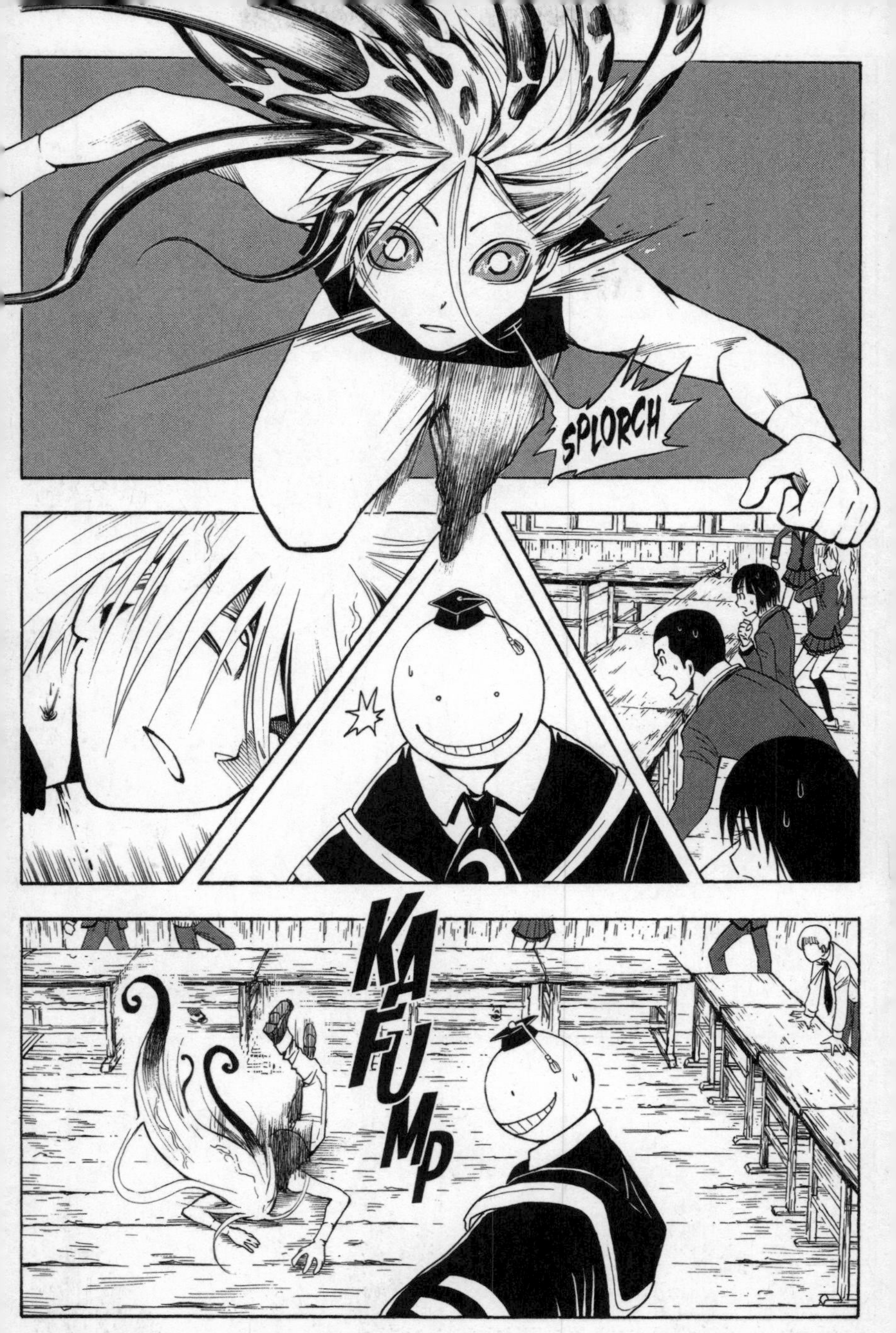
SPLORCH
KAFUMP

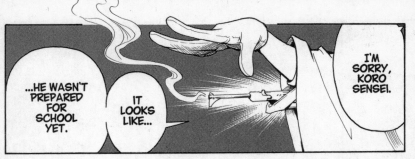

...HE WASN'T PREPARED FOR SCHOOL YET.

IT LOOKS LIKE...

I'M SORRY, KORO SENSEI.

I KNOW THIS IS HIS FIRST DAY HERE...

...BUT HE'LL HAVE TO TAKE SOME TIME OFF.

SKRTCH

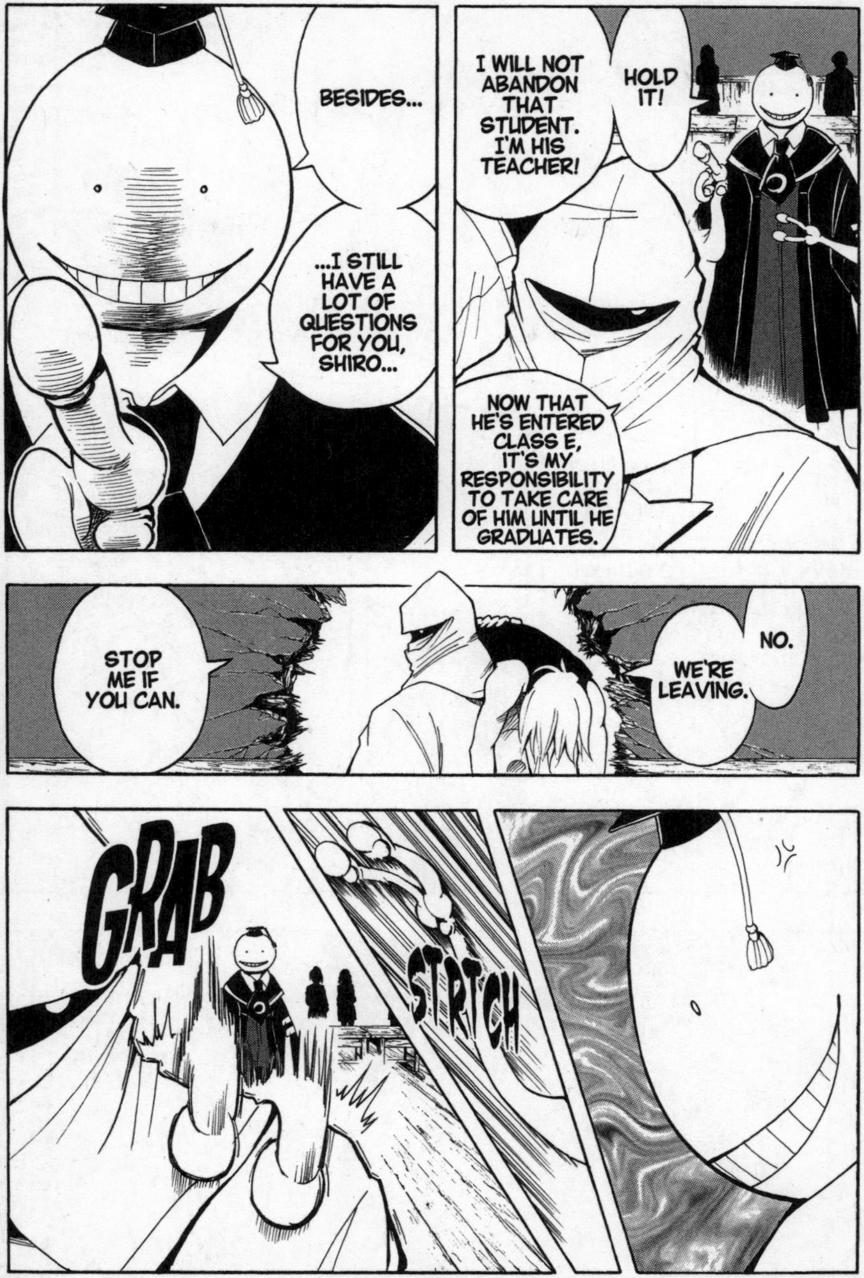
HOLD IT!
I WILL NOT ABANDON THAT STUDENT. I'M HIS TEACHER!
NOW THAT HE'S ENTERED CLASS E, IT'S MY RESPONSIBILITY TO TAKE CARE OF HIM UNTIL HE GRADUATES.
BESIDES...
...I STILL HAVE A LOT OF QUESTIONS FOR YOU, SHIRO...
NO.
WE'RE LEAVING.
STOP ME IF YOU CAN.
STRTCH
GRAB

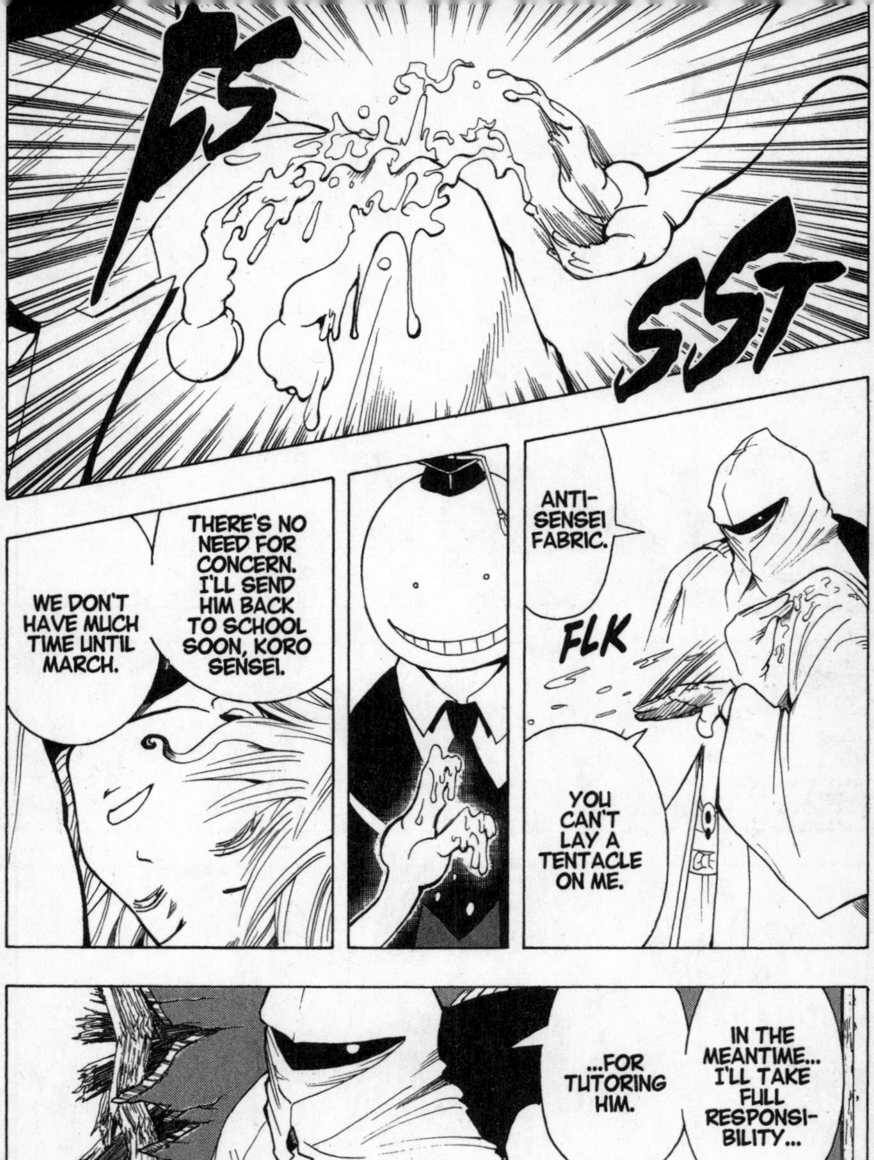
FS
SST
ANTI-SENSEI FABRIC.
FLK
YOU CAN'T LAY A TENTACLE ON ME.
THERE'S NO NEED FOR CONCERN. I'LL SEND HIM BACK TO SCHOOL SOON, KORO SENSEI.
WE DON'T HAVE MUCH TIME UNTIL MARCH.
IN THE MEANTIME... I'LL TAKE FULL RESPONSI-BILITY...
...FOR TUTORING HIM.

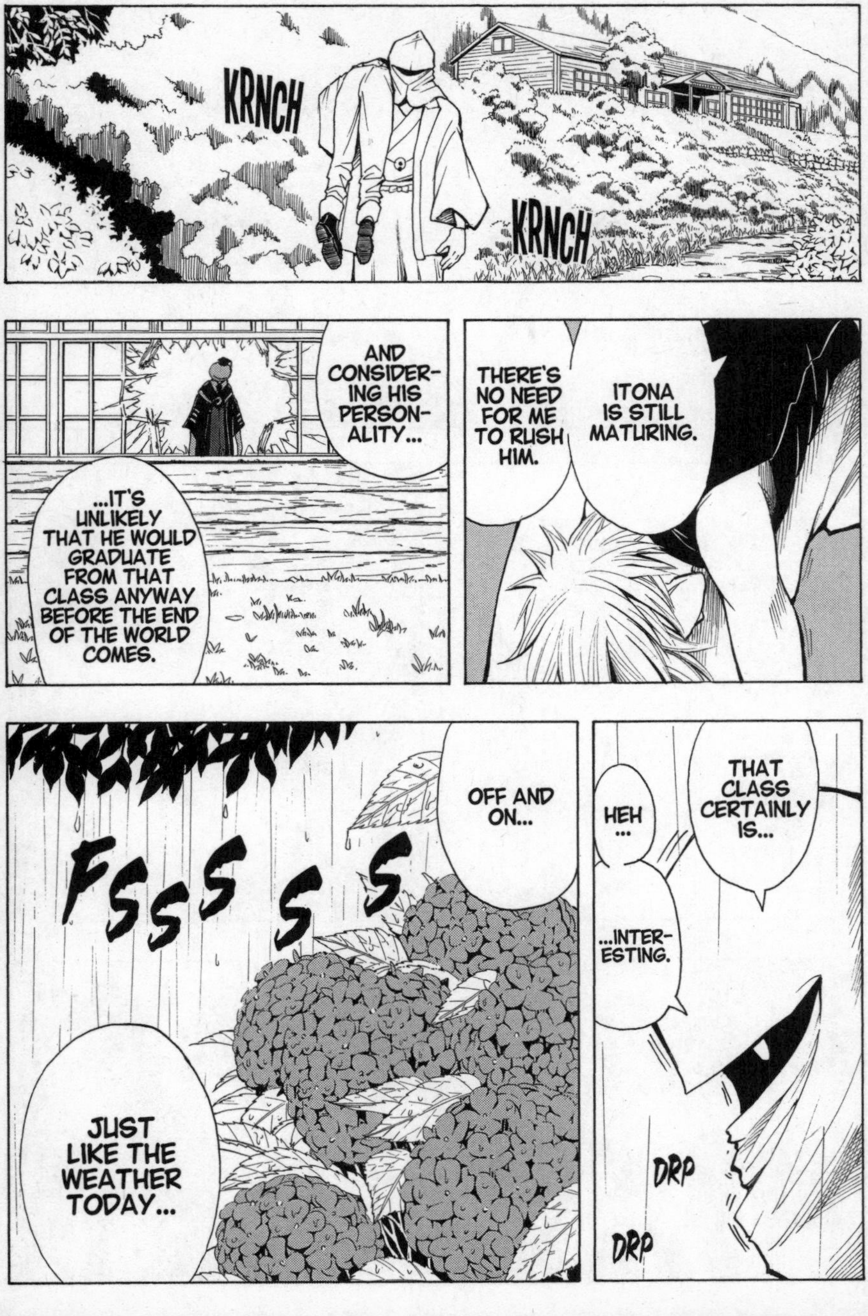
KRNCH
KRNCH
ITONA IS STILL MATURING.
THERE'S NO NEED FOR ME TO RUSH HIM.
AND CONSIDERING HIS PERSONALITY...
...IT'S UNLIKELY THAT HE WOULD GRADUATE FROM THAT CLASS ANYWAY BEFORE THE END OF THE WORLD COMES.
THAT CLASS CERTAINLY IS...
HEH ...
...INTERESTING.
DRP
DRP
OFF AND ON...
FSSSSS
JUST LIKE THE WEATHER TODAY...

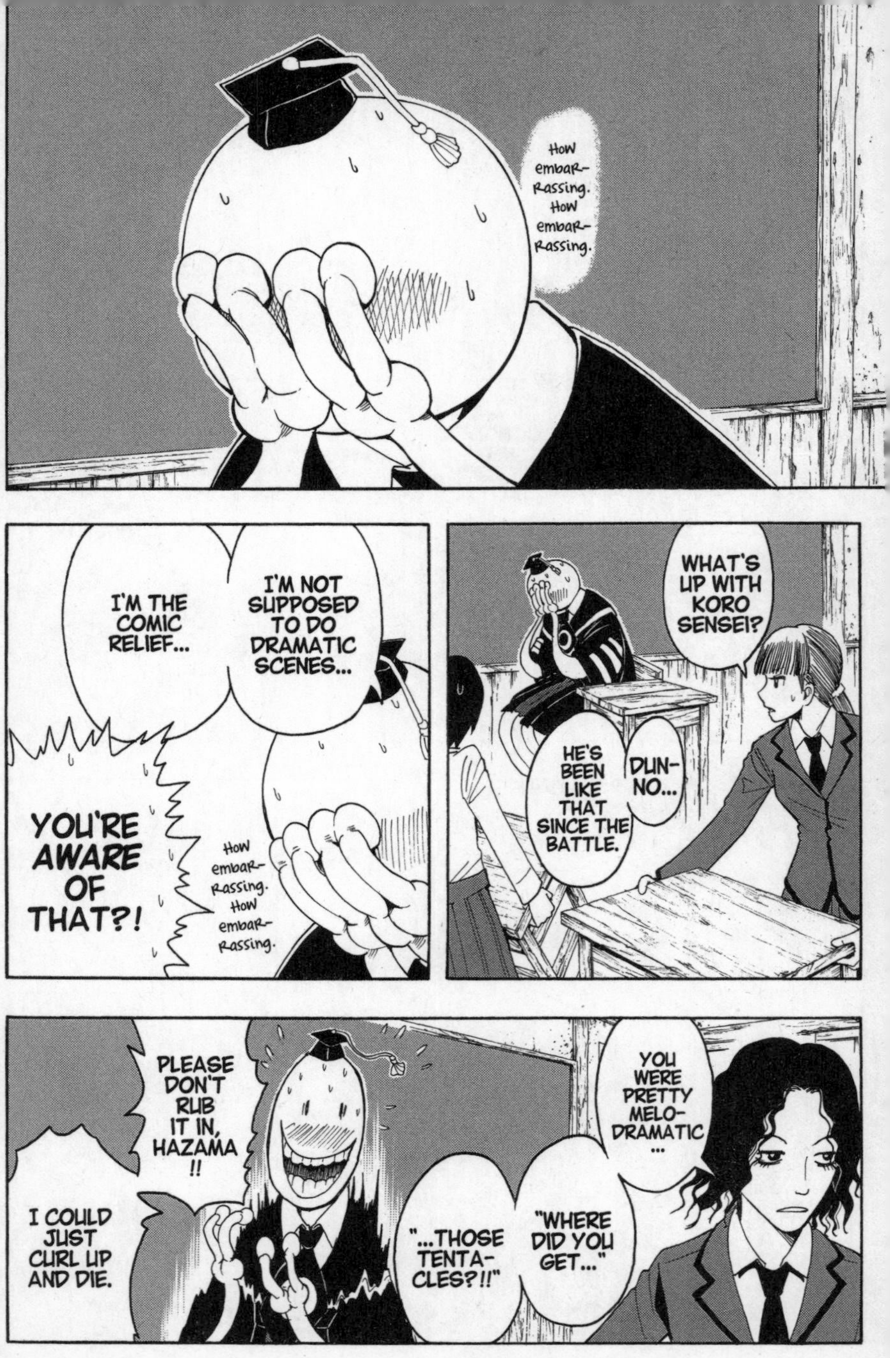
How embarrassing. How embarrassing.
WHAT'S UP WITH KORO SENSEI?
DUNNO...
HE'S BEEN LIKE THAT SINCE THE BATTLE.
I'M NOT SUPPOSED TO DO DRAMATIC SCENES...
I'M THE COMIC RELIEF...
YOU'RE AWARE OF THAT?!
How embarrassing. How embarrassing.
YOU WERE PRETTY MELODRAMATIC...
"WHERE DID YOU GET..."
"...THOSE TENTACLES?!!"
PLEASE DON'T RUB IT IN, HAZAMA!!
I COULD JUST CURL UP AND DIE.

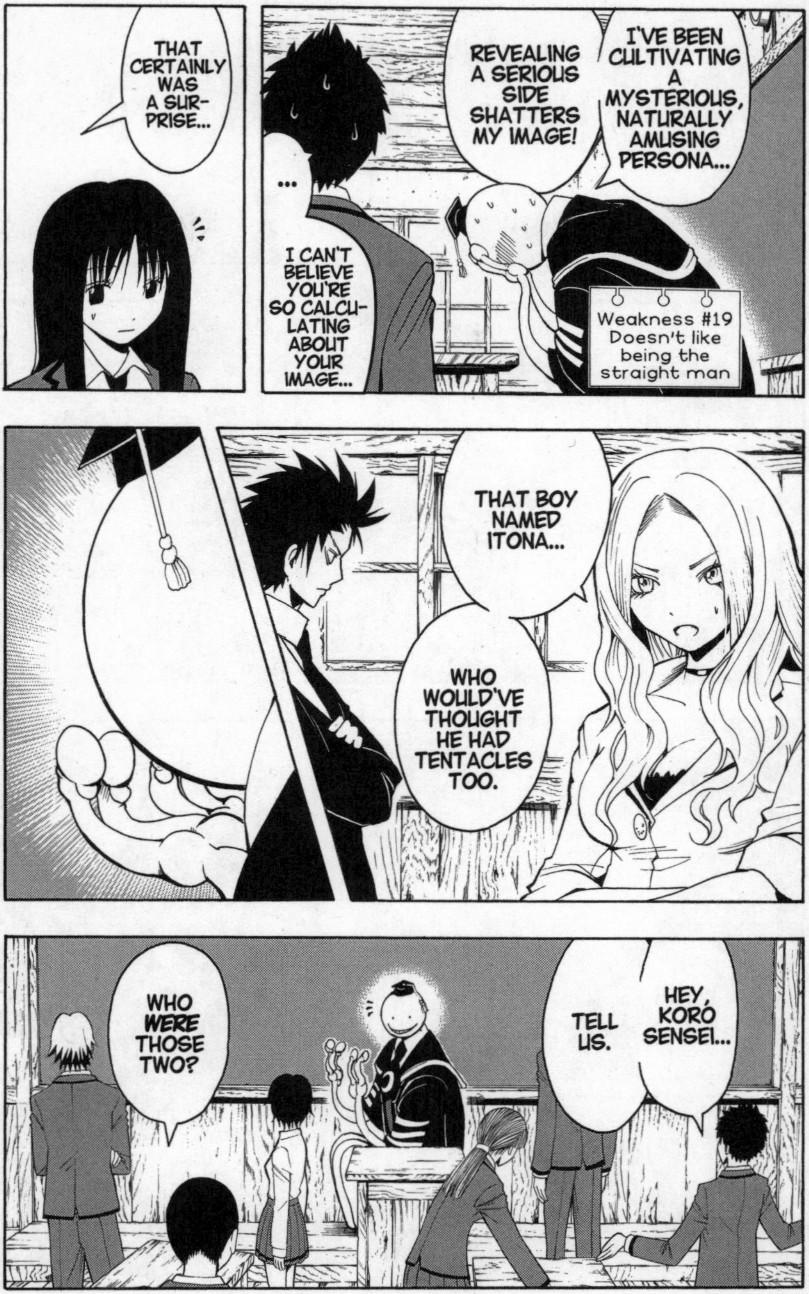
I'VE BEEN CULTIVATING A MYSTERIOUS, NATURALLY AMUSING PERSONA...
REVEALING A SERIOUS SIDE SHATTERS MY IMAGE!
...
I CAN'T BELIEVE YOU'RE SO CALCU-LATING ABOUT YOUR IMAGE...
Weakness #19 Doesn't like being the straight man
THAT CERTAINLY WAS A SUR-PRISE...
THAT BOY NAMED ITONA...
WHO WOULD'VE THOUGHT HE HAD TENTACLES TOO.
HEY, KORO SENSEI...
TELL US.
WHO WERE THOSE TWO?

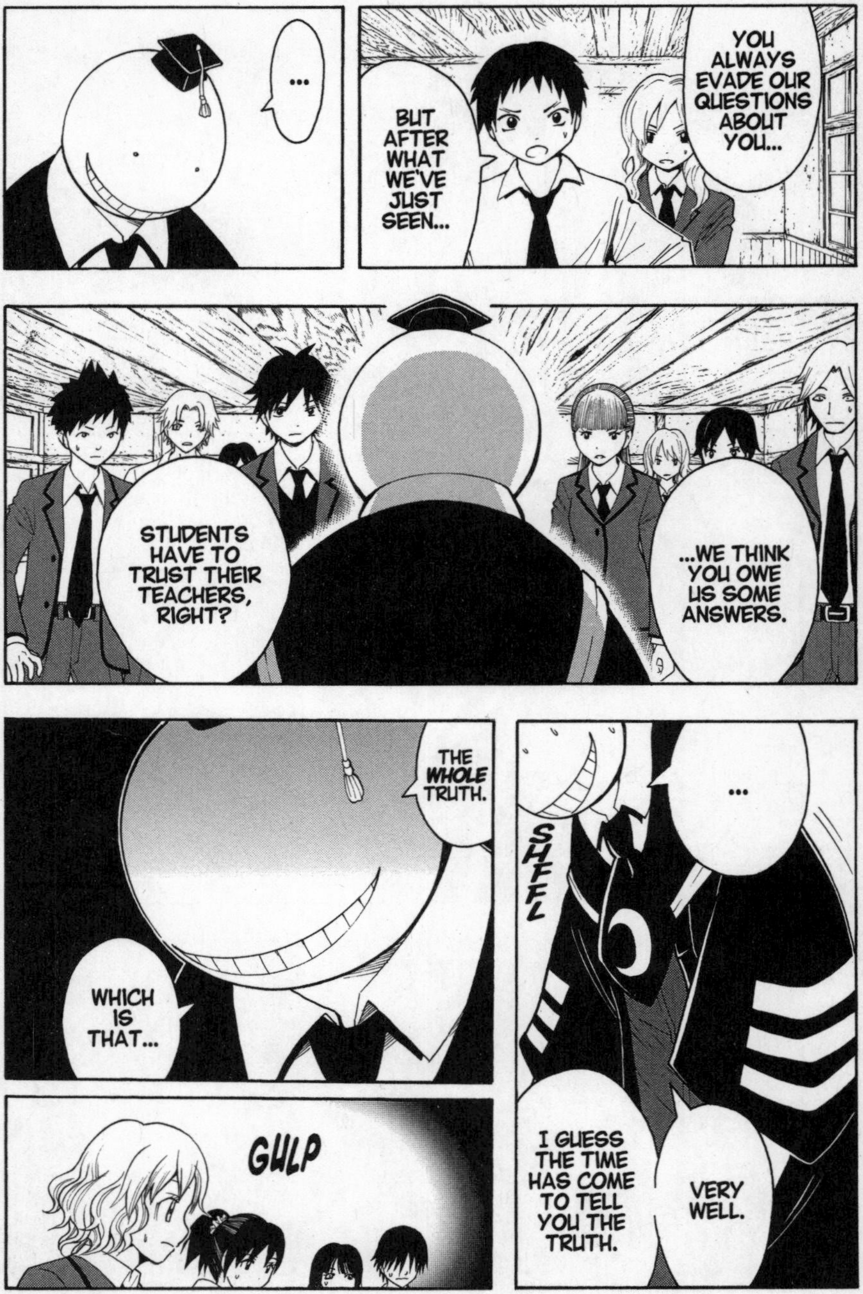

YOU ALWAYS EVADE OUR QUESTIONS ABOUT YOU...
BUT AFTER WHAT WE'VE JUST SEEN...
...
...WE THINK YOU OWE US SOME ANSWERS.
STUDENTS HAVE TO TRUST THEIR TEACHERS, RIGHT?
...
SHFFL
VERY WELL.
I GUESS THE TIME HAS COME TO TELL YOU THE TRUTH.
THE *WHOLE* TRUTH.
WHICH IS THAT...
GULP

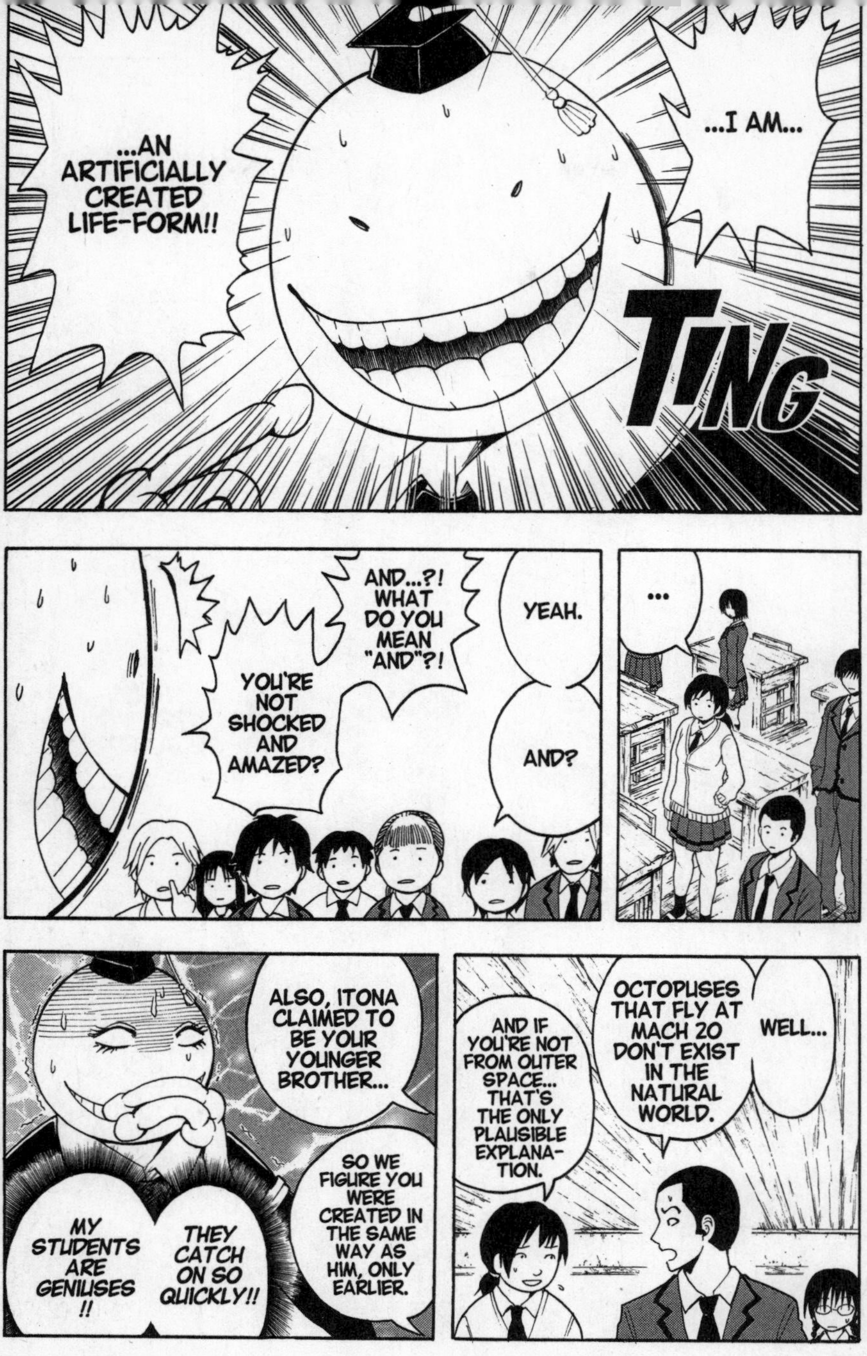
...I AM...
...AN ARTIFICIALLY CREATED LIFE-FORM!!
TING
...
YEAH.
AND?
AND...?! WHAT DO YOU MEAN "AND"?!
YOU'RE NOT SHOCKED AND AMAZED?
WELL...
OCTOPUSES THAT FLY AT MACH 20 DON'T EXIST IN THE NATURAL WORLD.
AND IF YOU'RE NOT FROM OUTER SPACE... THAT'S THE ONLY PLAUSIBLE EXPLANA-TION.
ALSO, ITONA CLAIMED TO BE YOUR YOUNGER BROTHER...
SO WE FIGURE YOU WERE CREATED IN THE SAME WAY AS HIM, ONLY EARLIER.
THEY CATCH ON SO QUICKLY!!
MY STUDENTS ARE GENIUSES !!

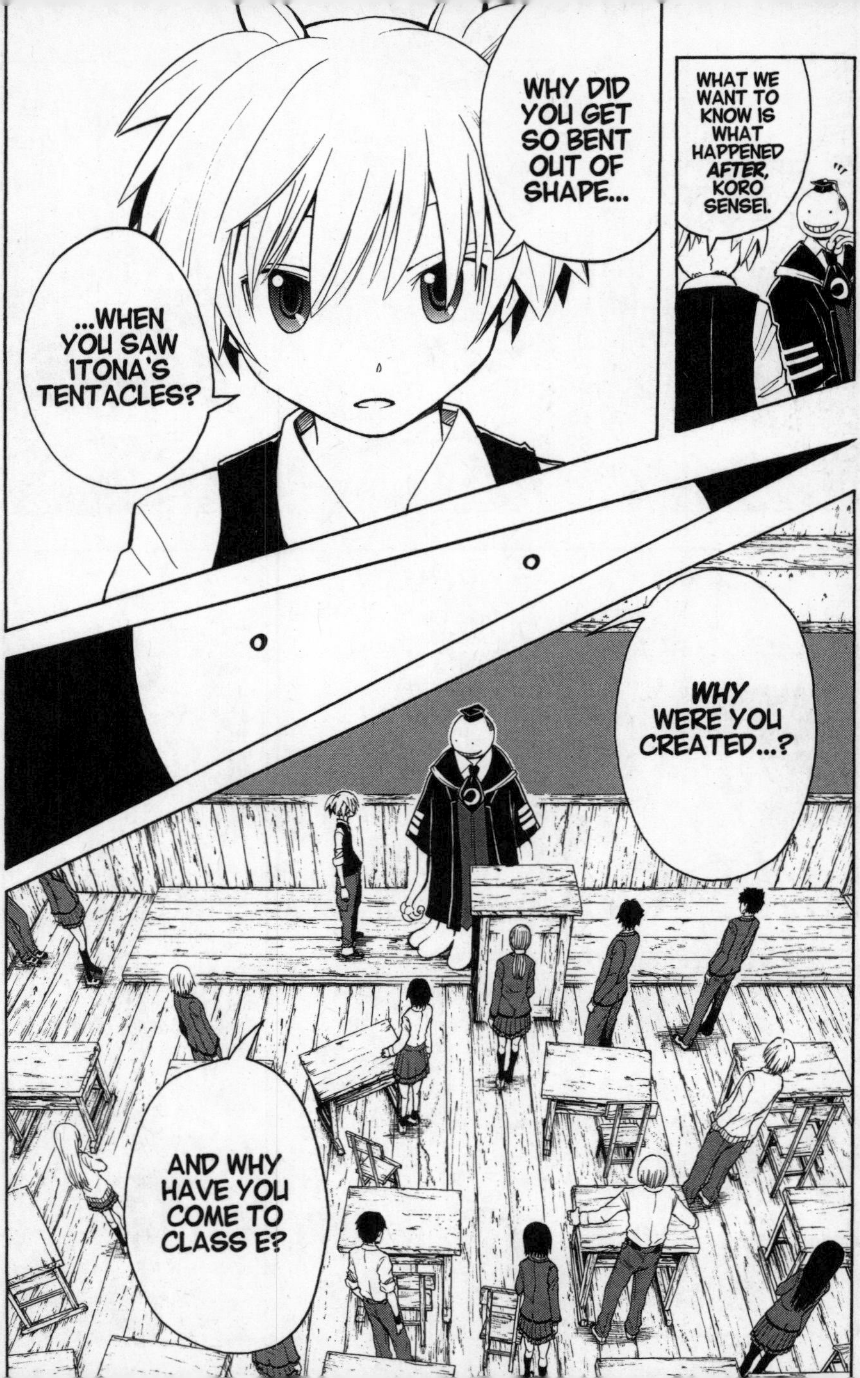
WHAT WE WANT TO KNOW IS WHAT HAPPENED AFTER, KORO SENSEI.
WHY DID YOU GET SO BENT OUT OF SHAPE...
...WHEN YOU SAW ITONA'S TENTACLES?
WHY WERE YOU CREATED...?
AND WHY HAVE YOU COME TO CLASS E?

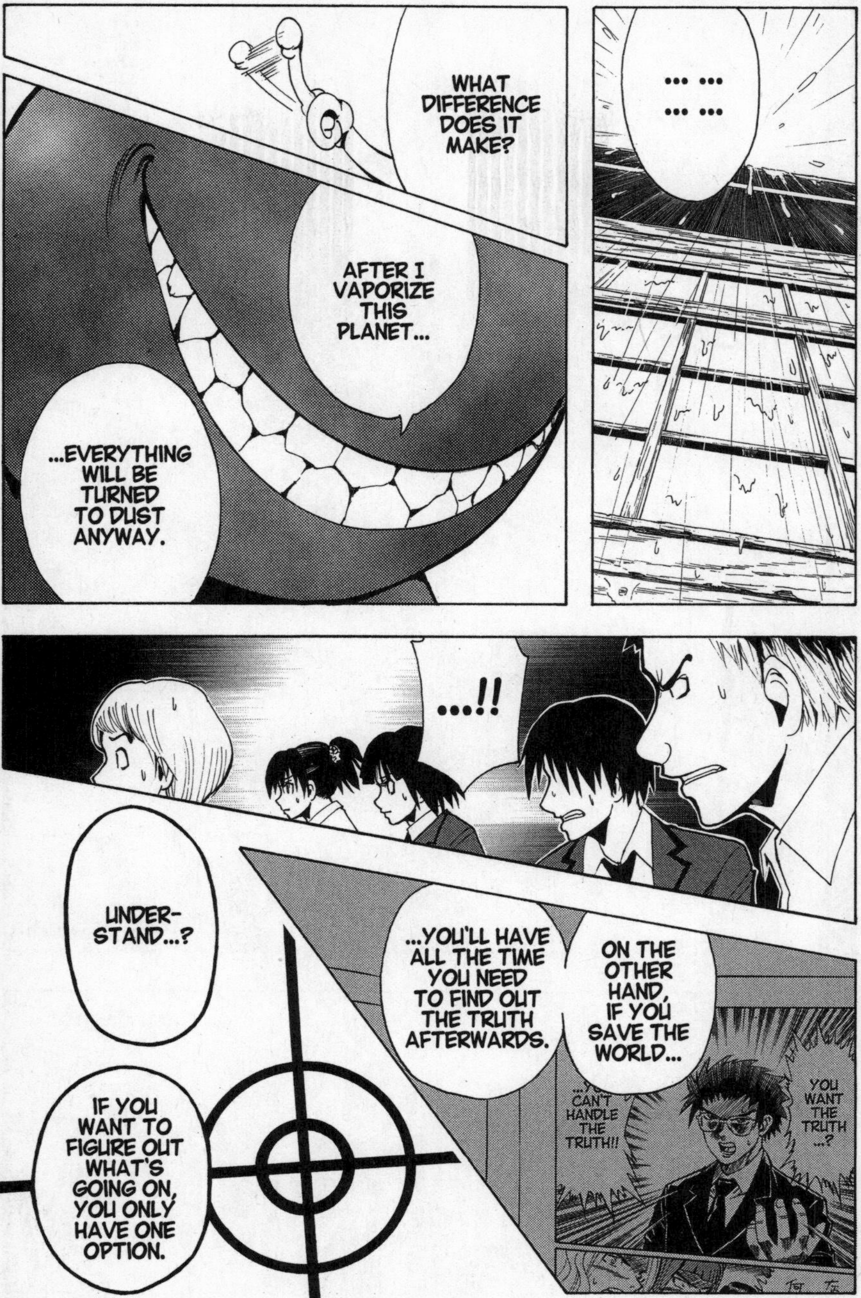

... ...
... ...
WHAT DIFFERENCE DOES IT MAKE?
AFTER I VAPORIZE THIS PLANET...
...EVERYTHING WILL BE TURNED TO DUST ANYWAY.
...!!
ON THE OTHER HAND, IF YOU SAVE THE WORLD...
...YOU'LL HAVE ALL THE TIME YOU NEED TO FIND OUT THE TRUTH AFTERWARDS.
YOU WANT THE TRUTH ...?
CAN'T HANDLE THE TRUTH!!
UNDER-STAND...?
IF YOU WANT TO FIGURE OUT WHAT'S GOING ON, YOU ONLY HAVE ONE OPTION.

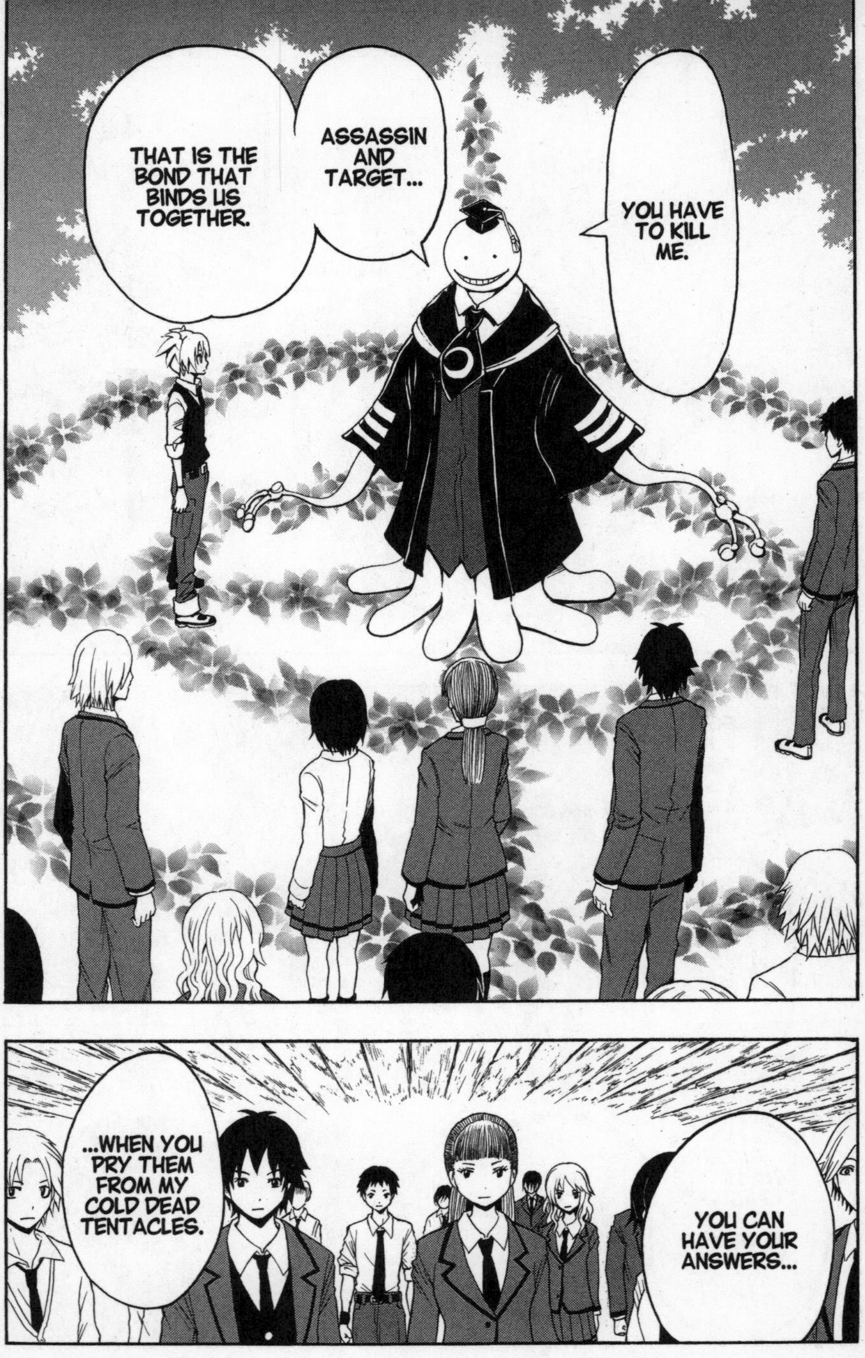
YOU HAVE TO KILL ME.
ASSASSIN AND TARGET...
THAT IS THE BOND THAT BINDS US TOGETHER.
YOU CAN HAVE YOUR ANSWERS...
...WHEN YOU PRY THEM FROM MY COLD DEAD TENTACLES.

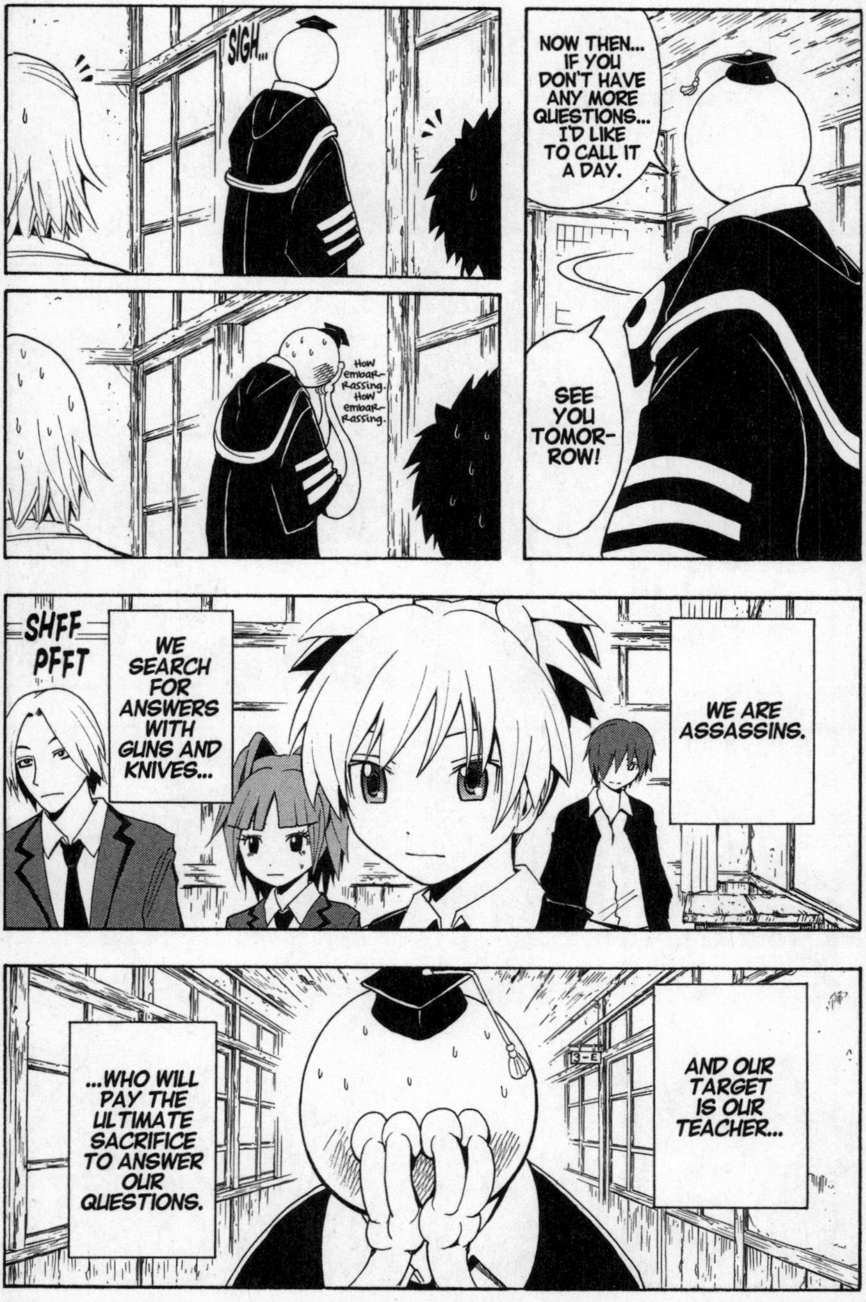
NOW THEN... IF YOU DON'T HAVE ANY MORE QUESTIONS... I'D LIKE TO CALL IT A DAY.
SEE YOU TOMORROW!
SIGH...
How embarrassing. How embarrassing.
WE ARE ASSASSINS.
WE SEARCH FOR ANSWERS WITH GUNS AND KNIVES...
SHFF PFFT
AND OUR TARGET IS OUR TEACHER...
3-E
...WHO WILL PAY THE ULTIMATE SACRIFICE TO ANSWER OUR QUESTIONS.

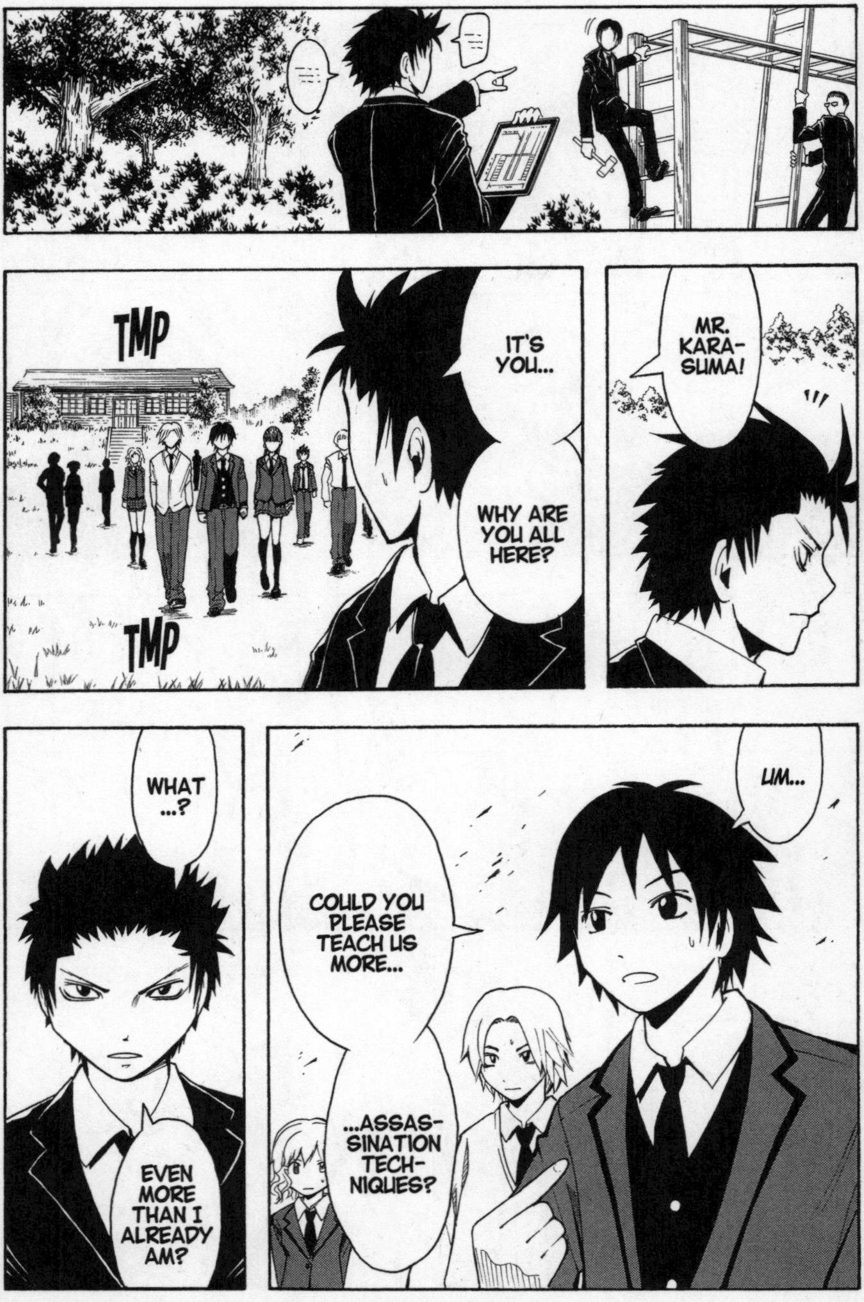
MR. KARA-SUMA!
IT'S YOU...
TMP
WHY ARE YOU ALL HERE?
TMP
UM...
COULD YOU PLEASE TEACH US MORE...
...ASSAS-SINATION TECH-NIQUES?
WHAT ...?
EVEN MORE THAN I ALREADY AM?

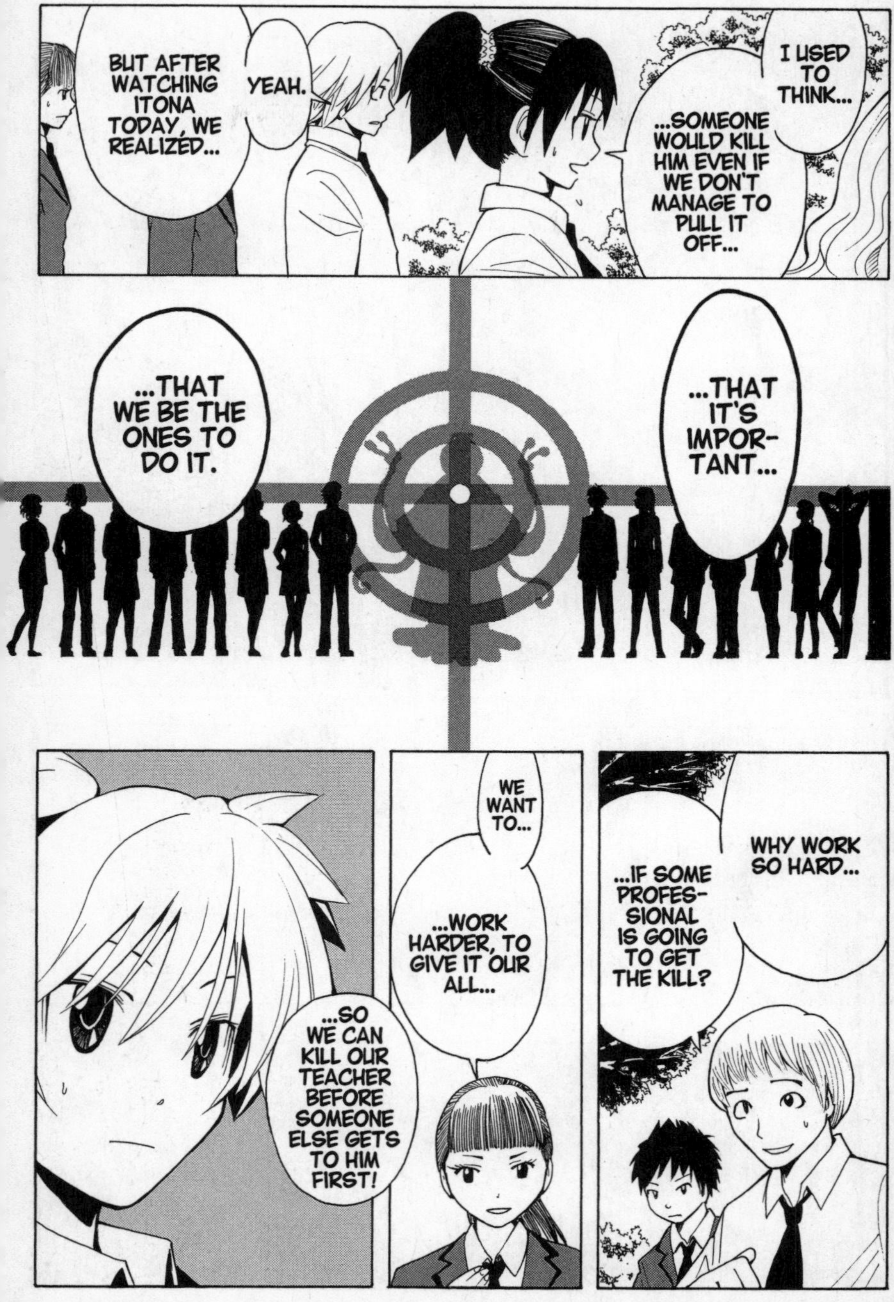
I USED TO THINK...
...SOMEONE WOULD KILL HIM EVEN IF WE DON'T MANAGE TO PULL IT OFF...
YEAH.
BUT AFTER WATCHING ITONA TODAY, WE REALIZED...
...THAT IT'S IMPOR-TANT...
...THAT WE BE THE ONES TO DO IT.
WHY WORK SO HARD...
...IF SOME PROFES-SIONAL IS GOING TO GET THE KILL?
WE WANT TO...
...WORK HARDER, TO GIVE IT OUR ALL...
...SO WE CAN KILL OUR TEACHER BEFORE SOMEONE ELSE GETS TO HIM FIRST!

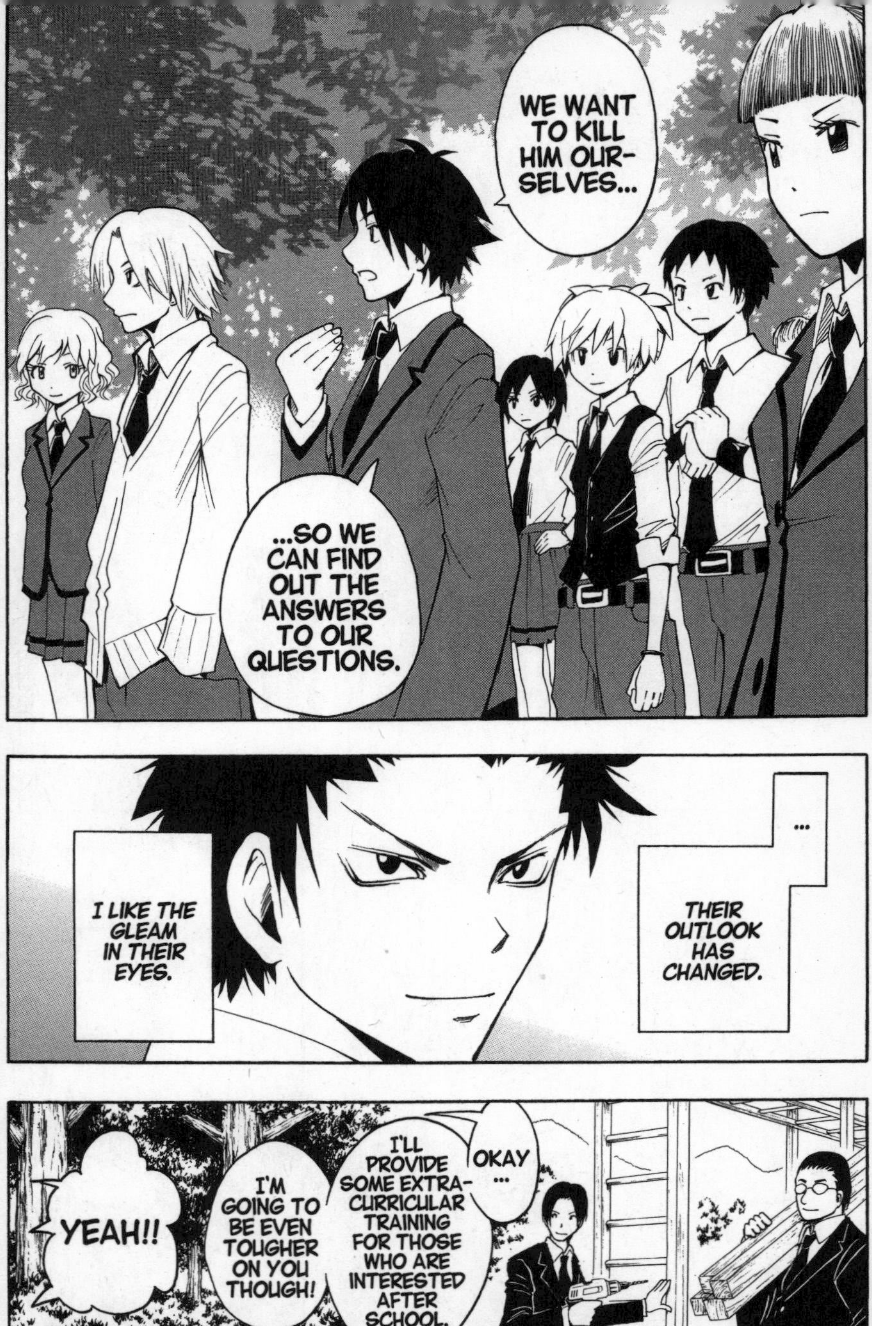
WE WANT TO KILL HIM OUR-SELVES...
...SO WE CAN FIND OUT THE ANSWERS TO OUR QUESTIONS.
...
THEIR OUTLOOK HAS CHANGED.
I LIKE THE GLEAM IN THEIR EYES.
OKAY ...
I'LL PROVIDE SOME EXTRA-CURRICULAR TRAINING FOR THOSE WHO ARE INTERESTED AFTER SCHOOL.
I'M GOING TO BE EVEN TOUGHER ON YOU THOUGH!
YEAH!!

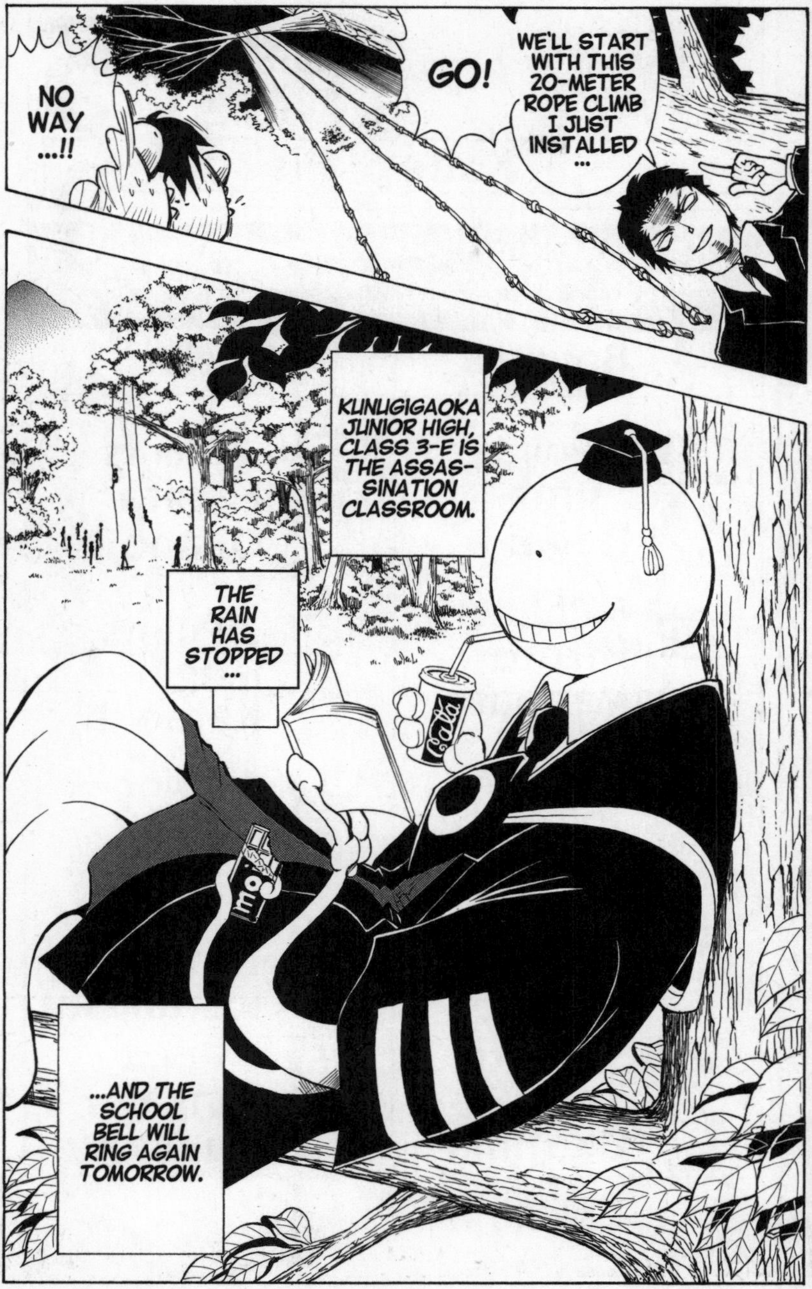
WE'LL START WITH THIS 20-METER ROPE CLIMB I JUST INSTALLED ...
GO!
NO WAY ...!!
KUNUGIGAOKA JUNIOR HIGH, CLASS 3-E IS THE ASSAS-SINATION CLASSROOM.
THE RAIN HAS STOPPED ...
...AND THE SCHOOL BELL WILL RING AGAIN TOMORROW.

Class 3-E
Best 5

Knife Skills

Karasuma Sensei's Mock Assassination Drill
(Clean Hit: 3 Points Grazing: 1 Point Hit working as a team:
1 Point per Person) Total Score from April to June

Boys	Girls
6 Points Yuma Isogai	**3 Points Hinata Okano**
5 Points Hiroto Maehara	**3 Points Meg Kataoka**
4 Points Tomohito Sugino	**1 Point Toka Yada**
3 Points Masayoshi Kimura	**1 Point Hinano Kurahashi**
3 Points Taiga Okajima	**1 Point Rinka Hayami**

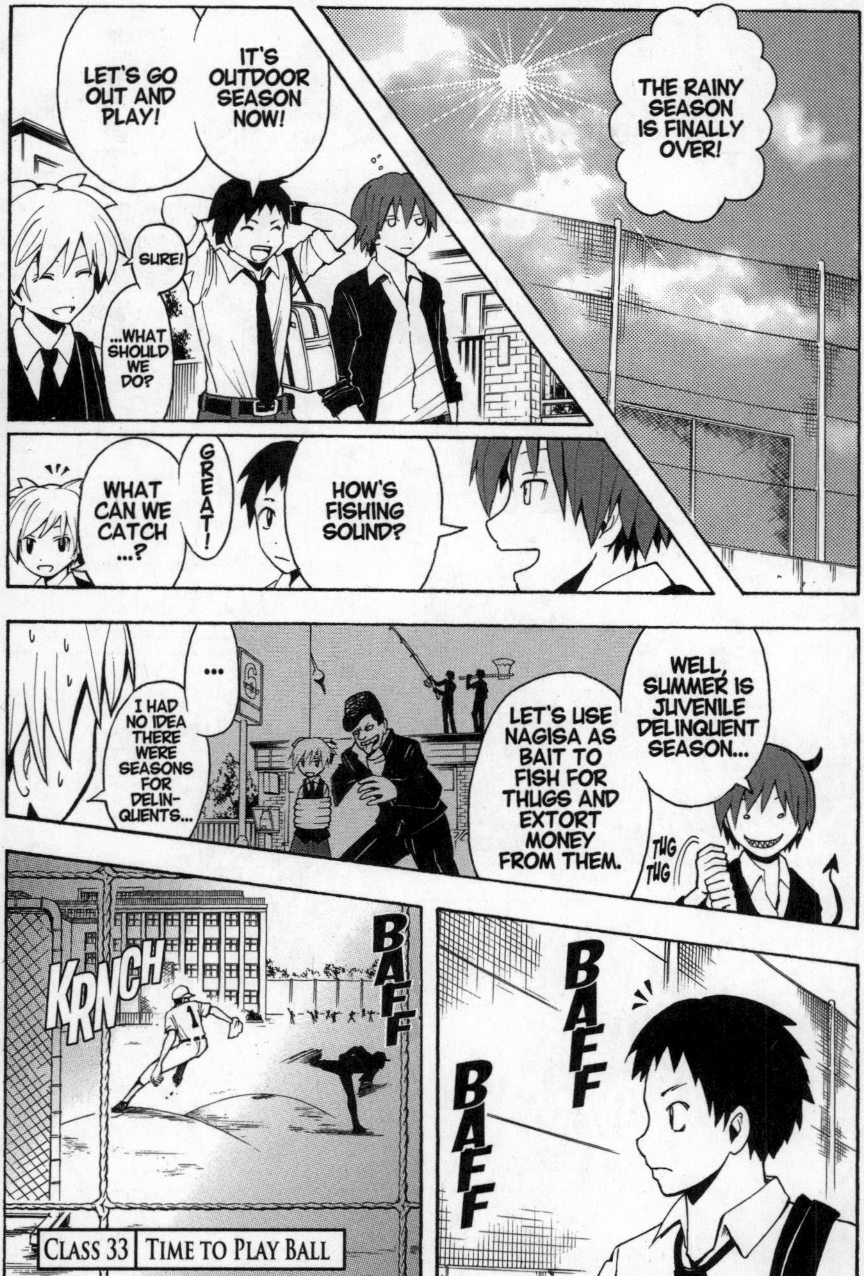
THE RAINY SEASON IS FINALLY OVER!
IT'S OUTDOOR SEASON NOW!
LET'S GO OUT AND PLAY!
SURE!
...WHAT SHOULD WE DO?
HOW'S FISHING SOUND?
GREAT!
WHAT CAN WE CATCH ...?
WELL, SUMMER IS JUVENILE DELINQUENT SEASON...
LET'S USE NAGISA AS BAIT TO FISH FOR THUGS AND EXTORT MONEY FROM THEM.
TUG TUG
...
I HAD NO IDEA THERE WERE SEASONS FOR DELINQUENTS...
BAFF
BAFF
BAFF
BAFF
KRNCH
CLASS 33 TIME TO PLAY BALL

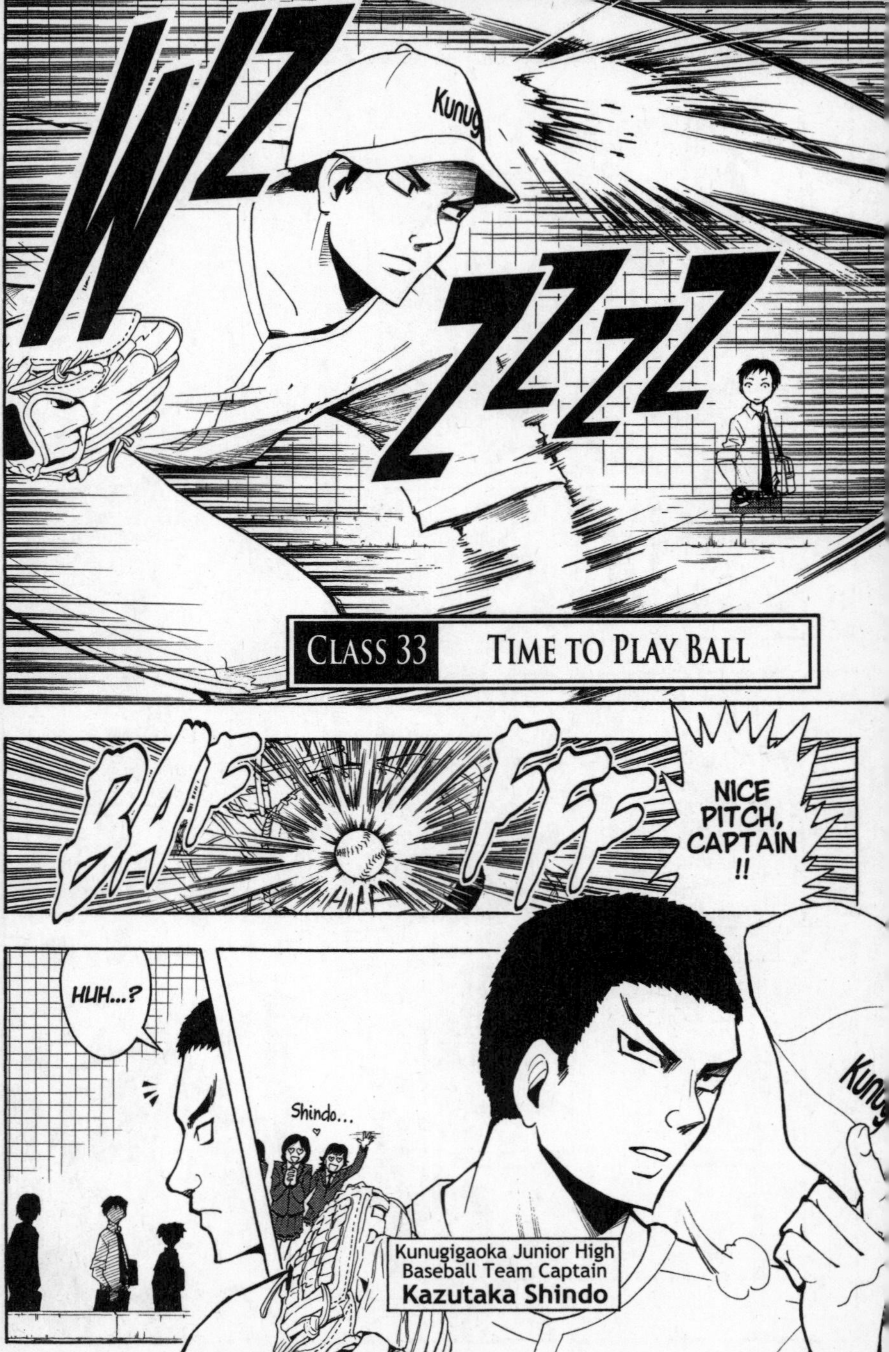
WZZZZZ
Kunug
CLASS 33 TIME TO PLAY BALL
NICE PITCH, CAPTAIN !!
BAFFFF
Kunug
Shindo...
Kunugigaoka Junior High Baseball Team Captain
Kazutaka Shindo
HUH...?

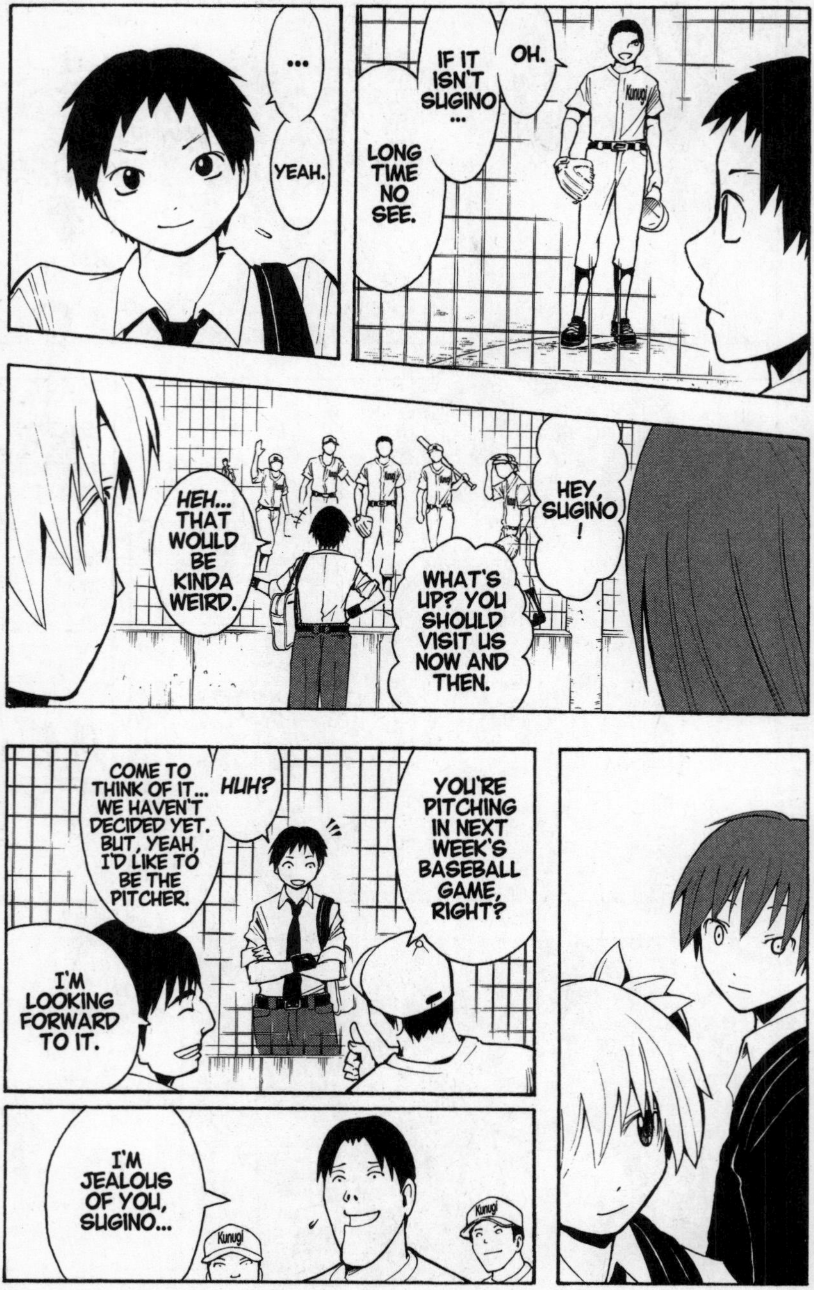
OH.
IF IT ISN'T SUGINO...
LONG TIME NO SEE.
...
YEAH.
HEY, SUGINO!
WHAT'S UP? YOU SHOULD VISIT US NOW AND THEN.
HEH... THAT WOULD BE KINDA WEIRD.
YOU'RE PITCHING IN NEXT WEEK'S BASEBALL GAME, RIGHT?
HUH?
COME TO THINK OF IT... WE HAVEN'T DECIDED YET. BUT, YEAH, I'D LIKE TO BE THE PITCHER.
I'M LOOKING FORWARD TO IT.
I'M JEALOUS OF YOU, SUGINO...

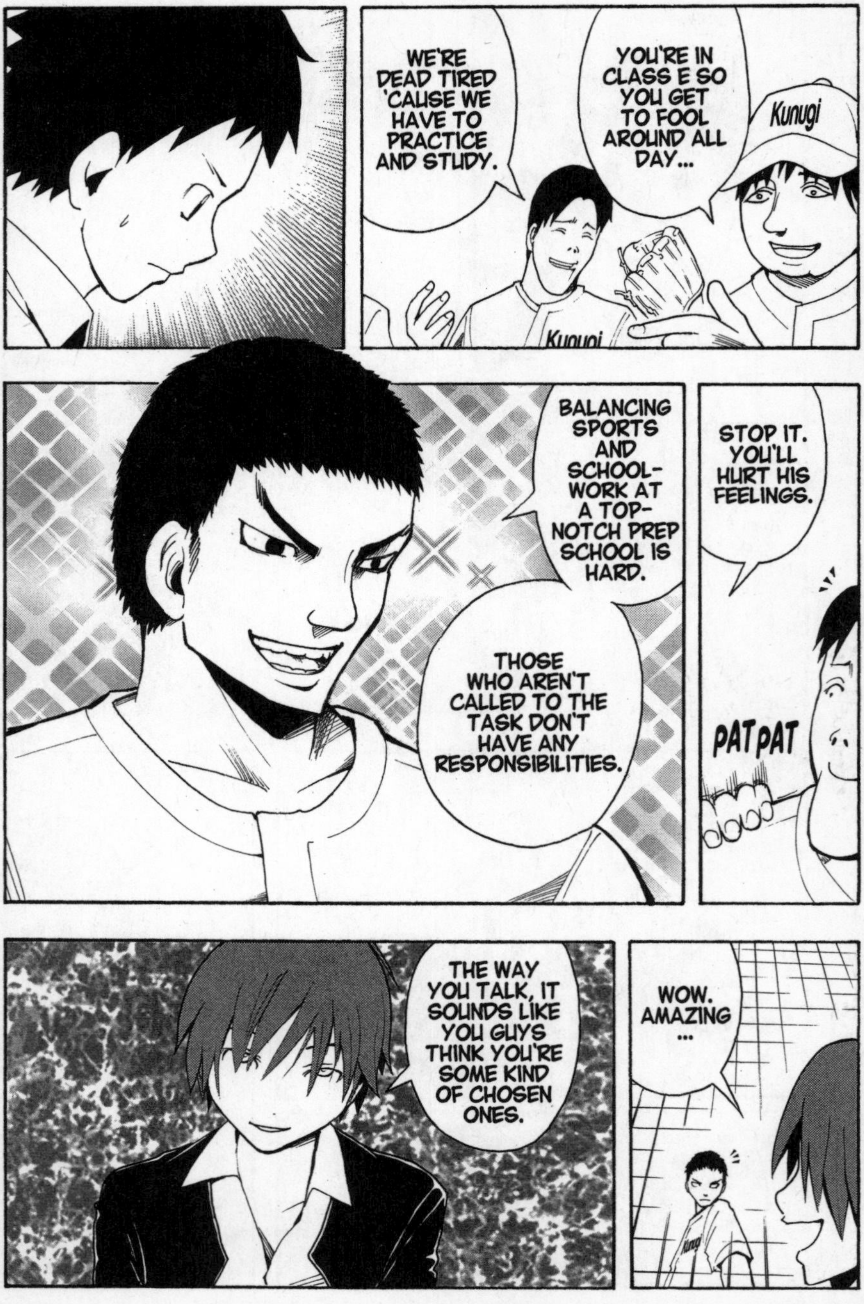

YOU'RE IN CLASS E SO YOU GET TO FOOL AROUND ALL DAY...
WE'RE DEAD TIRED 'CAUSE WE HAVE TO PRACTICE AND STUDY.
STOP IT. YOU'LL HURT HIS FEELINGS.
PAT PAT
BALANCING SPORTS AND SCHOOL-WORK AT A TOP-NOTCH PREP SCHOOL IS HARD.
THOSE WHO AREN'T CALLED TO THE TASK DON'T HAVE ANY RESPONSIBILITIES.
WOW. AMAZING...
THE WAY YOU TALK, IT SOUNDS LIKE YOU GUYS THINK YOU'RE SOME KIND OF CHOSEN ONES.

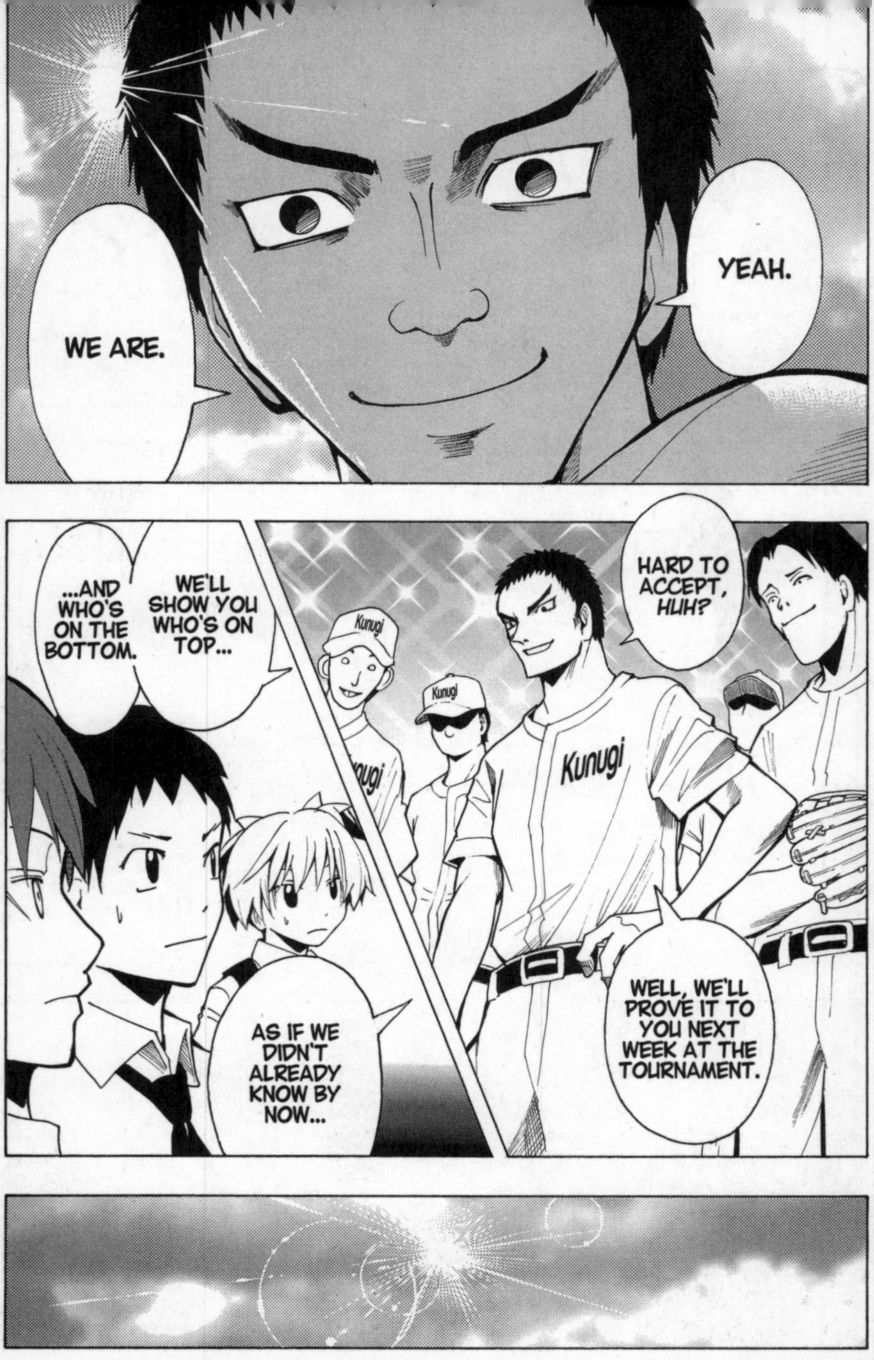
YEAH.
WE ARE.
HARD TO ACCEPT, HUH?
WELL, WE'LL PROVE IT TO YOU NEXT WEEK AT THE TOURNAMENT.
WE'LL SHOW YOU WHO'S ON TOP...
...AND WHO'S ON THE BOTTOM.
AS IF WE DIDN'T ALREADY KNOW BY NOW...

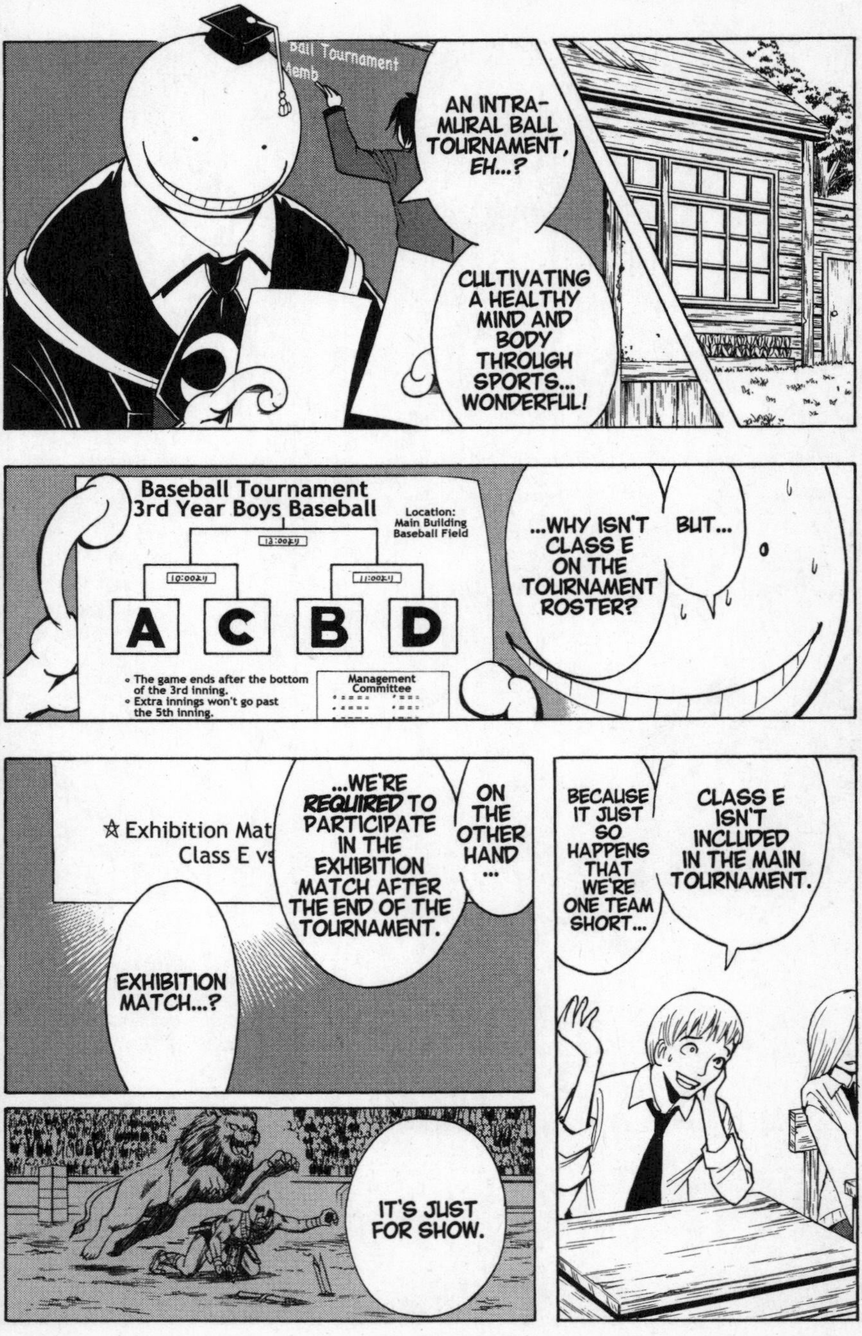
AN INTRA-MURAL BALL TOURNAMENT, EH...?
CULTIVATING A HEALTHY MIND AND BODY THROUGH SPORTS... WONDERFUL!
Ball Tournament
Memb
BUT...
...WHY ISN'T CLASS E ON THE TOURNAMENT ROSTER?
Baseball Tournament
3rd Year Boys Baseball
Location: Main Building Baseball Field
13:00より
10:00より
11:00より
A
C
B
D
• The game ends after the bottom of the 3rd inning.
• Extra innings won't go past the 5th inning.
Management Committee
CLASS E ISN'T INCLUDED IN THE MAIN TOURNAMENT.
BECAUSE IT JUST SO HAPPENS THAT WE'RE ONE TEAM SHORT...
ON THE OTHER HAND...
...WE'RE *REQUIRED* TO PARTICIPATE IN THE EXHIBITION MATCH AFTER THE END OF THE TOURNAMENT.
☆ Exhibition Mat
Class E vs
EXHIBITION MATCH...?
IT'S JUST FOR SHOW.

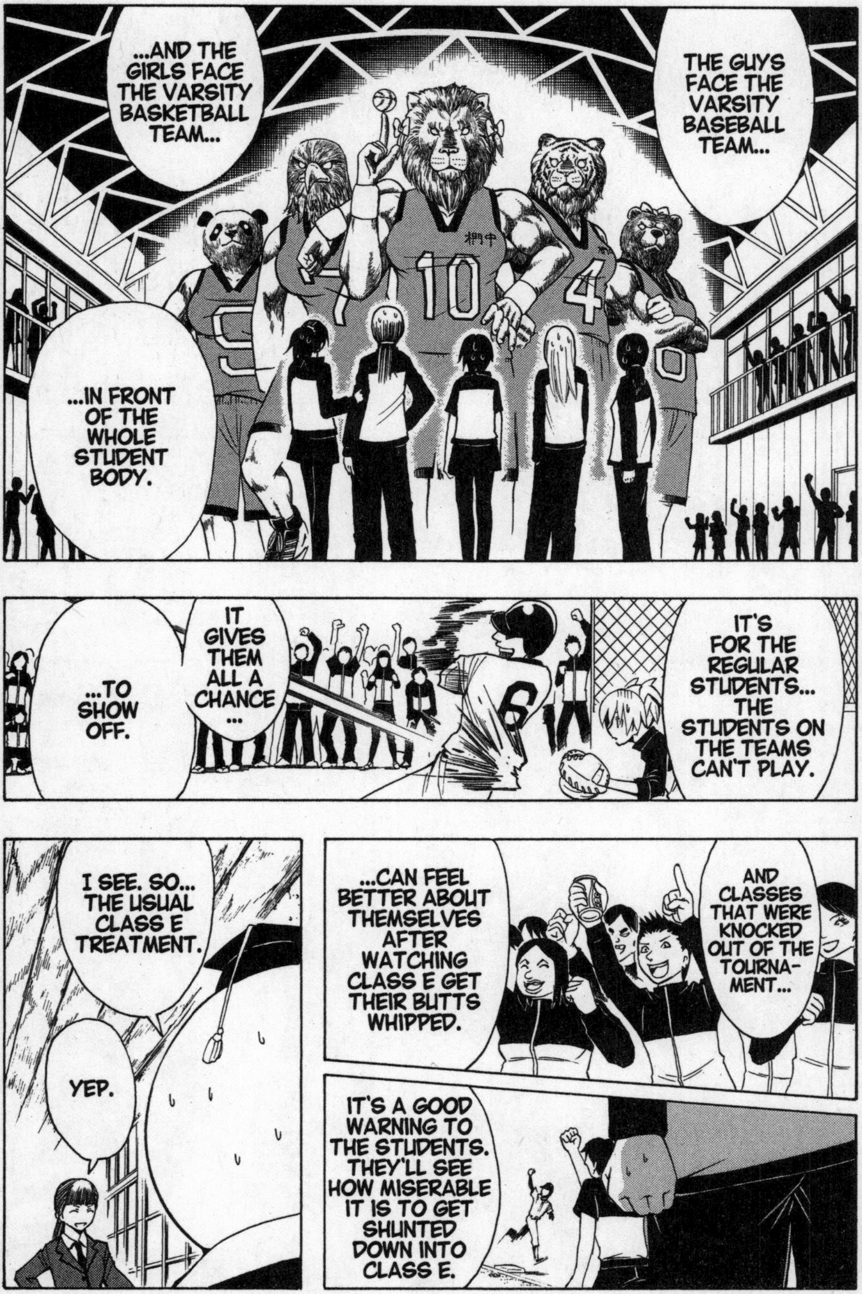
THE GUYS FACE THE VARSITY BASEBALL TEAM...
...AND THE GIRLS FACE THE VARSITY BASKETBALL TEAM...
...IN FRONT OF THE WHOLE STUDENT BODY.
IT'S FOR THE REGULAR STUDENTS... THE STUDENTS ON THE TEAMS CAN'T PLAY.
IT GIVES THEM ALL A CHANCE...
...TO SHOW OFF.
AND CLASSES THAT WERE KNOCKED OUT OF THE TOURNAMENT...
...CAN FEEL BETTER ABOUT THEMSELVES AFTER WATCHING CLASS E GET THEIR BUTTS WHIPPED.
IT'S A GOOD WARNING TO THE STUDENTS. THEY'LL SEE HOW MISERABLE IT IS TO GET SHUNTED DOWN INTO CLASS E.
I SEE. SO... THE USUAL CLASS E TREATMENT.
YEP.

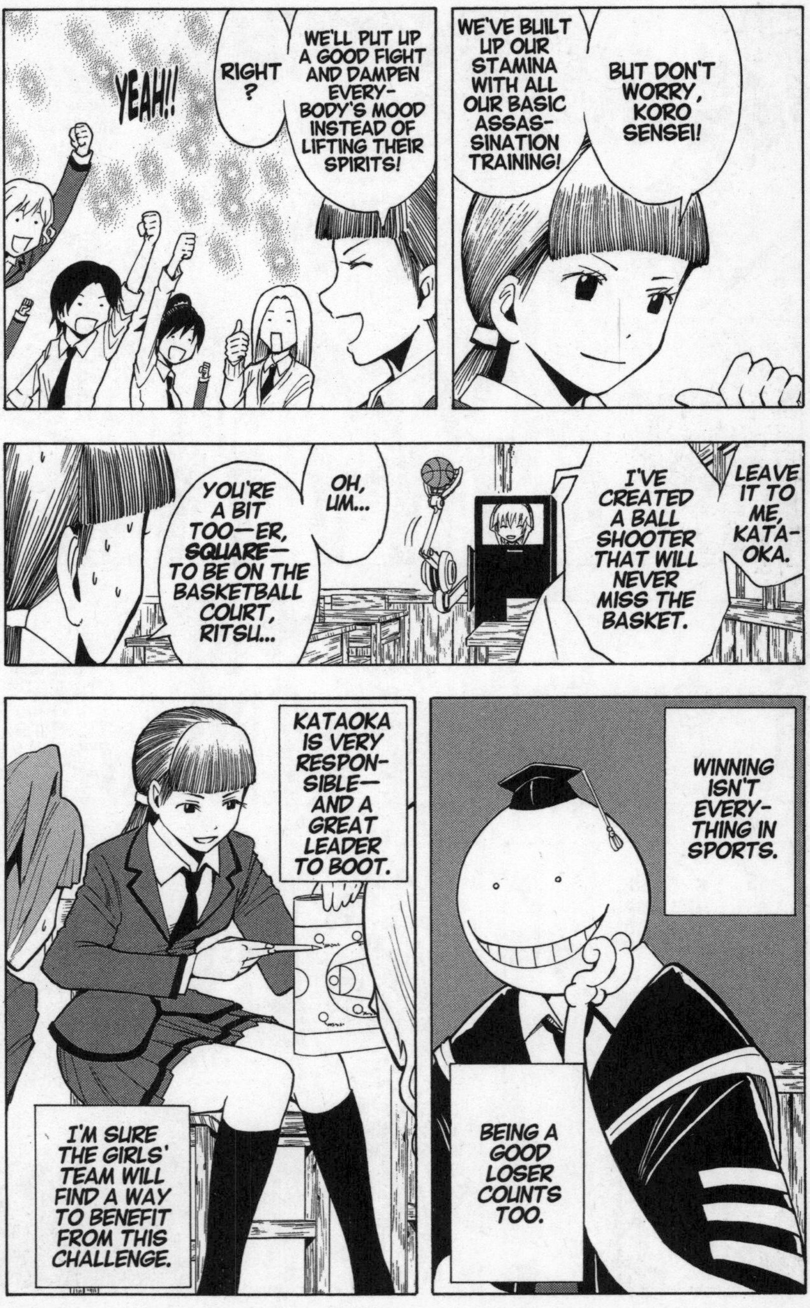
BUT DON'T WORRY, KORO SENSEI!
WE'VE BUILT UP OUR STAMINA WITH ALL OUR BASIC ASSAS-SINATION TRAINING!
WE'LL PUT UP A GOOD FIGHT AND DAMPEN EVERY-BODY'S MOOD INSTEAD OF LIFTING THEIR SPIRITS!
RIGHT?
YEAH!!
LEAVE IT TO ME, KATA-OKA.
I'VE CREATED A BALL SHOOTER THAT WILL NEVER MISS THE BASKET.
OH, UM...
YOU'RE A BIT TOO—ER, SQUARE—TO BE ON THE BASKETBALL COURT, RITSU...
WINNING ISN'T EVERY-THING IN SPORTS.
BEING A GOOD LOSER COUNTS TOO.
KATAOKA IS VERY RESPON-SIBLE—AND A GREAT LEADER TO BOOT.
I'M SURE THE GIRLS' TEAM WILL FIND A WAY TO BENEFIT FROM THIS CHALLENGE.

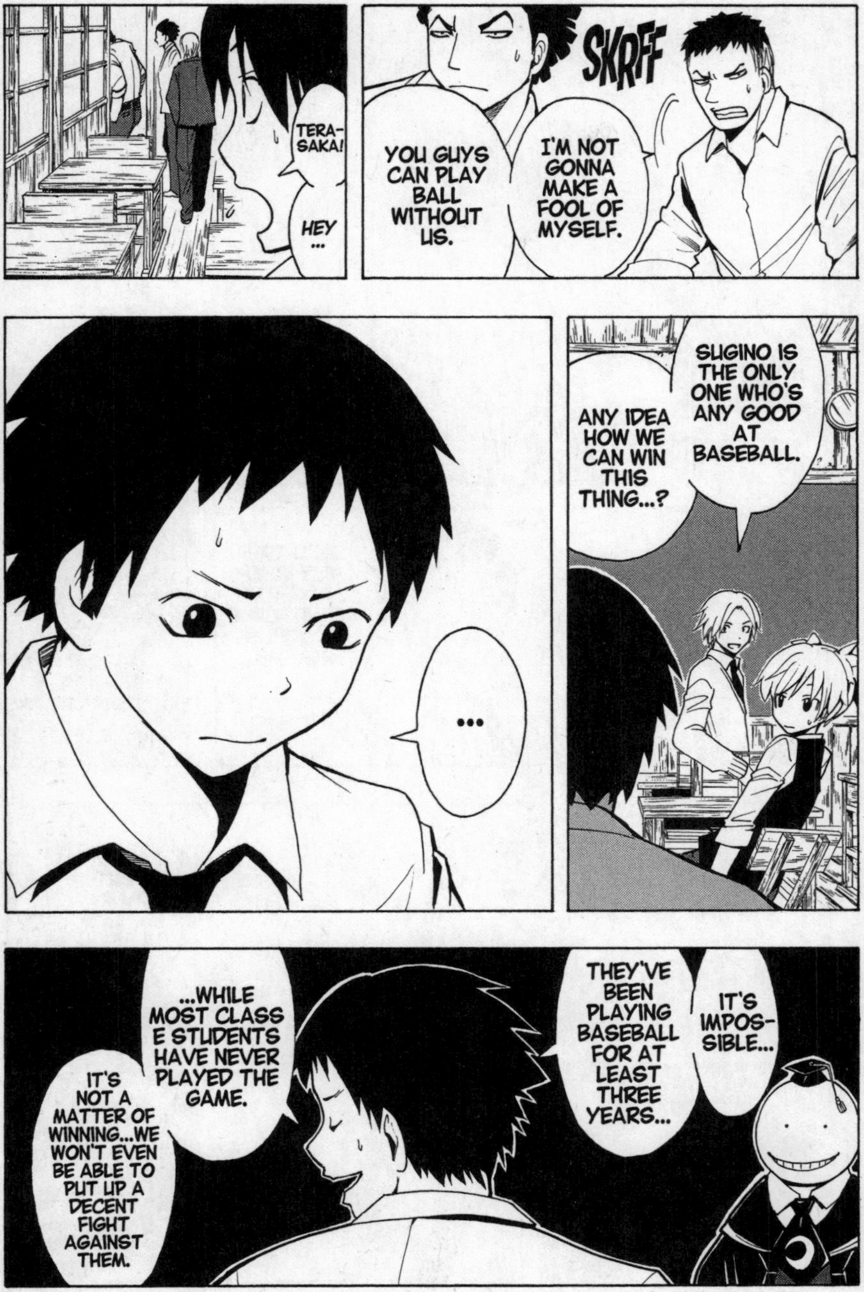
SKRFF
I'M NOT GONNA MAKE A FOOL OF MYSELF.
YOU GUYS CAN PLAY BALL WITHOUT US.
TERA-SAKA!
HEY ...
SUGINO IS THE ONLY ONE WHO'S ANY GOOD AT BASEBALL.
ANY IDEA HOW WE CAN WIN THIS THING...?
...
IT'S IMPOSSIBLE...
THEY'VE BEEN PLAYING BASEBALL FOR AT LEAST THREE YEARS...
...WHILE MOST CLASS E STUDENTS HAVE NEVER PLAYED THE GAME.
IT'S NOT A MATTER OF WINNING...WE WON'T EVEN BE ABLE TO PUT UP A DECENT FIGHT AGAINST THEM.

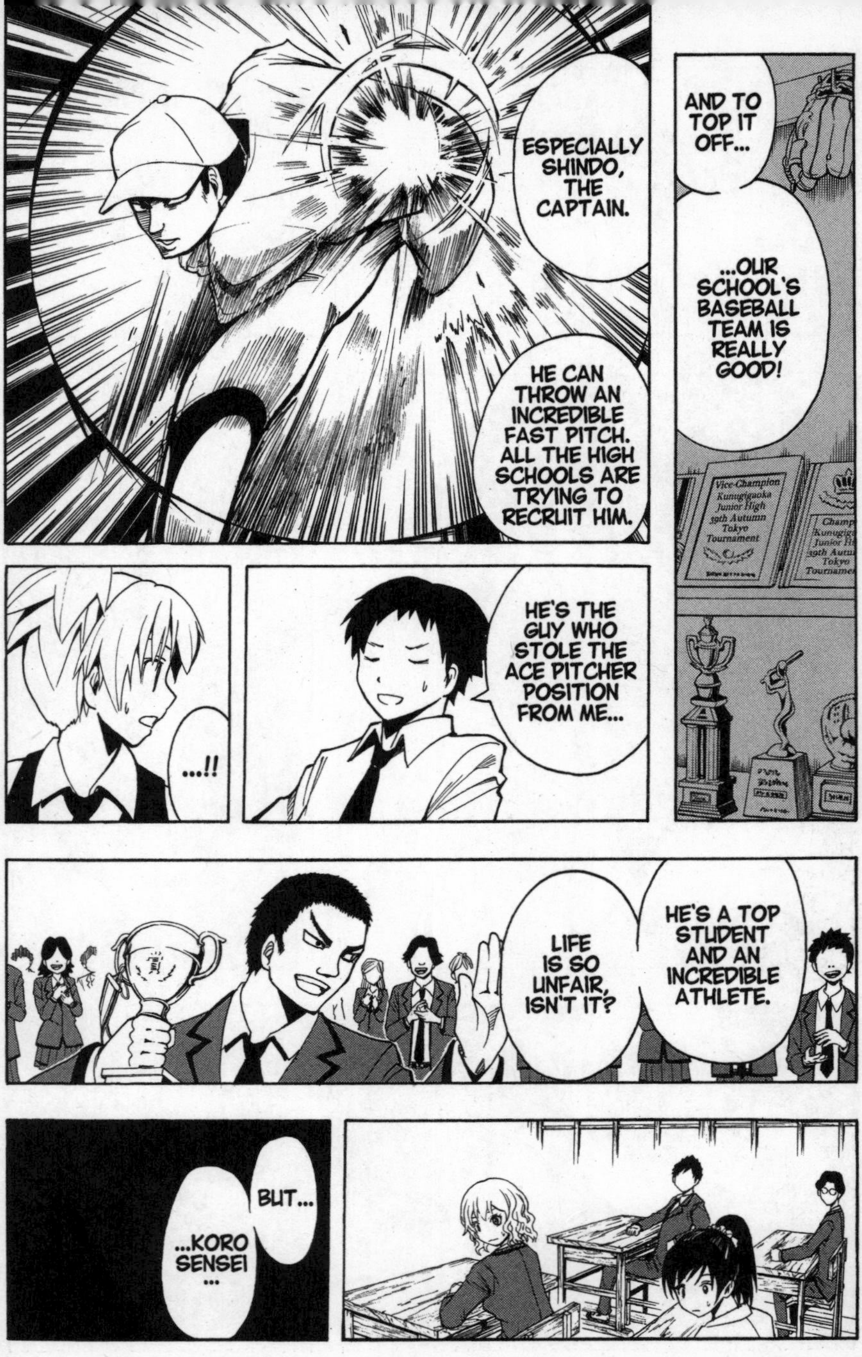

AND TO TOP IT OFF...
...OUR SCHOOL'S BASEBALL TEAM IS REALLY GOOD!
Vice-Champion Kunugigaoka Junior High 39th Autumn Tokyo Tournament
ESPECIALLY SHINDO, THE CAPTAIN.
HE CAN THROW AN INCREDIBLE FAST PITCH. ALL THE HIGH SCHOOLS ARE TRYING TO RECRUIT HIM.
HE'S THE GUY WHO STOLE THE ACE PITCHER POSITION FROM ME...
...!!
HE'S A TOP STUDENT AND AN INCREDIBLE ATHLETE.
LIFE IS SO UNFAIR, ISN'T IT?
BUT...
...KORO SENSEI...

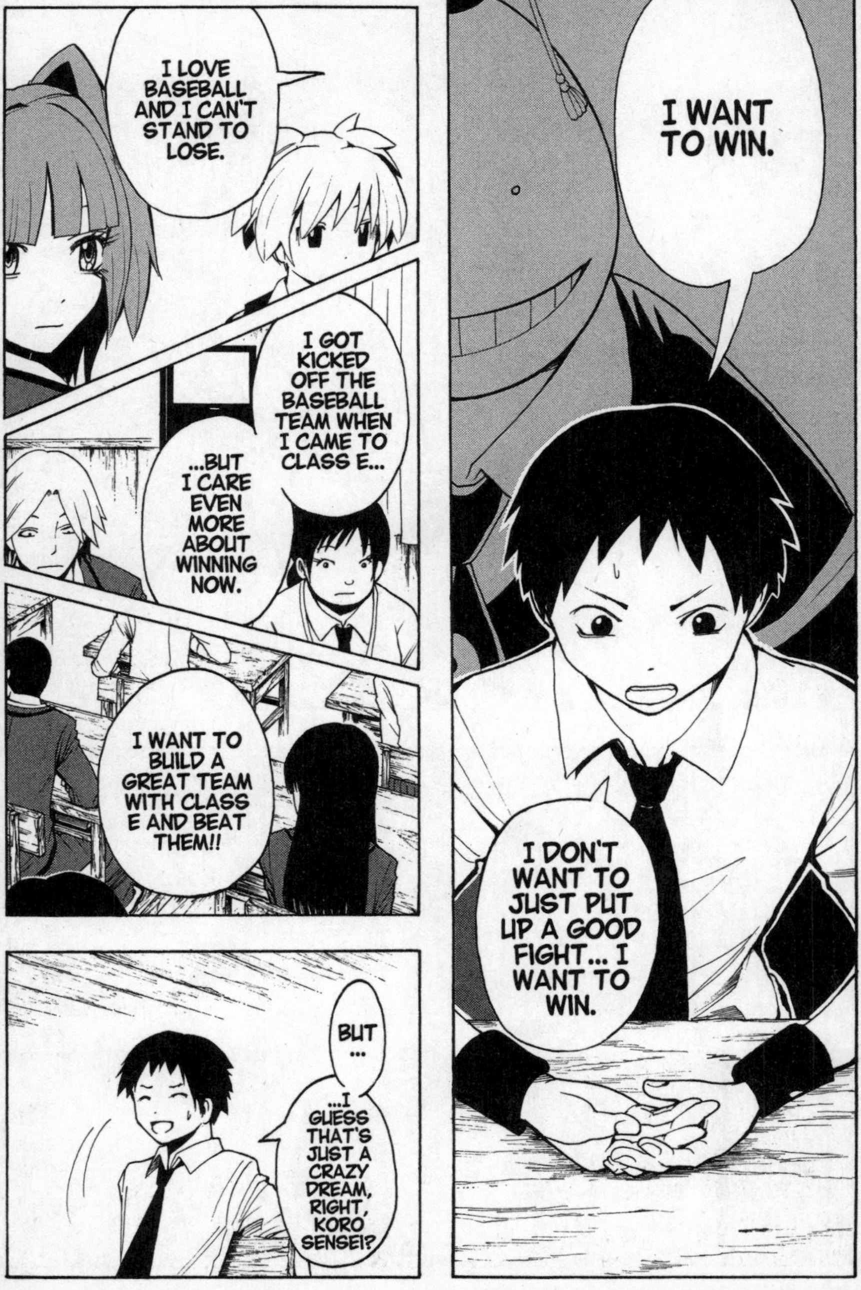
I WANT TO WIN.
I DON'T WANT TO JUST PUT UP A GOOD FIGHT... I WANT TO WIN.
I LOVE BASEBALL AND I CAN'T STAND TO LOSE.
I GOT KICKED OFF THE BASEBALL TEAM WHEN I CAME TO CLASS E...
...BUT I CARE EVEN MORE ABOUT WINNING NOW.
I WANT TO BUILD A GREAT TEAM WITH CLASS E AND BEAT THEM!!
BUT ...
...I GUESS THAT'S JUST A CRAZY DREAM, RIGHT, KORO SENSEI?

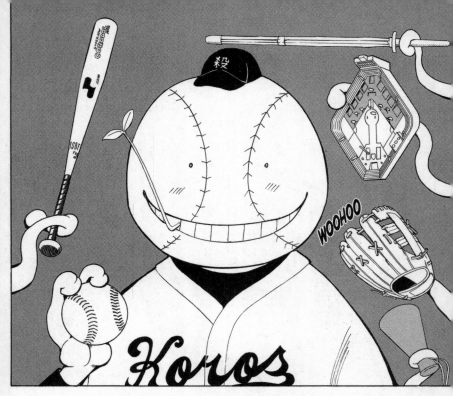

殺
WOOHOO
Koros
I CAN TELL YOU WANT TO PLAY BASEBALL TOO, KORO SENSEI...
EYEAH ...
HA HA HA HA HA HA...
I'VE ALWAYS WANTED TO BE THE HOT-BLOODED COACH IN THAT GUTS-AND-GLORY SPORTS MANGA SERIES!
I CAN'T PUNCH YOU, SO I'VE PREPARED A TRAY FOR ME TO FLIP OVER WHEN I GET MAD.
YOU'RE *TOO* WELL PREPARED !!

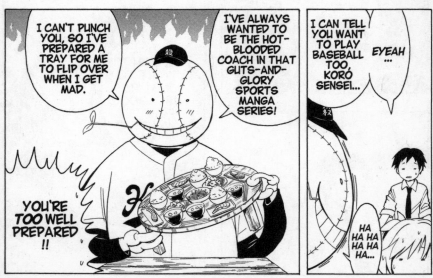

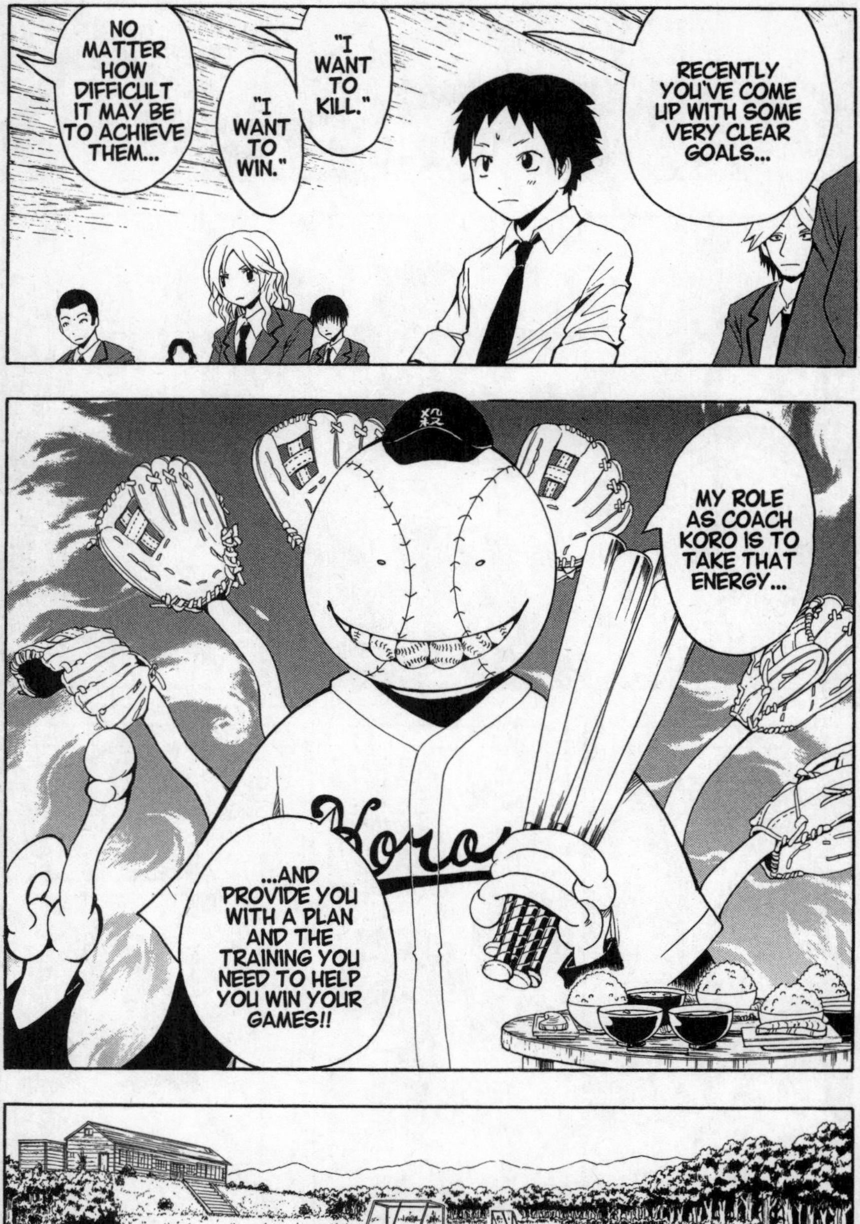
RECENTLY YOU'VE COME UP WITH SOME VERY CLEAR GOALS...
"I WANT TO KILL."
"I WANT TO WIN."
NO MATTER HOW DIFFICULT IT MAY BE TO ACHIEVE THEM...
MY ROLE AS COACH KORO IS TO TAKE THAT ENERGY...
...AND PROVIDE YOU WITH A PLAN AND THE TRAINING YOU NEED TO HELP YOU WIN YOUR GAMES!!

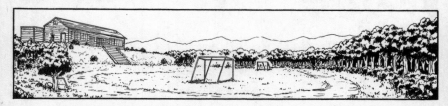

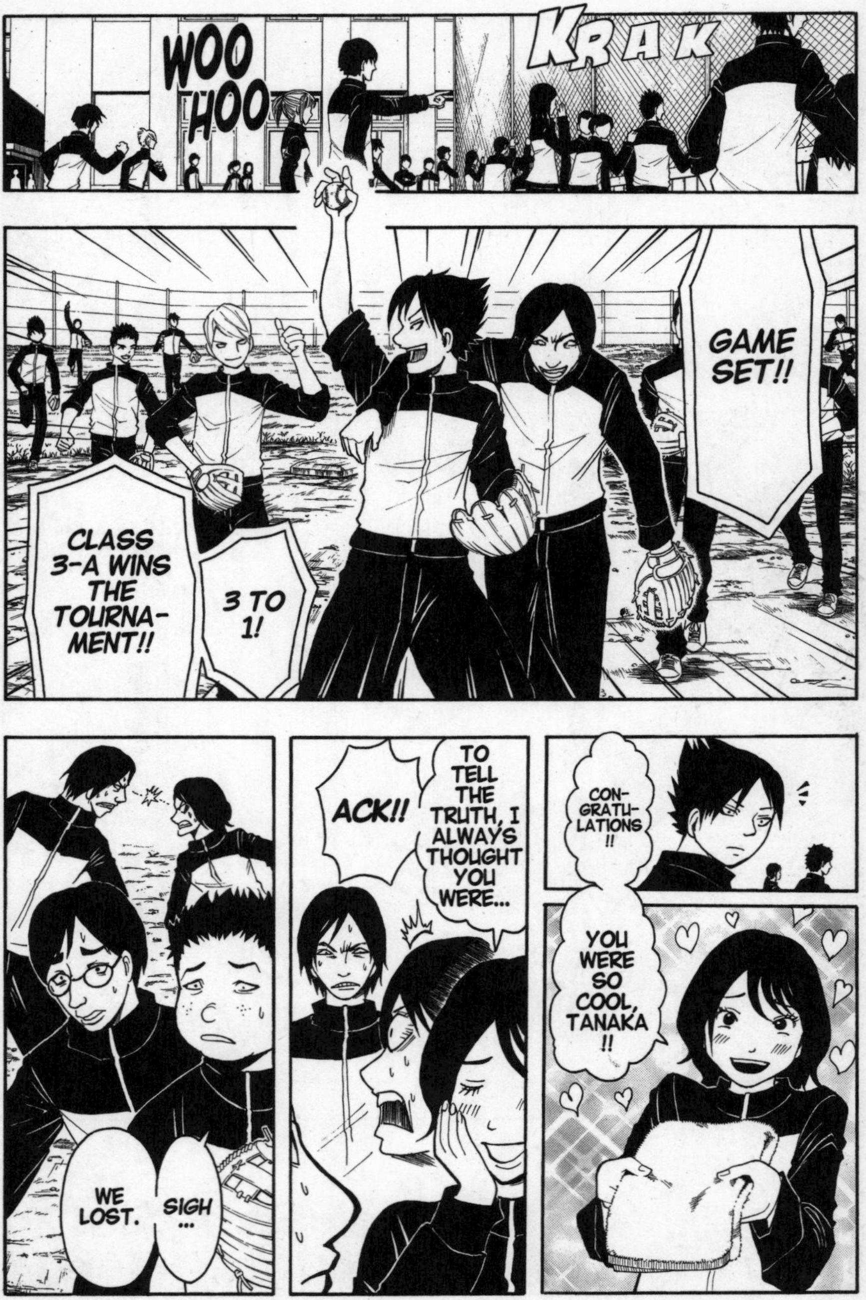
KRAK
WOO HOO
GAME SET!!
CLASS 3-A WINS THE TOURNAMENT!!
3 TO 1!
CONGRATULATIONS!!
YOU WERE SO COOL, TANAKA!!
TO TELL THE TRUTH, I ALWAYS THOUGHT YOU WERE...
ACK!!
SIGH...
WE LOST.

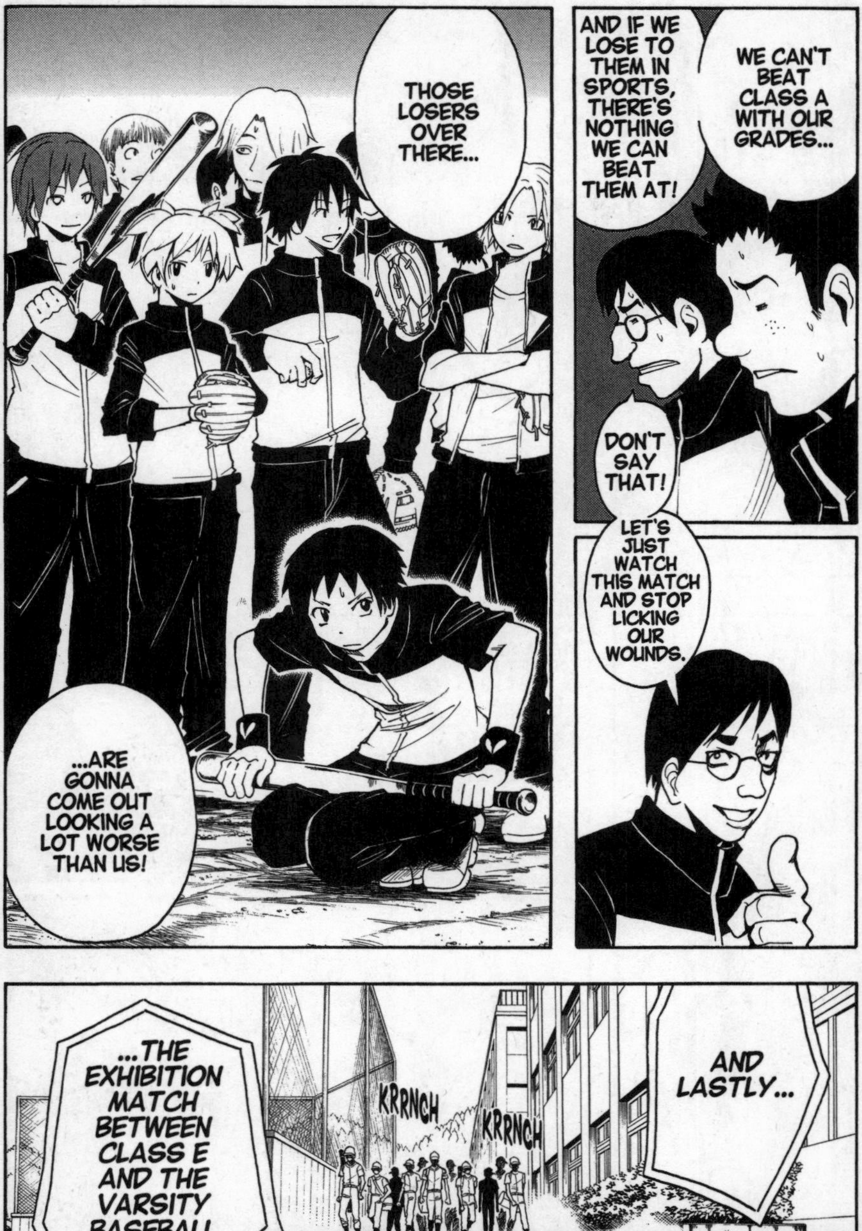
WE CAN'T BEAT CLASS A WITH OUR GRADES...
AND IF WE LOSE TO THEM IN SPORTS, THERE'S NOTHING WE CAN BEAT THEM AT!
DON'T SAY THAT!
LET'S JUST WATCH THIS MATCH AND STOP LICKING OUR WOUNDS.
THOSE LOSERS OVER THERE...
...ARE GONNA COME OUT LOOKING A LOT WORSE THAN US!
AND LASTLY...
KRRNCH
KRRNCH
...THE EXHIBITION MATCH BETWEEN CLASS E AND THE VARSITY BASEBALL TEAM...

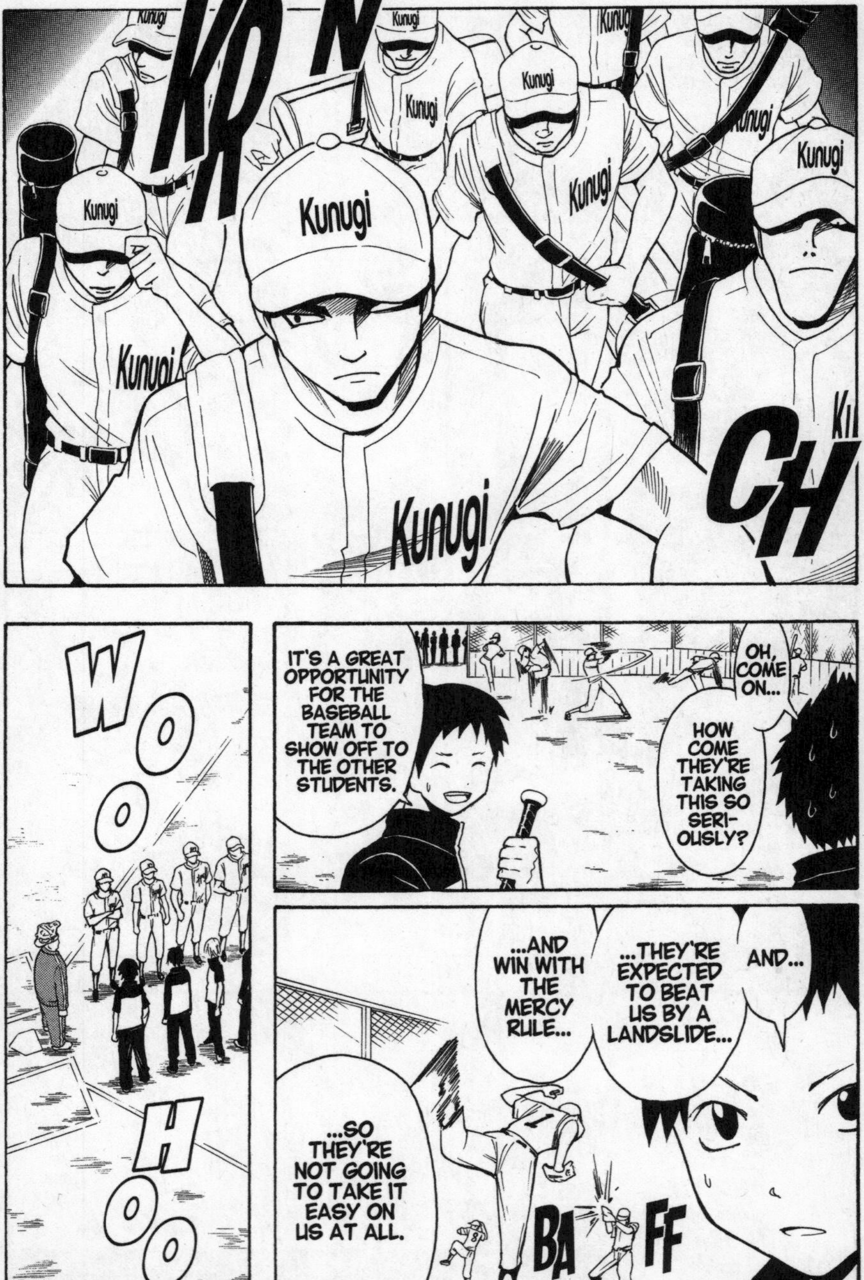
KR N CH
OH, COME ON...
HOW COME THEY'RE TAKING THIS SO SERI-OUSLY?
IT'S A GREAT OPPORTUNITY FOR THE BASEBALL TEAM TO SHOW OFF TO THE OTHER STUDENTS.
AND...
...THEY'RE EXPECTED TO BEAT US BY A LANDSLIDE...
...AND WIN WITH THE MERCY RULE...
...SO THEY'RE NOT GOING TO TAKE IT EASY ON US AT ALL.
BAFF
WOO
HOOO

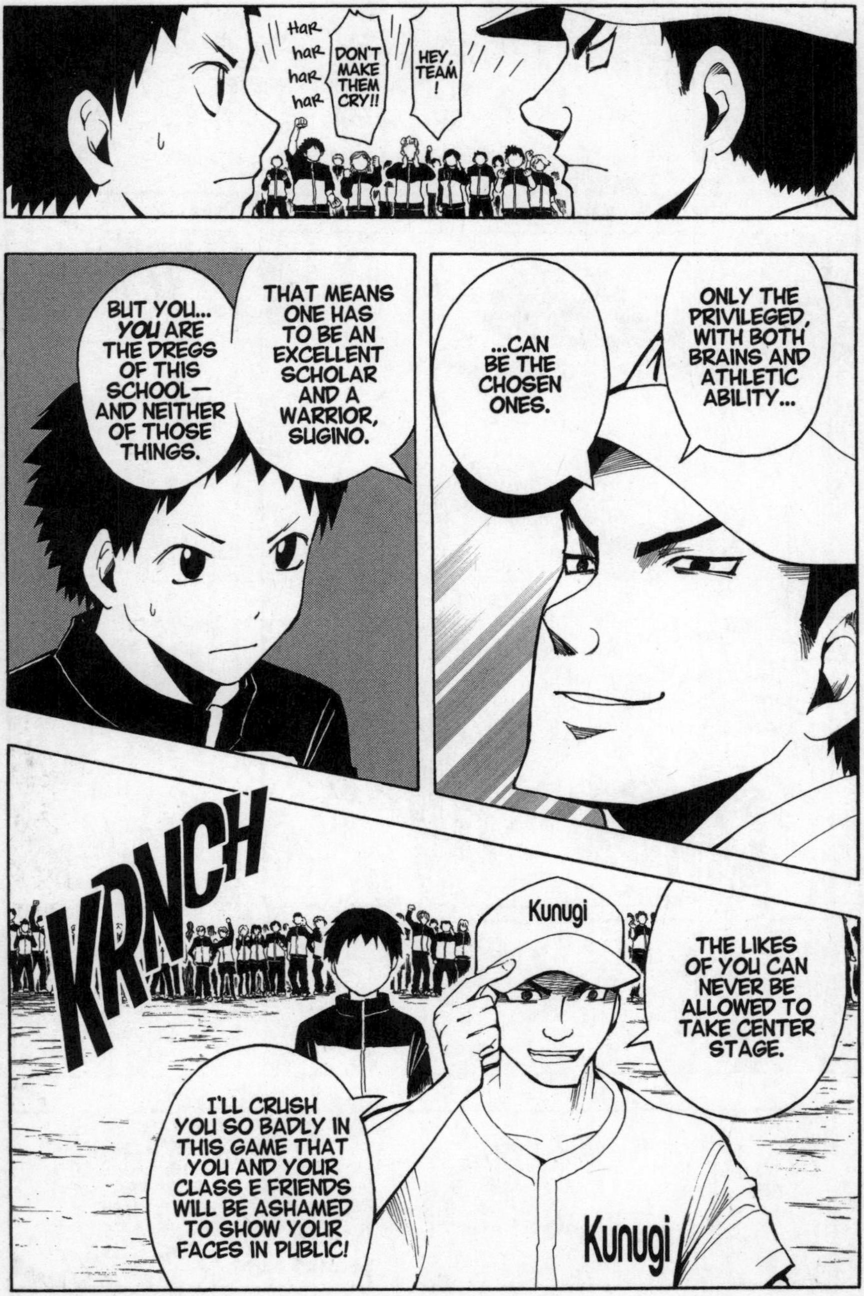
HEY, TEAM!
DON'T MAKE THEM CRY!!
Har har har har
ONLY THE PRIVILEGED, WITH BOTH BRAINS AND ATHLETIC ABILITY...
...CAN BE THE CHOSEN ONES.
THAT MEANS ONE HAS TO BE AN EXCELLENT SCHOLAR AND A WARRIOR, SUGINO.
BUT YOU... *YOU* ARE THE DREGS OF THIS SCHOOL—AND NEITHER OF THOSE THINGS.
Kunugi
THE LIKES OF YOU CAN NEVER BE ALLOWED TO TAKE CENTER STAGE.
KRNCH
I'LL CRUSH YOU SO BADLY IN THIS GAME THAT YOU AND YOUR CLASS E FRIENDS WILL BE ASHAMED TO SHOW YOUR FACES IN PUBLIC!
Kunugi

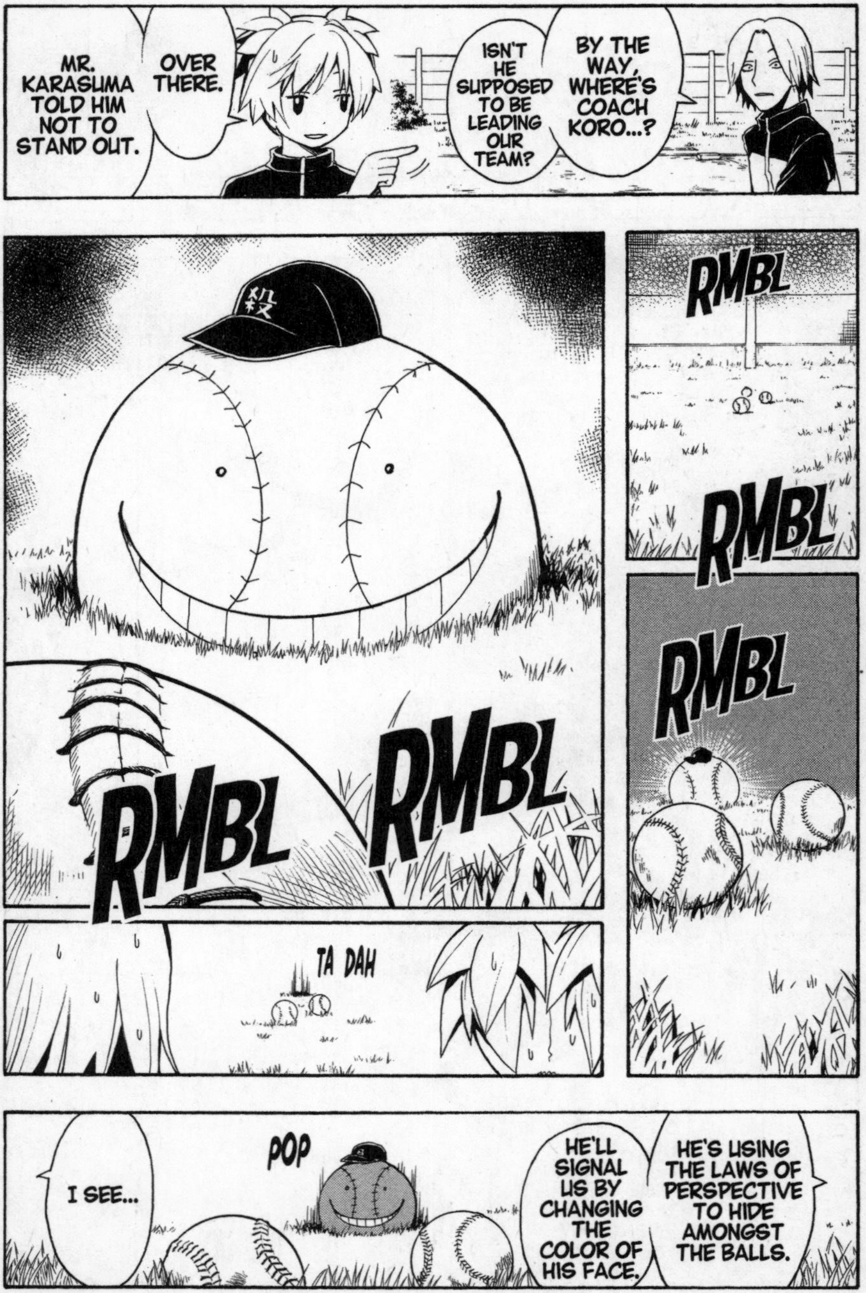
BY THE WAY, WHERE'S COACH KORO...?
ISN'T HE SUPPOSED TO BE LEADING OUR TEAM?
OVER THERE.
MR. KARASUMA TOLD HIM NOT TO STAND OUT.
RMBL
RMBL
RMBL
RMBL
RMBL
TA DAH
HE'S USING THE LAWS OF PERSPECTIVE TO HIDE AMONGST THE BALLS.
HE'LL SIGNAL US BY CHANGING THE COLOR OF HIS FACE.
POP
I SEE...

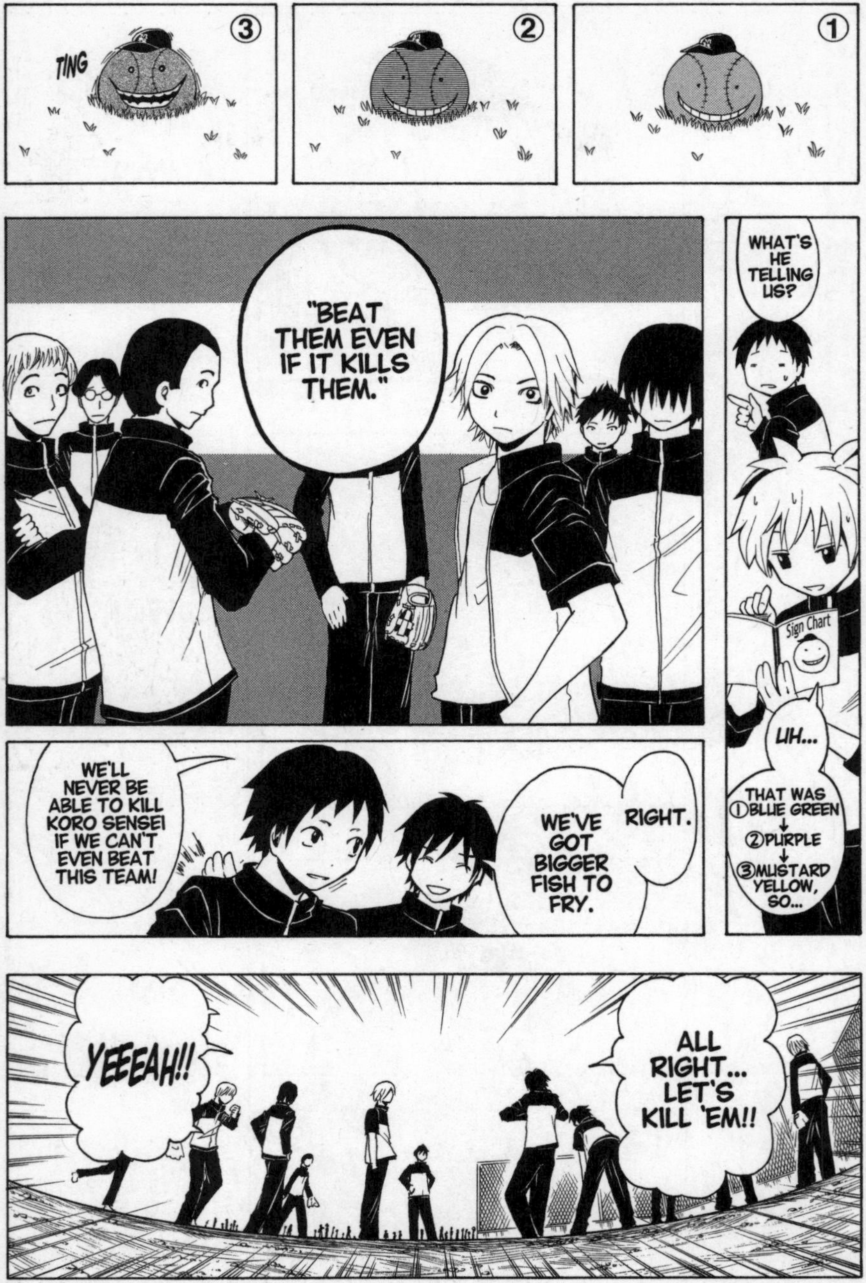
①
②
③
TING
WHAT'S HE TELLING US?
Sign Chart
UH...
THAT WAS ①BLUE GREEN ↓ ②PURPLE ↓ ③MUSTARD YELLOW, SO...
"BEAT THEM EVEN IF IT KILLS THEM."
RIGHT. WE'VE GOT BIGGER FISH TO FRY.
WE'LL NEVER BE ABLE TO KILL KORO SENSEI IF WE CAN'T EVEN BEAT THIS TEAM!
ALL RIGHT... LET'S KILL 'EM!!
YEEEAH!!

Slowly...

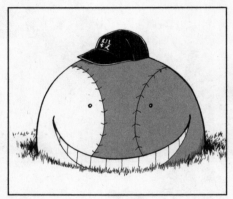

Slowly...

Go
slowly!!

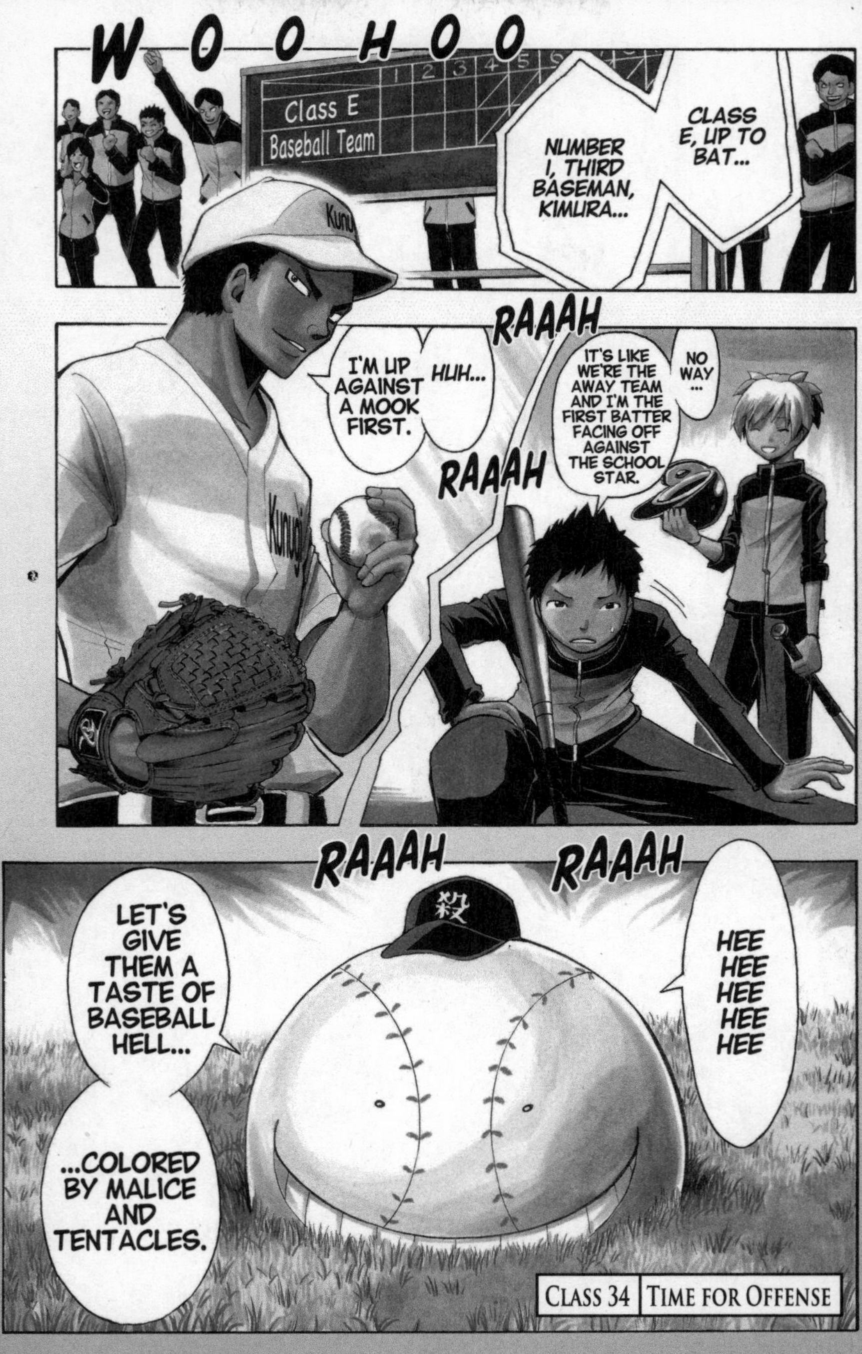
WOOHOO
Class E
Baseball Team
CLASS E, UP TO BAT...
NUMBER 1, THIRD BASEMAN, KIMURA...
NO WAY...
IT'S LIKE WE'RE THE AWAY TEAM AND I'M THE FIRST BATTER FACING OFF AGAINST THE SCHOOL STAR.
RAAAH
RAAAH
HUH...
I'M UP AGAINST A MOOK FIRST.
Kunugi
RAAAH
RAAAH
HEE HEE HEE HEE HEE
LET'S GIVE THEM A TASTE OF BASEBALL HELL...
...COLORED BY MALICE AND TENTACLES.

Class 34 Time for Offense

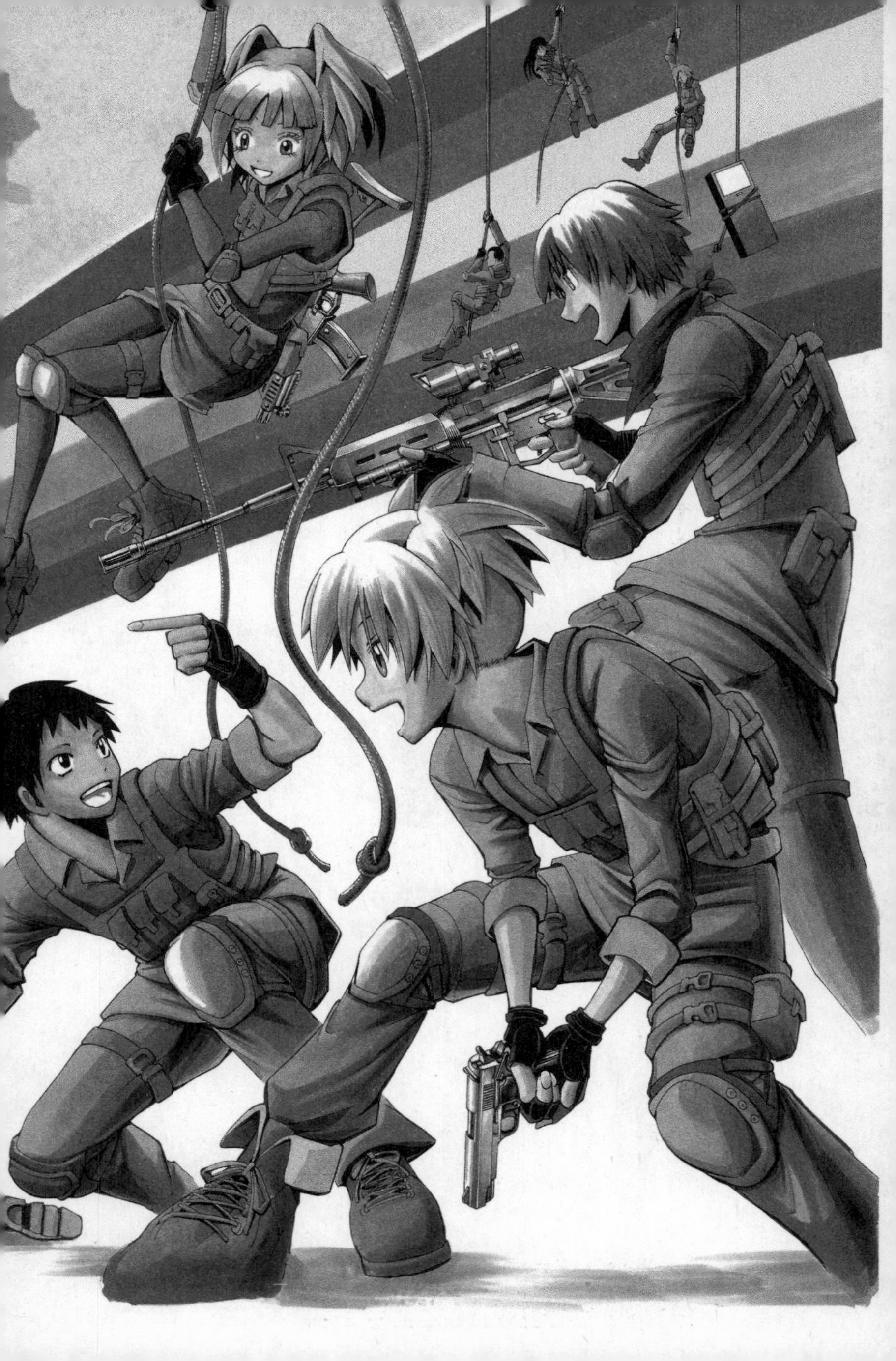

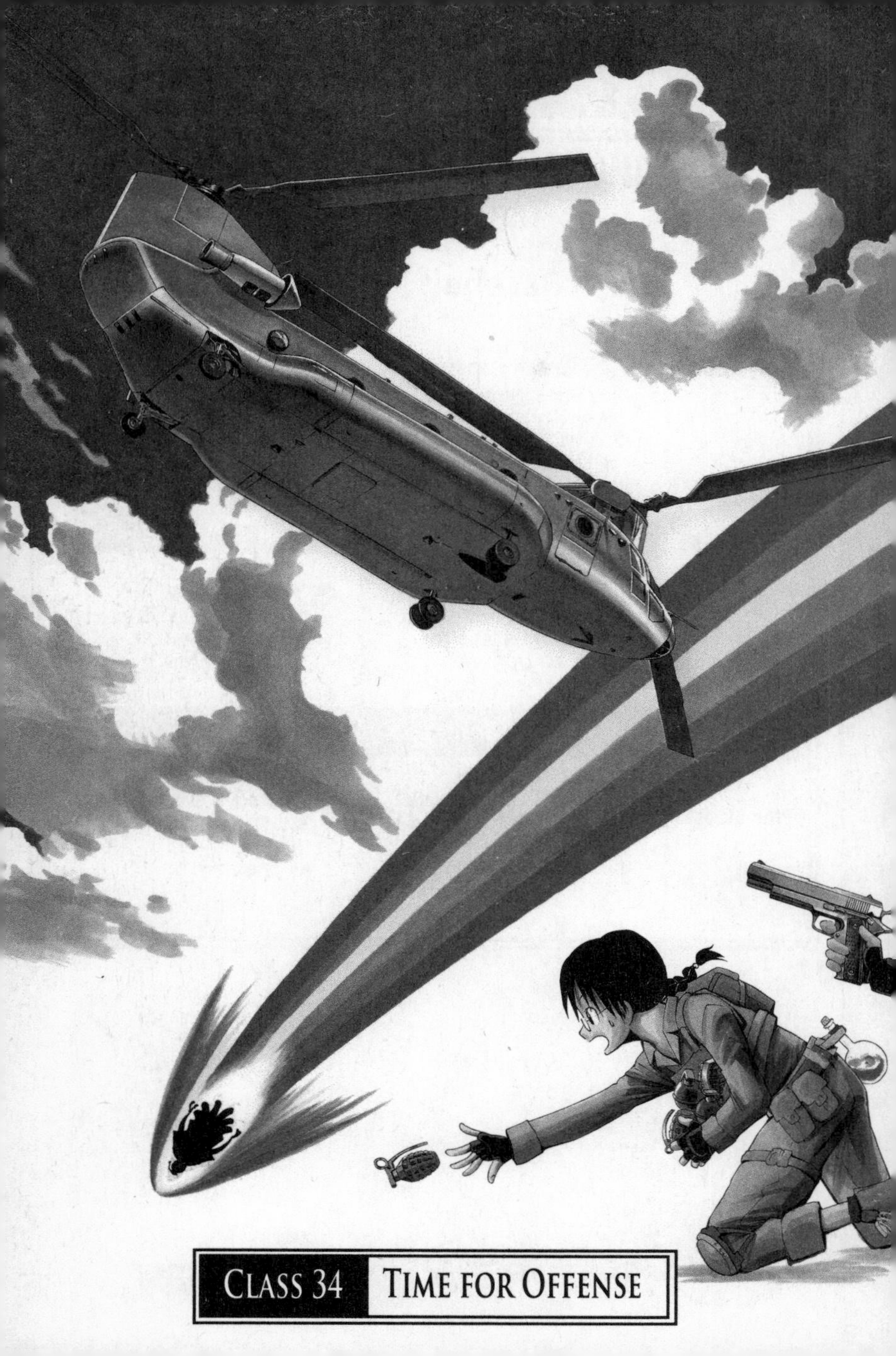

Class 34 Time for Offense

Kunugigaoka Junior High Bulletin Board

Ball Tournament Exhibition Match Rules

	Boys Baseball	Girls Basketball
Length of Game	● Three Innings (The game will continue up to the 5th inning if the score is tied at the bottom of the 3rd.)	● Three thirty-minute periods. (The game will be decided by a free throw if the score is tied.)
A Mercy Rule will be instituted so the spectators don't get bored.		
	● The game will be called after either side is ahead by 10 points.	● The game will be called after either side is ahead by 50 points.
Class E will be given handicaps due to their lack of skill.		
Handicaps	● Class E may divide their offense and defense.	● Class E may substitute as many players as they wish.

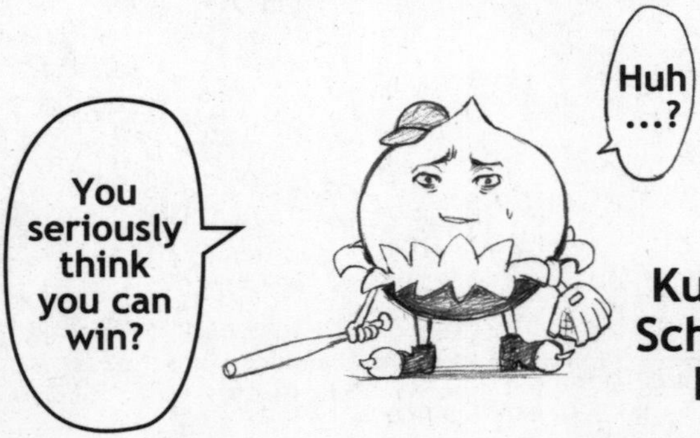
Huh ...?
You seriously think you can win?

Kunugigaoka School Mascot Kunudon

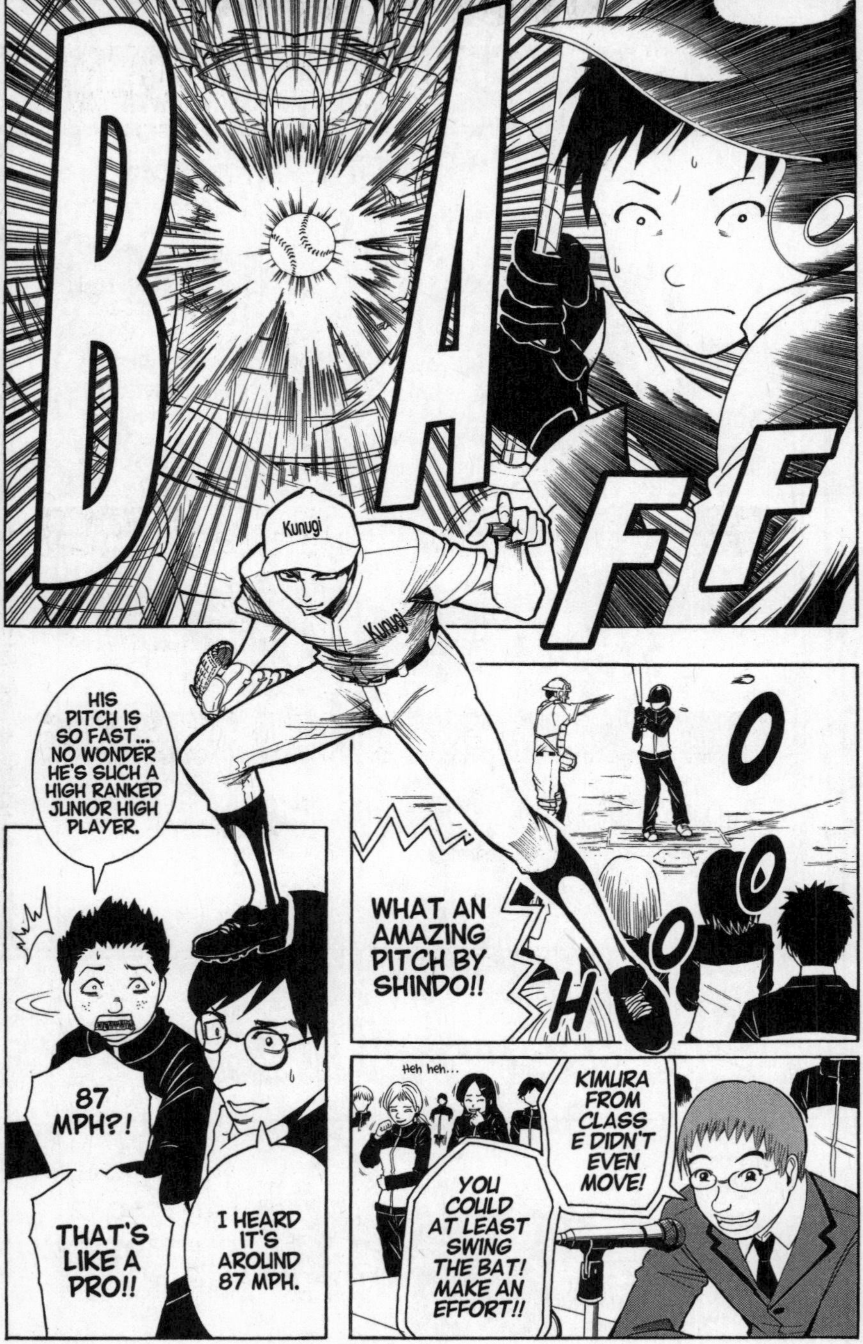
BAFF
WHOOOOH
WHAT AN AMAZING PITCH BY SHINDO!!
KIMURA FROM CLASS E DIDN'T EVEN MOVE!
Heh heh...
YOU COULD AT LEAST SWING THE BAT! MAKE AN EFFORT!!
HIS PITCH IS SO FAST... NO WONDER HE'S SUCH A HIGH RANKED JUNIOR HIGH PLAYER.
I HEARD IT'S AROUND 87 MPH.
87 MPH?!
THAT'S LIKE A PRO!!

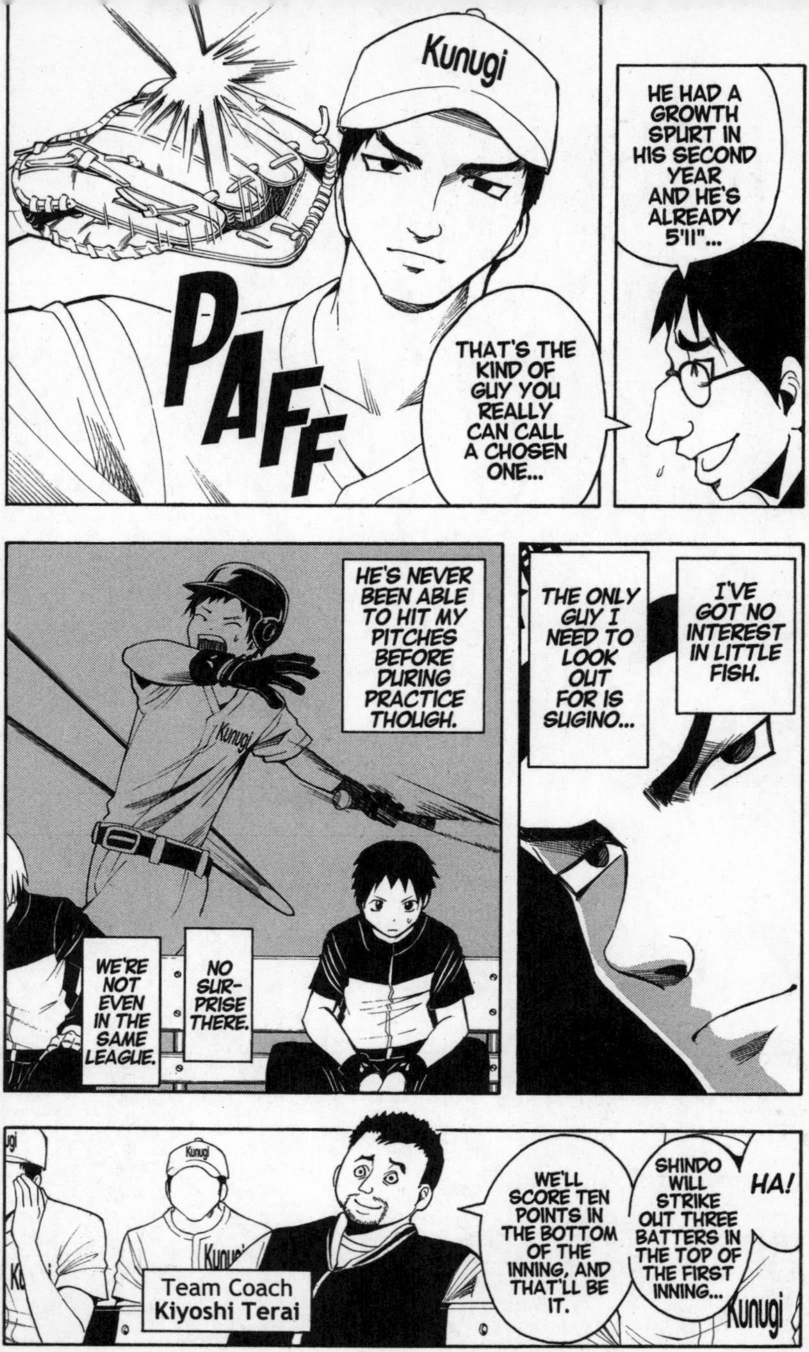
HE HAD A GROWTH SPURT IN HIS SECOND YEAR AND HE'S ALREADY 5'11"...
THAT'S THE KIND OF GUY YOU REALLY CAN CALL A CHOSEN ONE...
PAFF
I'VE GOT NO INTEREST IN LITTLE FISH.
THE ONLY GUY I NEED TO LOOK OUT FOR IS SUGINO...
HE'S NEVER BEEN ABLE TO HIT MY PITCHES BEFORE DURING PRACTICE THOUGH.
NO SUR-PRISE THERE.
WE'RE NOT EVEN IN THE SAME LEAGUE.
HA!
SHINDO WILL STRIKE OUT THREE BATTERS IN THE TOP OF THE FIRST INNING...
WE'LL SCORE TEN POINTS IN THE BOTTOM OF THE INNING, AND THAT'LL BE IT.
Team Coach Kiyoshi Terai

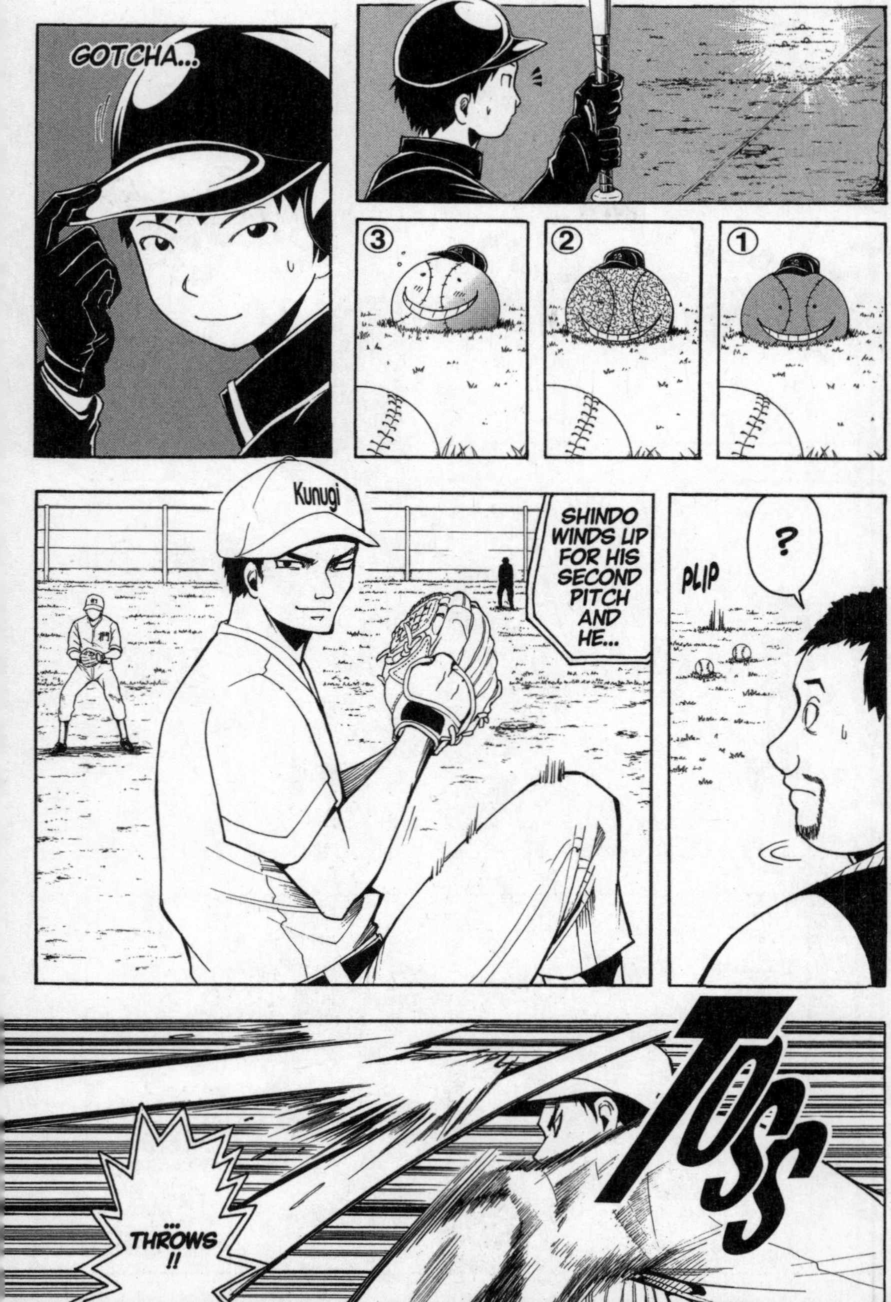

①
②
③
GOTCHA...
?
PLIP
SHINDO WINDS UP FOR HIS SECOND PITCH AND HE...
Kunugi
TOSS
...THROWS!!

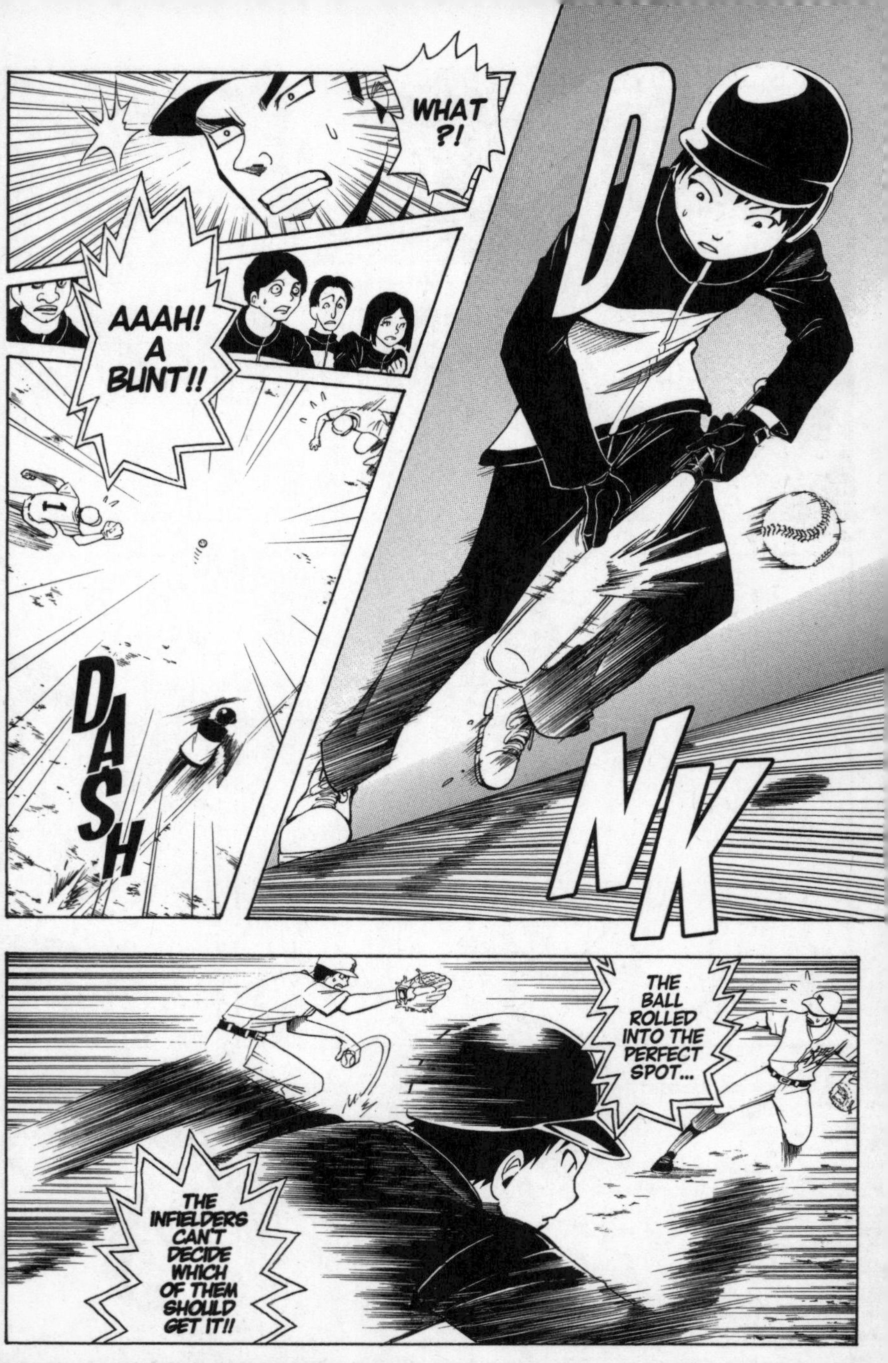
D
NK
WHAT?!
AAAH! A BUNT!!
DASH
THE BALL ROLLED INTO THE PERFECT SPOT...
THE INFIELDERS CAN'T DECIDE WHICH OF THEM SHOULD GET IT!!

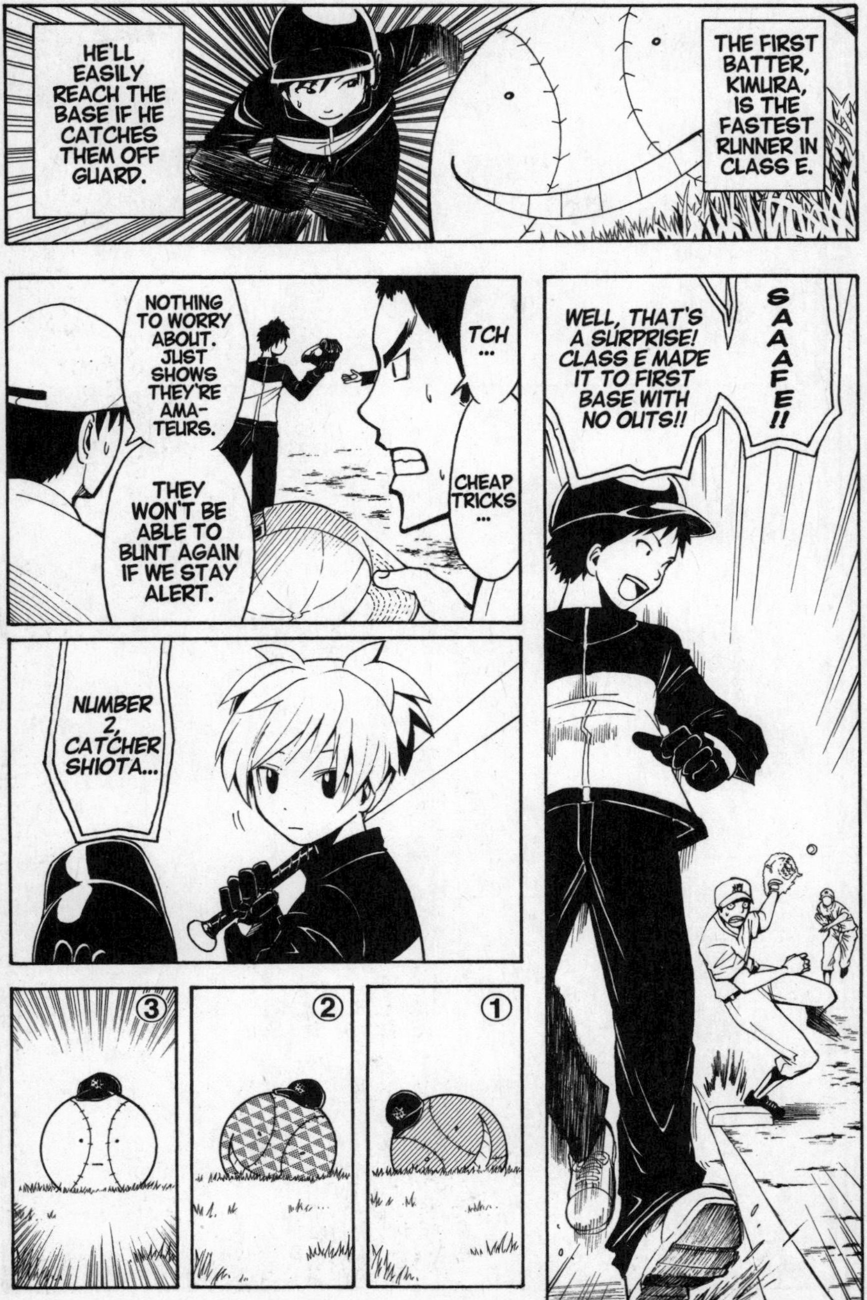

THE FIRST BATTER, KIMURA, IS THE FASTEST RUNNER IN CLASS E.
HE'LL EASILY REACH THE BASE IF HE CATCHES THEM OFF GUARD.
SAAAAFE!!
WELL, THAT'S A SURPRISE! CLASS E MADE IT TO FIRST BASE WITH NO OUTS!!
TCH...
CHEAP TRICKS...
NOTHING TO WORRY ABOUT. JUST SHOWS THEY'RE AMA-TEURS.
THEY WON'T BE ABLE TO BUNT AGAIN IF WE STAY ALERT.
NUMBER 2, CATCHER SHIOTA...
①
②
③

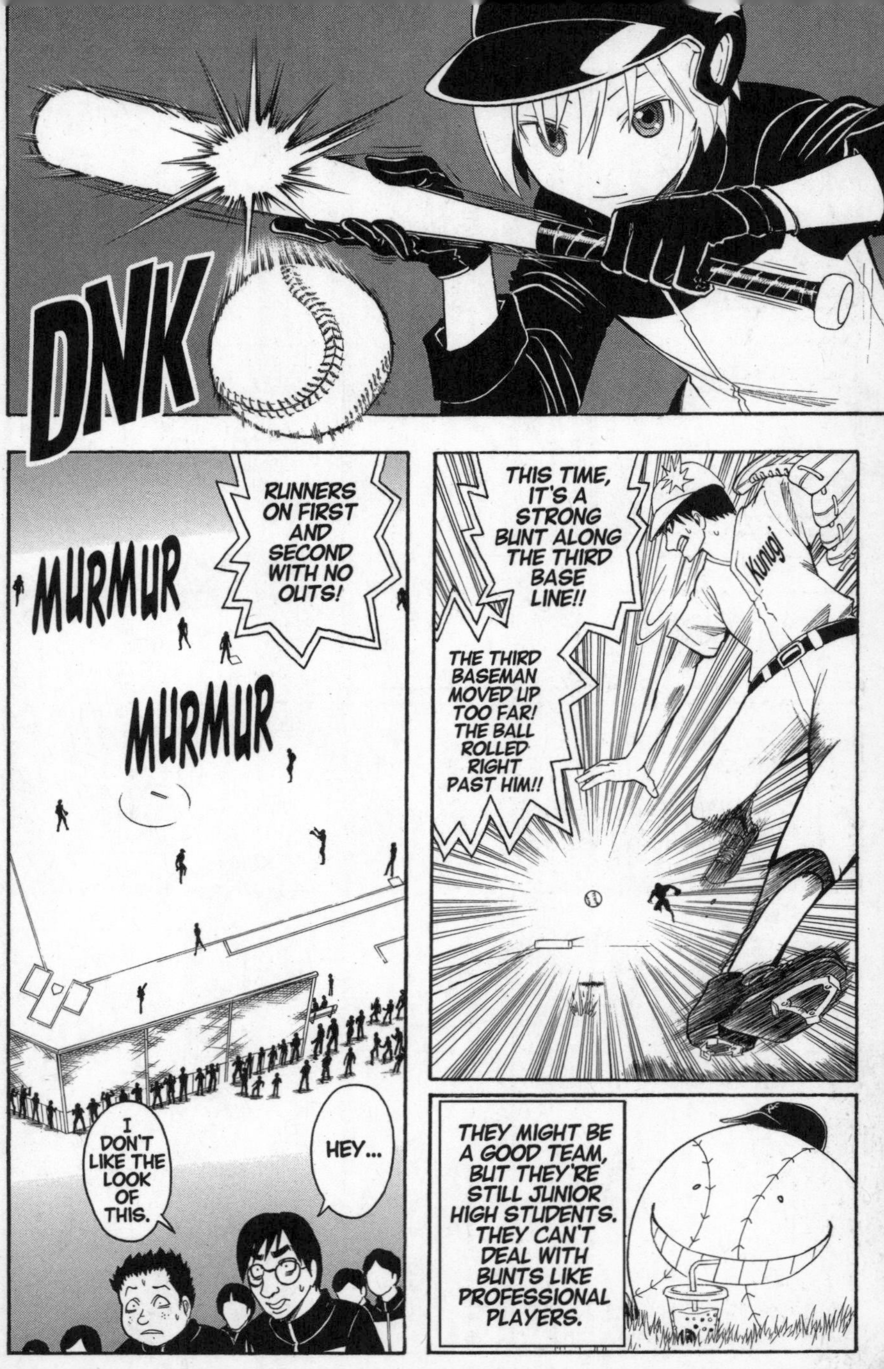

DNK
THIS TIME, IT'S A STRONG BUNT ALONG THE THIRD BASE LINE!!
THE THIRD BASEMAN MOVED UP TOO FAR! THE BALL ROLLED RIGHT PAST HIM!!
THEY MIGHT BE A GOOD TEAM, BUT THEY'RE STILL JUNIOR HIGH STUDENTS. THEY CAN'T DEAL WITH BUNTS LIKE PROFESSIONAL PLAYERS.
RUNNERS ON FIRST AND SECOND WITH NO OUTS!
MURMUR
MURMUR
HEY...
I DON'T LIKE THE LOOK OF THIS.

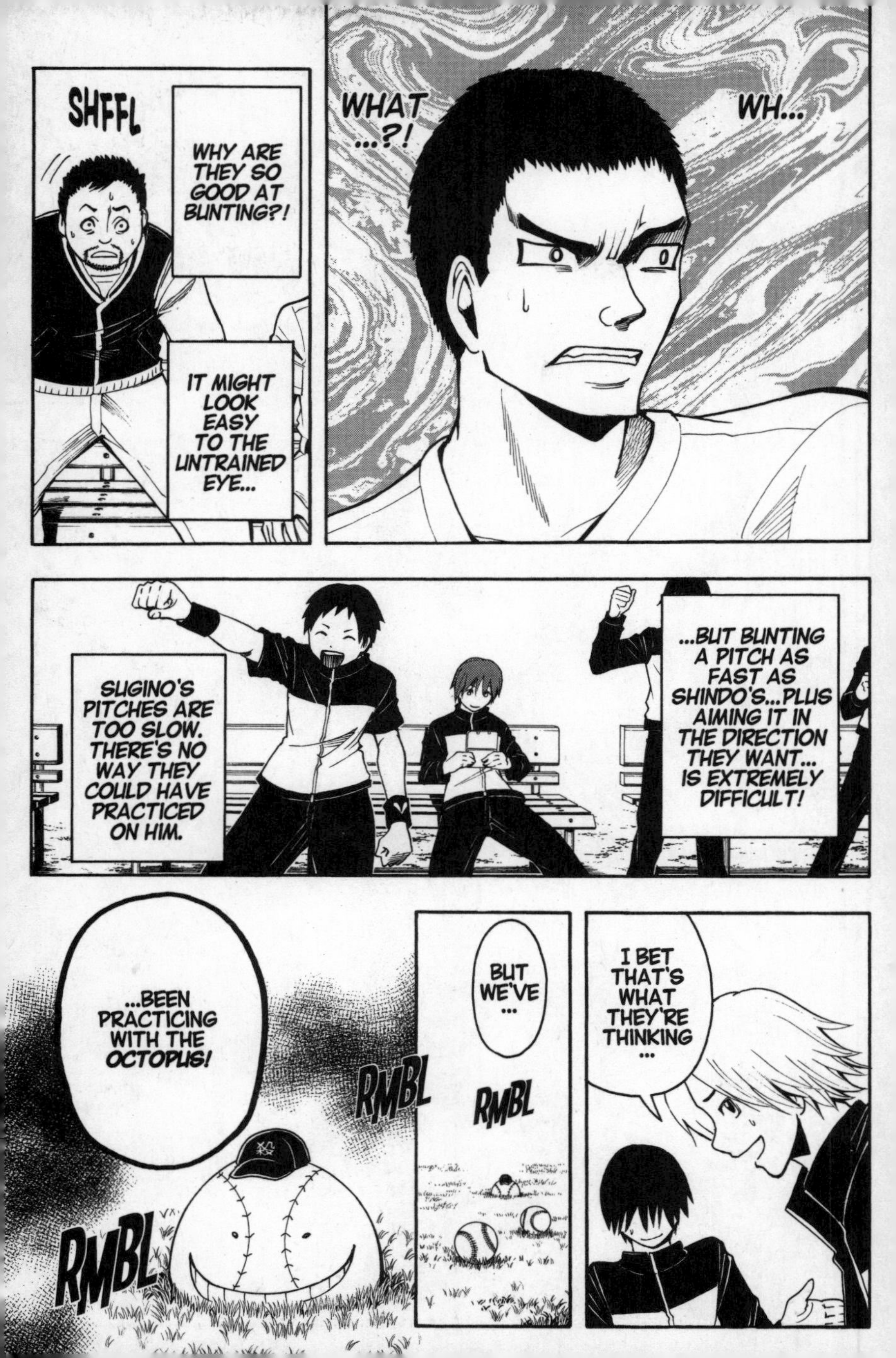
WH...
WHAT ...?!
SHFFL
WHY ARE THEY SO GOOD AT BUNTING?!
IT MIGHT LOOK EASY TO THE UNTRAINED EYE...
...BUT BUNTING A PITCH AS FAST AS SHINDO'S...PLUS AIMING IT IN THE DIRECTION THEY WANT... IS EXTREMELY DIFFICULT!
SUGINO'S PITCHES ARE TOO SLOW. THERE'S NO WAY THEY COULD HAVE PRACTICED ON HIM.
I BET THAT'S WHAT THEY'RE THINKING ...
BUT WE'VE ...
RMBL
...BEEN PRACTICING WITH THE OCTOPUS!
RMBL
RMBL

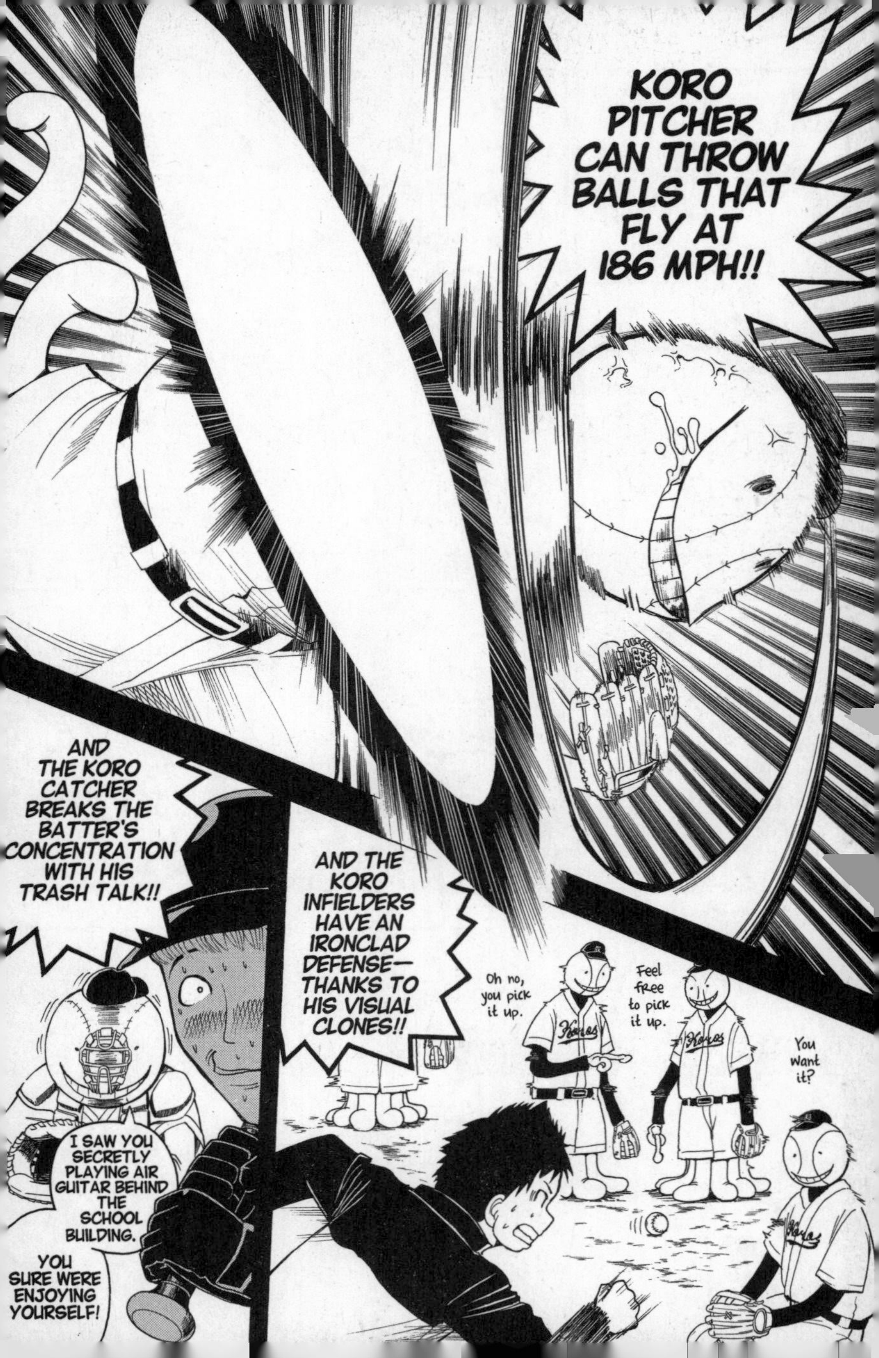
KORO PITCHER CAN THROW BALLS THAT FLY AT 186 MPH!!
AND THE KORO INFIELDERS HAVE AN IRONCLAD DEFENSE— THANKS TO HIS VISUAL CLONES!!
You want it?
Feel free to pick it up.
Oh no, you pick it up.
AND THE KORO CATCHER BREAKS THE BATTER'S CONCENTRATION WITH HIS TRASH TALK!!
I SAW YOU SECRETLY PLAYING AIR GUITAR BEHIND THE SCHOOL BUILDING.
YOU SURE WERE ENJOYING YOURSELF!

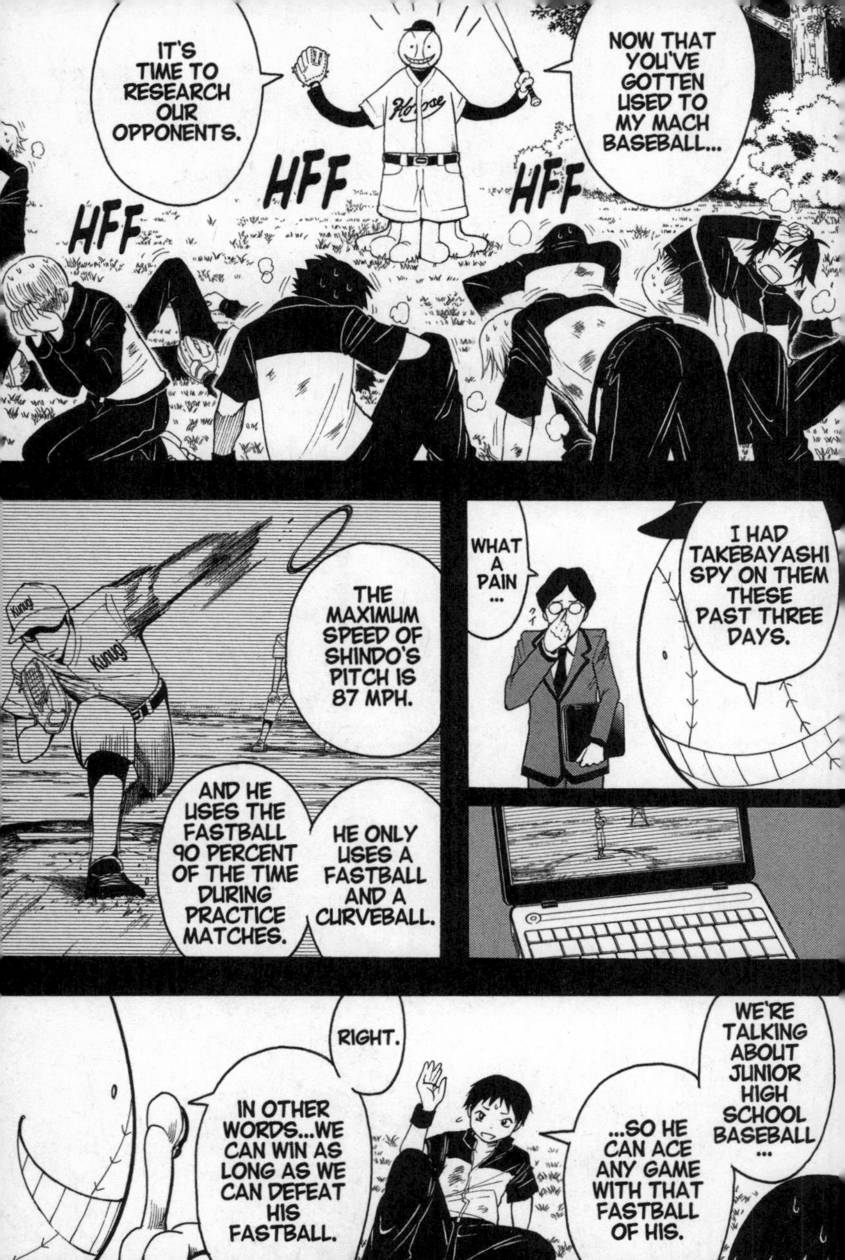
NOW THAT YOU'VE GOTTEN USED TO MY MACH BASEBALL...
HFF
IT'S TIME TO RESEARCH OUR OPPONENTS.
HFF
HFF
I HAD TAKEBAYASHI SPY ON THEM THESE PAST THREE DAYS.
WHAT A PAIN ...
THE MAXIMUM SPEED OF SHINDO'S PITCH IS 87 MPH.
HE ONLY USES A FASTBALL AND A CURVEBALL.
AND HE USES THE FASTBALL 90 PERCENT OF THE TIME DURING PRACTICE MATCHES.
WE'RE TALKING ABOUT JUNIOR HIGH SCHOOL BASEBALL ...
...SO HE CAN ACE ANY GAME WITH THAT FASTBALL OF HIS.
RIGHT.
IN OTHER WORDS...WE CAN WIN AS LONG AS WE CAN DEFEAT HIS FASTBALL.

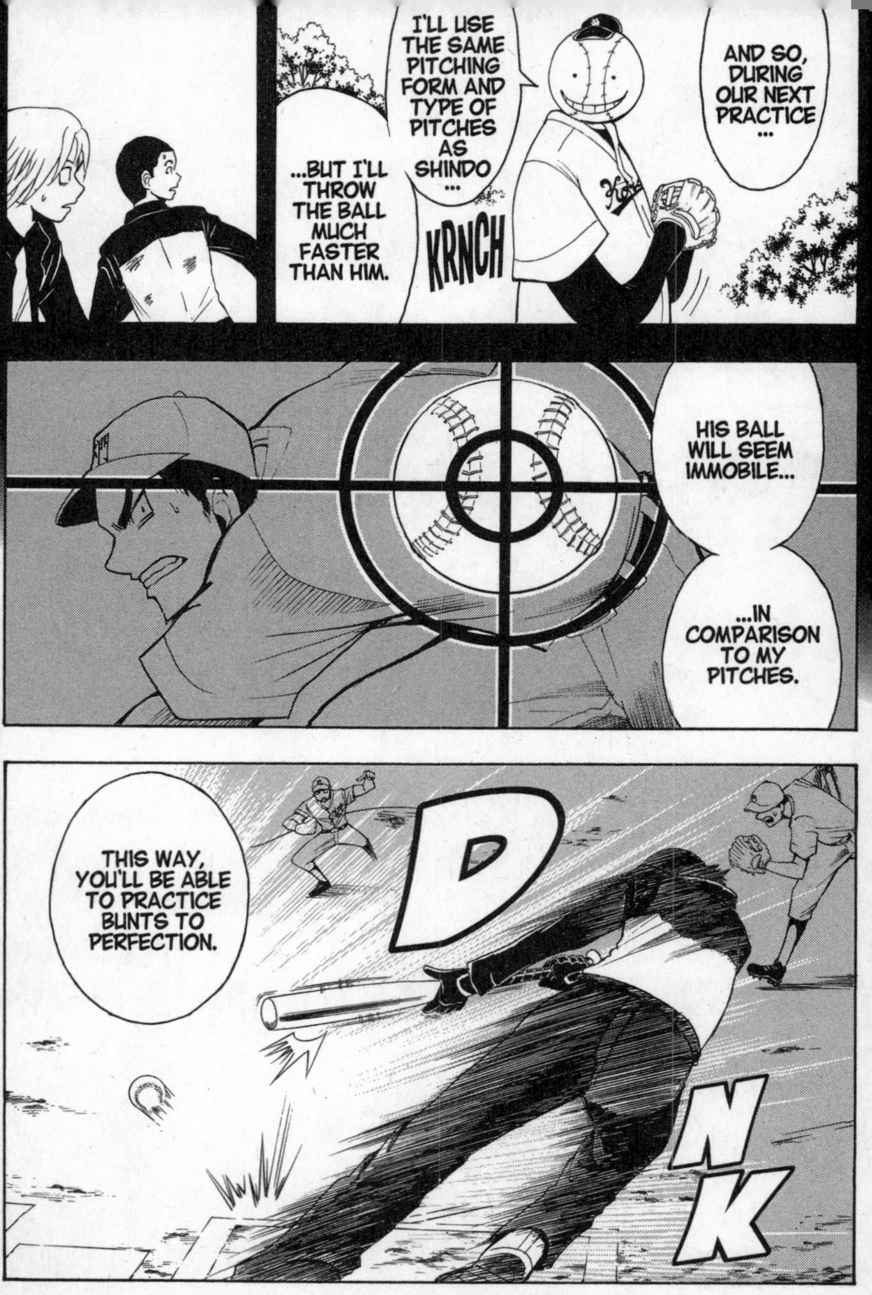
AND SO, DURING OUR NEXT PRACTICE ...
I'LL USE THE SAME PITCHING FORM AND TYPE OF PITCHES AS SHINDO ...
KRNCH
...BUT I'LL THROW THE BALL MUCH FASTER THAN HIM.
HIS BALL WILL SEEM IMMOBILE...
...IN COMPARISON TO MY PITCHES.
DNK
THIS WAY, YOU'LL BE ABLE TO PRACTICE BUNTS TO PERFECTION.

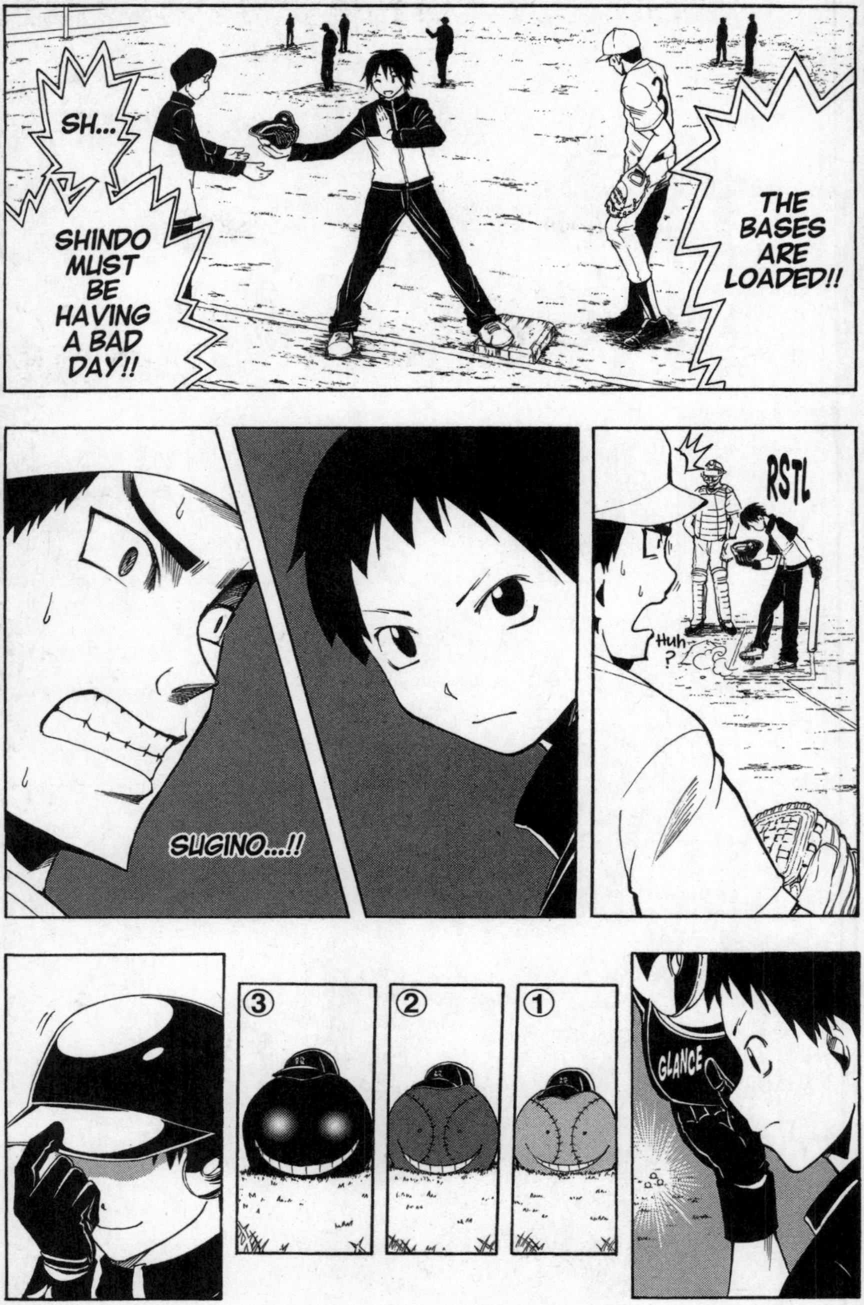
THE BASES ARE LOADED!!
SH...
SHINDO MUST BE HAVING A BAD DAY!!
RSTL
Huh?
SUGINO...!!
GLANCE
①
②
③

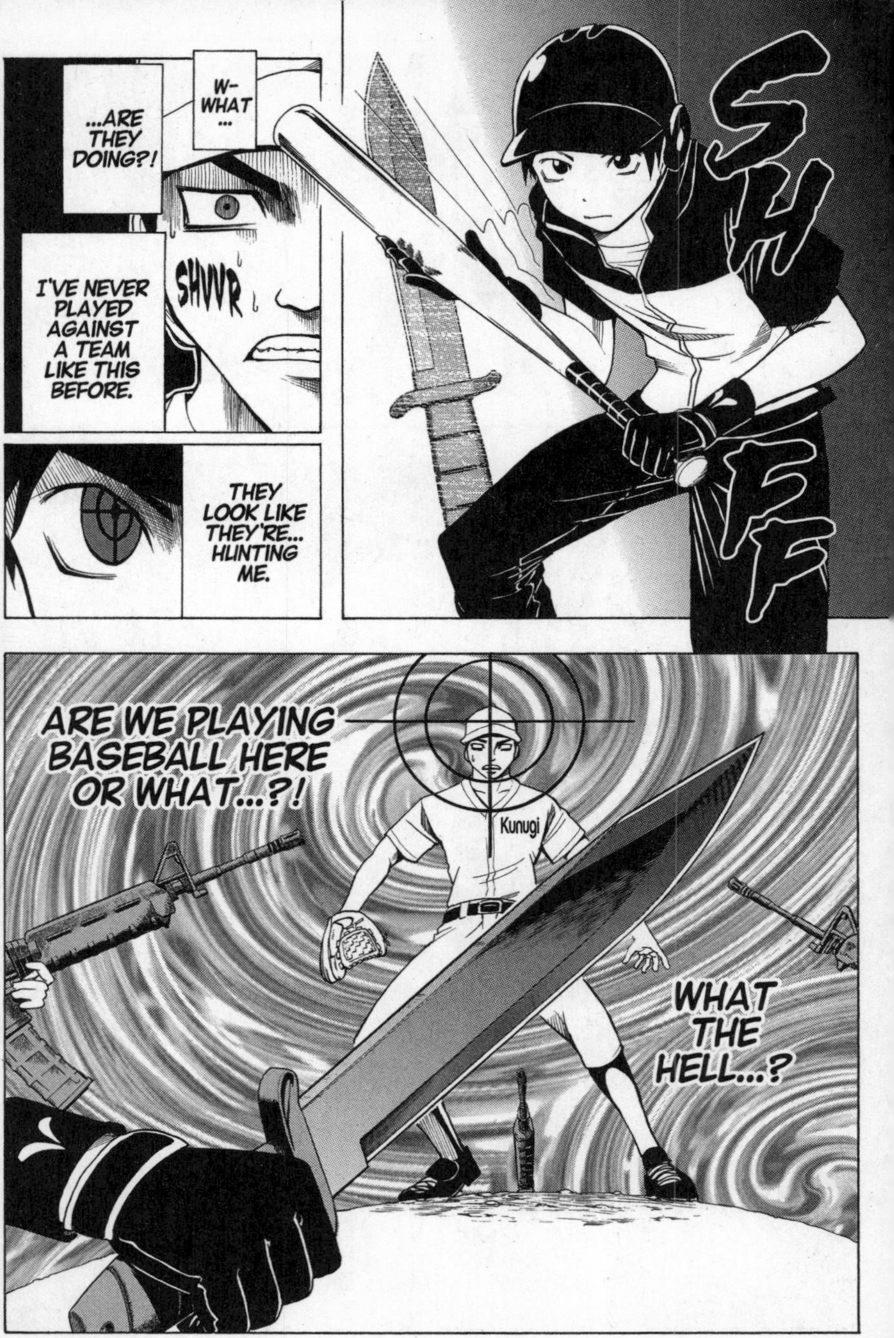
SHFF
W-WHAT...
...ARE THEY DOING?!
SHVVR
I'VE NEVER PLAYED AGAINST A TEAM LIKE THIS BEFORE.
THEY LOOK LIKE THEY'RE... HUNTING ME.
ARE WE PLAYING BASEBALL HERE OR WHAT...?!
Kunugi
WHAT THE HELL...?

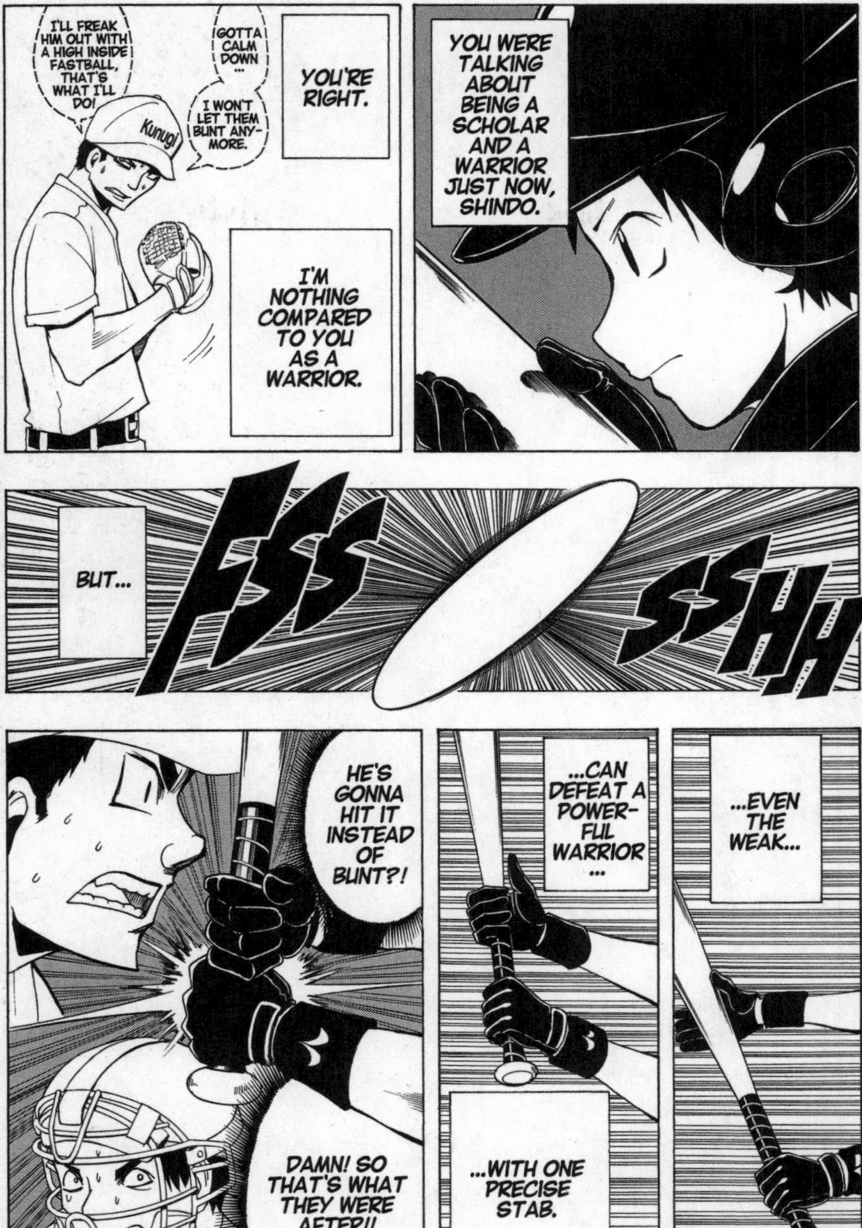
YOU WERE TALKING ABOUT BEING A SCHOLAR AND A WARRIOR JUST NOW, SHINDO.
YOU'RE RIGHT.
I'M NOTHING COMPARED TO YOU AS A WARRIOR.
GOTTA CALM DOWN ...
I WON'T LET THEM BUNT ANY-MORE.
I'LL FREAK HIM OUT WITH A HIGH INSIDE FASTBALL, THAT'S WHAT I'LL DO!
FSS
SSHH
BUT...
...EVEN THE WEAK...
...CAN DEFEAT A POWER-FUL WARRIOR ...
...WITH ONE PRECISE STAB.
HE'S GONNA HIT IT INSTEAD OF BUNT?!
DAMN! SO THAT'S WHAT THEY WERE AFTER!!
Kunugi

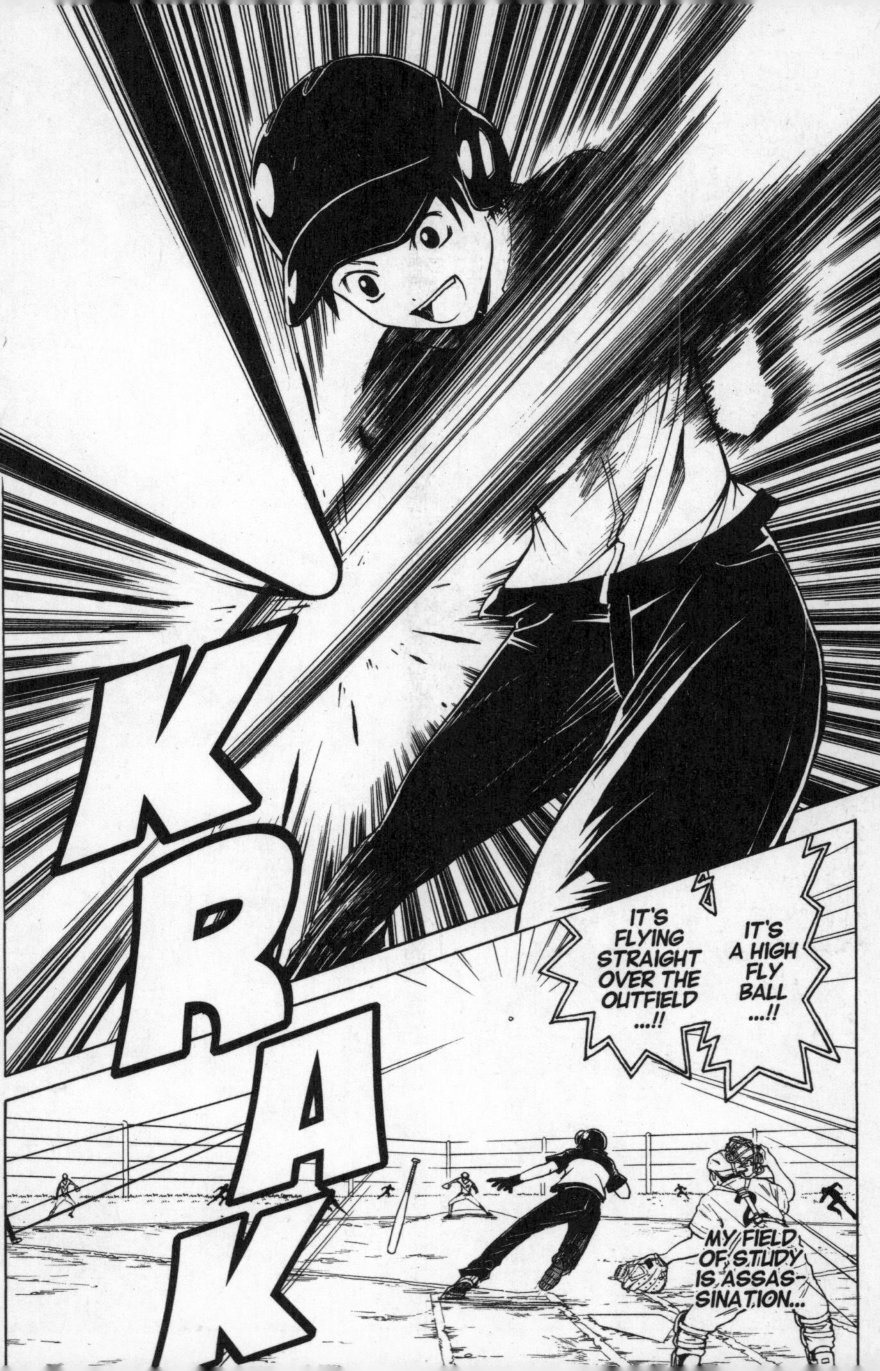
KRAK
IT'S A HIGH FLY BALL ...!!
IT'S FLYING STRAIGHT OVER THE OUTFIELD ...!!
MY FIELD OF STUDY IS ASSASSINATION...

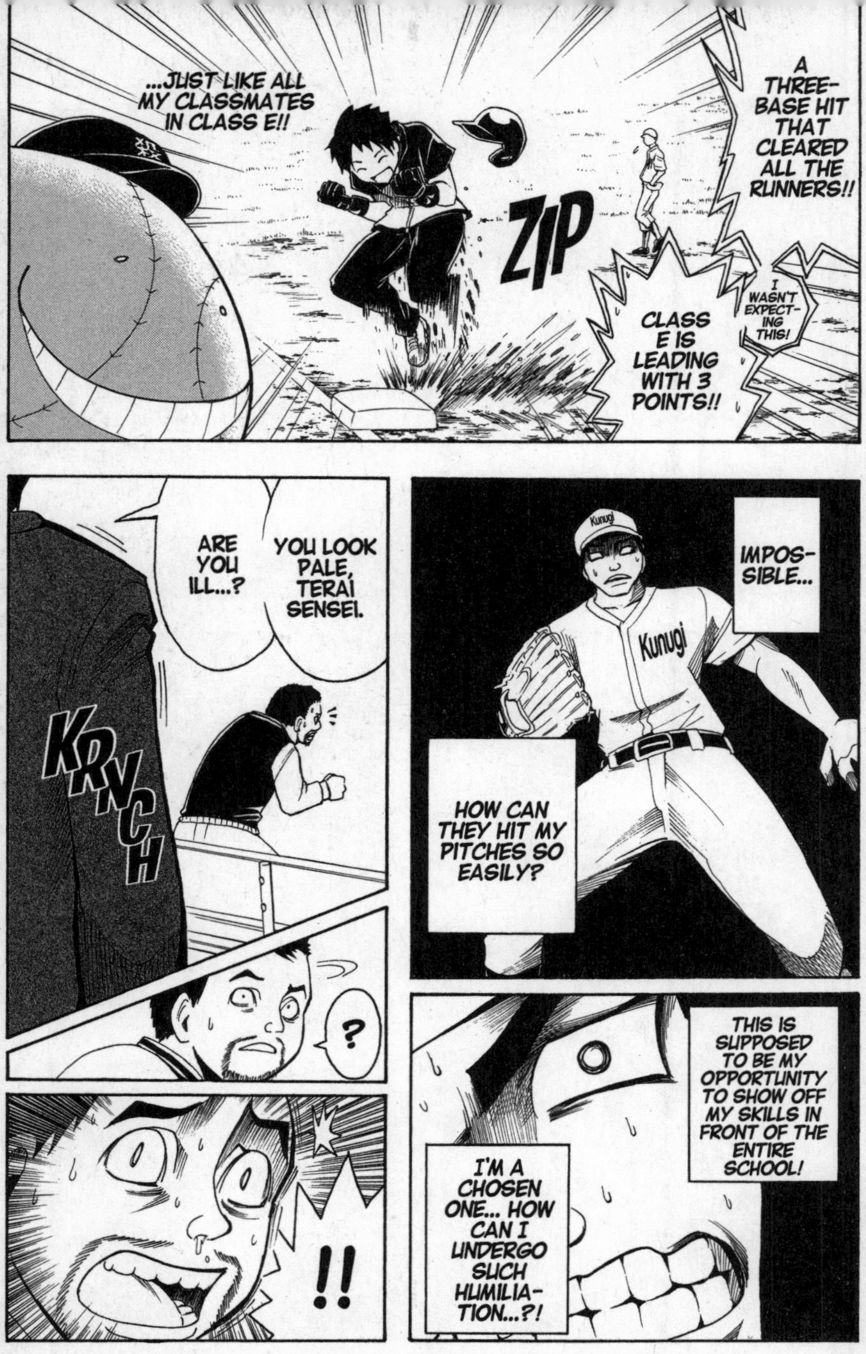
A THREE-BASE HIT THAT CLEARED ALL THE RUNNERS!!
I WASN'T EXPECTING THIS!
CLASS E IS LEADING WITH 3 POINTS!!
ZIP
...JUST LIKE ALL MY CLASSMATES IN CLASS E!!
IMPOSSIBLE...
HOW CAN THEY HIT MY PITCHES SO EASILY?
Kunugi
Kunugi
YOU LOOK PALE, TERAI SENSEI.
ARE YOU ILL...?
KRNCH
?
THIS IS SUPPOSED TO BE MY OPPORTUNITY TO SHOW OFF MY SKILLS IN FRONT OF THE ENTIRE SCHOOL!
I'M A CHOSEN ONE... HOW CAN I UNDERGO SUCH HUMILIATION...?!
!!

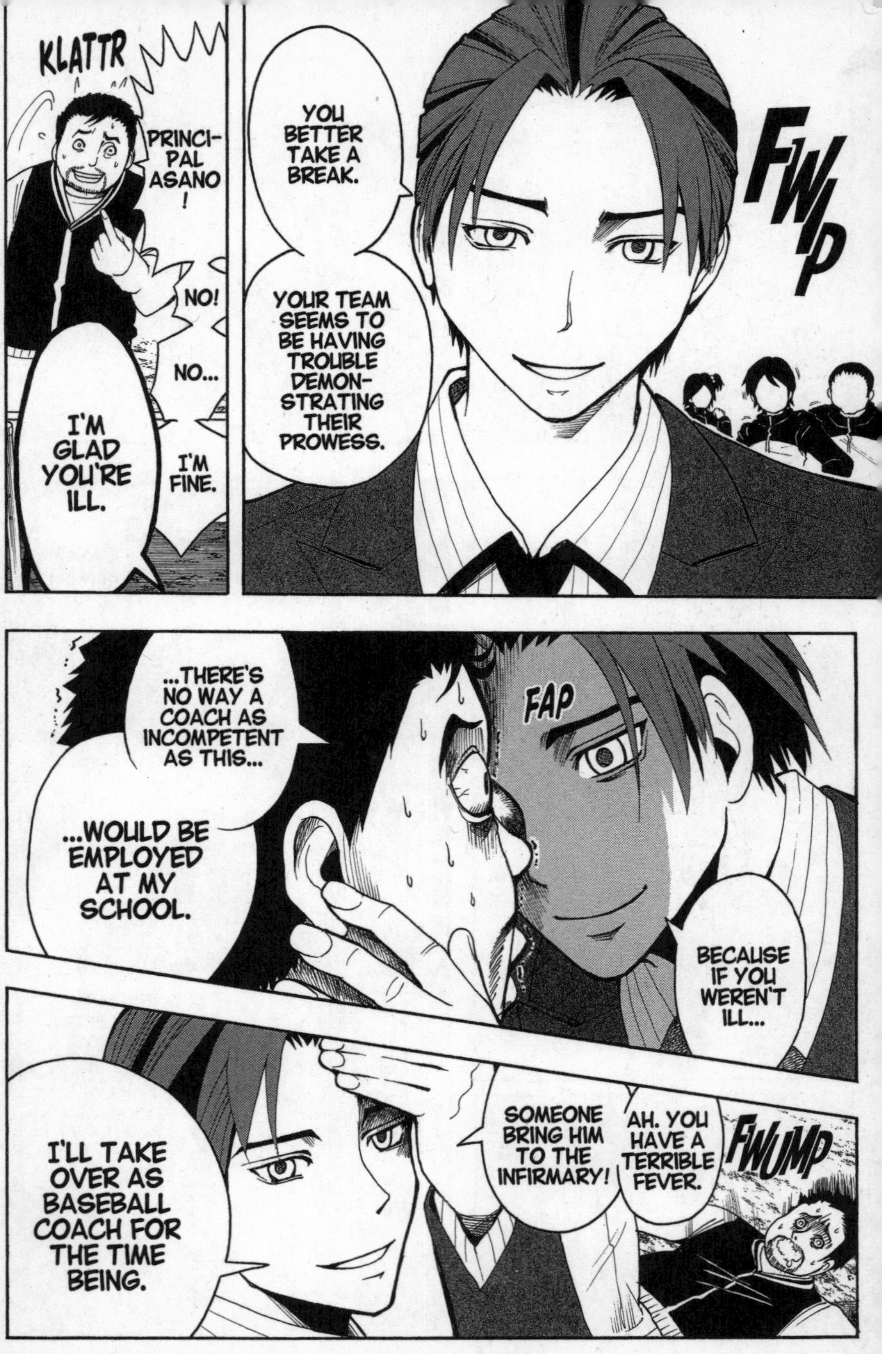
FWIP
YOU BETTER TAKE A BREAK.
YOUR TEAM SEEMS TO BE HAVING TROUBLE DEMONSTRATING THEIR PROWESS.
KLATTR
PRINCIPAL ASANO!
NO!
NO...
I'M FINE.
I'M GLAD YOU'RE ILL.
FAP
BECAUSE IF YOU WEREN'T ILL...
...THERE'S NO WAY A COACH AS INCOMPETENT AS THIS...
...WOULD BE EMPLOYED AT MY SCHOOL.
FWUMP
AH. YOU HAVE A TERRIBLE FEVER.
SOMEONE BRING HIM TO THE INFIRMARY!
I'LL TAKE OVER AS BASEBALL COACH FOR THE TIME BEING.

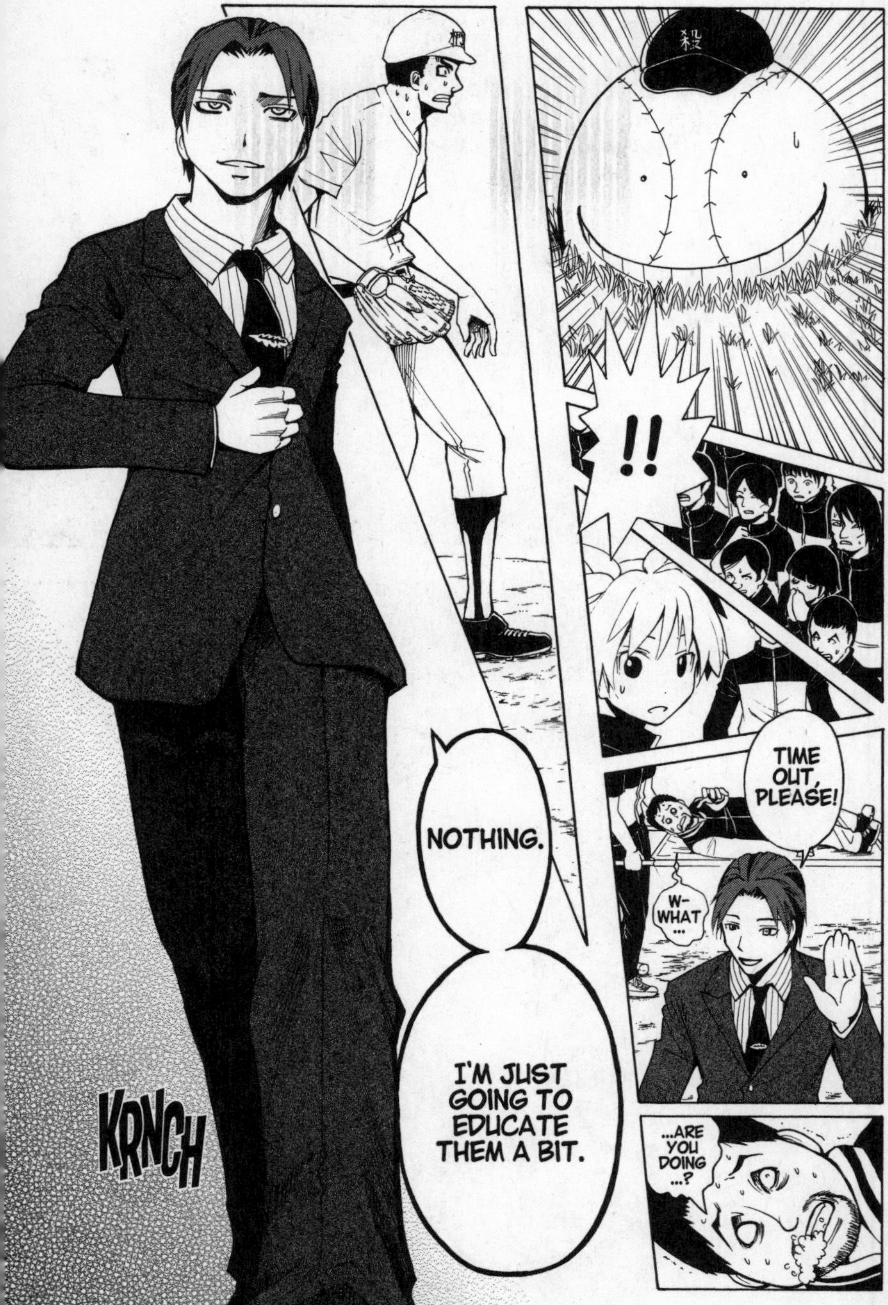
!!
TIME OUT, PLEASE!
W-WHAT ...
...ARE YOU DOING ...?
NOTHING.
I'M JUST GOING TO EDUCATE THEM A BIT.
KRNCH

Character Model: Nagisa

Nagisa was originally the main character of a different series. I'd like to write more about that somewhere near the final volume if I have the space.

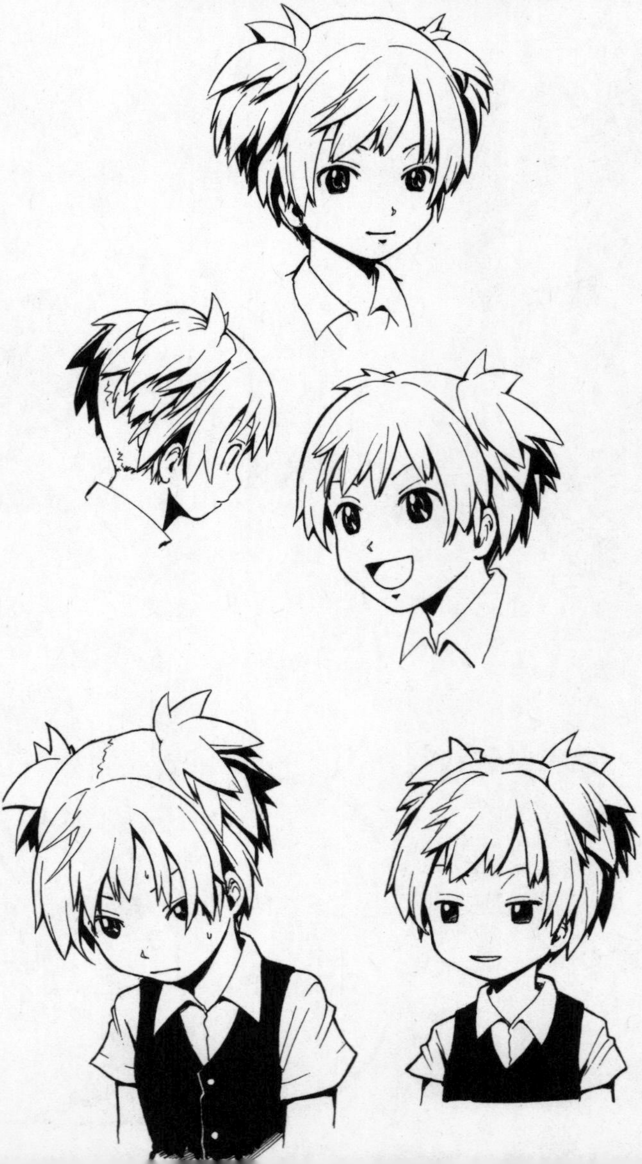

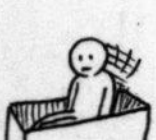

FROM
coffin...

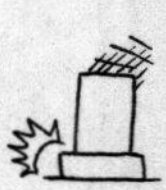

...to
grave.

When I didn't have a series, the next thing I had to do after waking up in the morning was to go to sleep at night.

I'm probably a hundred times busier now that I have a series, but I don't have a problem with that.

Based on my experience, we adapt to our environment once we're given a job to do.

Even if that job turns out to be assassin...!

—Yusei Matsui

Yusei Matsui was born on the last day of January in Saitama Prefecture, Japan. He has been drawing manga since elementary school. Some of his favorite manga series are *Bobobo-bo Bo-bobo*, *JoJo's Bizarre Adventure* and *Ultimate Muscle*. Matsui learned his trade working as an assistant to manga artist Yoshio Sawai, creator of *Bobobo-bo Bo-bobo*. In 2005, Matsui debuted his original manga *Neuro: Supernatural Detective* in *Weekly Shonen Jump*. In 2007, *Neuro* was adapted into an anime. In 2012, *Assassination Classroom* began serialization in *Weekly Shonen Jump*.

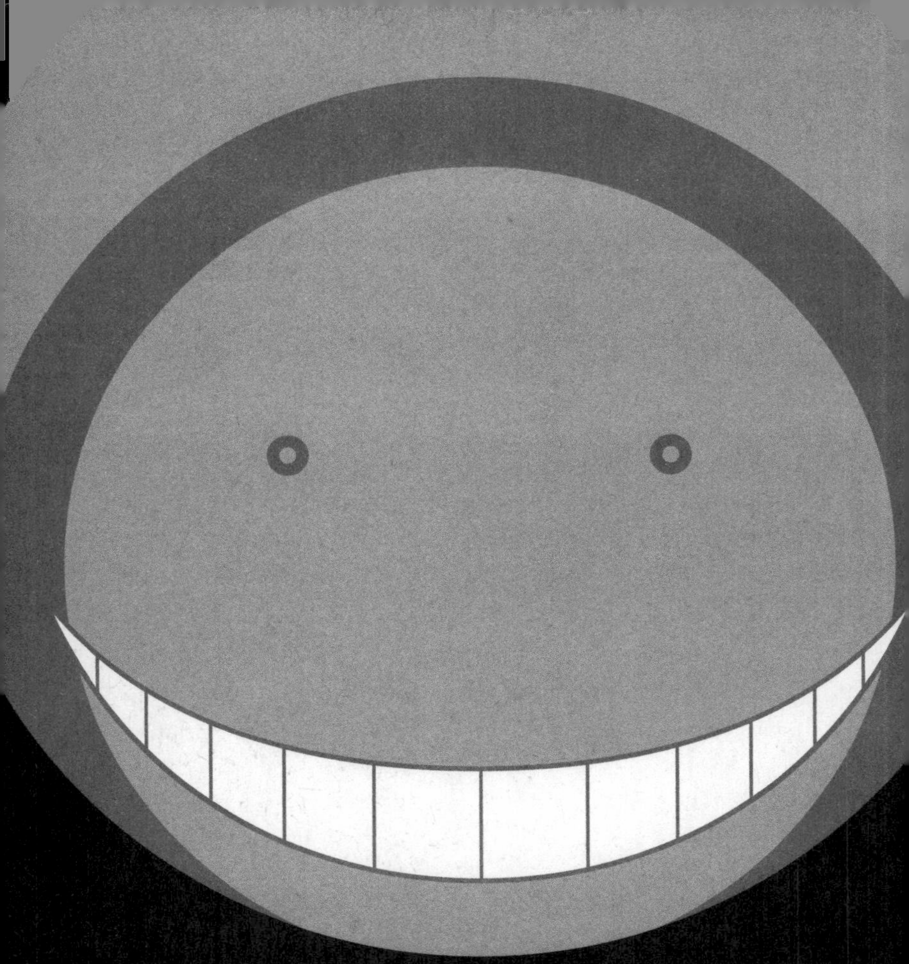

When you see the red circle on his face it means "correct." I asked him, "You don't have a girlfriend, do you?" And, sadly, the red circle appeared.

ASSASSINATION CLASSROOM

YUSEI MATSUI

4

TIME TO FACE THE UNBELIEVABLE

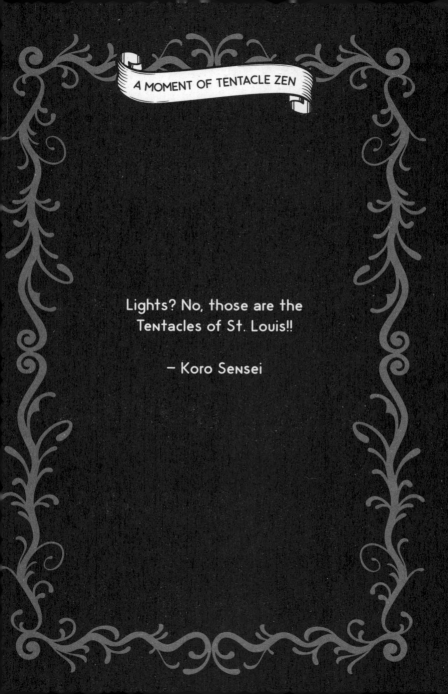

A MOMENT OF TENTACLE ZEN

Lights? No, those are the
Tentacles of St. Louis!!

— Koro Sensei

ASSASSINATION
CLASSROOM

Volume 4
SHONEN JUMP ADVANCED Manga Edition

Story and Art by YUSEI MATSUI

Translation/Tetsuichiro Miyaki
English Adaptation/Bryant Turnage
Touch-up Art & Lettering/Stephen Dutro
Cover & Interior Design/Sam Elzway
Editor/Annette Roman

ANSATSU KYOSHITSU © 2012 by Yusei Matsui
All rights reserved.
First published in Japan in 2012 by SHUEISHA Inc., Tokyo.
English translation rights arranged by SHUEISHA Inc.

The stories, characters and incidents mentioned in this publication are entirely fictional.

Published by VIZ Media, LLC
P.O. Box 77010
San Francisco, CA 94107

10 9 8 7 6 5 4
First printing, June 2015
Fourth printing, October 2017

www.viz.com

Syllabus for
Assassination Classroom, Vol. 5

Intramural relations are at an all-time low: Principal Asano wants to crush Koro Sensei's 3-E baseball team, while Koro Sensei wants to avenge Principal Asano's sabotage of 3-E's midterms. Then the government sends in a new Special Forces operative—a ruthless father figure who tests Karasuma's combat coaching skills. You'll never guess which student does him proud! And when Koro Sensei digs a swimming pool to help his students cool off, they discover a new weakness of his—as well as how cute their classmates look in swimsuits...

Available NOW!

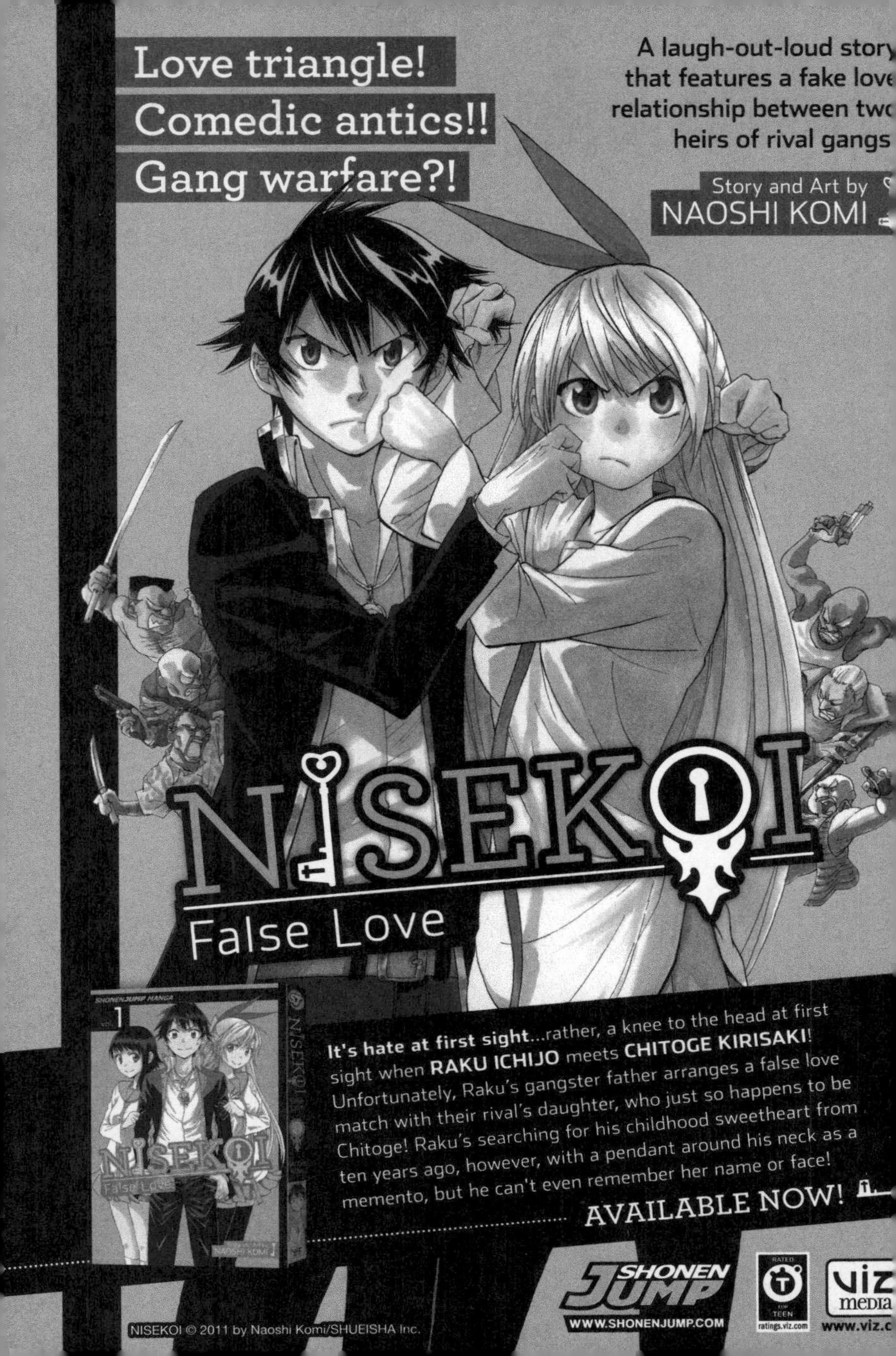
Love triangle!
Comedic antics!!
Gang warfare?!
A laugh-out-loud stor
that features a fake lov
relationship between tw
heirs of rival gangs
Story and Art by
NAOSHI KOMI
NISEKOI
False Love
SHONENJUMP MANGA
vol. 1
NISEKOI False Love
NAOSHI KOMI
It's hate at first sight...rather, a knee to the head at first sight when RAKU ICHIJO meets CHITOGE KIRISAKI! Unfortunately, Raku's gangster father arranges a false love match with their rival's daughter, who just so happens to be Chitoge! Raku's searching for his childhood sweetheart from ten years ago, however, with a pendant around his neck as a memento, but he can't even remember her name or face!
AVAILABLE NOW!
SHONEN JUMP
WWW.SHONENJUMP.COM
RATED T TEEN
ratings.viz.com
viz media
www.viz.c
NISEKOI © 2011 by Naoshi Komi/SHUEISHA Inc.

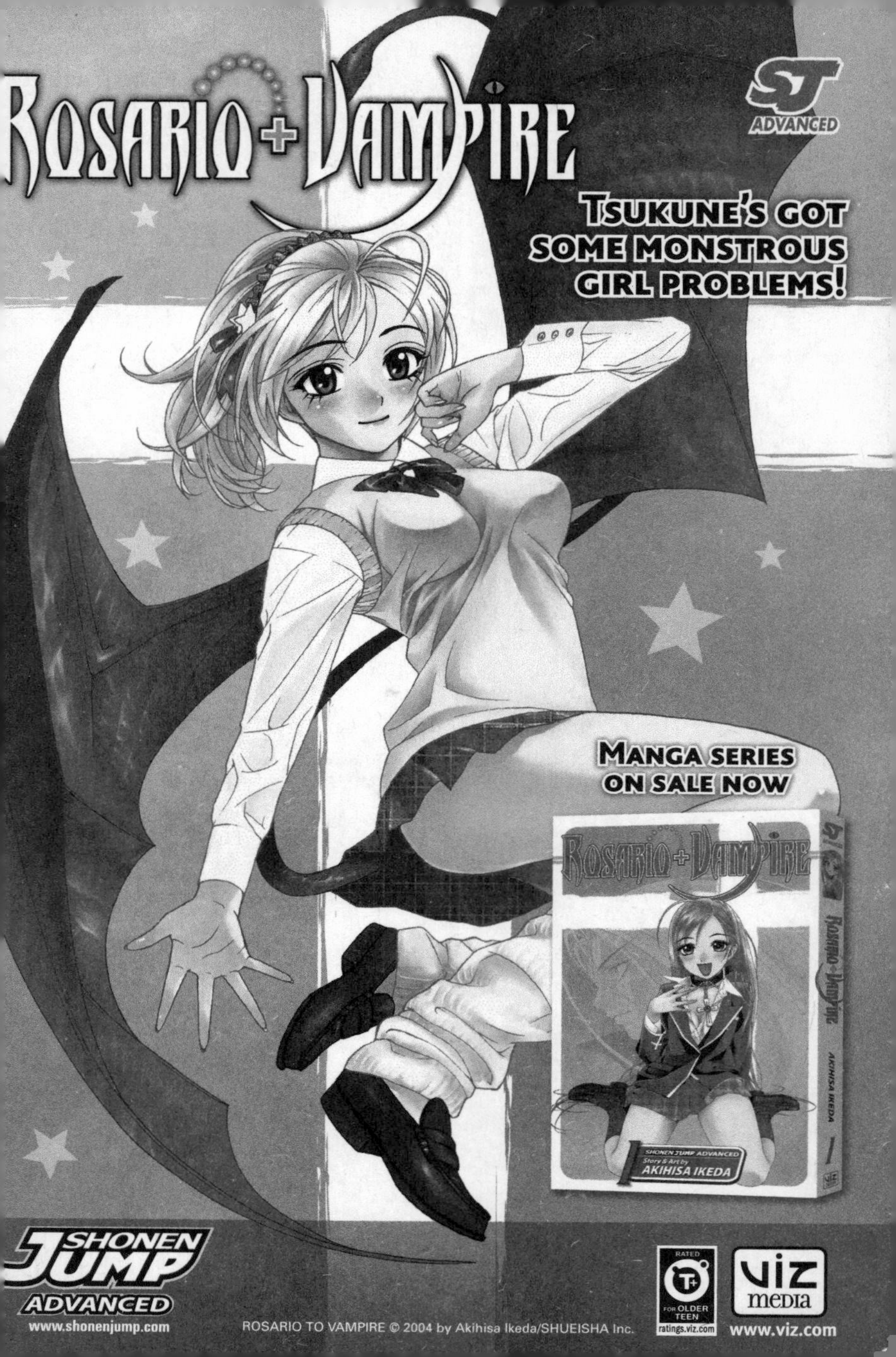
ROSARIO+VAMPIRE
SJ ADVANCED
TSUKUNE'S GOT SOME MONSTROUS GIRL PROBLEMS!
MANGA SERIES ON SALE NOW
ROSARIO+VAMPIRE
SHONEN JUMP ADVANCED
Story & Art by AKIHISA IKEDA
AKIHISA IKEDA
1
SHONEN JUMP ADVANCED
www.shonenjump.com
ROSARIO TO VAMPIRE © 2004 by Akihisa Ikeda/SHUEISHA Inc.
RATED T+ FOR OLDER TEEN
ratings.viz.com
VIZ media
www.viz.com